A DISTANT HERITAGE

A Distant Heritage

The Growth of Free Speech in Early America

LARRY D. ELDRIDGE

NEW YORK UNIVERSITY PRESS
NEW YORK AND LONDON

NEW YORK UNIVERSITY PRESS
New York and London

Library of Congress Cataloging-in-Publication Data
Eldridge, Larry D.
A distant heritage : the growth of free speech in early America /
Larry D. Eldridge.
p.   cm.
Revision of the author's thesis (Ph.D.)—Vanderbilt University,
1990.
Includes bibliographical references and index.
ISBN 0-8147-2192-3 (acid-free paper)
1. Freedom of speech—United States—History—17th century.
I. Title.
KF4772.E39   1994
342.73′0853—dc20
[347.302853]   93-5796
                         CIP

New York University Press books are printed on acid-free paper,
and their binding materials are chosen for strength and durability.

Manufactured in the United States of America

10   9   8   7   6   5   4   3   2   1

For Robin M. Rudoff
My first mentor. My long-time friend.

Contents

Charts   ix

Acknowledgments   xi

Abbreviations   xiii

Introduction: Leaving the Shadow   1

1 The Boundaries of Colonial Speech   5

2 Seditious Speech Law   20

3 The Nature of the Words   42

4 Between the Millstones   67

5 Sanctions in Decline   91

6 Λ Growing Leniency   114

7 Fruits of Circumstance   132

Notes   143

Bibliography   175

Index   195

Charts

1 "Bodily Correction" in New England and the South   97

2 Humiliation   103

3 Exclusion   107

4 Imprisonment   112

5 Fines of £5 and Over   117

Acknowledgments

Many people made significant contributions to this work. The most obvious, perhaps, are the members of my dissertation committee at Vanderbilt University. Paul Conkin, the dissertation director, imparted his work ethic and always treated me with tolerance, good humor, and respect. James Ely, the second reader, supported and guided me with a pleasant, energetic competence I admired from the start. Donald Winters, the committee chairman, became a friend of mine over the years, and I learned to value his insight as much as I enjoyed his whiskey. Douglas Leach taught me colonial history and gave me an appreciation for men like Francis Parkman and Samuel Eliot Morison—historians from older times with much to offer still. Joyce Chaplin came late to the project, but she was a ready source of new ideas and challenging questions.

Others made important contributions as well. Mel McKiven offered suggestions that proved invaluable as I revised the dissertation for publication. Jim Williams did the same, then went through the revision with a kind spirit and a relentless editorial eye. Michael Clark helped me polish the prose, and Carl Richard gave the manuscript a last critical read. As my assistants in the final stages of the project, Denise Montgomery and especially Carol McElroy greatly facilitated its timely completion. The work is better for the efforts of all these people, and to each I give a hearty thanks.

But the greatest contribution came from Virginia, my wife of many years. She remained enthusiastic and patient through the long dissertation process, listened attentively for endless hours as I talked through the project, and, as a professional librarian, helped me find and use the extensive materials I needed. Through it all, she shared the sacrifices more than the triumphs, the hardships more than the joys, and never once complained. Without her steadfast support, there would have been no book. This I will not forget.

Abbreviations

CSP	Calendar of State Papers, Colonial Series
CT/CR	The Public Records of the Colony of Connecticut
CT/PC	Records of the Particular Court of Connecticut
DE/KC	Records of the Kent County Court, Delaware
DE/RSC	Records of the Sussex County Court, Delaware
HAVEN	New Haven Colonial Records
MA/AAR	Massachusetts *Acts and Resolves*
MA/CAR	Massachusetts *Court of Assistants Records*
MA/CLM	Whitmore's *Colonial Laws of Massachusetts*
MA/DR	The Dudley Council Records (Massachusetts)
MA/DSS	*The Diary of Samuel Sewall*
MA/ECC	Essex County Court (Massachusetts) Records
MA/GCR	Massachusetts General Court Records
MA/HSC	Massachusetts Historical Society, *Collections*
MA/HSP	Massachusetts Historical Society, *Proceedings*
MA/JWJ	John Winthrop's Journal (Massachusetts)
MA/PCR	*The Pynchon Court Record* (Massachusetts)
MA/PlyCo	*Plymouth [County] Court Records* (Massachusetts)
MA/SCC	*Suffolk County (Massachusetts) Court Records*
MA/SP	*The Saltonstall Papers* (Massachusetts)
MA/WP	*The Winthrop Papers*
MD/A	*The Archives of Maryland*
MD/COA	*Proceedings of the Maryland Court of Appeals*
MD/PGC	*Court Records of Prince George's County, Maryland*

ME/PCR	*Maine Province and Court Records*
NC/HC	North Carolina Higher Court Records
NC/R	*The Colonial Records of North Carolina*
NH/PP	*Provincial Papers of New Hampshire*
NH/DRP	*Documents and Records Relating to the Province of New Hampshire*
NH/CHS	New Hampshire Historical Society, *Collections*
NH/SP	*State Papers of New Hampshire*
NJ/A	New Jersey Archives
NJ/BCB	The Burlington Court Book (West Jersey)
NJ/BPEJ	Records of the East Jersey Board of Proprietors
NJ/CCRC	Common Right and Chancery Court Journal
NJ/CMC	Records of Cape May County (New Jersey)
NY/ARS	*Minutes of the Courts of Albany, Rensselaerswyck, and Schenectady* (New York)
NY/BTR	Records of the Town of Brookhaven, New York
NY/CCM	*Calendar of [New York] Council Minutes*
NY/DH	O'Callaghan's *Documentary History of the State of New York*
NY/DRCH	*Documents Relative to the Colonial History of the State of New York*
NY/ECM	New York *Executive Council Minutes*
NY/HTR	Huntingdon [New York] Town Records
NY/JLC	*Journals of the Legislative Council of New York*
NY/KP	The Kingston Papers
NY/MC	Selected New York City Mayor's Court Cases
NY/NAR	*The Records of New Amsterdam*
NY/NTC	Newtown [New York] Town Records
NY/SAR	*Proceedings of the General Court of Assizes* and selected Supreme Court Minutes
NY/SC	Records of the *Supreme Court of Judicature of the Province of New York*
NY/WC	Minutes of the Westchester County (New York) Court of Sessions
PA/CCD	Chester County, Pennsylvania, Court Records
PA/PCR	*Minutes of the Provincial Council of Pennsylvania*
PA/PQS	Record of the Philadelphia County Court of Quarter Sessions and Common Pleas

PA/SAL	Pennsylvania's *Statutes at Large*
PA/UCC	Records of Pennsylvania's Upland County Court
PLY/CR	*Plymouth Colony Records*
PLY/OPP	William Bradford's *Of Plymouth Plantation*
RI/R	*Records of the Colony of Rhode Island and Providence Plantations*
RI/CT	Records of the Rhode Island Court of Trials
RI/ARB	Selected Bristol [Rhode Island] Town Records
SC/CCR	*South Carolina Chancery Court Records*
VA/BR-1	Virginia Burgesses Records (1619–1659)
VA/BR-2	Virginia Burgesses Records (1659–1693)
VA/BR-3	Virginia Burgesses Records (1695–1702)
VA/CSP	Virginia *Calendar of State Papers*
VA/EJC	*Executive Journals of the Council of Colonial Virginia*
VA/GCR	*Minutes of the Council and General Court of Colonial Virginia*
VA/LJC	*Legislative Journals of the Council of Colonial Virginia*
VA/SAL	Hening's *Statutes at Large* of Virginia

A DISTANT HERITAGE

Introduction: Leaving the Shadow

Historians have long stood in the shadow of a presupposition masquerading as a conclusion, namely that no political free speech existed in seventeenth-century America. Leonard Levy, an eighteenth-century specialist and still the premier historian of colonial free speech, summarized the state of scholarly opinion on the subject in his 1985 revision of *Legacy of Suppression*. After noting some seditious speech prosecutions on the Chesapeake, Levy observed that "in neighboring Maryland during the seventeenth century, there was as little freedom of expression as in Virginia." "A glance at New York and Pennsylvania," he continued, "indicates that speech and press were as unfree there during the seventeenth century as in the South." After citing a few more prosecutions, Levy turned his attention to New England. "The absence of freedom of speech in seventeenth-century Massachusetts, especially on religious subjects, is so familiar a fact that a mere reminder should suffice." "Liberty of expression," Levy announced with a daunting finality, "barely existed in principle or practice in the American colonies during the seventeenth century."[1]

Several interlocking assumptions have created that misguided "conclusion." Following Levy's work, it has been widely accepted that freedom of expression was strictly limited in the eighteenth-century colonies. From this besieged but resilient orthodoxy, it has been assumed as a matter of course that no freedom of expression would have existed in the century before. But that is a non sequitur, and it makes even less sense when we recall that Levy studied the press, not the freedom of individuals to criticize government. Published words, deliberately constructed and intended for wide dissemination, were inherently more dangerous to the state—and more severely proscribed and punished—than comments made in casual conversation. The seventeenth-century colonies had no "press." Analysis of free speech in that century inevitably centers on spoken, not published, words.

Historians also tend to extrapolate from known laws prohibiting and punishing seditious speech in the seventeenth century. Such laws, it is assumed, make plain that "free expression" was not tolerated. Yet no research has heretofore been done to determine the extent to which those laws were actually enforced, how that enforcement changed across the seventeenth century, or what such changes reveal about the relative freedom of expression experienced by early colonists.

The situation is only made worse by the handful of cases with which we are familiar. Richard Barnes's prosecution in early Virginia, probably the single most cited of all such cases, is a good example. Old Dominion authorities whipped and fined Barnes, ordered his arms broken and his tongue bored through with an awl, then banished him—all for seditious words against the governor.[2] But such cases were not representative of seditious speech prosecutions in early America. Indeed, they generally find their way into secondary works precisely because they were unusually colorful or startling. Using them as the standard to measure freedom of speech in the early colonies will never do.

To begin to write a history of free speech in early America, we must start from scratch. We must go to the original court records, laboriously sift out the seditious speech prosecutions they contain, then analyze those prosecutions. That is no easy task, to be sure. The court records are notoriously incomplete, difficult to access, and hard to digest. Many relevant records have been lost or destroyed, and even in their original state they omitted much important information. Indexes, when available at all, are typically incomplete and heavily biased toward genealogical interests. To compound the difficulty, colonial court records have a language and style all their own. Developing the skills to use them well takes time and patience. Put simply, the inherent difficulties and intimidating scope of such a project have long deterred systematic analysis of early colonial freedom of expression.

No longer. This work is based on a comprehensive examination of 1,244 seditious speech prosecutions drawn from the colonial court records of North and South Carolina, Virginia, Maryland, Delaware, Pennsylvania, East and West New Jersey, New York, Rhode Island, Plymouth, Massachusetts, Connecticut, New Haven, New Hampshire, and the Province of Maine.[3] Many of these are records from the higher colonial jurisdictions, including minutes of councils, assemblies, and provincial courts. I also sifted through records from eighteen county courts in ten different colonies, and some town courts as well, to compare seditious speech prosecutions at various levels. To the same end, I examined journals and diaries kept by individual magistrates. These contain information about cases at the lowest jurisdictional level—those heard by justices of the peace, who kept no official records. In addition, letters, papers, writings, and official communications from various colonial men of affairs complement this base of legal source material. Lord Bellemont, William Berkeley, William Bradford, Lord Howard of Effingham, Edward Johnson, Cotton Mather, William Penn, William Pynchon, Edward Randolph, Nathanial Saltonstall, Roger Williams, John Winthrop—all of these and others make valuable contributions.

With the mass of information extracted from these sources, I have been able to chart the nature and boundaries of free speech in the early colonies.[4] Put simply, I have discovered that colonists experienced a dramatic expansion of their freedom to criticize government and its officials across the seventeenth century.

Chapter 1 examines the nature of controls on colonial expression across a wide spectrum, then places seditious words within that context. Succeeding chapters explore seditious speech law, the kinds of cases actually prosecuted, juries, appeals, and other trial-related matters, important changes in punishment, and patterns of growing leniency in dealing with seditious speech. The work concludes with an answer to a broader question: freedom of speech clearly grew in the American colonies during the seventeenth century, but why? The answer lies in a fascinating confluence of historical developments. The seventeenth-century colonies simultaneously experienced a series of destabilizing trends and tumultuous events on the one hand, and the stabilizing effects of steady growth and development on the other. That ironic combination made colonists more outspoken in their criticism of authority and authorities, and made officials less able and less willing to punish seditious speech as they once had. In these complex and interrelated developments, colonists' freedom of speech grew. That growth in turn established the essential foundation in practical colonial experience for a flowering of dissent against English authority, and for the intellectual justification that sprang up around that dissent, in the eighteenth century.

The concluding chapter is titled "Fruits of Circumstance" for good reason. Free speech grew in the early colonies because of the unusual and fortuitous circumstances of the time. Had those circumstances been different, a quite different tradition might have developed. Indeed, long-standing freedom can easily contract as historical circumstances change, even in the presence of a supposedly strong and settled free-speech tradition. The McCarthy era and the intense interest in punishing "hate speech" and "politically incorrect" language in the 1990s offer ready reminders. To the extent that exploring how and why that process occurs is important, this study should have ongoing relevance.

ONE

The Boundaries of Colonial Speech

Governments regulate expression across a wide spectrum, and to accomplish varied ends. Ultimately, the goal is to maintain a well-ordered society—to uphold prevailing moral and social values, to preserve public peace, to maintain respect for authority. Colonial governments were no different. In this chapter I outline the various areas of expression that colonial authorities regulated and the reasons why they did so. I place seditious speech within a broader context, then explain the kinds of words they considered seditious. These tasks are essential. The broader goals and context within which officials defined and punished seditious speech add perspective. Without that perspective, crucial distinctions between slander and *scandalum magnatum*, to use one of many examples, would be difficult to understand. Drawing the boundaries of seditious speech is equally important, for it allows a delineation of the ways in which the limits of "political" expression changed across the century. Charting and assessing that change is the main purpose of this study.

A desire to maintain a moral society occupied a high place in the minds of colonial authorities. New England has gained special notoriety for this, in part because of the publicity accorded some particularly colorful cases. A Plymouth Colony court ordered Thomas Graunger hanged, for example, "for buggery with a mare, a cow, two goats, diverse sheep, two calves, and a turkey."[1] Graunger's creativity, it would seem, matched his energy. But such cases and the attention they inevitably attract tend to obscure the reality that all colonial governments established controls over morality, and not just early in the century. The 1691 Virginia statute outlawing "swearing, cursing, profaning God's holy name, Sabbath abusing, drunkenness, fornication and adultery," and New Jersey's 1698 prohibition against "all sorts of lewdness and profane behavior in word or action"[2] are but two of many examples. And, as those laws show, controlling personal behavior for moral ends meant more than regulating overt sexual activity. Alcohol abuse often commanded the attention of colonial leaders, and in every colony regulations against vulgar or obscene language stood alongside those outlawing profane and blasphemous words.

Colonial authorities also controlled what might otherwise be considered "aesthetic" expression on these same grounds. The Massachusetts Court of Assistants banished Henry Sherlot because he was "a dancing master and a person very insolent and of ill fame." Colonial regulations on dress were standard fare as well. Authorities commonly prevented colonists from wearing hubristically ornate or showy clothing. Sometimes, as in Nathaniel Washburn's case, dress could go beyond mere matters of godly humility. In December 1700, he appeared before the Plymouth County court in Massachusetts not just for "wearing woman's apparel in the public meeting house," but for doing so "in time of exercise on the Lord's Day."[3]

Officials regulated dress on other than moral grounds as well. They expected colonists to wear attire reflecting rank in society as much as godly humility. Upholding the social hierarchy in this way was important to colonial authorities. As early as 1634, Massachusetts officials outlawed the wearing of "new fashions, or long hair, or anything of the like," but throughout the century enforcement presented problems. The Bay Colony's Essex County court punished Samuel Weed in 1674 for "retorting and saucy language to the president of the court." "He might wear silver buttons if he paid for them," he had declared, "as well as any man in the country." Disagreeing, the judges fined the noxious Weed £1. New England's leaders combined penalties and lamentations, but as early as 1619 Virginia authorities sought a more practical approach. To prevent "excess in apparel," they taxed Virginia colonists based on the value of their clothes. "Every man shall be cessed in the Church for all public contributions," the law required, "if he be unmarried, according to his own apparel, if he be married, according to his own and his wife's, or either of their apparel."[4]

A decade later, in 1629, John Winthrop reminded Massachusetts colonists of what the Virginia authorities already knew. God "has so disposed of the condition of mankind," Winthrop said in his famous "Model of Christian Charity" sermon, "as in all times some must be rich, some poor, some high and eminent in power and dignity, others mean and in subjection." It was a sentiment echoed by all colonial authorities in the seventeenth century. In North Carolina, to cite one of many examples, Thomas Woodward expressed a similar view in a letter to Sir John Colleton on June 2, 1665. "To have some men of greater possessions in land than others will conduce more to the well being and good government," Woodward observed, "than any levelling parity."[5]

Colonial authorities attempted to maintain proper social hierarchy by controlling "expression" in many areas besides clothing, of course. Speech especially commanded their attention. Punishment for presumptuous or abusive language to "betters" was ubiquitous. Servants everywhere risked extension of their indentures and other penalties for being disrespectful to their masters. Children (especially in New England) faced the rigors of the law in deriding their parents. And wives were expected to be properly submissive to their husbands, "as the Church is unto Christ," and not use abusive or reviling language toward them. Margaret Jones, an early Virginia colonist, offers but one of many examples. In 1626 she and John Butterfield "had a falling out," as a witness described it, over who should be allowed to gather peas from a nearby plot. A witness "found her with her hair about her ears," and she later railed at her husband and called him a "base rascal" for his apparent lack of concern over her condition. Though rumpled, Margaret seems to have held her own, for Butterfield was "all bloodied over his face," and when Steven Webb stepped in, she had beaten him with a tobacco stalk. That may explain Mr. Jones's less than sanguinary response. Either way, the Virginia General Court ordered the woman tied to the back of a boat and dragged up and down the James River for her words and behavior.[6]

Regulating spousal exchanges involved more than preserving social hierarchy. Disrespectful language could lead to breaches of the public peace. Words of defamation or abuse, the reasoning went, tended to stir up "the objects of them to revenge, and perhaps to bloodshed."[7] Preventing such developments was another critical basis for controlling speech in the early colonies, and of course it applied outside the home as well. Authorities commonly punished colonists for slandering and defaming one another, for instance. The preamble to a 1647 Rhode Island statute nicely captured the colonial attitude toward this offense. "A good name is better than precious ointment," it stated, "and slanderers are worse than dead flies to corrupt and alter the savour thereof."[8]

Abusive language was something that lower-level officials—sheriffs, constables, collectors, and the like—regularly endured. That was perhaps inevitable, for such men represented government at its most personal and objectionable. They daily encountered colonists' angry retorts while collecting taxes, making arrests, serving subpoenas, levying attachments, enforcing forfeitures, and the like. Some abusive words were merely "slighting." In 1665 Joan Ford suffered nine lashes for calling a constable "horn headed rogue and slow headed rogue." Many years later, Maine judges sitting in Quarter Session fined John Nason £1.10 for "bidding the constable of Kittery go shit and his warrant too." Sometimes insults gave way to threats and even attacks. In 1659 John Matthews paid a 5–shilling fine after driving a Massachusetts constable off his land with a sickle. In 1685 some men assaulted the deputy sheriff at Albany, New York, "beating him, throwing him down unexpectedly and pulling a handful of hair out of his head." The flustered official produced the hair in court for evidence.[9]

Punishing abuse of lower officials illustrates colonial leaders' attempts to control words that threatened the public peace. It also highlights another rationale for controlling speech that motivated colonial authorities: a need to preserve the integrity of governmental institutions. As representatives of the legal system, such men had to be protected to keep that system viable. This was even more the case higher up, for if low-ranking officials often endured abuse as an intrinsic part of their jobs, colonial courts and judges could not tolerate it without impugning the government more broadly.

Authorities punished contempt to preserve the integrity of the courts. Contempts sometimes involved actions, including failure to appear when subpoenaed and the like. Most, however, were verbal, and most were spoken in court. Some people lost their tempers after losing civil suits or receiving penalties they considered too harsh. Others were merely drunk and obnoxious. Occasionally, sober colonists with the best intentions drew contempt citations for too forcefully arguing their cases. Judges often showed a willingness to bandy points and demonstrated considerable patience in dealing with such situations. In William Pynchon's Justice of the Peace Court, on December 9, 1684, Obadiah Abbee charged Goodman Booth with telling a lie. Pynchon ruled that the words did not "reach to a lie in the sense or words of the law," but Abbee "affirmed with violent expressions that Goodman Booth was liable to the law." At length, Pynchon offered up the bench with a flourish so that Abbee could be the judge instead, noting that in such a circumstance Abbee's opinion would carry force, but for now "it became him to rest in mine." Theatrics did not help. Abbee eventually became, in Pynchon's words, "so fierce and insolent, exceeding all bounds, that I was not able to quiet him till I writ his mittimus and sent him to jail for his contemptuous, insolent carriage and boisterous speeches." After a few hours, Abbee was freed at his brother's humble request.[10]

Punishment of contempt, like prosecutions for abuse of lower officials, helped preserve the integrity of the legal system. Colonial authorities sought to protect other institutions as well, including the colonies' official churches. Reviling ministers, deriding church practices, and denouncing the tithe were frequent offenses, and officials prosecuted these as a matter of course. Expressing unorthodox religious beliefs was also a fairly common offense, and prosecutions were not limited to New England by any means, nor to men alone. In 1652, the Maryland provincial court received a deposition from Phillip Land against Joan Mitchell. It seems she had the temerity to say there was "no hell but a bad conscience."[11]

Colonial authorities regulated speech in order to maintain moral society, social hierarchy, the public peace, and state institutions. They also did so to preserve government itself. In a sense, all efforts to control speech were intended to preserve the state, but most did so indirectly. Not so with "seditious speech," for in it officials saw a clear and immediate threat. Words that colonial authorities considered to be seditious fell into three broad categories: *scandalum magnatum*, government criticism, and false news.

In English law, *scandalum magnatum* meant slandering or scandalizing great men in the realm, including nobles, peers, and judges. In a few cases, colonial officials tried offenders for scandalizing English "great men." Edward Randolph stood trial in New Hampshire for a quip made while pleading a case against Mark Hunking in March 1679/80. Randolph, "being asked where the Earl of Danby was, answered that he was hanged for ought he knew." A "Special Court" held at Portsmouth by the president and Council judged the words "a great reflection upon such a great Minister of State." The court forgave the offense, accepting Randolph's claim that the words were merely "suddaine and rash" rather than an intentional defamation.[12] Such occasional cases aside, in colonial practice *scandalum magnatum* usually meant deriding or criticizing high-level colonial officials rather than English lords of the realm.

As in other prosecutions for verbal offenses, authorities often did not record the specific words, leaving only their own characterizations for posterity. The description could be as mild as the penalty, as when the Plymouth Colony court referred only to his "speaking evil of one of the magistrates" in fining Thomas Starr £1 in 1669. At other times, judges clearly showed their irritation in describing the offense. When Jan Jansen Van Amersfoort reviled New York officials after they called him to account for beating his wife in 1665, they noted his "dirty, contemptible, despicable treatment" of them. In 1687 Maine magistrates convicted Cornelius Jones of "diverse, base, ignominious, vile and reproachful speeches" against Edmund Andros, governor of the Dominion of New England. The judges ordered Jones to receive twenty-one "stripes on the bare skin, well laid on."[13]

More detailed records reveal that colonists sometimes challenged authorities' justice or competence. In 1648 the Maryland provincial court charged Captain Robert Vaughan with seditious speech against Governor Green. In an unguarded moment, Vaughan had commented that "whatsoever Captain Brent demanded in Court, or claimed to be his, was allowed to him by the Governor without further proof." Vaughan had made matters worse by adding a personal element, proclaiming in the presence of others "that he had no right of justice of the Green Governor (so nominating the Governor in a scoffing and scornful manner)." Vaughan apologized before the trial and a satiated Green deigned to "pardon the offense." [14]

Other *scandalum magnatum* cases were more purely insulting. Jonathan Thing and Thomas Norman provide notable examples. In 1655 Thing appeared before the York County court in Maine for aspersing one of its justices. In an argument with another colonist, he had said "no question you may cast my case there so long as Harry the Coachman sitts judge." Coachman and company gave Thing the option of paying a £12 fine or suffering twenty lashes. Thomas Norman had to choose between a £5 fine and ten stripes in 1672 for calling the Bay Colony's governor "old blue beard." [15]

Separating this form of seditious speech from slander can sometimes be tricky. *Scandalum magnatum* was a criminal violation, but slander had been a civil offense since 1606, so how authorities handled the case is generally a reliable guide. Occasionally, colonial officials appeared to treat obvious instances of *scandalum magnatum* as civil matters, and a handful of slander suits included criminal punishments, confusing the matter from a different direction. Such infrequent cases aside, colonial officials generally separated slander from *scandalum magnatum*. This was especially so in New England, where authorities most consistently distinguished the magisterial office from the person occupying it. John Winthrop reiterated the Puritan view of governmental authority in 1645. To counter grumbling over the magistrates' power, he told the Massachusetts colonists that "it is yourselves who have called us to this office, and being called by you, we have our authority from God." The "contempt and violation" of that office, Winthrop darkly added, "hath been vindicated with examples of divine vengeance." [16]

It also incurred the vengeance of temporal authorities, and not just in Massachusetts. Willing both to punish such "contempt and violation" and to distinguish the magisterial office from the person, New Haven authorities tried Henry Tomlinson in 1659. He had spoken against New Haven's Governor Newman while visiting in Connecticut and found himself in court for seditious speech when he returned home. Tomlinson argued that Massachusetts officials had recently dismissed a similar prosecution. No, the New Haven court countered, the Bay Colony case was one of personal slander "done on a particular account," while Tomlinson's was done "upon public respects," his words thus "tending to overthrow our government." [17]

Authorities in other colonies were not as consistently conscious of making the distinction as those in New England, but they did make it. After Bacon's Rebellion, Governor Jeffreys presented charges against Colonel Phillip Ludlow to the Virginia Council. Following a lengthy introduction outlining the evils of seditious speech, Jeffreys insisted that Ludlow should be punished for "contemning his Majesty's authority in me," as well as for "defaming, scandalizing and otherwise abusing my particular good name and reputation." A jury later found Ludlow innocent of "abusing the authority of his Majesty," but "guilty of scandalizing the Governor by saying that he was perjured and had broke several laws." [18]

Scandalum magnatum, by definition, applied to those of high rank or position and not to lower officials, though the words could be similar. Lower officials were generally uneducated, of limited means, and unable by virtue of ability or status to command the respect of the people or represent the dignity of the state. This held true in the colonies throughout the seventeenth century. In 1697, for example, Maryland's Provincial Council, recognizing that constables were men "who cannot well attend the said employ by reason of such their poverty," ordered the county courts "to choose able men that are richer and may better attend the said office." [19]

Authorities did not punish words against lower officials as seditious speech, but *scandalum magnatum* could apply at the opposite extreme: to the king. Such words could also be considered treason, and colonial officials sometimes found it difficult to distinguish the offenses. Consider the case of Arthur Mason, a "bisket baker of Boston." In 1666, while serving as a constable, Mason entered a Boston tavern to apprehend some men. An argument broke out. After being told he would arrest no one, Mason heatedly replied that he "would take the King himself" if sent to do so, intending to assert his devotion to duty rather than to degrade Charles II. Someone in the tavern reported the words, and Mason ended up before the Court of Assistants, hat in hand. The magistrates held a special hearing to determine if the words constituted treason, a crime punishable by death. The biscuit baker must have breathed a sigh of relief when the judges ruled his words a misdemeanor and released him with an admonition. Rare cases like this constitute *scandalum magnatum*. When colonial authorities prosecuted words against the king as capital offenses, the appropriate classification is treason. Seditious speech, in all its forms, was a misdemeanor.[20]

Religion offered some complications as well. Colonial authorities worked to control seditious words uttered within religious contexts as well as without. "Whilst I stay in the government," Governor Fletcher told the New York Assembly in 1693, "I will take care that neither heresy, sedition, schism nor rebellion be preached amongst you."[21] Officials throughout the colonies shared Fletcher's commitment, and many colonists stood trial for uttering seditious words with a religious element.

Sometimes colonists derided both religious and secular leaders. Jonathan Sprague suffered thirty lashes and a £10 fine for "reproaching the minister" and "reproaching and scandalizing the magistrates" in Suffolk County, Massachusetts, in 1674. Only the severity of Sprague's punishment made his case unusual, and that came partly from his simultaneous conviction for "lascivious carriages and attempting the chastity of Matitha Aldredge and Huldah Thayre." When Simon Smith, an Anglican minister in New York, married a couple without official permission in 1699, he found himself before the colony's Supreme Court. There he uttered "several scurrilous expressions to the scandal of his function, the abuse of the grand jurors, and diminution to the dignity of the court." After some discussion, the judges declined to punish the pertinacious parson, not wishing to offend the Earl of Bellemont to whom Smith was personal chaplain.[22]

Such cases illustrate that a religious dimension did not preclude criminal prosecution for seditious speech. Yet some cases involving words against civil and religious authority do not count as seditious for the purposes of this study. The Quakers, often tried for reviling ministers and magistrates, are a case in point. Colonial officials widely regarded them as a threat to civil government throughout the century, and not only in New England. Virginia still prohibited "the unlawful assembling of Quakers" in 1688, and as late as 1709 North Carolina authorities described Quakers as "a great disturbance to the peace in this Province and the hindrance of good laws." William Ledra's defense when on trial in 1660/61 demonstrates that challenging government and its officials was intrinsic to the Quakers' theology—not merely a manifestation of criticism or abuse. The Massachusetts Court of Assistants queried him on one of the charges: "You believe the scriptures to be God's word, how dare you then revile Magistrates and Ministers [?]" "It was not reviling," Ledra calmly replied, "to speak the truth." The honest spiritual beliefs of such people must be the reigning consideration. Quaker and similar prosecutions are not considered seditious speech cases in this study.[23]

The second broad category of speech that colonial authorities considered seditious was criticism of the government (including its laws, practices, and policies). Here, as in *scandalum magnatum*, a peripheral religious element was not uncommon. Take, for example, Richard Crab's words, which combined *scandalum magnatum*, government criticism, and religion. In 1658 the New Haven authorities convicted Crab for "clamorous speeches against the ministry, government and officers."[24]

Most government criticism contained no religious element, but cases could be complicated in other ways. Sometimes offenders spoke ill of courts, but stood trial for seditious speech because authorities interpreted their words as more than "contempt." In 1653 Edward Hull appeared before the New Haven Colony court. He had surpassed "his commission in harassing the Dutch" and was admonished after "speaking ill of the court which called him to account." Such prosecutions can be difficult to categorize because they come so close to simple contempt. Seditious speech always implied contempt of authority, yet contempt of court was a separate offense, designed—as we have seen—to protect the integrity of the judicial system. It was identified on the one hand by a statutory standing independent of seditious speech and on the other by its special characteristics. In particular, when judges summarily punished unspecified words spoken in court, the offense was clearly contempt and is excluded from this study.[25]

The interwoven cases of Swithen Wells and Mr. Wheeler demonstrate the distinctions made. Wells appeared before Maryland's Provincial Council on October 3, 1684, to be tried for seditious speech.

While on trial in Cecil County for killing a horse, a man named Wheeler got so carried away in defending himself that the judges "bound [him] to the peace" for contempt. At that, "Swithen Wells stood up and began to vindicate [Wheeler's] cause in such a manner as the court was forced to commit him." The judges did not punish Wells for contempt, but held him for trial on seditious speech charges because he had called them "fools, and ignorant fools, god damn their worships, god damn them all, etc." When Wells later apologized, the judges forgave him, unwittingly precipitating an instructive jurisdictional dispute in the bargain. The Council insisted that the Cecil County court had no right to dismiss Wells. The words did not merely impugn that particular court, they insisted, but reflected on "his Lordship's honor and dignity there (as in all other his Lordship's Courts of Justice) represented." The final disposition of the Wells case is unclear from the records, but the distinction between contempt and seditious speech is not.[26]

Colonial authorities considered other kinds of government criticism to be seditious besides words spoken against courts. They commonly prosecuted colonists for criticizing the colony laws, as well as for complaining too vociferously about the levying of taxes and customs. The Connecticut General Court fined John Wheeler £5 in 1678, for example, for saying that New London County officials "sit here to pick men's pockets." Criticism of the government often took more general forms. The Massachusetts Court of Assistants disfranchised Thomas Dexter, then set him in bilboes and fined him £40 in 1632 "for speaking reproachful and seditious words against the government here established . . . saying this captious government will bring all to naught."[27]

Colonial authorities regularly punished criticism, whether directed against government officials, against a specific law or policy, or against the government more generally. Authorities did not, however, attempt to quell what they considered legitimate complaints. The vehicle and manner of presentation proved critical in determining legitimacy. Two formal mechanisms for registering criticism, appeals and petitions, deserve special attention.

Appeals from court judgments, whether civil verdicts, criminal convictions, or administrative decisions, were an essential element of colonial justice. Yet they posed a problem for officials sensitive to seditious speech because appealing a court's decision inevitably impugned the judgment of the men on that court. Challenging the fairness or justice of a court or of individual magistrates was widely punished as seditious speech. To do so in a formal appeal was not. Henry Bennett's case illustrates the point. He lost a suit against William Fellows in the Bay Colony's Ipswich County court in 1659/60. He also lost his temper and ended up before the Court of Assistants. The justices fined Bennett £5 for "slandering and open traducing the court of Ipswich." He then filed an appeal formally repeating his charges against the Ipswich judges. Bennett lost the appeal, but the higher court adjudicated it without apparent concern over seditious words. John Griffin made a revealing attempt to avoid censure in 1673. He began his appeal in Essex County, Massachusetts, with the phrase "without any reflections upon or unto the said judge."[28]

Colonial authorities protected the right of appeal, but concern over abuses remained. In Virginia, the burgesses underscored the problem in 1684 when they asked the Council to repeal a law allowing appeals from the General Court to England. People like Sarah Bland, they argued, misused the right of appeal to "vex and molest" honest folks. Worse, colonists took advantage of such appeals "to libel and asperse the government." When this request got nowhere, the burgesses asked that only appeals involving sums larger than £3,000 sterling be allowed. The Council denied this also, though their decision had to do more with defending the royal prerogative than protecting the colonists' rights.[29]

Appeals provided avenues of criticism and relief only for people involved in the judicial system. The right of petition offered a much broader tool for redressing grievances. Individual colonists often used petitions for quite personal ends. A widow, Abiah Merchant, complained to the Virginia Council in May 1699, for example, about a curious and obviously important problem. "Living near the bounds between this government and that of Carolina," the record noted, she "is compelled to pay quitrents in both governments." More generally, colonists employed petitions in asking permission to establish new towns and churches, in requesting special exemptions from specific levies, laws or regulations, and in registering formal complaints about policies and officials. Though like appeals they often involved impugning government and its leaders, when properly and respectfully done petitions were entirely acceptable.[30]

Abuses were not. The North Carolina proprietors wrote Governor Sothell in 1691 from England, noting that "tumultuous petitions [are] prohibited by Act of Parliament here with a severe penalty upon such as shall break that law." The proprietors intended this as a prelude to serious criticism rather than a lesson in law. They chided Sothell for encouraging a petition to call an assembly to right supposed wrongs in the colony, adding "we know not how far such ill example in Carolina may influence his Majesty's subjects in his other American plantations." The other plantations had already anticipated that problem. To deter frivolous or counterfeit petitions, colonial authorities often required that each be signed by the petitioners, and accompanied by a filing fee.[31]

Even then, colonists sometimes seditiously abused their right to petition. In 1685 the people of Springfield and Suffield petitioned the Massachusetts General Court on a matter regarding taxes. Specie being scarce, they asked to pay in corn. The court granted the request, but warned that "sundry expressions therein do deserve sharp reproof." In 1680 the Virginia burgesses stiffened the regulations for presenting grievances. "It hath been too frequent by the practice of ill disposed and seditious persons," they explained, "to deliver to their burgesses, and they to the assemblies, scandalous and seditious papers, and to entitle and call them the grievances of the inhabitants."[32]

Proper appeals and petitions allowed colonists to mitigate the excesses and injustices of government without threatening its authority. Within government, parliamentary privilege functioned in the same way. That device allowed members of legislatures to speak words in session that would surely have landed them in trouble otherwise. The Carolina proprietors echoed the typical approach when they made special provision for elected representatives in the 1665 Articles of Agreement. Such representatives were free "to make any address to the Lords touching the Governor and Council or any of them or concerning any grievances whatsoever or for anything they shall desire without the consent of the Governor or Council, or any of them." Yet, as two exchanges between the Maryland Assembly and the governor and Council demonstrated, colonial authorities had not fully accepted free speech within the halls of government, even at the end of the seventeenth century.[33]

In March 1697/98, Maryland's governor requested a recommendation on a law regarding attorneys. The attorney general and two Council members wrote an opinion concluding that the law "should be burnt." The Lower House ordered the three arrested, insisting that each should be fined 10 shillings (to make the point) and that the written opinion itself should be publicly burned. The Council disagreed, and after considerable wrangling the matter was finally dropped without a resolution. Using the classic parliamentary weapon, the house exacted its revenge later by refusing to vote funds to pay the attorney general's salary.[34] The following November, roles reversed as Governor Nicholson angrily denounced a petition from the Lower House as "a seditious, scandalous libel" and ominously declared that he would not "protect them." No prosecution followed, though some months later a bolt of lightning hit the Lower House while it was in session and "strook down and grievously wounded several of the Delegates." The record is silent on whether that inclined the body to reconsider the value of the governor's protection. The members did, however, prudently order that leather water buckets be procured. Only a sudden rain shower had quenched the fire started by the lightning.[35] In another context, these would have been instances of seditious speech. Prosecutions for criticizing legislation and for seditious petitions were common enough. Yet these constitute instances of battling for power and prestige within government rather than outside threats to governmental authority. Such cases are not included in this study, participants' rhetorical invective notwithstanding.

Deriding public officials and criticizing government outside carefully constricted channels constituted a threat to government in the eyes of colonial authorities. If that sounds somewhat strange to modern ears, much more so does their fear and control of "false news." The seventeenth-century colonies had no newspapers, and official information came slowly, especially to those living away from the seat of government. The occasional notice read aloud in the town square or tacked to a post could hardly satisfy colonists ever curious about recent events. Private persons filled the void as news spread by word of mouth, usually from the ports inward. The chain of information stretched from the latest ship's crew to the most isolated planter, and in the process colonists regularly received and forwarded incomplete, exaggerated, or just plain wrong information. That was an accepted part of colonial life. Yet within this milieu, authorities recognized a danger to their governments and worked to limit that threat by regulating and prosecuting "false news."

"False news," knowingly spreading untrue reports, rumors, or information that endangered the government, appeared clearly as a crime in colonial law, as we shall see in the following chapter. Prosecutions, as we shall also see, were common for this offense, and that is not surprising, for it could be quite dangerous. For one illustration of how spreading false news could create problems for governments, consider the beginnings of Culpeper's Rebellion. Writing to the proprietors in 1680, the restored North Carolina authorities noted that John Culpeper was "a person that never is in his element but whilst fishing in troubled waters." He and others had gone about "poisoning the people's ears, unsettling and disquieting their minds, by diffusing and dropping abroad by their agents false and dangerous reports." In this way, they explained, the rebellion began.[36]

Colonial authorities, then, punished a wide range of speech they considered seditious. For offenses ranging from derogating public officials to criticizing government to spreading false news, people stood trial in every colony throughout the seventeenth century. Those prosecutions were inextricably intertwined with the reasons for controlling other kinds of expression. Because seditious words threatened government itself, they inevitably endangered the moral and social values that government protected, the public peace it sought to maintain, and the institutions it erected and protected to serve those ends. Punishing such words, in simple terms, preserved society. This basic logic was established in English seditious speech law in the thirteenth century and continued through the seventeenth, in England and in her colonies.

Seditious Speech Law

English seditious speech laws originated in the thirteenth century, eventually crossing the Atlantic to become established in the colonies. Those laws were the foundation upon which prosecution and punishment stood. They were also, in a sense, the one major constant in an ever-evolving universe of control over expression. To appreciate the important changes in freedom of speech that occurred during the seventeenth century, one must first understand the stable foundation the law provided.

The earliest stages of English seditious speech law date from the reign of Edward I, who ascended to the throne in 1272. Edward's rule marked an important turning point in English history. Under him, English government took on a form and permanence that lasted through to the rise of the Tudors at the end of the fifteenth century. Under Edward, summoning parliaments became the established manner of raising money and doing business, and he completed important judicial reforms begun by Henry II. Edward also promulgated a series of acts dealing with the position of the church and the great landholders, the regulation of trade, and the enforcement of public order. Those acts included England's first seditious speech law. The 1275 statute directed "that from henceforth none be so hardy to cite or publish any false news or tales whereby discord or occasion of discord or slander may grow between the king and his people or the great men of the realm." Anyone doing so, the law continued, "shall be taken and kept in prison until he hath brought him into the court which was the first author of the tale."[1]

The emphasis on false reports that directly disturbed the realm stood for more than a century, but by the reign of Richard II seditious speech statutes had begun to change. When rapid wage and price escalation followed the Black Death, Parliament restrained wages, but not prices. The resulting discontent brought about the Peasant's Revolt of 1381 and probably also led, in 1379, to the new direction in seditious speech law. The statute of that year abandoned the older emphasis on general lies and false reports, centering instead on false news about great men in the realm. It also defined the classes of persons who could be properly reckoned "great men" or magnates. The long-standing provision that offenders remain in jail pending discovery of the original author of the tale remained a part of the 1379 law, though it was soon changed. From 1389 on, when the originator of a false report could not easily be discovered, the disseminators of such tales were punished instead.[2]

During the 1300s, English authorities had established the basics of seditious speech law. By all accounts, officials rarely charged offenders under these statutes before the Tudors. Then prosecutions increased significantly. The Renaissance and the printing press combined to encourage and disseminate criticism just as the Tudor monarchy was struggling to stifle opposition and solidify its centralized control over the kingdom. By the 1530s, seditious speech usually involved derogating royal advisors or the ruling class more generally, dangerously misinterpreting the government's policies, or criticizing the sexual doings of the king. Judges could pillory, whip, or imprison offenders summarily. The modern equivalent of such words, as J. A. Sharpe has quite rightly observed, "if prosecuted with complete efficiency, would result in the incarceration of most of the population."[3]

Through the mid-sixteenth century, the Tudors preferred to prosecute seditious speech using a vague 1352 treason statute. This law made conviction easier because it imposed fewer procedural restrictions. A seditious speech conviction, for example, required the testimony of two witnesses, a rule which stood through the seventeenth century and applied in the colonies. Defendants sometimes went free because of this rule, even when they had clearly spoken the words alleged. Because of such cumbersome limitations, the large majority of early Tudor "treason" cases were, in reality, prosecutions for "seditious words uttered and overheard in public places." Judges often ordered punishments short of death, especially for less serious seditious words. Nevertheless, the chief complaint against Tudor treason law was that it made words used in everyday speech triable as treason.[4]

This led, in the reigns of Edward VI and Mary I, to statutes protecting the accused in treason prosecutions. Officials could no longer prosecute spoken treason, for example, past "a short period of limitation." These were coupled, however, with statutes designed to address seditious speech directly. A 1555 law made the penalty for "speaking seditious and slanderous words of the king and queen" the loss of both ears or a fine of £100, coupled with three months' imprisonment. Writing such words cost the offender one hand. Repeating words spoken or written by someone else was not quite so bad. For that, a person lost only one ear or paid a fine of 100 marks (about £65). Bloody Mary had little patience for repeat offenders. Anyone committing one of these offenses more than once suffered life imprisonment.[5]

A 1554 statute under Mary I, and a 1558 law under her successor, Elizabeth I, made it a misdemeanor "to speak or write with a malicious intent false and slanderous words of the king or queen." By 1580, writing such words was declared to be a felony, and speaking them a misdemeanor (but a felony on the second conviction). Elizabeth, ever sensitive about her claim to the throne, pushed a separate 1558 law making it treason to assert—in writing, printing, or by overt act—that she was not the rightful queen. A number of Englishmen met their deaths under that statute. To challenge Elizabeth's claim with spoken words, interestingly, was seditious on the first conviction, but treasonous on any subsequent conviction.[6]

These felony statutes "punished the expression of seditious opinion as a crime in itself." Before their promulgation, "the Crown did not possess a law that dealt specifically with seditious opinion, however expressed." Treason treated seditious opinion as evidence, and the old *scandalum magnatum* laws looked only at the "defamatory and therefore fractious consequences of language." The Tudor statutes remedied those weaknesses. Yet they did not outlast the

Tudors. When the most important felony statutes against seditious speech expired upon Elizabeth's death, Parliament did not reenact them for James I.[7]

Instead, James got a Star Chamber case, *de Libellis Famosis*, which defined and clarified the various forms of criminal libel, including seditious words. Lewis Pickering appeared before the Star Chamber in 1606, charged with writing a rhyme and letting a friend read it. The rhyme defamed Elizabeth I and Archbishop Whitgift, but Pickering argued that it was no libel because they were both dead. The judges disagreed. "The offense to the state dies not," they noted, even if the person does. Chief Justice Coke went on to distinguish simple slander and libel from defamation of great men and officials. The latter is more serious because "it concerns not only the breach of the peace, but also the scandal of Government." After all, "what greater scandal of Government can there be," he continued, "than to have corrupt or wicked magistrates to be appointed and constituted by the King to govern his subjects under him?" Nor could truth be a defense, Coke added, because the words' negative effect on the government remained the central consideration. The high court also clearly indicated that seditious speech constituted a misdemeanor, not a felony, and included under that heading "unpublished" words—whether spoken or appearing in manuscripts like Pickering's.[8]

The Star Chamber thus established the basic structure of English seditious speech law in 1606 with its *de Libellis Famosis* ruling. Important issues surrounding seditious speech as a crime, including distinctions between treason and seditious words and whether the offense constituted a misdemeanor or a felony, were thus settled on the eve of American colonization. This understanding of the offense remained throughout the seventeenth century, and colonists brought it with them to the New World.[9]

Colonial seditious speech fell into three broad categories: insulting or impugning government officials, criticizing government generally, and spreading false news. All caught the attention of colonial authorities, all had special statutes addressing them, and all carried legal penalties. Military regulations treated seditious words as mutiny, and the punishments were understandably harsh, reaching even to life itself under certain circumstances.[10] On the whole, however, a milder approach characterized statutes promulgated to control nonmilitary seditious speech. That was certainly true in the matter of speaking against government officials—an offense proscribed from earliest colonial days.

In his original instructions for Virginia on November 20, 1606, James I established that the Virginia authorities "should not suffer any person to withdraw" the colonists "from their due allegiance unto us, our heirs and successors, as their immediate sovereign under God." Anyone doing so, James added, would "be apprehended, arrested, and imprisoned until he shall freely and thoroughly reform himself." Unrepentant offenders were to be sent to England "to receive condign punishment." Few colonial speakers of sedition ever went to England for punishment, condign or otherwise. But Virginia authorities took the sentiment of the charter seriously, early establishing it in the law and occasionally adding measures designed to strengthen enforcement. In 1631, for example, the Virginia General Court ruled that "the first informer of any slanderous reports of the Governor or Council were to have the fine." [11]

Throughout the century, the firm prohibition against criticizing officials remained. On December 20, 1677, for example, the Virginia Council, noting a recent English statute, reaffirmed that anyone who "shall maliciously express, publish or declare any words to incite and stir up the people to hatred and dislike of his Majesty or the established government" would not only suffer the "punishment inflicted by common or statute law," but would also be "disabled to enjoy any place, office or promotion either civil or military." The law enjoined county court justices to enforce it on pain of paying double the fine the offender would have faced.[12] This statute came in the aftermath of Bacon's Rebellion, but it echoed established colonial practice. Every colony used exclusion from office as one form of punishment for seditious words.

The burgesses continued the law three years later, making the penalties more explicit and tougher. "Ill disposed persons" took it upon themselves "to asperse the government and defame the Governor and chief magistrates," the preamble noted, "which cannot but tend to the future disturbance of the peace and welfare [of the colony] if not timely prevented." To ensure timely prevention, the legislature ordered that anyone defaming the governor or attempting to "stir up the people to the dislike of any person appointed by his Majesty" would be sternly punished. Words against the governor brought an enormous fine of £500 sterling and a year in jail. Words against lesser officials, "councillors, judges, or principal officers," brought a fine of £100 sterling and three months in jail. In both cases, imprisonment would be without bail.[13]

Virginia was not alone in establishing a statutory foundation for punishing *scandalum magnatum*. Maryland authorities drew upon English tradition and the specific prohibitions of Cecilius Calvert. In the original commission to the governor and Council of Maryland on April 15, 1637, the second Lord Baltimore clearly provided that his own person be free from slights. He required that all colonists "honor, respect and obey him as they ought to do, upon pain of such punishment to be inflicted upon them, and every of them, as such high contempt shall deserve." So that none could claim ignorance of the ordinance, he ordered it proclaimed and published throughout Maryland. Baltimore also commanded colony authorities "to proceed with rigour against all contemnors and neglectors of the same . . . without favor." A year later, the Maryland Assembly established this sentiment in a law that would stand almost to the end of the seventeenth century. Among the various crimes designated as "enormous offenses within this Province," the legislators included "scandalous or contemptuous words or writings to the dishonor of the Lord Proprietary or his Lieutenant General [governor] for the time being or any of the Council." Reaffirmation of that sentiment came in the turbulent 1670s. In 1676 Philip Calvert, who had become the Third Lord Baltimore upon his father's death a year earlier, issued a special commission for a Grand Inquest to look into "mutinies, seditions, rebellions, etc." in Maryland. A manifestation, no doubt, both of the troubled times in the colonies and of Philip's desire to assert his suzerainty, the commission included a requirement that all "speaking of words against us or our dominion" over Maryland be tried "according to the laws and customs of the Kingdom of England and of this our Province."[14]

In 1647 the Rhode Island Assembly declared it a crime "for any man to use words of contempt against a chief officer, especially in the execution of his office." Any defendant convicted by a jury had to post a three-month behavior bond. Either Rhode Islanders remained exceptionally well-behaved in this regard or Rhode Island officials failed to enforce the provision strictly, for of all the New Englanders prosecuted for seditious speech in the 1640s, not one was a resident of "Rogue's Island" (as the colony's detractors called it). Not so in the 1660s. Rhode Island authorities reiterated their seditious speech law in 1663 and stiffened the allowable penalty. Not coincidentally, perhaps, the number of Rhode Island seditious speech cases went up notably in the 1660s. The law and the increase in prosecutions probably reflected the leaders' concern that all go smoothly in their bid to have the colony charter renewed by a restored Charles II. Indeed, the king's commissioners had come to New England precisely to assess the situation in general and the acceptability of such petitions in particular.[15]

The other New England colonies outlawed words against men in authority as well. The precise nature of New Haven's seditious speech law before 1656 is unclear. From the beginning, New Haven authorities emphasized "that the Word of God shall be the only rule to be attended unto in ordering the affairs of government in this plantation." Their *scandalum magnatum* prosecutions reflected the influence of that principle. In convicting Thomas Blatchley of uttering seditious words in 1646, for example, New Haven authorities noted that he was guilty of "neglecting the image of God in magistrates." A formal statement of New Haven's seditious speech law finally appeared in the Code of 1656. A wide range of penalties awaited anyone defaming a "Court of Justice, or any of the Magistrates or other judges of any such court within this jurisdiction in respect of any act or sentence therein passed." Offenders faced "fine, imprisonment, bonding to the peace, or good behavior, disfranchisement or banishment, according to the quality and measure of the offense." The marginal notation giving the scriptural reference for this law cites Exodus 22:28 rather than the traditional Deuteronomy 17:12. The latter required death for derogating magistrates; the former merely stated that "Thou shall not revile the gods nor curse the ruler of thy people." Where the softening attitude that implies might have led is speculation, for the tiny colony of New Haven was officially swallowed up by Connecticut in 1665.[16]

The 1656 New Haven statute was a near verbatim rendition of

Connecticut's seditious speech law. The Connecticut version had been established in the Code of 1650, also called "Mr. Ludlow's Code" after the man largely responsible for drafting it in the late 1640s. The Code of 1650 did not include binding to the peace or good behavior; New Haven authorities had added that possible penalty, perhaps borrowing from Massachusetts. It did include the other sanctions, banishment among them.[17]

From the earliest years, Massachusetts authorities maintained laws against criticizing officials. John Cotton's 1636 draft of proposed legislation on this issue required "reviling of the magistrates in highest rank amongst us, to wit, of the governors and council, to be punished with death." As his authority, Cotton cited I Kings 2:8, 9, and 46. The death penalty did not appear in the final version of the law in 1642 because it was thought too severe. Thomas Hutchinson, writing in the following century, claimed that John Winthrop personally erased the penalty from the original draft. Biblical issues aside, the Massachusetts authorities maintained laws against *scandalum magnatum* throughout the seventeenth century, reissuing the initial statutes in revisions of the laws from 1661 on. And they applied the law not only to ordinary colonists, but to magistrates as well, just as Connecticut did later.[18]

Other English colonies promulgated and enforced *scandalum magnatum* statutes in the seventeenth century as well. Pennsylvania's "Great Law," or "Body of Laws," of 1682 prohibited the offense. "If any person speak slightingly or carry themselves abusively against any magistrate or person in office," Chapter 32 proclaimed, they would either be fined a minimum of £1 or face "ten days imprisonment at hard labor." The Quaker colony reaffirmed the law periodically in the following years.[19]

The second broad category of seditious speech that concerned colonial authorities involved words against the government generally rather than against individual officials. That authorities separated this offense from *scandalum magnatum* is clear from various sources, including charters, oaths of fidelity, and prosecutions, in addition to colonial statutes. In the third charter of the Virginia Company, issued in March 1611/12, for example, James I noted that some colonists who had abandoned the plantation and made their way back to England defended their actions by disparaging the

Virginia government. Such unacceptable behavior had developed because Virginia officials had no "direct power or authority, by any express words in our former letters patents, to correct and chastise such offenders." James corrected this oversight in unequivocal terms when he issued the third charter. There, he fully empowered Virginia authorities to punish speakers of sedition "for the preventing of the like hereafter."[20]

Plymouth Colony's 1636 Freeman's Oath required that "you shall not speak or do, devise or advise any thing . . . that doth or may tend to the overthrow" of the colony. The revised oath of 1658 included the same pledge. On March 7, 1659/60, Plymouth officials disfranchised Isaack Robinson for "sundry scandals and falsehoods in a letter . . . tending greatly to the prejudice of this government." This followed a breach of not only the freeman's oath, but also a specific statute promulgated on June 7, 1659. The act required that "such as shall speak contemptuously of the laws" of the colony "shall lose their freedom of this corporation." Three months later the court refranchised Robinson, there having been "some mistake" about his offense.[21]

This Plymouth law highlights an important point. Speaking against the government included criticizing its laws as well as its exercise of authority more generally. Other colonies maintained similar provisions. We have seen that Massachusetts authorities punished offenders for deriding statutes from the 1630s on. Chesapeake leaders did as well. Virginia officials took the time to establish a law in 1664 providing specific punishments for "factious and seditious" colonists who took it upon themselves to be "contemners of the laws." A 1678 Maryland statute provided imprisonment for such people, and a tough 1672 Rhode Island law authorized three unpleasant options—thirty lashes, a fine up to £20, or as much as a year in jail—for those "speaking against such acts or orders [of the Assembly] openly."[22]

Colonial authorities commonly combined prohibitions against *scandalum magnatum* and criticism of the government more generally. A typical 1637 Massachusetts law allowed fines, imprisonment, disfranchisement or banishment for any colonist who "openly or willingly defame[d] any court of justice, or the sentences or proceedings of the same, or any of the magistrates or other judges of

any such court, in respect of any act or sentence therein passed."
Verbatim copies of this Bay Colony statute appeared in other colonies, as in Connecticut in 1672. Very similar versions surfaced periodically as well. As noted, New Haven incorporated this law into
its Code of 1656, adding "binding to the peace or good behavior" to
the list of possible penalties. In 1679/80, New Hampshire kept the
bond provision, but eliminated disfranchisement and banishment
as options. The 1671 and 1685 Plymouth statutes mirrored New
Hampshire's. Southern colonies also combined prohibitions against
scandalum magnatum and more general government criticism. In
1680, for example, Charles II issued a pardon and indemnity for
most participants in Bacon's Rebellion. But he added a clause designed specifically "to prevent the licentious defamation of the government and magistracy" of Virginia.[23]

The Maryland prosecution of Gerrard Slye illustrates how these
two offenses could be combined in a single case. Slye stood convicted for seditious words against Governor Nicholson and the
Maryland government in 1698. In a petition for clemency, Slye
noted that "he looks upon it as one of the greatest misfortunes of his
life to be brought under the circumstances he at present lies." One
wonders if he meant having spoken the words or being convicted
for them. Either way, his petition emphasized the words spoken
against the governor, who held the pardoning power. Governor
Nicholson replied that he took the "offense to be as well against the
government," adding that "if he thought it only against himself he
would have scorned to have kept him in prison half an hour." The
governor then asked the Council's advice. They all agreed that the
petition sufficed for mercy in the *scandalum magnatum* portion
of the offense, but insisted that clemency for words against the
government required a separate petition. In the second petition,
Slye begged forgiveness for that part of his offense, noting that his
words had "by some of the people in the Province been improved to
that degree as to breed some discontents in the minds of some of
the inhabitants whereby your Excellency's government might have
received some trouble." Such a development he "never in the least
imagined or intended." The provincial court forgave Slye's transgressions, released him from prison, and ended his bond obligation.[24]

Seventeenth-century colonial authorities regulated a third category of seditious speech as well—false news. Historically, this offense had been linked with *scandalum magnatum*, centering on the spreading of false tales about great men in the realm. In the early colonies "false news" came to mean false tales about important officials on the one hand, and false reports about events and the government on the other. Officials clearly separated both variants of false news from defaming or vilifying officials and from criticizing government more generally.

Laws prohibiting false news appeared less often than other seditious speech statutes, but they did appear. A case in point is the South Carolina act of 1691, designed "to punish persons which divulge reports to the dishonor of the Right Honorable Lords Proprietors." A similar Maryland statute, passed by the Assembly on April 8, 1671, allowed a fine or corporal punishment for "any such idle and busy-headed person [who] shall forge or maliciously publish or invent any false reports or tales of any of his Lordship's Justices" of the provincial or county courts. That defendants stood trial before the justices they had offended could not have strengthened their prospects for acquittal. Whether legislators regularly revived the act is not clear, though the 1684 Assembly did specifically continue the law in force. And three years before, in 1681, Maryland authorities issued a proclamation to note that "diverse good laws are now in force against divulgers of false news, rumors and reports, though (we fear) either forgotten by the people, or neglected to be executed by the magistracy." Officials intended the proclamation to remind "all the good people of this our Province to take notice of the said laws."[25]

Interestingly, prosecutions for the variant of false news involving untrue tales about officials occurred entirely in the South. Most were in Maryland in the 1670s and 1680s. Rumors ran rampant in those years that the proprietor and fellow Catholics within Maryland were behind recent Indian depredations. They conspired with the Indians, the story went, to destroy the Protestants in the colony. Maryland authorities had issued their 1681 proclamation precisely to stem the spread of such rumors. Virginia had a few such cases, and by the 1690s, Old Dominion authorities took care to outlaw both *scandalum magnatum* and false news about officials, but did so in separate statutes. Two 1693 laws so illustrate. In that year, the General Court approved both "An Act against divulgers of false news," and "An Act Punishing offenders for defaming the Governors, Councillors, and other principle officers."[26]

In the colonies as a whole, however, false news usually did not involve words that defamed individual leaders. It more often meant a very different offense—spreading false reports that were dangerous or damaging to the government generally. The Massachusetts authorities gave this transgression independent statutory standing as early as 1645. "Every person," they wrote, "of the age of discretion, which is accounted fourteen years, who shall wittingly and willingly make or publish any lie which may be pernicious to the public weal ... shall be punished." Plymouth authorities recognized the offense as a separate crime as well by 1653, even borrowing the language of the Puritan statute, differing in only two respects. The Pilgrims made the age of discretion sixteen years instead of fourteen, and allowed judges greater leeway in assessing penalties. They continued the law in June 1660. By the 1690s the language of the acts had changed, but authorities continued to regulate the offense. A Massachusetts law of 1692/93, for example, provided penalties for all who "make or spread any false news or reports with intent to abuse and deceive others." Conspicuously absent was the lengthy preamble against the evils of lying that had preceded the 1645 law.[27]

The Middle Colonies also prohibited this form of false news. The 1664 "Duke's Laws" of New York established clear penalties for anyone "who shall wittingly or willingly forge or divulge false news whereof no certain author" could be produced. "The minds of the people are frequently disquieted and exasperated" by such stories, the act explained. A first offense brought a 10-shilling fine, a second £1. Offenders unable to pay the fine faced the humiliation of the stocks or a public whipping of up to forty lashes. A 1684 statute reaffirmed this stance almost word for word. The thirty-eight fundamental "laws agreed upon in England" prior to the formal planting of Pennsylvania included a false news provision. "All scandalous and malicious reporters, backbiters, defamers and spreaders of false news, whether against magistrates or private persons," law number thirty declared, "shall be accordingly severely punished as enemies to the peace and concord of this Province." Pennsylvania officials hung a copy of these laws, including number thirty, in every court in the colony and had them read aloud at the formal opening of the Provincial Council each March. Authorities reaffirmed the false news statute at least five times between 1682 and 1700.[28]

The Southern colonies maintained statutes regulating the more general form of false news as well. We have seen that one reason for the Virginia Company's 1612 third charter was the spreading of scandalous and false reports in England, to the endangerment of the enterprise. This kind of false news continued to occupy the minds of Virginia authorities throughout the century. In 1649 the burgesses made the spreading of "false reports and malicious rumors . . . tending to the change of government, or to the lessening of the power and authority of the Governor or government" virtually synonymous with treason, allowing the death penalty for the offense. The statute, made in the year Charles I lost his head, did not distinguish originators from mere repeaters of news.

The fear and uncertainty following Charles's execution passed in the following years, and Virginia's subsequent false news laws reflected the change. A March 1657/58 statute allowed a fine of 2,000 pounds of tobacco against "any person who shall forge or divulge any false or dangerous news tending to the disturbance of the peace of this colony" unless he named the author of the report. Essentially the same act passed in March 1661/62, though reference to disturbing "his majesty's liege persons in this colony" signaled the restoration of the Stuart monarchy. The basic law continued in Virginia at least through 1702.[29]

Maryland and South Carolina established false news legislation as well. Maryland officials appear to have used *scandalum magnatum* laws and other means to prosecute seditious speakers until well past midcentury. By 1671, however, the Assembly had passed a clear false news law, providing a fine of 2,000 pounds of tobacco for "what person or persons soever shall forge or divulge any false reports (tending to the trouble of the Province)." Maryland authorities also promulgated some unusually specific false news laws. In the 1680s the Assembly twice saw the need for legislation against those who said the government did not support trade. In 1695 the

Assembly authorized prison sentences for those who said Carolina and Pennsylvania were better places to live, and (perhaps not coincidentally) for anyone spreading rumors that taxes were about to be raised in Maryland. South Carolina authorities had their own problems in the 1690s as well, and those led to a false news law emphasizing words that endangered the government generally. On June 21, 1692, they ordered that any person who "presume[d] to publish any false news or utter any seditious or scandalous words tending to the disturbance of the peace of this government" would "suffer three months imprisonment without bail or mainprise." [30]

Containing the spread of false rumors proved difficult. Various means had been attempted. The most common included rewarding people who reported others for spreading such rumors and lessening or eliminating penalties for those revealing from whom they had heard the report. Sometimes officials even investigated to determine the true originator, but that tactic must have been as aggravating and time-consuming as it was fruitless. I have found no cases that resulted from such an investigation in any colony. [31]

Authorities from Kittery to Charleston showed their frustration. After Charles II's restoration, his commissioners questioned the willingness of Bay Colony officials to prosecute spreaders of false news. All things considered, these doubts probably had some foundation in truth, but so did the reply. They stood ready to silence "all scandalous and false rumors that have been raised," the General Court intoned, but it was "extremely difficult, if not impossible to trace those wild and absurd rumors to their first fountain, every reporter commonly contributing some addition to the stream." [32]

Southern authorities struggled with the same problem. In 1685 Virginia's governor expressed the difficulty attending false reports in terms that would have drawn knowing nods from New England officials. "The rise and growth of sedition and faction proceeds and increases," he observed, "by the over licentiousness of the people in their discourses." They relate "their own vain imaginations and conceit," he continued, "which being once on foot, though altogether suggested by particular biased persons, is esteemed as news." It is then "infused into the giddy headed multitude, which afterwards becomes the rule and square of their actions." "Over licentiousness" might have been an ungenerous description of people's inability to resist improving a good story, but the governor's basic point certainly stood.[33]

These, then, represented the three basic types of seditious speech colonial authorities sought to control through legislation. *Scandalum magnatum*, criticism of government more generally, false news of both types—all occupied the minds of officials. Those laws had two especially notable general characteristics that deserve consideration here: a remarkable consistency from colony to colony, and a clear pattern of response to changing circumstances.

On the matter of consistency, leaders in every colony worked to regulate each type of seditious speech, and they used strikingly similar statutes and methods to enforce that regulation. A New Hampshire colonist passing through the Chesapeake late in the century would not have been confused by a Maryland proclamation against criticizing the government or its officials. Nor would a Virginian in port at Boston or a South Carolinian visiting New York have considered those colonies' seditious speech statutes out of the ordinary—in the 1660s or the 1690s.

Colonial authorities also demonstrated a notable consistency in the types of punishments authorized against seditious speech. Statutes in all colonies allowed officials to exact fines and take bonds. Offenders everywhere faced humiliation, disfranchisement, and banishment. Those options became less viable as the century progressed, but that was true from Pemaquid to Pamlico. And the crack of the whip echoed through Hartford's town square as readily as it drifted across Albemarle Sound when speakers of sedition took their stripes "well laid on."

Leaders in every colony also assumed as a matter of course that there would be a broad consensus on what constituted seditious speech and how it could be punished. That assumption was well-founded. Petitions and complaints revealed colonists' clear knowledge of the law. In Essex County, for example, Massachusetts residents petitioned authorities in 1671 to settle a church dispute lest it "break forth into open factions and mutinies." As part of the argument for intervention, the petition quoted a Bay Colony statute authorizing punishment for "every person whatsoever that shall revile the person or office of magistrates or ministers."[34] More broadly, the vast majority of prosecutions began after ordinary colonists reported words they understood to be seditious. And defendants on trial for seditious speech attempted various defenses— ranging from drunkenness and claims of being misunderstood to loss of memory and outright denial—but none argued that laws regulating seditious speech were improper or confusing.

True, occasional disagreements arose. Sometimes these came over a petition worded too strongly or an appeal argued too strenuously, but those were differences in degree, not in kind. Petitions and appeals, after all, typically involved criticism of government or its officials. And in the very rare case where a defendant seemed genuinely ignorant of the offense (and properly penitent upon being made aware of his fault), officials normally dropped the charge. This happened, for example, with Andries Gardenier in 1684. When the sheriff came to collect taxes from him in Albany, New York, he said "the Devil gave the Assembly power to give away his money, and that they were all fools." In court he claimed he had not thought the words seditious. The judges let the prosecution fall.[35]

Seditious speech laws in all colonies maintained the misdemeanor status of seditious speech. Rare exceptions did occur: Virginia during the English civil wars; Massachusetts briefly flirting with the death penalty in first drafting its laws; military regulations in time of war; occasional confusion over whether certain words constituted treason. These aberrations aside, seditious speech, in all its forms, was a misdemeanor in the colonies in the seventeenth century. The Star Chamber's 1606 *de Libellis Famosis* ruling obtained on both sides of the Atlantic and stood through 1700 and beyond.

Historically, seditious speech regulations, in England as well as in the colonies, also tended to appear in response to changing circumstances. In 1533, when Henry VIII divorced Catherine and married Anne, a statute made it treason (recall the confused legal status of seditious speech under the Tudors) to speak against the new marriage in writing and misprision of treason to do so with spoken words. Henry stiffened the law three years later as murmuring grew, making both spoken and written words against the marriage treasonous. In 1547 it became treason to assert that Henry was not the head of the English church, in writing on the first offense, verbally on the third. A 1558 law made it treason to say that Henry and Anne's daughter, Elizabeth, was not the rightful queen. Under a 1661 statute, criticizing the restored Charles II was deemed treasonous, and some judges even "claimed that the publishing of a seditious libel was nearly an act of treason."[36]

Times of danger sometimes brought increased levels of prosecution as well as new laws. England in the latter part of the seventeenth century saw a "great frequency of prosecutions for political libels and seditious words," especially in the 1680s.[37] This basic pattern held across the Atlantic as well. As in England, insecure times produced surges of prosecutions in the colonies. Massachusetts during the 1630s and Maryland following the Ingle Rebellion are two examples. Changing times produced variations in colonial seditious speech statutes as well. Virginia, Rhode Island, and Maryland offer some practical illustrations.

After Charles I's execution in 1649, Old Dominion authorities made the spreading of reports or rumors "tending to change of government, or to the lessening of the power and authority of the Governor or government" liable to the death penalty. By 1657, the law had become both milder and more general. It allowed fines of up to 2,000 pounds of tobacco for spreaders of false or dangerous news, but no penalty if the defendant divulged the author. In 1661/62, and again in 1673, authorities continued the statute and let the punishment stand, though with an additional behavior bond for offenders who maliciously invented or spread such news.[38]

Immediately following Bacon's Rebellion, Berkeley's government initiated a stiffened seditious speech law. "Seditious and scandalous libels," it began, are "the usual forerunners of tumult and rebellion." None "shall presume to speak, write, disperse or publish by words, writing or otherwise," it continued, "any matter tending to rebellion, or in favor of the late rebels or rebellion." Men who violated this new statute would, for the first offense, pay a fine of 1,000 pounds of tobacco, and spend two hours in the pillory "with capital letters of their crimes affixed on their foreheads or breast." The second offense doubled the fine and kept the pillory and paper provision. The third offense changed things entirely, for with it the words went beyond sedition and became treason. The law made separate provision for women. They received twenty lashes for the first offense, thirty for the second, but were not to suffer the pillory. In each case, the whipping would be set aside if the erring woman could pay the fine normally taken from men. The third offense brought no options. Habitual offenders of both sexes stood trial as traitors.[39]

Rhode Island's original seditious speech act came in 1647, authorities there apparently seeing no need for one earlier. It "declared that for any man to use words of contempt against a chief officer, especially in the execution of his office, is against good manners, and misbehavior." The statute authorized a maximum penalty of a three-month behavior bond, amount unspecified. Officials thought the law needed reiterating during the Interregnum. "Ill affected and rude persons" had apparently increasingly vilified "such as are in place of office" and their speech "tends much to the disparagement, not only of the government here established, but also reflects upon the State and Commonwealth of England, our honorable protectors." The renewed law of 1652 did not specify a penalty, but it did stipulate "that whosoever uttereth such words" be punished in any town of the colony. After the Restoration, the Rhode Island Assembly reinstated its original law, complete with the "misbehavior" language and the allowance of behavior bond. Interestingly, under the new law an offender could in addition "be fined by his peers," in an amount unspecified. No longer would seditious speech be prosecuted in the town courts, but only in the Court of Trials, the colony's highest jurisdiction. In April 1672, widespread complaining about taxes in the colony led to a harsher law. The act ordered that anyone "appear[ing] by word or act in opposition to such rates and impositions made from time to time by the General Assembly of this colony," or any other laws, especially if spoken in town meetings, "shall be proceeded against for high contempt and sedition." Offenders faced up to thirty lashes, up to £20 as a fine, or up to a year in the House of Correction.[40]

Changing circumstances drove some colonial leaders, including those in Rhode Island and Virginia, to toughen their seditious speech laws. But circumstances could push change in other directions. Maryland's seditious speech law, for example, disappeared entirely in the decade following the Glorious Revolution. That did not occur without a long fight and two changes of governors.

Led by the new royal governor, Sir Lionel Copley, the Maryland Council fired the opening salvo on May 24, 1692. Sitting as the Upper House, the Council informed the Lower House that the colony's long-standing seditious speech statute, "being of great import and concernment to the peace of this Province," needed to be toughened.[41] The House complied, forwarding a revised bill with three provisions. "Divulgers of false news" would be fined up to 4,000 pounds of tobacco. Those "defaming and evil speaking of the Governor" would pay a fine of 10,000 pounds of tobacco and endure "12 months imprisonment without bail." A fine of 6,000 pounds of tobacco and three months' imprisonment without bail awaited those convicted of "defaming the Councillors, Judges, Justices or other principal officers." The Council responded in writing a few days later. "The penalties asserted for the breach of this Act the Board think too slight and mean," the note began. We "know no reason why the same care should not be taken to preserve the authority and respect due to" Maryland's officials, they added, "as in Virginia and other neighboring colonies who have thought fit to enforce the same by a far greater penalty than was proposed." To help the Lower House "consider thereof and provide accordingly," the Council forwarded its own revised version.

House members preferred milder penalties for both false news and *scandalum magnatum*. They called for a reduction in the allowable amercement for spreading false reports and maximum fines of 6,000 pounds of tobacco for defaming the governor and 3,000 for defaming other high officials. The Council accepted a reduction in the false news fine from 4,000 pounds of tobacco to 2,000, but strongly opposed reductions on the other provisions. After days of wrangling, the House finally gave in, sending the Council "the Act against divulgers of false news amended in the penalties, 10,000 pounds for 6,000 pounds and 5,000 pounds for 3,000 pounds." The Council accepted a slight reduction in the fine for speaking against officials below the rank of governor. That did not end the dispute. The House, having capitulated on the matter of fines, refused to include imprisonment as a sanction. "This House do humbly conceive," they told the Council on June 2, "that the penalties of 10,000 pounds and 5,000 pounds tobacco now inserted are high enough considering the law is perpetual." Even on this matter the House members could not sustain their view, though they did wrangle some concessions.

The final bill, "assented to by the House, June 4th 1692," included a mixture of compromise provisions. The false news fine would be 2,000 pounds of tobacco or less (rather than 4,000) if the defendant could not produce the author. "If it appears to the Court that he did maliciously publish and invent the same," however, an additional behavior bond of unspecified amount could be required. For defaming the governor, offenders would face a fine of 10,000 pounds of tobacco. The words "or less" were added, satisfying the House. To satisfy the Council, imprisonment accompanied the fine, though for six months instead of twelve. Bail or mainprise still did not apply. Defaming councillors and other principal officers brought three months' imprisonment without bail or mainprise (as the Council had wanted), but the fine was reduced from 6,000 pounds of tobacco to 5,000 (less than the Council had sought, but up from the 3,000 pound figure the House had pushed). An added concession to the House allowed the fine to be less if in the opinion of the judges the offense deserved milder treatment.

Under this statute, Maryland authorities prosecuted eighteen speakers of sedition in 1692. The number declined dramatically in the following years. Eight stood trial in 1693, two in 1694, none in 1695. Only one colonist appeared in court for seditious speech in Maryland in 1696, and only one in 1697. The mood of the House in working to limit penalties for the offense mirrored a more general attitude of growing leniency within the colony. Indeed, even the Council itself seems to have become accustomed to accepting some degree of criticism over the years after 1692. Francis Nicholson, who arrived as governor in the summer of 1694, and under whom the capitol was moved to Annapolis the following year, finally told the members of the Council flatly in 1698 that even though "they will suffer themselves to be so abused, yet he must take care to prevent it." [42]

Nicholson, a former lieutenant-governor both of Virginia and the fallen Dominion of New England, was as good as his word. Though he had presided over four years of peace and quiet, a time when very few colonists appeared before the Provincial Court for seditious speech, the year 1698 saw a dramatic upsurge in such cases. Court documents recorded nineteen prosecutions for seditious speech in that year alone. That upsurge can be misleading, however. Most of the offenders were part of a tightly knit group—supporters of John Coode, opposed to Nicholson. Tempers flared after Nicholson beat Coode with a cane "for unseemly conduct" during church services, and a coalition formed to discredit and unseat the governor. He responded by prosecuting a number of them under the 1692 seditious speech statute.[43]

The spate of prosecutions led to a reaction after Nathanial Blackiston replaced Nicholson as governor in 1698/99. When revising the laws a few months later, the House excluded the 1692 statute against false news and *scandalum magnatum*. They sought the act's repeal because "its great latitude" led to abuses, "of which," they pointedly observed, "we know several examples." The omission did not escape Governor Blackiston's attention, but he was no Nicholson. "I am as little fond of keeping it on foot," he wrote the members of the House, "as it seems grateful to you to drop it." Blackiston then added a comment that would very much characterize his governorship. "When you know me better," he told them, "you will find me ever very ready to take off any oppression you shall in the least seem to be uneasy under." Beginning right away, he allowed the 1692 statute to lapse in accordance with the Assembly's wishes, leaving the colony without a seditious speech law until a milder one could eventually be substituted.[44]

Francis Nicholson did not go far away after Blackiston replaced him. Moving down the Chesapeake, he became governor of Virginia that same year. Perhaps still smarting from his running battle with the Coode faction, he issued a proclamation shortly after his arrival in the Old Dominion. Various laws had not been adequately enforced in the past, he announced, but they would be under his administration. Virginia's 1661 statute against seditious speech appeared prominently among the laws the new governor singled out for more rigorous enforcement.[45]

Seditious speech law stretched across time and distance from the dim days of the thirteenth century under Edward I to the dawning of the eighteenth century in the English colonies. A sense of the character and development of that law provides valuable context from which to view seventeenth-century changes in colonists' free-dom to criticize government and its officials. Yet the law itself liberated few people. Its basic ingredients remained the same in 1700 in most colonies as they had been in 1606 in the Star Chamber. What changed was less the law than attitudes toward it, less legal theory than practical implementation, less statutory sanctions than actual treatment of offenders.

THREE

The Nature of the Words

Early colonial authorities sought to control expression across a wide spectrum in the interests of maintaining ordered society and stable government. Within that spectrum, laws against seditious speech of various types figured prominently, and they retained their essential elements throughout the seventeenth century. Yet the gulf between theory and practice, between statute and enforcement, was substantial. In this chapter we will explore how colonial officials put seditious speech law into practice. We will examine the types of actual cases officials pursued and assess changes in the nature of the words prosecuted across the century, in the colonies as a whole and within the major regions.

In some instances, the type of a case cannot be determined from its meager representation in the records. In 1672 Stephen Whitman escaped and fled Maryland after being arrested "for speaking seditious words in his house," the exact nature of which went unrecorded. In 1681 Thomas Matthews, a West Jersey resident, uttered various "scandalous expressions" against William Penn. The Pennsylvania governor demanded that West Jersey authorities either fine Matthews £500 sterling or else affix a paper to the Burlington courthouse door expressing his offense, then banish him for six months and permanently disable him from holding any public office. But Matthews went unpunished, and he continued to asperse Penn at his leisure in the following weeks. A Rhode Island grand jury presented John Greene for speaking unspecified seditious words in

1668. After he acknowledged "that he is heartily sorry for using and uttering such words," the Court of Trials forgave Greene and released him.[1]

Such cases occurred infrequently. Over 90 percent of the prosecutions comprising the analytical base for this study are of a known type. Some even encompassed several known types. Cornelis Van Dyke said something to a fellow New York resident in 1683 that very nearly got him into trouble. The comments sparked an investigation into his having spoken "words to the prejudice of the King, the Duke [of York], the government, or the authority or the laws thereof." The justices at Albany seemed intent on casting a wide net, but it came up empty. Van Dyke went unpunished. Virginia authorities ordered a search in 1677 for the author of an anonymous petition they considered "highly scandalous and injurious, not only to the late honorable governor, Sir William Berkeley, Knight, but to the honorable Council of State, to the whole House of Burgesses, and," lest anyone be left out, "to the whole government and magistracy of this colony."[2]

Most offenders spoke less ambitiously. Such was certainly the case with words directed at individual officials, which came in various forms. Some were clearly of a personal nature, though not specifically recorded. Edward Adams and Samuel Cock appeared before the Albemarle County court in North Carolina on April 3, 1684. Both had "used very opprobrious language towards" Thomas Miller, a member of the court. Adams's unspecified words must have been the worse of the two offenses, for he paid a fine of 2,000 pounds of tobacco. Cock paid only 1,000 for his crowing. On July 10, 1683, Richard Webber petitioned the governor and Council of New Hampshire seeking forgiveness for his "abusive words against the honored Deputy Governor." His comments arose "from a testy and peevish nature that he retains within himself," Webber noted, "which he is heartily sorry for." Connecticut's General Court fined Bevill Waters £5 in 1692 for "sundry ill reflections made upon the Honored Governor and other members of the court."[3]

Far more colonists stood trial for speaking personal words of an identifiable nature, and authorities prosecuted these in every colony throughout the century. Insults were a staple. John Lee boldly affronted no less a personage than John Winthrop, governor of Massachusetts, in 1634, "saying he was but a lawyer's clerk," and demanding "what understanding had he more than himself." That Lee had also enticed the governor's maidservant "to go with him into the cornfield" would not have encouraged leniency. The magistrates ordered him whipped and fined £40. In a cooler temper the following day, they reduced the fine to £10.[4]

Similar offenses occurred elsewhere in New England. After posting a £10 appearance bond, Thomas Roberts went before the Rhode Island Court of Trials on March 8, 1658/59, for calling the magistrates fools. The judges accepted Roberts's apology after he explained that he had been drunk when he spoke the words, then fined him 5 shillings for drunkenness. Seabank Hog later found trouble in New Hampshire for even more pointed words, and no liquor to blame. "The Governor and the rest of the Gentlemen were a crew of pitiful curs," a witness had heard her say in 1684, "a parcel of pitiful beggarly curs." "And as for John Tufton," the witness added, "she said she could take down his breeches and whip his ass." What became of the case, the outspoken Ms. Hog, or the constable's breeches is uncertain. All of the New England colonies except Connecticut recorded instances of this variety of seditious speech.[5]

Middle Colony records contain such cases as well. When a New Jersey constable tried to arrest Thomas Wright for hog stealing in 1686, Wright exclaimed that "the Justices are all fools to send for him and that the Province stood in need of better government." He paid a 30–shilling fine for the words. In 1699 Henry Barnes was presented in Pennsylvania's Chester County for saying "he cared no more for constables nor justices than the dirt under his feet." Edward Southrin complained against John Avery on September 18, 1678. Avery had called the New York magistrate a "rogue and beggarly rogue" and a "pitiful, lousy rascal," adding, "I hold it beneath me to sit with such a pitiful fellow as thou art." Not that far beneath him, it turned out, for three weeks later Avery accepted a justice of the peace commission and sat with Southrin hearing cases. Governor Andros apparently declined to act upon the complaint.[6]

Southern authorities took a dim view of such insults as well. In 1693 the Maryland Council ordered Henry Jowles to post a huge behavior bond of £500 sterling, and to find two sureties, each worth an additional £500 each. During a conversation in Jacob Moreland's Calvert County store, Jowles had unwisely revealed his feelings about Nehemiah Blackiston, councilman and soon to be governor. "By God there is another pitiful fellow," Jowles had said of Blackiston, adding that he had many letters from Blackiston, and he intended to "keep them to wipe his arse." [7]

Years earlier, in 1674, Giles Bland called Thomas Ludwell, Virginia's General Court secretary, a "pitiful fellow, puppy, and son of a whore." Before Ludwell could register a protest, Bland gave him considerably more to complain about. He nailed one of Ludlow's gloves to the State House door along with "a most false and scandalous libel." The libel was thorough. "The owner of that glove," it announced, "was a son of a whore, mechanic fellow, puppy and a coward." The Assembly considered the words, both spoken and written, not just a private slander but "a public affront as well because the said Secretary was a public minister." For the personal slander, the General Court ordered Bland to ask forgiveness of Ludwell publicly, "which he did, but in so slight and scornful a manner as rather showed contempt of the Secretary and the whole court than a submission to their order." To satisfy for his affront to Ludwell as a public official, the court fined Bland £500 sterling. [8]

Seditious speech within the general category of words spoken against officials included not only insults but also charges of incompetence, unfairness or disloyalty. These I call "misprision" charges for economy's sake. In 1639 Jeffrey Ferris lost a civil suit in Connecticut and had to pay Richard Westcoat two bushels of corn because "his fence is found to be insufficient, and his cows were proved to be in Mr. Westcoat's corn." Upon hearing the decision, he angrily accused those making the award of bias and refused to pay. The court fined Ferris £1 for his words. Among the serious offenses charged against John Scott, a Long Island resident on trial in the same Connecticut General Court in 1665, was that he had been heard charging a colony official with "villainous and felonious practices" while in office. The court fined Scott a large, though unspecified, sum. [9]

In Rhode Island, John Briggs appeared before the Court of Trials in the fall of 1663 for saying that the governor of the colony, Benedict Arnold, "had gone about to subject the colony of Plymouth."

After Briggs conceded that he had no grounds for the accusation, the judges fined him £7 and required an additional £10 behavior bond. Captain Abraham Read appeared before Virginia authorities in 1653 for charging that Governor Bennet had so improperly handled two Dutch ships "that he would be called home into England and there they would deal well enough with him." Read confessed the words, but insisted that "he was only moved with the languages of others" and bore no malice toward the governor. Unconvinced or unsympathetic, the General Court jailed Read until he paid a fine of 10,000 pounds of tobacco and cask. He later petitioned to have the fine remitted "in regard the petitioner and his wife and children are now fitter objects of pity than punishment." Further south, William Billings took ten lashes at the whipping post in 1685 for loosely charging William Wilkison, a North Carolina justice of the peace and sometime Council member, with bribery.[10]

Among those forms of seditious speech directed at officials, insults and misprision charges predominated. Yet some less common forms deserve mention. Occasionally an offender stood trial for speaking words against dead officials. In a characteristically succinct notation, Plymouth authorities recorded on October 27, 1675, that "Thomas Lucase, for reviling some deceased magistrates, and for being drunk, was sentenced to be whipped at the post, which accordingly was performed." George Buttler fared better. In 1683 he appeared before the Maryland Council for several times uttering "most scandalous and opprobrious speeches reflecting both upon his Lordship [Charles Calvert] and his father of noble memory [Cecilius Calvert, d. 1675] to the derogation of their honors and breach of his Lordship's peace." Buttler denied the charge at first, but thought better of it after sitting in jail for three days awaiting trial. Before the Council, he confessed—taking care to mention his own "forlorn and miserable condition" and that of "his poor wife, big with child," all to good effect. The Council accepted Buttler's submission and freed him.[11]

Offenders sometimes threatened officials. The Connecticut General Court banished John Dawes in 1653 for his "threatening, malicious speeches against Mr. Hopkins his person, for his executing of justice (when he was Governor), on the said Dawes' wife." William Munsey sat a chilly half-hour in the stocks on December 12, 1688,

when the Maine Court of Quarter Sessions convicted him "for giving scurrilous and threatening language" to Francis Hooke, a justice
of the peace. What became of Shadrack Walton's case is uncertain,
but Peter Coffin, a New Hampshire councilman, made very clear in
his 1699 deposition that he took exception to Walton's "misbecom-
ing, reviling language," and even greater exception when Walton
"threatened to break the deponent's [Coffin's] head." [12]

On occasion, threats against lower-level officials mixed with seditious words. John Young was specifically empowered to impress a
horse in Maryland when "sent to St. Mary's County upon Express
for his Majesty's service." He attempted to do just that in the summer of 1698 at Elizabeth Wilson's home. But she "came out with a
case knife and swore she would cut his hand off if he did not
loose the horse." Young produced a special warrant signed by the
governor authorizing the impressment. Elizabeth Wilson looked at
the warrant and replied curtly that the governor could "kiss her
arse." Young found another horse, and Wilson found herself before
the provincial court for seditious words. [13]

Out of the 880 seditious speech cases of a known type gathered
from the Southern Colonies, New York, and New England, 503
contained some personal element. Of this group, 204 (40.6 percent)
do not admit of more specific classification. Court secretaries described the words sufficiently to identify seditious speech directed
against officials, but not fully enough to get at the precise nature of
these "personal" words. Fully identifiable prosecutions for words
against colonial officials thus number 299. A handful of these cases,
spread across the century, centered on threatening officials, with a
few scattered prosecutions for libeling dead magistrates. But the
large majority (91.3 percent) involved either words insulting an
official or misprision charges. For the century as a whole, and in the
colonies taken together, the two types proved to be closely balanced.
Insults numbered 142 (47.5 percent) compared to 131 (43.8 percent)
misprision charges. No consistent pattern emerged. In all regions,
one decade rich with insult prosecutions followed another with few
of them. In overall proportions, New England and the South were
notably similar. For the Northern colonies, 47.7 percent of all prosecutions for words against officials involved insults, while 46.5 percent centered on misprision. In the South, the order was reversed,

but the numbers were almost identical with 46.2 percent insults and 47.2 percent misprision. New York alone showed a marked difference. There 50 percent of all *scandalum magnatum* cases were of the insult variety, while only 23.7 percent involved charges of misprision. Why this is so remains unclear.

Dividing the New England and Southern cases into pre- and post-1660 groupings helps reduce the confusion caused by wide short-term fluctuations. When viewed from that perspective, North and South do appear different. The Southern colonies experienced a mild decline in insult prosecutions (50 percent before 1660 to 44.8 percent after) with an even milder corresponding rise in misprision cases (from 46.4 percent before 1660 to 47.4 percent after). In sharp contrast, New England's insult-type prosecutions increased dramatically from 38.7 percent before 1660 to 56.3 percent between 1660 and 1700. The decline in misprision cases proved equally dramatic, falling from a pre-1660 average of 56 percent to a post-1660 average of 37.5 percent (declining even further in the final three decades to an average of just 26.8 percent). That New England trend may have reflected the decline of the Puritan ethic and a growing secularization of attitudes toward status and authority.

An unusual form of *scandalum magnatum* involved utterances against the king. In 1670/71 John Cowin appeared before Plymouth authorities, charged with seditious speech. "He scorned to be in subjugation to any English man," Cowin had declared, adding "that there was never any King in England that was an English man but one crookedbacked Richard, a crooked rogue." A jury acquitted Cowin. In 1689 Thomas Broome repeatedly reproached the king in private conversations in Virginia, calling him a rogue and a villain among other things. Broome also habitually compared William III to Oliver Cromwell, "making the result of the comparison to render Cromwell an honest man and a saint, in respect to the King." The words, following a growing trend later in the century, went unprosecuted.[14]

Nor was the queen safe from aspersions, even in the grave. In 1699, five years after Mary died of smallpox at the age of thirty-two, Samuel Grey appeared before the Virginia Council for writing "a certain scandalous, false, malicious, and seditious libel" aspersing both William and "the late Queen Mary of blessed memory." Grey, a minister in Middlesex County, had told others that the paper was "put into his pocket by some idle rascal or other at town," but decided against trying that explanation on the Council. Instead, he humbly apologized and sought mercy. The Council accepted the apology and remitted the offense.[15]

David Lloyd was not so fortunate. He stood trial before the Pennsylvania Council in 1700 for "unparalleled misdemeanors and affronts against his majesty." In a disagreement over an attachment, Lloyd—a member of the Council—took the marshall's commission and held it up to the people standing around. "Do you think to scare us with a great box (meaning the seal in a tin box) and a little Babie (meaning the picture or effigies [of the King] aforesaid)[?]," he asked. "Fine pictures please children," Lloyd added, "but we are not to be frightened at such a rate." For these and similar expressions against William III, the Council unanimously voted to suspend Lloyd from the body until he had been tried on the charges.[16]

Most of the sixty-four recorded cases of seditious words against the monarchy came at periods of English governmental crises. Only four prosecutions occurred before the Restoration, two in New England and two in the South, all in the 1640s during the English Civil War. In the 1660s with the reestablishment of the Stuarts, the colonies witnessed a dozen such prosecutions—nine in New England, two in the South, one in New York. The number dropped to two in the 1670s and early 1680s, and then took a dramatic upsurge with the Glorious Revolution. The late 1680s saw twenty-four such cases, and the early 1690s followed close on with another twenty-two.

Words against the English king represented only 7.3 percent of all typeable seditious speech prosecutions, but that should not obscure the notable regional variations. A majority of the cases (51.6 percent) appeared in the Southern colonies, and constituted 11 percent of all Southern prosecutions across the century. The proportion soared during the 1680s in particular, going from no prosecutions in the 1670s to 21.5 percent of all Southern cases of a known type during the next decade, falling somewhat to 17.9 percent in the 1690s. That is not surprising considering that Virginia had been a royal colony since 1624 and that half of Maryland's prosecutions for words against the king occurred after 1691, the year in which the

Calvert's proprietary became a royal colony (remaining so until 1715).

Nor is it surprising that New England officials were the least likely to punish words against the king, doing so only seventeen times before 1700—a mere 3.9 percent of their region's seditious speech prosecutions of a known type. The Bay Colony, thoroughly dominant in New England throughout the seventeenth century, remained historically separated from (even hostile to) royal rule until the 1690s. Two contemporary comments make the point nicely. "The King's authority and power must in no sort be lessened," a Virginia gentleman wrote in 1674, "for the New England disease is very catching." New York's Governor Fletcher captured the same spirit in referring to Connecticut nearly two decades later in a letter to the Earl of Nottingham. "The government is a republic; they are enemies of the Church of England and no friends to monarchs."[17] Excepting a brief upsurge in prosecutions for words against the restored Charles II during the 1660s (when authorities remained on their best behavior pending charter reviews), in no decade did such cases constitute more than 5.3 percent of seditious speech prosecutions in New England. The 1620s, 1630s, and 1650s brought none at all.

Falling between New England and the South, New York prosecuted a total of fourteen cases involving words against the king. That constituted 9.5 percent of all the colony's seditious speech prosecutions of a known type before 1700. In plain numbers, it nearly matched New England's eight decades' worth of cases in just thirty-five years; in relative terms it came close to the southern colonies' 11 percent proportion of typeable cases.

The second broad type of seditious speech involved words spoken against the government more generally, rather than against officials. Such words covered a wide range. Common among them were utterances against the practices, decisions, or instruments of colonial courts. The Massachusetts Court of Assistants fined Ensign Jennison £20 for "upbraiding the court with injustice" on October 6, 1634, then remitted the amercement six months later after he submitted and acknowledged his offense. For "vile expressions, tending to the defaming the court for doing justice according to their light," New Haven colony authorities fined John Charles £20 in

1646. They showed none of the Bay Colony officials' leniency with Jennison.[18]

In 1675 John Ogle found trouble in New York for speaking against a New Castle magistrates' order directing that two dikes be constructed next to some local marsh land. After an official read the order aloud in church, Ogle "in an arrogant manner" said "we will not make Hans Block's dike, nor the other dike either." He disliked being forced to do this work without wages for Block, one of the officials making the order. Others took Ogle's side, grumbling their support aloud, and as the situation grew nasty, the magistrates wisely gave up trying to arrest him. After things quieted down, confirmation of the order was posted on the church door. A few days later, Magistrate Block met Ogle on the street. As they discussed the recent incident, Block noted that the order had been confirmed and published, ending the matter. "I care no more for your order, than for this dirt on the street here," Ogle hotly replied, kicking the ground for effect. On July 23, the Provincial Council sent some soldiers to New Castle to keep the peace. They arrested Ogle the next day for his seditious words.[19]

Twenty years later, Griffith Jones, a new immigrant from Maryland, appeared before the Philadelphia County Court of Quarter Sessions and Common Pleas. In a disagreement with the justices about a petition, in open court Jones "turned his back [on them] and sat down and said let them be burned." The justices summarily jailed Jones for contempt. He had already paid a fine of 2 shillings and 6 pence for lying in court. More serious charges came fast behind. The county grand jury presented Jones on four counts of seditious speech, each of a different kind. He criticized the courts of the province, spread false news (a category we will examine in detail later in this chapter), spoke "slightingly of the magistrates of this county," and derogated the colony laws. The court required Jones to post a personal bond of £40 and to find a surety for an additional £20, all to guarantee his good behavior pending appearance for trial.[20]

Colonists sometimes falsely accused each other of this form of seditious speech. On April 5, 1688, Frederick Ellis claimed that two of Maryland's Somerset County commissioners had shown disrespect for a letter written by the members of the Maryland Provincial

Council. Upon investigation, the Council cleared the men and ordered that Ellis either "publicly in the Provincial Court ask them pardon" or take a lashing from the sheriff of St. Mary's County. His choice was not recorded.[21]

Words against the government took other forms besides criticizing courts and their doings. Sometimes colonists spoke against colonial laws. Numerous Stonington residents presented a remonstrance to the Connecticut General Court in 1675. The colonists criticized colony officials for "acts, orders or laws passed by them prejudicial to peace, exposing their liberties to hazard, the consequences whereof brings them to an amazement." The General Court judged that "such practices ought to be crushed," menacingly adding that the legal penalties for such offenses included fines, prison, and disfranchisement. The point made, the court released most of the remonstrants after they had retracted their declaration. Captain George Denison, the group's leader, did not fare so well. The judges fined Denison £10 and disabled him from holding any office in the colony for the indeterminate future. Two years later, he formally asked the court to remit his fine. In consideration of his distinguished service during King Philip's War, the judges agreed.[22]

On occasion, offenders derided imperial laws, especially those governing trade. In 1696, for example, Charles Carroll appeared before the Maryland Court of Appeals for "sleighting and condemning" one of the Navigation Acts and for accepting several barrels of beer into his warehouse knowing they had not passed customs. The judges let the seditious words pass, but tried Carroll for evading import duties. A jury convicted him, and the court confiscated the beer.[23]

Some offenders spoke against the jurisdiction of the prevailing authorities. At times, such challenges were directed at particular courts. In 1670 Maine's York County court admonished Walter Gyndall "for vilifying and abusing of the Commissioners of Falmouth and Scarborough," insisting that "they had no power to try [cases] above forty shillings, with other abusive words." Sometimes colonists spoke against the jurisdiction of colony authorities more generally. Elias Stileman, Richard Martin, Major Richard Waldron, and William Vaughan did just that in the fall of 1684. At John Partridge's house in New Hampshire, they told Thomas Thurton that neither he nor his superior, Edward Randolph, collector of the customs for the king in the colonies, had "any thing to do in this province," adding that they were rogues. And when Thurton attempted to enter a room where the four men were meeting, Vaughan "came then to me, and struck me on the head with his hand and kicked me down the stairs, asking me whether I came thither for a spy, and shut the door, keeping me out." If anyone prosecuted the men, the records did not preserve the cases.[24]

Unusual situations could occasion words against the right of an entire colony government. In March of 1664/65, Colonel Nathaniel Utie and Alexander D'hyniosa, governor of the Delaware River settlements before their capture by the English in the Second Anglo-Dutch War, got into an argument over the disposition of some tobacco in Maryland. Mutual recriminations flew as the exchange grew heated. Utie claimed D'hyniosa had stolen and sold a Negro slave. The Dutchman retorted that the "turne coate" Utie had twice switched sides during the Fendall uprising. Utie angrily defended himself, asserting none too gently that the king, and not Lord Baltimore, was the "Absolute Lord" of the province. Ambiguities in the proprietary form of government complicated the point, but Utie was basically correct. Even so, the Maryland authorities characterized his statements as "contemptuous and scandalous words uttered by him against his Lordship's rule and government here."[25]

Seditious speech sometimes involved words against the home government. Lord Bellemont wrote on May 15, 1699, of an exchange between him and a member of New York's Provincial Council. The councillor said that a bill just passed by the New York Assembly would not be approved in England, even if it took £20,000 to obtain the defeat. When chided, the man merely replied that if the amount proved insufficient, £40,000 would certainly suffice. "I was so provoked," Bellemont later observed, "that I was about to suspend him" for "this so abominable reflection on the government of England." Instead, the miffed governor wrote to the Board of Trade. Disgusted because the belief that "money will do anything at Court" is "so common a one here," Bellemont penned an exhortation: "I hope your Lordships will take effectual care to put all imaginable discountenance on it."[26]

Words against local colonial government were far more frequent.

Prosecutions for aspersing colonial assemblies, if less common in the seventeenth than in the eighteenth century, did occur. William Dyre "reflected upon the General Assembly" of Rhode Island in a 1665 petition to the royal commissioners for New England. Calling the words "most dishonorable and dangerous to the Government," the Assembly forced Dyre to make a formal, written apology. He "doth crave pardon for this his transgression," Dyre dutifully wrote, "being anxiously desirous to walk inoffensive to all." The Assembly agreed to pardon Dyre with the expectation that "he and all others will be more circumspect for the future." They then attached the apology to Dyer's original petition and sent both along to the commissioners.[27]

Thomas French appeared before the Burlington court in New Jersey on August 9, 1686, for a letter he wrote "whereby he accuses and impeaches them [the Governor and Council] and the General Assembly of the Province." The letter, which French admitted writing, was read aloud in court. Given the opportunity to acknowledge his offense, French refused. A jury convicted him, recommending a fine not exceeding £5. When the judges asked "if he be satisfied in the jury's verdict and recommendation," French grumbled that he could not afford even "two pence." Irritated perhaps, they fined him £10 and ordered that his property be sold to pay it.[28]

Disagreement over taxes could lead to seditious speech. Benjamin Nason appeared before the Maine Court of Sessions on March 31, 1684/85. Nicholas Frost, a constable, had been going from place to place collecting the "rates due to the Proprietor and the Country." When he came to Nason's home Frost got a cold reception. Nason proved "very insolent and imperious in his carriages, and as dangerous in his speeches, tending to mutiny," so the justices fined him £1, assessed 5 shillings in court costs, and required a £10 behavior bond. When Nason the firebrand became Nason the supplicant, they reduced his fine to 10 shillings.[29]

Among prosecutions for seditious speech against the government rather than officials, the most common involved charges for characterized but unspecified words. These ranged from the earliest years of settlement through the end of the century and occurred in all the colonies. John Rolfe, the man credited with introducing tobacco cultivation into Virginia, charged Captain John Martin in 1619 with writing a letter which "taxeth him both unseemly and amiss of certain things wherein he was never faulty," adding for good measure, "and besides casteth some aspersion upon the present government." That government, Rolfe noted (perhaps a bit transparently), "is the most temperate and just that ever was in this country, too mild indeed for many in this colony, whom unwonted liberty hath made insolent." The burgesses thought the charge serious enough "to be referred to the Council of State." Martin's was but the first of many such Old Dominion cases.[30]

Other colonies had their share as well. Massachusetts colonists hardly had time to get settled before Henry Lynn "wrote into England falsely and maliciously against the government and execution of justice here" in 1631. Lynn suffered a whipping and banishment. John Stockbridge paid a 10–shilling fine in 1638 "for disgraceful speeches tending to the contempt of the government" of Plymouth. The amercement might have been less had he not uttered "jeering speeches to them that did reprove him" for the offense. Considering her other offenses, Margery Rendell got off easy with an admonition and a £1 fine in Maine after "abusing the government, saying there is none" on March 11, 1650/51. She also stood convicted of living with a man out of marriage, lying, and threatening Thomas Withers' wife, and was suspected of incontinence with Thomas Spleney.[31]

In 1699, the Pennsylvania Council examined two men, Major John Donaldson and Joseph Wood, about some seditious letters. Donaldson had written the lieutenant-governor, and Wood had written the secretary of the Council, both in some way discouraging the holding of elections. The Council concluded that both letters constituted "a great indignity and high misdemeanor against the government," adding that they were "of a very ill consequence, and may tend to the subversion and overthrow of the frame and constitution of this government." Donaldson claimed that he wrote the governor privately and "intended no reflection or ill to the government thereby." The Council accepted this explanation and released him. Then Joseph Wood stepped forward. His letter to the secretary being read aloud, he answered that he had no intention of defaming the government. "What he wrote was only jocular," Wood explained, and he "was sorry that he had given them any offense thereby." He, too, "was dismist."[32]

Among seditious speech cases of a known type, 432 (49.1 percent) involved words against the government. Of those, 151 included words against officials as well. The number of prosecutions for words against officials alone is thus 352, and the number for words against the government alone is 281 (40 and 31.9 percent of all typeable cases, respectively). Across the seventeenth century, words against officials were more common than general type words in all but two decades, the 1660s and the 1690s. New England and the South were similar, with significantly higher proportions of "personal" cases. In striking contrast, New York's proportions were exactly reversed. That may reflect the presence of large numbers of Dutch residents unhappy with English government generally rather than with specific officials.

Interestingly, the inclination to group both personal and general types of seditious words together in a single prosecution declined across the century, indicating a greater consciousness of the differences between them. From a high of more than one in four cases (26.3 percent) in the 1630s, such "dual" prosecutions dropped steadily each decade to a low of just one in ten before 1700. No significant regional differences occurred. The proportion of dual prosecutions was very similar in the three regions, ranging from 18.1 percent of typeable cases in New England down to 14.2 percent in New York.

Among prosecutions for seditious speech containing some general element (even if words against officials were included), two variations predominated in all regions: words derogating colonial courts, and those spoken against the government as a whole. In New England and the South, words against the government comprised the larger share, strikingly so in the South at 70.3 percent; words against courts were proportionately few. New York exhibited a directly opposite pattern, prosecuting words against courts almost twice as often as those against government as a whole. Here again the presence of a large Dutch population may help to explain the divergence. Dislike of English control among these people tended to surface when government most directly intruded into their lives—in collection of taxes on occasion, and in legal proceedings much more often. Differences between Dutch and English law and procedure provided fertile ground for Dutch complaints after the 1664 English takeover.

Across the century in the colonies the incidence of prosecutions for words spoken against the government as a whole increased through the 1660s, declined markedly in the next two decades, then surged back in the 1690s to end the century on an upswing. One might expect cases of this kind to be prominent in a decade of revolutions in England and the colonies rather than plummet as they did in the 1680s. But colonial officials opted not to prosecute this form of seditious speech during the most turbulent years precisely to avoid stirring up discontent at a time when the legitimacy of government was uncertain.

The third basic category of seditious speech prosecuted in the seventeenth-century colonies was false news. The origins of seditious speech law in thirteenth-century England tied the offense closely to great men of the realm, as we have seen. Spreading false reports or rumors that defamed these men undermined the government, and that basic view remained as the offense gradually came to be applied to government officials. What is perhaps most surprising about this transgression (which I call the "old" or traditional form of false news) is its sheer rarity in the colonies. Only nine of 880 typeable cases involved false reports concerning officials. The sole New England case of this sort came during King Philip's War in Massachusetts. Richard Scott appeared before the Court of Assistants in 1675 for sending a letter to Major Savage "wherein many untruths and several reproachful [words] were written." Scott testified that Ezekial Fogg wrote the letter, and Fogg was later tried and fined £5 for it. Middle Colony authorities occasionally prosecuted such cases. In 1684 William Clark, a member of the Provincial Council, filed a complaint against fellow Council members John Edminson and William Darvall for spreading "false reports of things done amiss in open court." The Council released Darvall a week later because "the things suggested were not proved against him." Nothing further is recorded of the Edminson case. Presumably evidence against him proved insufficient as well.[33]

Most prosecutions for spreading false news about officials occurred in the South, and most of those came between 1678 and

1691. Richard Covill, a London-based ship captain, visited Maryland in 1678. On returning to London, he "falsely and maliciously reported that the Governor of this Province had by order from his Lordship the Proprietary imposed an Oath of Fidelity on the people of this Province." The supposed oath required Marylanders "to swear allegiance to his Lordship against all Princes whatsoever and more especially against his Sacred Majesty our Sovereign Lord the King of Great Britain." Covill remained out of the Maryland courts' reach, so the Council took a different tack. "In vindication of his Lordship's honor and innocence against so black an aspersion," they published an official declaration refuting Covill's lie. Covill does not appear again in the records. Perhaps he wisely avoided Maryland's jurisdiction in the future.[34]

Captain John Jennings, commander of an English naval vessel, entered Virginia's Lower Norfolk County court on May 7, 1691. Jennings and his men dragged away John Porter, a civil defendant then arguing his case before the bar. Jennings later tried to "extenuate or lessen his crime" by spreading "a false and scandalous report that the Justices were sitting about a table drinking strong drink" when he took the prisoner. Various witnesses testified to the contrary. William Crawford never saw "any manner of drink, strong or weak, in the Court House." There was not even "any pot, cup or vessel to contain drink" in the court, Thomas Butt added. Not to be outdone, Thomas Hodges claimed that not only was the court free of liquor, but he could not recall that "he saw, or tasted one drop of strong drink in the town that day." The testimony notwithstanding, Jennings seems to have escaped punishment, not only for dragging Porter from court, but for the false news he spread about the justices afterward.[35]

A more common form of false news involved spreading reports relating to events rather than to particular officials, a newer form of the offense. As in the traditional form, New Englanders rarely appeared for this transgression, accounting for only one of the fifty-seven known cases. The Connecticut Council jailed John London on January 11, 1675, pending further consideration of his case. He had left the army without permission, and began not only "falsely calumniating the officers of our army," but also spreading "many false and notorious lies, to the great prejudice of the colony," per-

haps to make his desertion appear justified. Jail gave London time
to reflect. When called before the Council he fully acknowledged
his offense, and upon his "promise of returning to the army and
doing good service there, the Council saw cause to release him from
his imprisonment."[36]

The Middle Colonies produced some of these kinds of cases.
Peter Clock, an attorney, appeared before the New York Supreme
Court in 1695 on a charge preferred by the attorney general. Clock
"hath lately spoken many words to the disturbance of government,"
the charge read, "saying the Queen is dead and nothing can be
legally done in the Assembly now sitting." For "spreading false
reports in the country," the court ordered Clock to post a £20 behavior bond and to find a £20 surety. John Windower, another convicted speaker of sedition, became Clock's surety.[37]

Among Southern cases of this kind, Virginia prosecutions predominated. The case of the Virginian, Colonel William Diggs, offers
an unusually detailed and instructive example. In 1693, Maryland
authorities informed Virginia's governor of Diggs's seditious utterances, and Diggs soon found himself before the Council. When
visiting Maryland, Diggs had spread a remarkably detailed, and
plausible, tale. James had sent proclamations into England announcing "a general free pardon to all not excepting Doctor Burnett, but
only the Bishop of London, and the Lord President" who had partic-
ipated in his ousting. James and his supporters in England had
reached an agreement, the story continued, under which Angli-
canism would remain the official state religion but James would be
allowed to practice Catholicism. A great many "men of quality" and
others thus anxiously awaited James's return to the throne. Evidence
of that, according to Diggs, had been unexpectedly discovered two
years before, during King William's War. After the French were
defeated and James failed in his attempt to regain the Stuart throne
in 1691, "there was several thousands of horses found in England
accoutered for war" which none came forward to claim. The tale did
not stop with Maryland and England. Many in Virginia, including
Governor Andros and the Council, opposed the Oath of Supremacy
and looked forward to James's return. Indeed, this "was very publicly talked on in Virginia and in England without any notice taken
thereof." Andros had even shown Colonel Diggs "the proclamations

which he brought out of England with him," and "had delivered already several copies thereof to some persons in Maryland."

Misty-eyed nostalgia about a fugitive king was one thing. But a story like this was dangerous in an age when official news traveled slowly and uncertainly, and in which European circumstances remained at once unstable and of great import. Consider that Zachary Whitpain found himself on the verge of prosecution in 1688 when he arrived in Pennsylvania, spreading the amazing story that a Dutchman had invaded England and taken the Stuart throne. Only his steadfast sticking to the story and willingness to put it in writing, then swear to it, kept Whitpain out of trouble for the short term. Eventually, official word that the fabled Prince of Orange had indeed become England's William III ended the suspicion and suspense.[38] News that James had made a deal to regain his throne could have easily fired revolts, just as news of William's invasion had a few years before. Malcontents became rebels readily enough when assured that legions of supporters awaited the call to arise. Worse, in the face of such apparently overwhelming odds, government supporters might lack the resolve to prevent an overturn attempted by an emboldened few.

In that context, the Council order that Diggs stand bound in £10,000 sterling pending his appearance for a full hearing is less startling. Not surprisingly, Diggs appeared some months later as ordered. When originally questioned, he had equivocated. Now he resolutely denied having spread the story. Lacking a confession, and having no evidence but one man's testimony, which "would not be sufficient in law to convict," the Council was forced to release Diggs.[39]

Other Southern colonies prosecuted this newer form of false news. The Grand Council of South Carolina tried William Popell in 1692 for "spreading false, dangerous and seditious rumors and reports concerning the government of this province." Popell, the deputy provost marshall, had said that the House of Commons "voted that the two late pretended Parliaments in the time of the government under Seth Sothell" were legal. Popell confessed, and the Council ordered him to post a £200 behavior bond and to find two £100 sureties, so to remain bound for the space of one year.[40]

Rarely, false news cases involved unspecified words. John Sollers appeared before Maryland's Provincial Council in 1688 "for divulging false news." What Sollers said went unrecorded, but his explanation must have satisfied the Maryland authorities. "Being fully heard," they tersely noted, he "was discharged." A much more widely known fellow faced similar charges in 1693. Edward Randolph, "Surveyor General of their Majesties' Customs in the North Parts of America," fled from Maryland to Virginia in that year to avoid prosecution "for uttering and divulging several false and mutinous speeches and reports." He appears not to have been tried for the offense, the fervor of Maryland's Governor Copley notwithstanding. Indeed, William Anderson, the Virginia justice who issued a hue and cry for Randolph's apprehension and return to Maryland, was himself suspended from office by the Virginia Council, his actions being "adjudged unwarrantable and in contempt of the [Virginia] government."[41]

Sometimes, false reports led to investigations to find the original author and extinguish the rumor at its roots. The idea was anything but new. In 1515 a written libel so incensed Henry VIII that he ordered three men to view every volume of every book dealer in London in an attempt to match the handwriting. Finding the source of spoken words proved more difficult, as Maryland authorities learned in 1678/79. In the kitchen of the governor's house, John Burdett whispered in John Lewellin's ear that Christopher Rousby had called the proprietor a "traitor to his face" and that the proprietor was involved in treasonable activity. Before the Maryland Council, Burdett admitted speaking the words, but claimed he had heard them from Thomas Smith. Smith later appeared and said he got the story while aboard a ship when he overheard a discussion between Thomas Price and Arthur Hart. The court ordered the men to appear and answer the charge, but there the trail ends. Price and Hart were not arrested, perhaps because their ship had already sailed in the meantime. The ship's home port was in Maryland, so the Council could have pursued the case later. If they did, it went unrecorded. More likely they grew weary of trying to sort out the tangled web of who said what, who added which part, and who started the whole thing.[42]

Several years later, the Pennsylvania Provincial Council decided to mount a search after reading "part of a scurrilous invective libel against Robert Turner, a worthy member of this Board." Turner had formerly been a provincial judge, and the paper, representing the traditional form of false news, "very abusively reflected upon him in the execution of that office, in such matter as to our certain knowledge is most abominably false and untrue." On September 8, 1687, the Council unanimously ordered that with "all convenient speed, course shall be taken for the discovering of the forgers, or first contrivers, as well as the publishers of the same, that they might be brought to condign punishment." As in the Maryland case, the record does not preserve the final outcome of the search.[43]

Searching for the author of a false tale proved a cumbersome and often fruitless business, so it is not surprising that officials increasingly sought other ways to deal with the problem. From time to time, they passed new laws or reactivated old ones restricting such loose talk. They sometimes specifically encouraged greater diligence in enforcing statutes, new or old, as when Maryland's government made a special effort in 1696 "to prevent the dispersion of false reports about the province." Infrequently, officials stiffened penalties for spreading false reports. Toward the end of the century, Old Dominion authorities took a carrot and stick approach. In a 1690 letter to Maryland's Governor Blackiston, Virginia's Lieutenant-Governor Nicholson recommended the best course of action. "Here we have offered rewards for all true news," he wrote, "and punishment for all false reports." Officials sometimes simply investigated rumors and announced the finding that they were false. New York officials did that in 1689. So did New Jersey authorities in 1695.[44]

Sometimes officials issued proclamations and made announcements to counter false rumors. English authorities took this course from time to time. In 1695, "to prevent any mistaken or malicious information" from being spread about, the Privy Council issued an official statement regarding a failed plot against the king. A decade earlier, Whitehall drafted a letter to be forwarded to each colonial government announcing the Duke of Monmouth's defeat. "All this we tell you," the letter concluded, "lest false reports should be spread by the malicious." Such official news was much welcomed in the colonies. "We received with joy the news of the suppression of the [Monmouth] rebellion," Virginia's Governor Lord Howard of

Effingham wrote, "as we have been terrified by reports of another kind from New England which emboldened many bad subjects here." The proclamation, he added, "deterred others from spreading false reports."[45]

Colonial officials, as Effingham's last comment indicates, found proclamations useful as well. A rumor began to circulate through Pennsylvania in 1689 that the governor and Council intended to overturn the charter and rule arbitrarily. The maligned authorities posted copies of a formal denial throughout the colony. That calmed things for a while, then another rumor began to spread a few months later. The French and Indians were in league with the Papists in Maryland, the story went, and they were attacking New England to the north as well. The Council met to discuss the rumor, concluding that Pennsylvanians were safe "if we can but keep quiet among ourselves." A proclamation might stir things up more.[46]

Several years later, Maryland had pressing problems of its own in the form of Indian depredations. In 1697 a Maryland woman had been "washing off butter at the stream" when two Indians attacked her. She ran, but as she tried to scramble over a fence they caught up and beat her unconscious. When she awakened, she found "her scalp all taken off except a little hair left on her forehead." The description is from Captain Brightwell's report, and he added another grisly detail. "Her right breast has been ripped up by the indians with a knife" so that "the wind puffed out like a pair of bellows." Such stories only grew with the telling, so "I would have you take care," Governor Nicholson cautioned Brightwell, "to observe the directions of the law about divulging false news concerning the indians." Warnings were fine, but sensational news could hardly be kept quiet for long.[47]

Interestingly, the propensity to issue official denials of false reports rather than prosecute the people who spread them grew significantly across the century. Before the 1670s, such proclamations were virtually unknown. By the 1680s, they became commonplace. And by the 1690s, the number of formal proclamations defusing false reports in the colonies actually surpassed the number of offenders being prosecuted for spreading those reports. Why that happened is not hard to understand. By the end of the century, officials had become increasingly concerned about not irritating or angering ordinary colonists if it could be helped. A colonial governor made the change all too clear. In 1695, when a false rumor began to circulate in New York, the governor ordered both the colony records and a formal refutation to be published. This, he significantly noted, was "for the satisfaction of the common people." Officials earlier in the century would not have made such a proposal, particularly for such a reason. The "common people," after all, were to be "subject to their rulers," in John Winthrop's endlessly echoed phrase. Both Winthrop and his view, however, belonged to an earlier time.[48]

As for false news prosecutions, they were virtually unknown in the colonies before 1660. Though never a major proportion of seditious speech cases in the seventeenth-century colonies, false news prosecutions climbed steadily from a low of only .7 percent of typeable cases in the 1660s to almost one in six cases (15.1 percent) by the 1690s. The Southern colonies had the lion's share with 68.4 percent, while New York lagged far behind with 24.6 percent, and New England produced only 7 percent. Less than one percent of New England's seditious speech cases involved false news. Not much, particularly when compared to New York's 9.5 percent, and the South's even stronger 13 percent. Curiously, overall, only 15.8 percent of the cases involved reports spread about important officials (the "old type" of false news), while 73.7 percent were prosecutions for spreading reports about events (the "new type" of false news). (The numbers do not add up to 100 percent because insufficient information makes some false news cases impossible to categorize.) This pattern obtained in all three regions, the new type of false news predominating in New York, the South, and New England. The numbers are small, absurdly so for New England, yet the thoroughly one-sided proportions are notable.

For centuries, false news law and prosecutions in England had centered on the spreading of false reports about great men in the realm, evolving in the seventeenth century to apply to governmental officials. Though this form of the offense appeared in the colonies, it was vastly overshadowed by the newer form of spreading false reports about events. Why? When combined with the reminder that most false news cases occurred later in the century and in the South, it seems probable that the practical threat to governmental stability posed by rumors of revolution and Indian conspiracies led officials toward greater concern for quashing loose stories of this type. Certainly most of the recorded cases centered on these and related problems. In addition, colonial officials had a ready and reliable method of dealing with seditious words spoken against them in the form of *scandalum magnatum* prosecutions. Even as false news prosecutions proved superfluous in punishing words against officials, they increasingly became the preferred method of dealing with potentially destabilizing tales about political, religious, and military developments.

The types of seditious speech colonial authorities prosecuted, then, changed significantly across the seventeenth century. Among *scandalum magnatum* cases, insults remained a staple, but misprision gained ground outside of New England. More importantly, perhaps, misprision charges everywhere increasingly led to investigations, and punishment followed only when the charges proved baseless. There the early foundations of allowing truth as a defense in seditious speech cases were slowly and quietly laid—in the century before John Peter Zenger's famous New York trial. Prosecutions for the second major category of seditious speech, words against the government generally, revealed an interesting pattern of fluctuation. Officials concerned about upsetting the population often opted not to prosecute such cases amid unsettled times when the legitimacy of government could be questioned, then picked them up again as consensus was once again established. At the same time, the propensity to combine words against officials with words against the government declined markedly, indicating a growing consciousness of the differences between the two. Interestingly, aside from fluctuations, no major changes occurred in general-type seditious speech cases. The reason may well be that as maintaining personal respect for individual magistrates became less tenable, a growing concern for simple governmental stability took over. Keeping society intact was the prime goal, even if society itself became less respectful, less submissive, and more impudent in the process. Ironically, in making that compromise, authorities may have inadvertently solidified the hold of the new impertinence. That, alas for those frustrated officials, may have been inevitable. In reacting instinctively to save the society they knew, they actually helped create a society alien to them in one of its most important elements:

attitude toward authority and government. Prosecutions for the third form of seditious speech, false news, came increasingly to center on reports about events, less on rumors about individual officials or great men. Moreover, officials increasingly elected to make public refutations of false reports rather than punish the people responsible for them—so much so that by the 1690s, such refutations actually outnumbered prosecutions.

In all of this, habitual respect for authority clearly declined across the seventeenth century. At the same time, the people themselves came to pose a more profound threat to government than they had before. Organized opposition, not just emboldened mobs, had unseated two kings and various colonial governors in this century. No wonder officials backed off of general prosecutions in times of governmental crisis and increasingly investigated misprision charges rather than punishing accusers out of hand.

FOUR

Between the Millstones

Throughout the seventeenth century, colonists well understood William Hoskins's observation that to be a defendant drawn into the criminal justice system was to be "ground as copper between two millstones."[1] Here we will explore the nature of that system as seditious speakers confronted it, from discovery and arraignment through trial and conviction. What courts were like, conflicts of interest, procedural protections, availability of attorneys, the role of juries and appeals—each will command our attention in turn. Though many aspects of the system remained essentially static across time, in some areas—especially the increasingly successful employment of juries and the growing use of appeals—colonists faced considerably less "grinding" at the end of the century than they had at the beginning in seditious speech prosecutions.

In general, colonists came face to face with the legal system soon after their offenses came to light. Most often, other colonists reported the transgressions. In a 1661 petition to the Massachusetts General Court, Thomas Coleman, Timothy Dalton, and nine other residents of Hampton charged that Edward Colcord had for some time "viciously lived to himself, and disorderly towards others." Worse, "by subtle contrivances and underhand practices he hath hitherto evaded the hand of justice." By contrivances perhaps less subtle, after aspersing a magistrate and "foreseeing his condign punishment," Colcord "made an escape and ran away from the town where he lived." Not that this bothered the petitioners. On the contrary, after Colcord fled, "the places adjacent quickly perceived by their peace and quietness what a blessing it was to be freed from such an incendiary." But he later returned and "hath anew vilified the chiefest of our magistrates and abused them by opprobrious terms." The petitioners wanted Colcord punished. The General Court referred the case to the Hampton County court. There Colcord was convicted "of many notable misdemeanors and crimes, some against authority and some against persons in authority." The judges fined him £5 and jailed him until he posted a behavior bond. In addition, to curb Colcord's nasty habit of suing people and not paying assessed costs when he lost, the court barred him from bringing suits in the future without first posting a performance bond.[2]

Individual colonists reported seditious words more often than groups, and not usually by filing such lengthy petitions. Sometimes colonists falsely accused each other. On March 13, 1661/62, the Connecticut General Court fined John Blackleich £30 for derogating some magistrates. "The heinousness of the transgression deserves a fine of an hundred pounds," the judges noted, but they satisfied themselves with less because of "some weakness" in the evidence. Upon further investigation the court concluded "that there is too much appearance of prejudice in the testimonies that have been presented," finding it suspicious that two men overheard the alleged words while "lying in wait." In the end, the judges acquitted Blackleich of the charge and withdrew the fine, suspecting instead that the two wily witnesses "are guilty of the crime they testify against Mr. Blackleich." George Seith faced a curious variation of the false accusation problem in Pennsylvania in 1693. Complaining to the Provincial Council that four officials had defamed him, Seith produced a letter they wrote as his proof. Their letter characterized him as "crazie, turbulent, a decryer of magistracy, and a notorious evil instrument in church and state." The Council took the unusual step of giving Seith "a certificate of his good behavior" that he could carry to clear his name as the need arose.[3]

False accusations proved to be an infrequent problem. Colonists usually reported seditious words they had actually heard. Many occurred in casual conversations. Four men testified against Jonathan White, Speaker of the House in Pennsylvania, on May 17, 1684, for speaking seditiously. While the men were visiting White in his home, he said "that the proposed laws were cursed laws," adding in his frustration, "hang it, damn them all." Such conversations did not always come to light right away. Edward Earle waited years before reporting in 1698 that William Pinhorne, a member of the New York Council under Governor Fletcher, had spoken against the king. "In 1691 or 1692 I was at William Pinhorne's house," Earle testified, "when a book being produced with a picture of the Prince of Orange, Pinhorne asked was it not a pity that such a hump-backed, crook-nosed Dutch dog should rule the kingdom of England." Hanna Earle testified to the same. Though Pinhorne vigorously denied the charge, he was suspended from all offices in the colony.[4]

Not all seditious words were reported by parties to the discussion at hand. Maryland's well-known Josias Fendall soon regretted hiring John Bright in 1681 "to mall some rails for him at his plantation." While hewing the logs, Bright overheard the tempestuous Fendall speak some seditious words and wasted no time reporting them. Nor by any means did seditious speech always occur in casual conversation. Heated arguments sometimes occasioned such words. Less than a month after Edmund Andros arrived in Boston to take up the governorship of the Dominion of New England, Richard Wharton and Edward Randolph found themselves in a confrontation while "going up the street towards Mr. Usher's" house. Arriving to examine a fellow in the constable's custody, the two councillors came upon Captain George, Captain Saintloe, and the constable—all embroiled in a loud argument. Amid the yelling, George struck the constable, and he and Saintloe tried to rescue the prisoner. Wharton ordered the mariners "to be peaceable or otherwise he should be constrained to raise the town" against them, whereupon they turned on the interfering magistrates. George shouted many "reflective and abusive speeches, both upon the government, and Mr. Randolph." Saintloe threatened Wharton "with some unkind treatments if he caught him on the water, with many other scurrilous and abusive" words. George also "threatened Mr. Randolph's officers," especially Erasmus Stephens who "if he saw him upon the water passing by his ship he would take him aboard and whip him till he were raw." To "maintain the authority of the government," Wharton jailed the contumacious captains pending a hearing.[5]

The streets of Albany, New York, proved as ready a stage for seditious speech as those of Boston. On the night of February 8, 1683/84, a very drunk Jan Cloet stumbled about the street, pretending to be the town crier. The assemblymen "bought up all the land," he loudly and repeatedly announced before "cursing and abusing" not only them, but the governor as well. When the townspeople came out of their houses to investigate, they found Cloet slumped against a wall, still making his drunken announcements. As they bent close to identify him, he tried with uneven success to blow out their extended candles. Later, in county court, a sober and perhaps embarrassed Jan Cloet humbly submitted himself to the bench. The judges set the charges aside with a warning that the matter might be reopened if he offended in the future.[6]

Taverns offered a fertile environment for vilifying authority. In 1680, two men found themselves in trouble in Elizabeth Town, New Jersey, for words they had spoken in Jonas Wood's ordinary the night before. Dissatisfied with the loss of Governor Philip Carteret, William Taylor and John Curtis "utter[ed] many railing and invective speeches against Sir Edmund Andros and his government." At least one magistrate and several assemblymen were in the pub at the time. Emboldened perhaps by drink, Taylor repeated the words even after "Mr. Justice Ward bid him hold his tongue." Both men were arrested the next day and remained imprisoned at the fort pending trial. What became of Curtis is unclear, but Taylor appeared before the Council on August 13, "craving pardon for what past [sic] and engaging a reformation." The Council accepted Taylor's submission and dismissed him after he posted a behavior bond.[7]

Determining a defendant's exact words remained an inherent problem in trying seditious utterances. The phrase "or words to that effect" in depositions and presentments is common testimony to the difficulty, and the problem certainly added to the pressure for a confession or acknowledgment of wrongdoing that often characterized these prosecutions. The difficulty sometimes clouded discovery just enough to prevent effective prosecution. Maryland's Provincial Council received information about "several mutinous and seditious speeches" spoken by Major Edward Dorsey "on board

Captain William Hill's ship in the presence of Mr. Thomas Cornwall" in 1692. During questioning by the Council, Cornwall admitted that "several high words passed between them," and that as a result he did "retort something by way of reprimand to the said Dorsey but what the words positively were he cannot truly call to mind." The testimony of others aboard the ship proved no more precise, and the Council dropped the prosecution.[8]

Written seditious words involved no such problems. In Plymouth Colony, William Nicarson got into trouble in 1666 for writing two letters to the governor of New York complaining that Plymouth officials treated the inhabitants unfairly. The letters included "sundry expressions of a scandalous nature, tending to the great defamation of Thomas Hinckley, of Barnstable, Assistant, as that he denied him justice notwithstanding his oath to God and the King." The court ordered Nicarson and his three sons-in-law, who admitted subscribing to the letters, to make a public acknowledgment vindicating the Plymouth authorities. Caught off guard by the discovery of the letters (which were read aloud in court), Nicarson quickly apologized, publicly acquitting Hinckley "from the imputation of the said crimes, or what else may in either of the said letters reflect upon him to his defamation." He also paid a £10 fine, and his sons-in-law paid £5 each.[9]

If written words were easier than spoken ones to prove in court, discovering them could still present difficulties of its own. We get a glimpse into how these were obtained from a 1638 complaint of George Burdett, then on the Piscataqua, to Archbishop Laud in London. Massachusetts authorities managed to get copies of his previous letters to Laud, procured it seems by Mr. Vane and sent over. Irritated, Burdett "cannot believe it was with [Laud's] consent." New York authorities took a more direct approach to discovering seditious writings in 1689. In May of that year, the Council ordered "all letters and messengers from New England to be stopped and sent to New York to prevent the stirring up of faction." Eight months later, Jacob Leisler ordered that all messengers and letter carriers, not just those from New England, be stopped and searched for evidence of any designs against his government of the colony. The approach was hardly original. North Carolina's Governor West "ordered that no letters be carried off before he sees them" on March

21, 1670/71. He aimed to prevent "reflections upon the government" in the form of complaints to the proprietors. The Caribbean colonies offered older precedents.[10]

The large majority of seditious speech prosecutions began after ordinary colonists reported words they had heard. Cases of written words, whether in petitions, personal papers, or pamphlets, were comparatively rare. Equally rare were words spoken in the presence of magistrates, the occasional angry outburst in court or drunken disparagement in a tavern notwithstanding.

A pretrial investigation usually followed the discovery of seditious words. A justice of the peace normally conducted this preliminary investigation, often in his home, determining whether the charge seemed sufficiently supported by the evidence to proceed. He commonly examined physical evidence (if any), took witnesses' depositions, and questioned the accused. Sometimes a constable, sheriff, or marshall was dispatched to search premises or belongings. When Dr. Robert Child ended up in trouble for seditious words against Bay Colony authorities in 1646, some of the key evidence against him came from papers found stored in his trunk in anticipation of going to England. This whole preliminary business of searches and questioning could be abbreviated considerably if the defendant committed the offense in the presence of authorities. That applied to all crimes, including seditious words—something the Pennsylvania Council pointedly affirmed in 1689. When an offense was "done in the view of one Justice," they observed during a debate over a seditious speech prosecution, that not only justified immediate arrest, but generally "was sufficient for conviction."[11]

Justices of the peace, sitting alone, also determined guilt and ordered punishment for minor offenses. Seditious speech, though a misdemeanor, was an exception to that rule. Single magistrates did not ordinarily try seditious words. In such prosecutions, the examining judge either jailed or bailed the accused pending trial at the next appropriate court. Few defendants faced pretrial incarceration. Inadequate jail facilities, the considerable expense, and the hardship to defendants' families all militated against such a course. As a rule, authorities reserved custody without bail for colonists thought likely to flee and those accused of capital offenses.

Whether held in custody or bound over, offenders usually came to trial quickly. When two Virginia defendants remained in jail ten months pending trial for piracy in 1690, they insisted that "such delays are odious in law." "By Magna Charta chapter 29," they added, "it is ordained that no freeman shall be imprisoned or disseised of his freehold or liberties, or justice denied or deferred." The authorities rejoined that the fault lay with the petitioners' deliberate attempts to delay trial in hopes of release. Trials before individual magistrates normally took place within a day or two. Trials in town courts were rarely delayed more than a few weeks. Crimes serious enough to require a full panel of judges could wait up to ninety days for disposal, for these went before county courts which ordinarily met quarterly. The higher jurisdictions—provincial courts, general courts, and the like—adjudicated the most serious matters. In criminal cases, that meant felonies as a rule, though seditious words were commonly tried in these high tribunals. Offenders unlucky enough to be arrested just after the end of a session and held without bail could wait months in jail pending trial—longer if evidence or participants crucial to the case proved unavailable at the scheduled trial date, or if other pressing business used up the court's time. On the whole, however, colonial officials would have agreed with the view of the Maryland Council on the issue of pretrial delays. In 1696, they ordered lower courts not to adjourn until all their business was finished. Doing so, they explained, often forced postponements of cases, and "delay of justice is in effect as bad as denying thereof." [12]

Once an offense serious enough to be heard by a panel of magistrates had been discovered and investigated, preliminary testimony taken, and the offender imprisoned or released on recognizance, the stage was set for trial. Though details varied, courts followed a fairly standardized general manner of proceeding. Rhode Island practice in 1647 offers a useful illustration. The presiding judge began court by dealing with persons under bond to appear, continuing or releasing their obligations. Next, criminal defendants came into the courtroom. Each offender stepped to the bench when called by name, listened as the indictment or presentment was read aloud, and pled when asked. Guilty pleas brought an immediate assessment of punishment. If they pled not guilty, offenders could choose to be tried by the bench or by a jury. If they chose a jury trial, the presiding judge called twelve jurymen forward and asked the accused "if he have any thing against them." If so, others came forward. When seated, the jurymen took their oaths and trial proceeded. Few trials lasted more than a few minutes. After criminal matters had been disposed of, the court went on to civil actions and other business.[13]

Colonial courtrooms were nothing like the calm, well-ordered halls of justice we tend to envision. Often people appeared late or drunk, if at all. Judges left the bench at their leisure as cases were argued, and even got into fistfights in open court with litigants they disliked. In general, colonial courtrooms were bustling, noisy places—unbearably so at times, crowded as they were with colonists, each intent on his own problems and huddled in the back of the courtroom discussing his own case with friends, family, and supporting witnesses. As early as 1637, the Connecticut General Court had to order "that whosoever doth disorderly speak privately during the sitting of the court with his neighbor or two or three together, shall presently pay one shilling, if the Court so think meete." It was a problem colonists everywhere understood all too well. Less common but equally revealing were incidents like the Henry Higgs affair. In Maryland in 1684, Higgs angrily denounced the Cecil County court's treatment of a defendant. Ignoring repeated admonitions to be quiet, Higgs instead pushed his way to the front and presumptuously took a seat with the judges. There he began "calling for drink, swearing he was come to drink with them," and, with his hat on—as the secretary noted twice—"swore God damn them, he was come to drink a bowl of punch with them and such like discourse." Guffaws no doubt filled the courtroom. The Council made Higgs post £45 sterling in bonds and security for his good behavior and future appearances. In light of such incidents, it is less surprising that in 1677 Virginia colonists themselves sought a law requiring "that no drink may be sold within a mile of the [Northampton County] courthouse at any of the court sitting days."[14]

Rowdy and raucous as courts could be, colonial authorities on the whole preserved fundamental procedural protections, including the common law rights to be free from forced self-incrimination and double jeopardy, and statutes of limitation. In seditious speech prosecutions, however, officials proved willing to bend the rules on such protections when necessary. The New Jersey Council faced a difficult situation in 1686, for instance, because of their extremely short statute of limitation in seditious speech cases. John Duty appeared before the governor and Council at two o'clock in the afternoon on October 26 "for speaking sundry words of evil import against his present majesty the King of England [James II], and being examined utterly denied the same." So they called in Peter Prew, the informer, and questioned him. As it happened, Prew had not "made his complaint within eight and forty hours as the law directs, but has delayed the same for several months." But after lengthy "debate with the House of Deputies touching and concerning the premises," it was agreed that Duty should be bound over to stand trial at the next Court of Sessions. The outcome of the case went unrecorded.[15]

Seditious speech defendants did more consistently enjoy the protection of another rule, one that had stood since the 1500s in English law. When an accused speaker of sedition refused to confess, the rule prohibited conviction without the testimony of at least two witnesses. The Tudors had used treason statutes to prosecute seditious words in part to avoid the difficulties imposed by this rule. But colonial (and English) authorities enjoyed no such leeway after the Star Chamber distinguished the offense from treason in 1606. Plymouth officials had to release Robert Ransome, for example, on March 1, 1669/70, when he came to trial "for speaking wicked and reproachful words against the governor and magistrates" of the colony. "Although they were persuaded that the accusation spake like unto the said Ransome's language," the secretary rather tortuously recorded, he was legally cleared, "there being but one witness appearing against him in that case."[16]

Other colonies also released seditious speech defendants without trying them if only one witness came forward. In 1660, Thomas Hinson narrowly escaped punishment in Maryland. A Virginia Puritan who migrated to Maryland with his wife and three children in 1649, Hinson sympathized with Parliament in its struggle against Charles I in the English Civil War. His anti-Stuart views very nearly got him into trouble in 1660 when Charles II returned to the throne. According to Mary Baxter, on a cold February court day in Kent County, Hinson, who had been writing in another room, "came into the court house to dry the writing at the fire." Only John Winchester and Baxter were in the room as Hinson entered. While standing at the fireplace, Hinson quipped to Winchester, "now we are in his Majesty's dog house." Baxter, "finding herself aggrieved at those words answered that his Majesty did not use to keep dogs in any courthouse where justice use to be administered." Winchester, who might have been a witness against Hinson, instead joined him, replying to Baxter that "there was a great many dogs in the house." Because no one else testified to the seditious words, Kent County authorities declined to prosecute either man.[17]

Occasionally, seditious speech defendants availed themselves of more technical legal protections. In May 1685, John Berry, a convicted speaker of sedition currently under bond, refused "to answer or appear" before the New Jersey Court of Common Right. He objected to "the *scire facias* as not being legally summoned according to the exigency of the said writ." The court conceded "that the same was not served with that formality as the law doth require," and gave Berry the option of challenging its legality or of letting it pass. Refusing the olive branch, he opposed the writ. When convicted of affronting and abusing Edward Randolph "in the execution of his office" in 1682, Timothy Armitage appealed the conviction, arguing that the English law upon which the decision was based had not actually been published in Massachusetts. The General Court allowed the appeal even though similar Massachusetts laws were in effect. That may well have been a measure of their attitude toward Randolph more than an indication of their attention to "legal niceties."[18]

Such cases aside, mere technicalities did not often prevent authorities' pursuit of seditious speakers. Henry Johnson appeared before the Maryland Council for spreading a seditious rumor in 1678/79. While they were out hunting together, Johnson told John Mould of a supposed "plot betwixt my Lord and that Irish fellow Talbott." "There is forty [Irish] families to come in under the pretense of seating Susquehannah River," Johnson said, "but that forty families will prove in the end to be forty thousand to cut the Protestants' throats." The Provincial Council ordered Johnson and Mould to appear, but five months later the sheriff of Baltimore County returned the order with a note on the back. Having received the paper after its date of execution had already expired, he wrote, "I could not summons the persons within mentioned to appear at a certain time." Undaunted, the Council ordered the warrant "issued afresh."[19]

David Konig has argued that cases came increasingly to be decided on legal technicalities under the Dominion of New England because Andros insisted that colonial practice conform to English law. While seditious speech cases involving technicalities were uncommon, they did appear more at the end of the century than at the beginning, and they did constitute a significantly greater percentage of prosecuted cases in the later years. Whether that merely coincided with a more general procedural trend, or was part of the century's softening attitude toward seditious words, is impossible to know. Either way, it contributed to the colonists' growing freedom to criticize government and officials by helping limit discretionary use of the legal process against offenders.[20]

Colonial prosecutions for seditious speech exhibited a number of common characteristics. They were rarely long delayed, as we have seen. And they, like most trials, were almost universally brief. That is not surprising, considering the sheer volume of cases that courts handled. In its July 1664 session, Maine's York County court did a typical volume of business. The first day of the session, the court heard eleven presentments, tried eleven criminal cases, including one of seditious speech, handled thirty-two civil actions (seventeen decided by juries, four of which the judges later overturned), and finished the day by issuing ten court orders, mostly related to highway maintenance.[21]

Seditious speech trials shared other characteristics as well. Most took place in virtual minefields of conflict of interest. Members of juries often personally knew one or more of the participants in cases they heard. Far from being a disqualification, this was considered an advantage because it helped them measure the honesty and character of the persons before them, whether witnesses, criminal defendants, or prosecuting officials. This approach, reflecting a very different conception of fairness than prevails today, was normal in all sorts of trials in the seventeenth century—in England and her colonies.[22]

Nor would modern perceptions of "objectivity" apply to the judges. The same men sat the bench at all levels of jurisdiction within colonies, from the simple Justice of the Peace courts of no record, through the town and county courts where more significant cases were tried by justices sitting together, to the General Courts, the highest colonial jurisdictions. That could lead to practical complications. Higher courts occasionally could not conduct business because so many of their justices were busy deciding cases in lower courts, and vice versa. Having the same men judge at all jurisdictional levels created other difficulties besides scheduling problems. True, this approach guaranteed a degree of consistency in treatment and procedure throughout a colony's court system, but it also meant that judges often heard appeals of cases they had decided, and sometimes even adjudicated cases in which they were personally concerned. The practice continued throughout the century in seditious speech cases. Martha Wearing stood trial before West Jersey's Burlington court in 1699 for "having spoken abusively and contemptibly of Thomas Revell, Justice." The bench, including Revell, convicted Wearing and fined her for the words.[23]

Attorneys very rarely appeared to defend those accused of seditious speech. That was not unusual, for lawyers were comparatively rare in the colonies generally. Julius Goebel observed that neither attorneys nor juries were common in criminal trials in colonial New York. Brad Chapin went even further in his assessment, arguing that "in no case did the accused have counsel" in colonial criminal trials before 1660. John Beattie has made the same basic point about Surrey, England, though with a bit less force. He found that few defendants put up much of a defense there, most simply pleading guilty even by the eighteenth century, and that fewer still had any counsel at all. In England the idea of counsel for the defense began to develop in the 1680s when the judicial system became highly politicized and a fair trial seemed increasingly less plausible to Englishmen. That was especially the case with treason prosecutions. Interestingly, Beattie has found that sedition trials constituted something of an exception to the general rule that attorneys for the defense were rare. Such cases often involved defense counsel by the 1720s, foreshadowing the widespread use of lawyers in other cases.[24]

Throughout the seventeenth century, colonists and officials alike revealed an ambivalent attitude toward attorneys. Most accepted and appreciated the important role lawyers could play. Rhode Island authorities offered a good illustration of this when they empowered attorneys to practice in 1668/69. A criminal defendant might be innocent, they observed, "and yet may not be accomplished with so much wisdom and knowledge of the law as to plead his own innocence." On the other side, barratry was widely despised. Pennsylvania's Council voiced the common concern in 1686. "For the voiding of too frequent clamours and manifest inconveniences which usually attend mercenary pleadings," the body forbade anyone from handling another's case for pay. Perhaps no single reference captures the colonial ambivalence about lawyers quite so succinctly as Edward Randolph did in a 1689 letter to England. "I have wrote you," Randolph noted, about "the want we have of two, or three, honest attorneys, (if any such thing be in nature)."[25]

No such uncertainty marked colonists' attitudes toward trial by jury. Indeed, reverence for this ancient right was very much in evidence throughout the early colonies. In an address to the governor, Maryland's House of Delegates captured the spirit in which Englishmen on both sides of the Atlantic viewed the right in the seventeenth century. "Juries are always accompted an especial bulwark," they observed, "to protect our liberties and privileges from arbitrary government." The Carolina proprietors shared that view. They wrote the Carolina Council in 1676 about the extradition of Thomas Miller to Virginia. "Upon this occasion we think fit to mind you," they wrote, "that we utterly dislike trying and condemning any person either in criminal or civil cases without a jury." New York officials agreed. They arrested Francis Rombouts, former mayor of New York City, in 1681 because he had denied John Tuder "a lawful trial by jury." Such a denial was, after all, "contrary to Magna Charta, the Petition of Right," the "dignity and honor" of the crown, and "the law of the land."[26]

As that last phrase indicated, beyond general statements of support lay colonial laws guaranteeing the right to trial by jury. All the colonies maintained such statutes, and they stood from the earliest years of the seventeenth century to the very end. The first law preserved in Plymouth Colony's records guaranteed the right to trial by jury. Chapter XVII of the West Jersey "Concessions" stipulated that no one could "be arrested, condemned, imprisoned, or molested in his estate or liberty, but by twelve men of the neighborhood." Pennsylvania established laws requiring jury trials on demand and punished any for "maliciously purposing the weakening of the aforesaid liberty." And in the fall of 1693, Virginia authorities approved "an Act appointing all trials to be by Juries." That merely continued the Old Dominion's commitment to the right to trial by jury that appeared in her earliest charters and Governor Wyatt's famous 1621 ordinance.[27]

Juries served in various capacities in the early colonies. Besides settling civil actions and criminal prosecutions, they were commonly impaneled to determine cause of death. Most towns and counties also had "presenting juries." These typically consisted of twelve to twenty-four men, appointed to the position for a year. Each man had the responsibility to keep track of offenses in his neighborhood. When court convened periodically, these men met and formally "presented" neighbors for alleged crimes. Presentments covered offenses as wide-ranging as the activities of ordinary colonists. Drunkenness, lying, fighting, illegitimate pregnancy, theft—all these transgressions and many more occupied the presenting juries. Trials of a sort did follow presentments, but in practice presentment virtually guaranteed conviction. In the lower courts especially, most business centered around such presentments throughout the seventeenth century.[28]

Grand juries handled a wide range of matters. At the county level in New England, they functioned like presenting juries, members sitting "a full twelve months before they are released." Pennsylvania grand juries assigned lots for the county fairs held twice a year, laid out roads within their respective counties, and controlled county taxation just as the Assembly did for the province as a whole. West Jersey grand juries controlled local taxation and laid out roadways, like their Pennsylvania counterparts, and occasionally decided unusual matters. In 1686, for example, one had to determine whether a fellow in a "lunatick state" was capable of handling his own affairs.[29]

Trial juries, those which most concern us here, were a very different matter. Their sole concern was deciding civil and criminal cases put before them. Trial juries generally consisted of twelve men throughout the English colonies, though sometimes the number could be less, especially in sparsely populated areas. In 1665, for instance, the people of Maine consented to seven-man juries if more men could not be had. Indeed, the Duke's Laws of 1664, under which New York was originally ruled, provided that juries would ordinarily be made up of six or seven men, and twelve only at the judge's discretion. But that was unusual. Jury constituencies varied, but on the whole they had to be made up of a defendant's peers and of colonists who were not criminals. Jurors had to be adults, and usually property owners, though nonfreemen were allowed to sit on juries in some colonies. Under certain circumstances, women juries were empaneled, but that was rare. It never happened in seditious speech cases.[30]

Trial juries were normally appointed in the morning to hear all cases, both civil and criminal, coming before the court that day. Jurors traditionally listened to numerous cases, often as many as one to two dozen, before "retiring and taking the aforesaid business into their serious cogitations" at the end of the day. This practice inevitably led jurors to confuse facts and to forget key testimony. Not surprisingly, it began to change around 1700 in England; juries started retiring after each case. The same process took place in the colonies.[31]

Defendants enjoyed a legal right, during the selection process, to challenge jurors they believed to be biased against them, and they employed that right on occasion. Most cases proceeded without challenges, however, and challenges were not always automatically accepted in any event. When Thomas French went on trial before the Burlington court for writing seditious letters in 1686, he claimed "his case is determined before hand." The judges replied that "if he can make it appear by any of the jury who are to be his judges, or anything to object against them, they shall be put by." But "in regard he makes no such thing appear, nor makes any particular objections of the jury," the trial proceeded.[32]

Challenges were not intended to build an impartial jury, but to cull out jurors inimical to the defendant's interests. As we have seen, objectivity in the modern sense was neither a reality nor a goal in seventeenth-century legal proceedings. Janet Monroe's comment in 1694 is particularly instructive in this regard. When she went on trial for her life for infanticide, West Jersey authorities gave her the opportunity to challenge the impaneled jurors. The jurors "are strangers to her," Monroe observed. "But," she added revealingly, "she freely accepts them" anyway. She would have preferred jurors who knew her for the otherwise decent person she was, but disinterested ones presented an acceptable alternative.[33]

Juries decided a wide variety of cases, but were not widely used in criminal prosecutions, especially in misdemeanor trials. According to John Murrin, West New Jersey used juries most, followed in descending order by Rhode Island, Pennsylvania, North Carolina, Plymouth, Massachusetts, Maine, Connecticut, Virginia, and New Haven. More to the point here, in all of these colonies except Rhode Island the trend during the seventeenth century was away from using juries and toward summary judicial proceedings. In Plymouth Colony, for example, "the frequency of the demand for a criminal jury steadily declined over time despite the steady growth in population." "In Massachusetts, Connecticut, and Maine," Murrin adds, "civil juries flourished from the start, but trial by jury for noncapital crime all but disappeared before 1660." New Haven completely abolished trial by jury from its inception and gave no sign of changing that policy. Historians of crime and punishment in the colonies generally share Murrin's conclusions.[34]

The reasons why jury trials were the exception in criminal prosecutions, seditious speech cases included, are not hard to find. In the first instance, trials were expensive. Every colony established standard allowances for jurors, ranging from a few pence to a few shillings a day, and jurors took these allotments seriously. John Nevell, a jury foreman in Maryland's Charles County court, refused in 1664 to render the verdict in one case until the jury was paid. Defendants in criminal cases paid these costs, which sometimes equaled or exceeded the potential fines involved. With the amount required for jurors, it is hardly surprising that jury trials proved to be significantly more expensive than trials before the bench. In Connecticut, even at the end of the seventeenth century, the numbers made the point plainly. In 1699 trials by jury in that colony cost defendants three times as much as trials before the bench alone.[35]

Besides the expense of jurors, defendants had to pay an array of other costs. Filing papers, having summonses issued, getting the verdict officially recorded—all of these, and many other aspects of process, had fees attached. Witnesses had to be reimbursed for time and expenses as well. Those costs simply formed part of the judicial system, but such a system, it should be noted, clearly worked against the poor. Few of the "lesser sort" could afford to be a party in civil suits on either side. That alone must have made them subject to considerable intimidation from more well-to-do colonists in many aspects of everyday life. And when accused of a crime, a poor man could ill afford to pay jurors, witnesses, and the myriad expenses of a defense. It comes as no surprise that most criminal defendants, seditious speakers included, simply confessed and let the judges punish them. After all, when it came to obtaining justice, "tis possible," in the words of one Rhode Islander, that "the toll may prove to be more than the grist." Many a poor defendant would have quietly grumbled agreement.[36]

Other factors besides cost discouraged legal defenses. Criminal defendants faced formidable odds. Overall, on both sides of the Atlantic, acquittal rates were low in the colonial period. Peter Hoffer noted a 70 percent conviction rate for felonies in eighteenth-century Virginia, and fully 100 percent for lesser offenses. That compared to lower conviction rates in colonies to the north. On average, some 45 percent of serious offenders stood convicted in Massachusetts. John Murrin maintains 90 percent, but that would include minor transgressions. The figure for New York stood at 50 percent. J. M. Beattie noted a 61 percent conviction rate for Surrey, England. Nor did juries help offenders, for they were—by all accounts—no more likely to acquit criminal defendants than judges. That in itself no doubt helps explain why so few defendants elected trial "by god and country."[37]

Even if a jury did acquit an offender, the judges might very well refuse to accept the decision, and that, too, discouraged the use of juries. Magistrates commonly set aside jury verdicts they believed unjust or improper, though not everyone supported that judicial power. Thomas Arnold, a member of a jury at the Rhode Island Court of Trials in 1669, certainly qualified. When the judges disagreed with the jury in a case, Arnold insisted that there were more jurymen than judges and that a majority vote should decide the issue. "Which reasoning of his seemed to be soe redickelous as declared him to be unsuitable to serve," the judges commented just before replacing him on the jury. Arnold was ahead of his time. By law, judges could set aside jury verdicts in England in the seventeenth century, and, though the 1690s saw some question about this in Maryland, the rule applied in the colonies as well.[38]

In overturning jury verdicts, judges did not necessarily subvert justice. On the contrary, they often worked to ensure fairness and to maintain equal application of the law in the face of colonists ignorant or dismissive of it. Indeed, precisely because of the distinction in learning between jurors and judges, a long tradition existed of allowing juries to determine matters of fact, but leaving matters of law to the bench. That rule occupied a particularly important place in seditious libel trials and could be central to seditious speech cases as well. When Josias Fendall went on trial in Maryland for seditious words in 1681, the jurymen, upon retiring, asked "to have the act of assembly with us to see what it directs." "You have not to do with that," the Chief Justice snapped, "you have only to find whether or not the words have been spoken accordingly as the prisoner is charged." The humbled jury returned shortly with their verdict. "We find Josias Fendall guilty of speaking several seditious words without force or practice, and if the honorable Court think him guilty of the breach of the act of assembly we do, or else not." The judges fined Fendall 40,000 pounds of tobacco and banished him from the colony.[39]

Not only did judges commonly overawe juries and occasionally disallow jury verdicts, but they sometimes actually punished jurors for their verdicts. That, too, would have discouraged the average defendant considering a trial by God and country. The practice of punishing jurors for verdicts stopped in England after 1670, though judges continued to intimidate jurors and could in many ways steer juries. In the colonies, Julius Goebel claimed, punishing jurors persisted "until 1670, and possibly later." Later indeed. In 1675 Jacob Jesson sat on a Massachusetts Bay jury and found himself in trouble before the Court of Assistants for dissenting from the other jurors "and not giving the court a satisfactory reason." Jesson wrote a petition complaining that the judges in the case had threatened him with fine and imprisonment. "I know of no law that requireth jury men to be of the same mind with the Magistrates," Jesson noted, "nor no oath that is given to us to oblige us so." If the offended justices frowned at this point, they surely scowled at what followed. "But this I know," he continued, "that jury men do take oaths to give in a just verdict according to law and evidence, which can be understood no otherwise than according to their best judgment, and not according to the judgment of the bench." The jury's decision should stand whether or not the bench agrees because the judges, after all, are not the defendant's peers, and the law says a man is to be tried by his peers. That sharp piece of logic driven home, Jesson twisted the blade. "To make a jury say as the bench sayeth is to mock the law," he concluded, "and to make jury men but noses of wax." On November 18, the unhappy magistrates publicly admonished Jesson for his "high reflections, and abusive expressions . . . tending to the debasing authority amongst us," and jailed him pending payment of a £10 fine.[40]

Expense and uncertainty, then, discouraged criminal defendants from using juries to decide their cases. Most merely conceded adjudication to the bench, stood convicted, and relied on the salubrious effects of abject submission. Yet seditious speech prosecutions in the seventeenth-century colonies departed from the general pattern in two important ways. In stark contrast to other criminal prosecutions, colonists tried for seditious words increasingly availed themselves of the right to trial by jury as the century progressed, and— even more striking—they increasingly won those cases.

Certainly the basic assessment that jury trials were uncommon in criminal misdemeanor cases holds for seditious speech. Overall, colonial juries clearly decided less than one in seventeen seditious speech prosecutions. Yet even as colonists moved away from juries in criminal cases generally, juries became increasingly common in seditious speech trials across the century. Up through 1660, juries decided only .54 percent of seditious speech cases in the colonies as a whole. Between 1660 and 1700, however, the figure jumped eighteenfold—to about 9 percent. Whether that trend continued into the eighteenth century awaits further research, but clearly the latter half of the seventeenth century witnessed a dramatic increase in the use of juries in seditious speech cases.[41]

At the same time, colonists increasingly won acquittals from juries. When tried for seditious words before magistrates in the seventeenth century, Southern colonists stood less than a one in one hundred chance of being acquitted. The situation was even worse to the north. Not a single New Englander went free when tried for seditious speech by judges only. Juries proved more accommodating. North and south, an offender who opted for a jury trial stood a much better chance of being acquitted. Southerners tried by jury for seditious speech won their cases in better than one in five instances. Colonists in New England fared even better. Nearly two out of three jury trials for seditious speech ended in acquittals there. In both regions, a very substantial difference.

Perhaps we should not too quickly conclude that colonial juries were inherently fairer than magistrates, or even more disposed to tolerate seditious speech. It seems reasonable to suppose that offenders willing to pay the considerable additional expense of a jury trial were more likely to have strong cases, hence more likely to be acquitted in the end. From another direction, because of the expense of jury trials, they tended to be used by wealthier offenders. Such men may have had higher status and more influence within the community, hence more likely enjoyed an attendant degree of immunity (or at least benefit of doubt) unobtainable by lesser men. That said, however, it should be noted that the proportion of wealthy seditious speech defendants does not appear to have grown in the latter part of the century.

Even when convicted, whether at the hands of a jury or the bench, all was not necessarily lost. An offender could still appeal to a higher jurisdiction. On both sides of the Atlantic, the right of appeal sometimes proved essential to correct wrongs done at lower levels, whether by juries or judges.[42] That obviously valuable role notwithstanding, the thing itself invited difficulty. Without some limitations, the right would result in most cases being appealed, for losers would naturally like another chance. That would be a disastrous burden on any court system. As a result, colonial officials restricted appeals in ways designed to reduce the inherent difficulties of the right without seriously undermining its legitimate role.

Restrictions took many forms. Most often, authorities charged filing fees to reduce frivolous appeals. Though typically small at a few shillings, such fees occasionally became intrusive. In 1686, for example, Edmund Andros drastically increased New Hampshire's appeal fees, from 4 shillings to over £1.6 sterling, adding fuel to detractors' claims that the Dominion of New England encouraged injustice. Officials used other means to minimize appeals as well. As early as 1678, the Virginia General Court stipulated that appeals could no longer "embrace new material." Massachusetts authorities under Dudley allowed appeals of cases amounting to less than £2 from Justice of the Peace courts to county courts "and no higher." In 1678 New Jersey allowed appeals from town courts only for criminal cases extending "to life or member." From 1645 on, the Bay Colony made appeals readily available, but doubled a losing appellant's previous punishment. New York authorities refused to allow appeals filed more than two weeks after the original decision. Nor would they hear appeals from the courts of other colonies where New York colonists thought themselves aggrieved, for that "would be a matter of such high consequence as every man discerns where it must end." Any appeal to the Pennsylvania Council had first to be heard in the county of its origin. New Haven courts allowed no appeals whatsoever in criminal cases, though they "did accept requests for mitigation of the imposed sentence." Colonial officials also required appellants to post appeal bonds which were forfeited if they did not pursue the appeal within a reasonable time. Such bonds were common, especially for inherently expensive appeals to England, and they were required from the lowest to the highest judicial tribunals.[43]

Colonial restrictions on appeals of all kinds had the desired effect. Erwin Surrency's comment that "no appeal was possible in a criminal case in the colonial period" is an overstatement. Yet it points in the right direction. Appeals of criminal cases in the colonies were rare. Outside of Massachusetts, Brad Chapin has observed, "there were virtually no appeals to the New England general courts," and most of those involved requests to reduce fines imposed by lower courts. Civil cases tended to be appealed in greater numbers because they more often produced differences between judges and juries, and because the winner would normally expect the loser to bear the costs of the appeal.[44]

What was true of criminal cases in general was true of seditious speech prosecutions in particular. Some were appealed with unclear results. Richard Waldron appeared before the New Hampshire

Court of Sessions in 1683 and was there "fined £5 for mutinous words spoke at a trial, between him and Mason, and fined £10 for words spoken to the dishonor and contempt of his Majesty." He was a man of considerable stature within the colony, so it is hardly surprising that when he "desired leave to appeal" his sentences the court granted his request. What came of the appeal is not clear, but Waldron died most gruesomely in 1689 at the hands of marauding Indians. Other colonists clearly won appeals. Richard Wilkinson and John Cutler were among them. In 1640 Wilkinson appealed to the Virginia General Court after his conviction "for speaking contemptuous words against Captain John Upton," commander of Isle of Wight County. He asked and received Upton's personal forgiveness in the meantime, then cleverly had William Boulke submit a deposition attesting to the personal apology. The tactic worked. Seeing evidence of his submission, the General Court ordered "that the said Wilkinson be clearly acquitted and discharged of the said fine." John Cutler appeared before the Massachusetts Court of Assistants in 1691, appealing a £20 county court fine "for reproachful words by him uttered against the present authority." Cutler probably had disparaged the new royal government, but a jury acquitted him.[45]

More often, seditious speakers lost appeals. Samuel Hunt appealed his conviction at the Ipswich County court for seditious words in 1664. The Massachusetts General Court denied the appeal and admonished Hunt "to humble himself," but added that they had no objection if the Ipswich magistrates saw fit to abate his sentence. James Richards appeared before "a Special County Court" held by three justices at Hartford, Connecticut, on August 27, 1667. After questioning the right of this court to sit, Richards was ordered to "appear after dinner before the Court to answer for his expressions." He refused to do so "without a [formal] summons." The court fined Richards £20, having "judge[d] such expressions in their own nature to be tending to the weakening of the hands of authority" as well as "a very evil example and encouragement to others in such practices." Richards appealed. The Special Court had proper authority to sit and judge cases, the Connecticut General Court decided in the appeal, though the law on this point was confusing and needed clarification. The appellant, they added, "might in an humble manner have presented his apprehensions that his case was not under cognizance of that court." Richards being half right, the judges remitted half his fine. When he pressed the point and asked that the other half be removed as well, "this was voted in the negative." Richards paid the remaining £10.[46]

Whether won or lost, appeals of seditious speech convictions were rare, constituting only about 3 percent of all cases for which a disposition is known. New Englanders were more likely to appeal such convictions (3.49 percent of regional cases) than Southerners (2.36 percent). I found not a single appeal of a seditious speech conviction in New York during the seventeenth century. Regarding long-term trends, colonists appealed no seditious speech convictions before the 1640s and only one percent by the 1650s. Yet the proportion of such appeals went up significantly as the century progressed—to 2.46 percent in the 1670s, to 5.68 percent in the 1680s, and finally to 7.01 percent in the 1690s. Whether that trend continued into the eighteenth century remains to be seen, but colonists in the seventeenth century certainly became increasingly willing to challenge convictions for seditious words. The numbers were not large, but they were clearly growing. Were colonists more likely to win appeals later in the century? It is impossible to draw a dependable conclusion because the cases clearly won on appeal are few and fit no clear pattern.

Colonists prosecuted for seditious speech in the seventeenth century faced courts very unlike what we envision today and stepped into a system of justice tilted heavily against the accused. That system placed a high premium on deference, submission, and acknowledgment of wrongdoing. It remained largely unconcerned with pervasive conflicts of interest. And it generally took a dim view of defense counsel, the use of which indicated a defendant's lack of remorse and implied that presiding magistrates would not safeguard the just interests of the accused. Procedural protections, including statutes of limitation, prohibitions against double jeopardy, and the two-witness rule, helped balance the system—but they were unevenly applied in seditious speech cases. Juries offered a bright spot as colonists increasingly used them and increasingly won acquittals during the seventeenth century. Appeals, too, became more common as the years passed. Still, even by the end of the century, by far the larger share of seditious speech defendants stood convicted and mounted no appeals. To them, punishment was the central, dominant concern.

FIVE

Sanctions in Decline

Colonists tried for seditious words in the 1600s more often than not found themselves convicted and facing punishment. Early in the century, that prospect was a looming terror, for the possibility of disfigurement and other hardly less alarming forms of corporal punishment was very real. Short of those, profound public humiliation, banishment, prison in chains, and other penalties most frightening to contemplate awaited. The situation was very different by the end of the century. By the 1690s, very few seditious speech defendants need have trembled when before the bench, for use of all the truly menacing sanctions had declined dramatically through the years. Outlining that decline is the main object of this chapter.

The penalties colonial authorities employed against seditious speech in the seventeenth century included a group described by contemporaries as "bodily correction." These encompassed various punishments, all involving physical violence, but excluded stocks, pillory, and similar penalties, which inflicted a degree of physical discomfort, but for which humiliation remained the distinguishing characteristic. "Bodily correction," on the other hand, included lashings and more macabre inflictions—cutting or nailing the ears, breaking legs or arms, tongue boring, and the like.

By far the most common of this group was the whipping. Authorities whipped women as well as men, and they employed lashings in punishing a wide range of offenses. Theft, drunkenness, religious infractions, sexual transgressions, wife abuse—these offenses and others commonly led to the whipping post. Constables or sheriffs normally administered court-ordered lashings, though authorities occasionally allowed offenders to do so in lieu of their own penalties. Sometimes very high-ranking officials carried out the sentences personally. John Endicott, for example, whipped Thomas Gray for drunkenness in 1639. Endicott, an assistant at the time, later became governor of the Bay Colony.[1]

The severity of whippings depended largely on the person administering them. Courts determined the number of lashes, but a lighter hand meant less pain and presumably less penance—something colonial authorities well understood. So in seditious speech cases, as in others, judges sometimes took care to ensure appropriate harshness. In 1636, for example, Massachusetts authorities ordered that Peter Bussaker be whipped with twenty lashes for "slighting the magistrates." He had impudently insisted that for a punishment they "could but fine him." Perhaps to emphasize their view of the matter, the judges ordered that the lashes be "sharply inflicted."[2]

More often, we may suppose, the expectation of a sturdy application of force was understood. Such seemed to be the case with Edward Erbery, who appeared before the Maryland legislature for seditious speech in 1666. According to William Calvert, who preferred the charges, "Erbery called the whole house a turdy shitten assembly" and "said we are a company of turdy fellows (meaning the Lower House) and were ashamed of the place from whence we came." Erbery had been drinking. Encouraged perhaps by the ale, he warmed to the denunciations and continued, brushing aside all objections. "A company of Rogues and Puppies," he called the Assembly, "and there is not one in the Country deserves to keep me company but Charles Calvert, who owes me ten thousand pounds of tobacco." Erbery then passed out, only to awaken the next morning in jail. Later, before the Assembly, he meekly insisted that he had been "in drink" and could remember nothing of his speech the night before. "No person of full age," the Assembly retorted, "shall take advantage of drunkenness in such case." Even so, his defense might have brought some leniency if combined with a sober apology had it not been for a conversation he had that morning. Upon awakening, Erbery had complained about being tied up. When asked if he knew why he was bound, Erbery proudly insisted "that he

remembered all what he said last night and that he was not drunk."
When confronted with this testimony, Erbery stammered that "he
remembers not that ever he spoke such words." The Upper House
ordered that Erbery "be tied to the Apple tree before the House of
Assembly and be there publicly whipped upon the bare back with
thirty-nine lashes."[3]

Authorities in other colonies used the lash as well, though Maryland seems to have been unique in employing an apple tree. The
Pennsylvania Council ordered Anthony Weston whipped "at the
market place on Market day three times, each time to have ten
lashes, at 12 of the clock at noon." Weston had displayed "great
presumption and contempt of this government and authority" by
drawing up a set of seditious proposals in 1683. Twelve years later,
Ellinor Moline appeared before the North Carolina Council for
speaking "against the Honorable Deputy Governor and Government" of the colony while "aboard a foreign vessel." It could not
have helped her case that she spoke her words "to the Honorable
Deputy Governor's face." The court ordered Moline "punished by
receiving fifteen stripes upon her bare back." She quickly wrote
a humble petition to the court indicating that she was "heartily
sorrowful" for the words she had spoken and craving pardon. This
delayed punishment until the next court meeting, but the Council
ultimately agreed with Moline's confession that she was "unworthy
of the least favor." She took her fifteen lashes that afternoon.[4]

On the whole, only 8 percent of the punished seditious speakers
in this study received a whipping as all or part of their penalty, and
this was a sanction in decline. The 1630s saw more than one in four
(25.8 percent) go to the whipping post, but by the 1690s the figure
had dropped to a mere 3.5 percent. Though both New England and
the South exhibited that general decline, marked regional distinctions appeared. New Englanders tasted the whip twice as often as
Southerners after speaking against the government or its officials
(almost one in ten of the Northern colonists as compared to one in
twenty Southerners). New York colonists virtually never did; for all
the years between 1664 and 1700, less than one percent took lashings for seditious words. The century also witnessed a notable decline in the number of lashes inflicted. The number is not specified
in most cases before the 1640s, but that rarely happened afterward.

The average number of lashes in the 1640s was thirty; by the end of the century, that figure had been cut in half to fifteen, the turbulent 1670s providing the only aberration in an otherwise steady decline.[5]

Some differences between men and women appeared. Women on the whole received slightly fewer lashes than men for seditious speech, enduring an average of seventeen lashes with a range of nine to twenty-five. Men took an average of eighteen lashes, with a range from nine to thirty-nine. Actual whippings seem not to have differed significantly according to gender, for seditious speech or other offenses, except in the cases of pregnant women. Officials normally delayed their whippings until they had been "delivered of child." Women constitute only 3.5 percent of all seditious speakers, yet they provide a substantially higher proportion (17.8 percent) of those suffering whippings as a punishment. That probably reflected their inability to afford amercements independently—a conclusion supported by colonial law and practice. Sometimes statutes ordered lashes for female seditious speakers only if they could not pay a fine. More often, judges gave women that option, and married women's husbands normally paid their fines.[6]

Less common than whippings was the simple, if gruesome, penalty of ear cutting. It involved grasping the ears and cutting them with snippers or a knife. The order for this messy sanction was usually general enough to allow some leeway to the person carrying it out. Depending upon his enthusiasm, the ear or ears might merely have the top portion cut off cleanly ("cropping" as it was called), or they could be cut flush with the head, leaving only holes. One can just imagine the hygienic, not to mention aesthetic, ramifications of such a procedure. Again depending upon the enthusiasm of the punisher, the severed portion could be returned to the offender to be sewn back on. That was unusual, however, and more than one colonist probably wore his hair long to hide ears mutilated for a past indiscretion. The macabre sanction, intended as a mark of infamy, had been used in England (and in Europe generally) for centuries to punish various offenses, including seditious speech. In 1553, to cite but one example, Gilbert Pott had his ears nailed to the pillory at Cheapside, London, then had both ears cut off "for seditious and traitorous words." A trumpeter blew and then a description of Pott's offense was read aloud, all as the executioner severed his ears.[7]

Colonial officials did not hesitate to continue this tradition. Though Philip Bruce claimed that in seventeenth-century Virginia only slaves "who had shown an incorrigible disposition to run away" had their ears cut, one of the first colonists to endure the ignominy was Captain Richard Quaile, and he was no slave. For unspecified seditious words in 1624, Virginia authorities ordered Quaile to be stripped of his commission, to have his sword broken, then to be "sent out of the port of James City with an axe on his shoulder afterwards to be brought in again by the name of Richard Quaile, Carpenter." After this, Carpenter Quaile was to be "set upon the pillory with his ears nailed thereto and they either cut off or redeemed by paying a fine" of £100 sterling. Nailing an offender's ears to the pillory often preceded ear cutting—perhaps because in addition to maximizing discomfort it made the job of severing the ears from a jerking, screaming offender easier. Ear cutting was not unique to Virginia. The Massachusetts General Court took exception to Philip Ratcliff's "speeches against the government and church at Salem" in 1631, to cite a New England example, and ordered him to be "whipped, have his ears cut off, fined forty pounds, and banished out of the limits of this jurisdiction." Ratcliff, according to John Winthrop's journal entry, was a servant and a man of "most foul, scandalous invectives."[8]

No seditious speaker faced death as a punishment, but other forms of bodily correction, including mangling tongues and breaking limbs, did appear on occasion. In 1625, the Virginia General Court tried Richard Barnes for "base and detracting speeches concerning the governor." Besides disarming and banishing Barnes, the court ordered both his arms broken, after which he ran a gauntlet of forty men required to beat him with their rifle butts. As if the beatings, fractures, and banishment were not enough, the court also ordered that Barnes have "his tongue bored through with an awl," a macabre if fitting penalty for a crime of words. One can only guess what effect a hole in the tongue might have, depending upon the size of the hole, the sharpness of the tool, and the driller's skill. Barnes may well have suffered cruel jokes about his slurred speech and sloppy eating for the remainder of his life. In any event, boring through the tongue with a red-hot iron was the preferred procedure elsewhere, perhaps because it resulted in fewer infections.[9]

Hot irons were used in another way as well—to brand offenders. Adulterers, blasphemers, and felons of all sorts could be branded. The mark often went on the face or the hand to maximize the shame and to more readily identify the person as a serious offender in the future. Specific letters identified the offense as well as the offender. These varied among jurisdictions, but common ones included "R" for rogue, "T" for thief, "M" for manslaughter, "F" for forgery, and "B" for burglary. Some colonies apparently kept brands with an "SL" ready for punishing seditious libel, but of more than sixty-score cases of seditious speech I have uncovered, not one resulted in a recorded branding.[10]

One form of corporal punishment used mostly in disciplining soldiers was the wooden horse. Offenders with hands tied behind sat on the sharpened edge of a board placed too high for their feet to support their weight. They remained "in the saddle" for a specified time, usually less than half a day. Sometimes authorities ordered a shorter but more intense ride. Such was the case for the only seditious speaker known to have suffered this penalty in the seventeenth century. William Warran found himself in trouble on Jamaica "for slighting an order of his Majesty's Council" in 1668. The unfortunate fellow had to ride the wooden horse for only one hour, but with three heavy muskets tied to each ankle and a paper on his back announcing his crime. That Warran was a soldier simultaneously convicted of "giving his superior officer base language at the head of the troop" no doubt explains the use of this sanction. People had been known to die from riding the wooden horse for extended periods, and it fell largely into disuse by the end of the seventeenth century.[11]

Authorities rarely used bodily correction penalties alone in punishing seditious speakers in the early colonies. Generally, officials incensed enough to inflict bodily injury for words against them or the government had already pronounced a litany of more commonplace sanctions. Indeed, all but one such offender suffered at least three additional punishments, ranging from fines to banishment. The single exception was George Pidcock. After convicting Pidcock of uttering seditious words in 1651/52, Plymouth authorities gave him the choice of paying a fine or suffering some form of corporal punishment.[12]

Chart 1
"Bodily Correction" (n = 53) as Percentage of All Punished Cases in
New England and the South

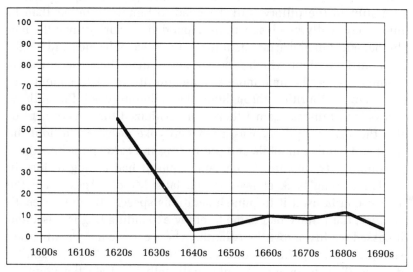

Bodily correction (whippings aside) never constituted a significant proportion of penalties for seditious speech. Only 3.3 percent
of all such offenders in the colonies before 1660 suffered one or
more of these. None did between 1660 and 1700, even as the colonial population grew and the number of seditious speech cases
escalated. Chart 1 plots colonial use of all forms of bodily correction
(including whipping) in punishing seditious speech across the century. It graphically illustrates the decline in such sanctions as a
proportion of all punished cases. The common association of greater
harshness in punishing crime with the South does not hold for
seditious speech cases. Indeed, New England authorities actually
used bodily correction more often—both in real numbers and as a
percentage of punished cases—than Southern ones. In punishing
seditious speech, New York officials used whipping only once between 1664 and 1700 and other corporal punishments never. For
that reason, that colony is excluded from the chart to avoid the
misleading effect it would have on the illustration of long-term
trends.

Far more common, especially in the early part of the century, were "humiliation" punishments. These included a number of penalties that ranged from being forced to ask forgiveness for an offense to a stint in the pillory—all designed to humiliate rather than to injure physically. Such sanctions depended primarily upon the medicinal effect of embarrassment in the presence of friends and neighbors, an ingredient which increasingly limited their usefulness as colonial society became more mobile and diverse, less community centered. Authorities throughout the colonies used the pillory, stocks, and bilboes against those who criticized the government or its officials. The pillory was a wooden yoke designed to hold the head and hands immobile and protruding and to keep the body bent uncomfortably forward at the same time. It had a long history in England, going back at least to the later Middle Ages when the Tower courts used it to punish seditious speech. By the sixteenth century, the pillory had come to enjoy expanding English use, and it passed readily across the Atlantic, where every colony maintained statutes requiring the erection and maintenance of this and similar devices. Two of many examples will help illustrate the point. In 1693 the Virginia Assembly ordered every county in the colony that did not already have a pillory and stocks promptly to erect some. The Duke's Laws of 1664, under which New York (and Pennsylvania before establishing its own code) operated, required that every town provide both pillory and stocks for the punishment of malefactors.[13]

Nor were colonial authorities shy about using these devices to punish seditious speech. Consider the case of William Munsey. On December 12, 1688, he appeared before the Maine Court of Quarter Sessions held at Wells, bound over from Francis Hooke's Justice of the Peace court "for giving scurrilous and threatening language to the said justice." Four men—Joseph Hill, Samuel Hill, Ephraim Tebbets, and John Hanscomb—had hoodwinked Munsey out of his property. The four ended up in court "for coming in Indian habits, and firing a gun, to frighten William Munsey & family out of his house, whereby they took possession." Eventually, Tebbets and Hanscomb paid 10–shilling fines for their part in the business. The Hills, presumably the chief offenders, paid £1 each. Before Justice Hooke could settle the matter, however, Munsey lost his temper and vented his anger. Had the case been one of contempt, Hooke would have handled it himself. But he thought the words more significant than that and forwarded the case to the justices in quarter session. Upon hearing the case, they ordered Munsey to spend a half-hour in the pillory.[14]

Stocks were a wooden yoke fastened around an offender's ankles. Offenders normally sat on a low bench with legs directly forward and feet protruding through the yoke. Sometimes stocks included another yoke to hold the wrists like the pillory, but not the head. That at least protected the face from the rotted food and other flying debris that sometimes accompanied the jokes and insults offenders had to endure. On occasion, officials combined pillory and stocks, known as being "laid neck and heels," which produced a doubly uncomfortable effect. Luke Eden and Thomas Ewer had the misfortune to experience that discomfort for their words. The Virginia General Court ordered Eden set in stocks and pillory "in the marketplace" for abusing the governor and Council in 1625. Plymouth authorities took exception to Thomas Ewer's seditious words in 1659 and gave him a taste of what Luke Eden had endured years earlier. More commonly, speakers of sedition faced one or the other. In 1676 Jan Conell and Dirck Albertse Bradt spread a false report in New York that "300 men was lying at Westerbrook and had come here with the intention of asking permission to drive away the river Indians." When the story came "to the ears of the Indians," many fled. Conell and Bradt were arrested and brought before an "extraordinary session" of the Albany court. The best defense they could muster was to claim "that it was not done with such evil intention as is assumed" before begging the court's mercy. The judges fined the two men, then ordered them to spend an hour each in the stocks.[15]

Given the discomfort and humiliation deliberately associated with stocks and pillory, it is perhaps not surprising that every colony had to deal with a degree of vandalism of the devices. Delaware's experience was typical. In 1680 Alexander Humphry and five friends paid fines of five hundred pounds of tobacco each after they mischievously stole the Kent County stocks. Four years later, Robert Johnson "carried away part of the stocks and flung it down the [river] bank" in Sussex County. He bragged of the deed to Arthur

Starr and Henry Urbanck, who informed county officials. Johnson not only vandalized the stocks, but boasted that he would have chopped down the whipping post as well except that he had no axe at the time.[16]

More durable but less common were the "bilboes"—a rod of iron a few feet long with ankle cuffs attached. A chain trailed from one end and was ordinarily bolted to the floor or wall of a prison or to a post, often raised enough to force the offender to lie supine with feet held high. Bilboes functioned in much the same way as stocks, and could do "effectually with one bar what a prison cell does with many." The device was common on English ships in the seventeenth century. It never gained wide use in the colonies, where abundant wood could easily be worked into pillory and stocks, but iron was scarce and required greater skill, effort, and expense to fashion into bilboes. Given the scarcity of the device, it is not surprising that few offenders of any kind suffered it in the colonies. Among speakers of sedition, only three endured the bilboes in the seventeenth century—all after appearing before the Massachusetts Court of Assistants in the 1630s. Thomas Knower was set in the device for threatening an appeal to England on April 3, 1632. The following March, Thomas Dexter was "set in the bilboes, disfranchised & fined £40" for criticizing the Bay Colony government. Six years later "Robert Shorthouse was set in the bilboes for slighting the magistrates in his speeches."[17]

Other types of humiliation penalties included having a paper or sign announcing the offense attached to the offender or read aloud as he stood in public or endured additional punishment. In 1640 Francis Willis, clerk of the Charles River County court in Virginia, said that the members of the General Assembly "did things imbecilely which he would alter," adding that "the commissioners did such unjust things there [in Charles River County] as they durst not show their faces to answer at James City." Among other punishments, the court ordered Willis "to stand at the Court door with a paper on his head expressing his offense." One can just imagine the congestion created as people passing through the door stopped to read the announcement and perhaps chuckle before moving along. John Smith appeared before the Rhode Island Court of Trials in 1662 for "speaking words of reproach against Mr. Benedict Arnold, president, which words did absolutely tend to his disparagement in the execution of his office." He had wrongly accused Arnold of sending out a warrant for the arrest of Mrs. Ayres, and then privately sending word so that she could escape. Smith confessed and begged mercy. The judges, who sought "not the destroying but the reforming of such as are in legal sort reformable," ordered Smith to write out his confession and personally "fasten it upon the post of the door at the entrance of the prison porch at Newport," near where he and his wife lived. Benanuel Bowers would have appreciated some of that leniency. In 1677 the Massachusetts General Court convicted Bowers for having his wife write "a paper of scurrilous verses, superscribed to Thomas Danforth, magistrate" which seditiously defamed Danforth and the Bay Colony magistrates generally. Not appreciating Bowers's literary contribution, the judges ordered him publicly whipped twenty lashes as a declaration of his offense was read aloud.[18]

One might reasonably doubt the value of writing out an offender's crime in an age when few if any observers could read. Indeed, that was probably why declarations of offenses were sometimes read aloud, as in the Bowers case. It was also probably part of the reason colonial authorities sometimes ordered offenders to make verbal acknowledgments of their crimes publicly. This sanction at once humbled miscreants and affirmed the authority of government, and that dual role is evident in its use in the seventeenth-century colonies.

It was used widely in the early decades of the century. In Massachusetts one in five seditious speakers in the 1630s and 1640s had to acknowledge wrong as all or part of their punishment. On March 6, 1637/38, for example, Bay Colony magistrates fined Thomas Starr £20, then ordered him "to acknowledge his fault the 14th at the General Court" for saying that a statute regulating swine "was against god's law, and he would not obey it." Through the 1660s, Virginia judges demanded a public acknowledgment in almost one in ten cases. William Hatcher referred disparagingly to Edward Hill, the Speaker of the House of Burgesses, in 1654, saying "that the mouth of this house is a Devil." They ordered Hatcher to "upon his knees, make an humble acknowledgment of his offense unto the said Col. Edward Hill and [the] Burgesses of this Assembly."[19]

By the 1660s, use of this penalty had declined markedly as colonial governments became more stable. New York was an exception. Its only seventeenth-century seditious speech cases involving public acknowledgment occurred in the 1660s, the turbulent decade of its initial capture from the Dutch. The prosecutions of William Lawrence and George Wood are good illustrations. In 1666 the New York Court of Assizes fined Lawrence and ordered him to "acknowledge his fault" publicly for "speaking seditious words against the Government." Three years later, after George Wood uttered some seditious comments, the judges of the Newtown town court gave him the choice of paying a fine of 18 shillings, or one of 8 shillings combined with "an acknowledgment to the court of his wrong." Wood apparently took the second option and gave them 10 shillings' worth of satisfaction.[20]

The 1670s witnessed a brief resurgence of the use of public acknowledgments in the colonies as the difficult and uncertain years surrounding King Philip's War in New England and Bacon's Rebellion in Virginia threatened the stability of government. Old Dominion officials nearly tripled the use of public acknowledgments, for example, demanding them in 27.3 percent of their seditious speech prosecutions during the unsettled 1670s.

But the 1670s were an aberration. The 1680s and 1690s saw a return to the pattern that had been established by midcentury. No New England speaker of sedition had to acknowledge personal fault in the final decades of the 1600s. In the Southern colonies, use of this penalty declined to insignificance as well. Indeed, the only speaker of sedition to suffer it in any colony in the 1690s was Thomas Rooke. In 1693 the Virginia House of Burgesses ordered him to "on his bended knees acknowledge his offense, and beg the pardon of the House in such words [as] shall be appointed." In a rare instance, the record contains the complete formal statement Rooke read before the burgesses. He had "not only greatly abuse[d] Mr. Matthew Kemp, a worthy member of this worshipful house, by diverse unbecoming and gross words and speeches not fit to be repeated," but also had "utter[ed] and declare[d] several expressions against the honor of the members of this House in general." The acknowledgment ended with a plea for clemency and a promise to maintain "all due reverence towards the representatives of this

Chart 2

Humiliation (n = 95) as a Percentage of All Punished Cases

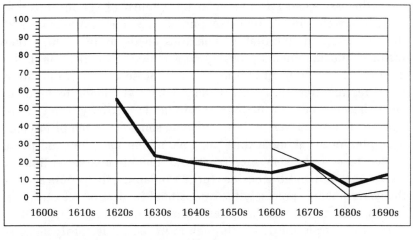

—— New England and the South   **—** New York

their Majesties' most ancient colony and dominion." After some consideration of his "hearty contrition," the burgesses discharged Rooke.[21]

Humiliation penalties declined significantly across the seventeenth century in all the colonies, as Chart 2 illustrates. The line indicating New England and Southern humiliation punishments shows a dramatic decline from the 1620s to the 1630s, followed by a slower decline between the 1630s and the 1690s, a mild aberrational rise in the 1670s notwithstanding. New York revealed a similar experience. Humiliation penalties there went from a high of 26.7 percent of punished cases in the 1660s to 17.4 percent in the 1670s, then dropped to zero in the following decade before ending the century with 3.6 percent in the 1690s. The overall decline in their use was due no doubt in part to the erosion of communal standards of behavior and discipline in the presence of expanding population and increasing mobility. Indeed, humiliation penalties declined across the century for all sorts of crimes, not just seditious speech.

Nor was this limited to the colonies. J. A. Sharpe has observed that the two centuries between 1550 and 1750 saw a move away from humiliation penalties in England. Because of that general trend, it is difficult to draw conclusions about the boundaries of free speech from analysis of humiliation punishments in isolation. Nevertheless, when considered in the context of significantly declining severity in all types of punishment for seditious words, the reduction in humiliation penalties sheds useful light. Other historical developments probably contributed to the decline in the use of such sanctions in seditious speech prosecutions. Humiliation penalties required the scorn of neighbors and friends in order to work; because of that, using them proved particularly tricky when "political" crimes were at issue. Placing someone in the pillory, for example, for speaking against the government in a time and place where most onlookers merely shared the offender's sentiments would accomplish little besides further inflaming the people against the government—precisely the opposite of its desired effect. Given the ongoing crises and the general unsettledness of government in the colonies from the 1670s through the 1690s, it is hardly surprising that authorities would seek less risky forms of punishment.[22]

Colonial authorities employed a third group of punishments in chastising seditious speakers as well—a group specifically designed to deprive transgressors of rights or privileges. Barring offenders from military or civilian offices, disfranchisement, banishment—all fall under the rubric of "exclusion penalties." This type of sanction proved especially effective with well-off offenders. Gentlemen could not be given corporal punishment as a matter of custom and law; as a matter of financial reality, fining them often proved insufficiently painful. George Catchmey's 1653 comment to Robert Taylor in Maryland is illustrative. After forfeiting 10,000 pounds of tobacco, Catchmey quipped that the loss "was but a flea biting to him." That amounted to about £100 sterling at the time, a very large flea indeed, so Catchmey's brag may have been bluff. Yet it makes the point. For rich men, exclusion penalties often proved more useful than fines. They were useful as well in controlling government officials who got out of hand. In 1643 the Virginia General Court disabled some commissioners from further holding office after they challenged a councillor. The Pennsylvania Council put David Lloyd out of his position as clerk of the province in 1688 when he refused one of their orders and offered them "a high contempt" with various "unseemly and slighting expressions."[23]

More ordinary colonists sometimes experienced this sort of penalty, as did Abraham Corbett—tavern keeper, chronic malcontent, bigamist, and speaker of seditious words. A resident of Portsmouth, New Hampshire, Corbett appeared before the Massachusetts General Court in 1666 (the Bay Colony then had jurisdiction over New Hampshire) for "a seditious practice, stirring up sundry the inhabitants of the place where he lives to discontent against the government and laws here established." He stood convicted of that offense and of "entertaining in his house such persons as are his complices in these his proceedings." The judges fined Corbett £20, exacted an additional £100 behavior bond, prohibited him from further "retailing of beer, cider, wine, or liquors," and ordered that "he shall also be disabled from bearing any office in the town where he lives, or in the Commonwealth."[24]

Such cases notwithstanding, putting someone out of office was not a common penalty for seditious speech. Overall, fewer than one in twenty colonial cases ended with this punishment, though almost twice as many offenders endured this sanction before 1660 as after. Regional differences emerged. New England authorities exacted this penalty in only 2.2 percent of the seditious speech cases tried in their region for which a punishment was recorded. Southern officials, by contrast, punished such offenders with this sanction in almost one in ten (9.7 percent) prosecutions. In neither instance is the proportion of total cases large, but the difference between the two regions is curious. Why it occurred is unclear, for the pool of Southern seditious speakers seems not to include a disproportionately larger number of officials than the Northern one. New York concluded 7.2 percent of its seditious speech cases by putting someone out of office, but the number was inflated by an aberrational bulge in the 1660s, the conquered province's first decade. The average proportion from 1670 through 1700 was just 2.9 percent.

When punishing seditious speech, authorities disfranchised even fewer offenders than they barred from office. Overall, fewer than 2 percent of all offenders lost their voting privileges as a punishment. New York officials disfranchised no seditious speakers. Among the other colonies, the proportion was higher in New England (2.1 percent) than in the South (1.5 percent)—perhaps because fewer Southern offenders were freemen, or because more received other punishments instead. Of course, such percentages meant nothing to the offenders being punished. In 1677 the Connecticut General Court fined George Phillips £5 and disfranchised him for accusing the Hartford County court of "oppression and opposing a poor aged cripple," as well as "unmercifulness, presuming to declare them guilty before God, etc., urging the oppression to be so heavy as would sink a Christian state." Repeating the charge loudly and often, Phillips used up the Connecticut authorities' patience. He lost his right to participate in the colony's political affairs.[25]

Arguably the most severe exclusion penalty was banishment. Sometimes officials banished offenders out of the jurisdiction "on pain of death," meaning that they automatically would be hanged upon returning. New England authorities used this sanction in the seventeenth century against religious nonconformists of various stripes, Quakers especially. But Puritans were not the only ones who banished people, and Quakers were certainly not the only people banished. Maryland officials banished an entire ship's crew in 1659 because they were "apt to raise mutiny and sedition within this province" if allowed to remain. Captain North and Richard Collet faced similar sanctions. North arrived in Plymouth colony in the summer of 1643 and soon found himself in trouble. The captain "gave out some speeches tending to sedition and mutiny," notably "that he would make garters of their guts, and that as little while as he had been here he could have a hundred men at his command, or words to like effect." The Plymouth authorities ordered North "to remove himself out of this government within a month or two next ensuing." Richard Collet was banished from Maryland after he presented a seditious petition in 1655. The provincial court gave Collet, the manager of a Virginia gentleman's Maryland holdings, six weeks "to appoint another in his room" and leave.[26]

Authorities never pronounced banishment as a penalty in large numbers of seditious speech prosecutions, and the use of this sanction declined markedly across the seventeenth century. The years before 1660 saw about one in fifteen seditious speakers banished. That figure dropped to a mere 1.4 percent in the last four decades of the century. That is no great surprise. Banishment, like humiliation punishments, declined as a penalty for all sorts of crimes through the seventeenth century, not merely in the American colonies, but

Chart 3
Exclusion (n = 66) as a Percentage of All Punished Cases

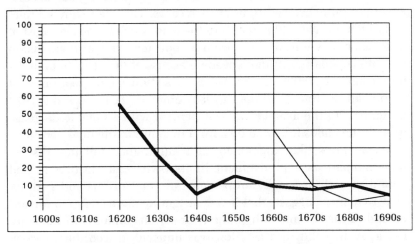

— New England and the South   — New York

in Europe as well, marking the continuation of a long-term trend. A closer look, however, reveals more than participation in that general pattern. In the colonies, banishment fell into relative disuse early and it was, from the beginning, largely a New England phenomenon. Almost one in four colonial seditious speakers suffered banishment in the 1630s. The figure never climbed above 4 percent in any decade after that. And more than two-thirds of all the banishments (68.4 percent) occurred in New England (more than half of those in the 1630s alone). The early Puritans showed themselves as willing to suppress secular criticism as religious dissent in preserving their Holy Commonwealth.

Chart 3 plots the percentages of exclusion penalties of all types in punished seditious speech cases. The marked decline in their use is striking. Equally striking, though not shown by the chart, is that Southern authorities used these more than Northern ones. One would expect the community-oriented New Englanders to have used such penalties more often than the scattered and more individualistic Southerners. The oddity is an accident of the grouping technique. Southern officials leaned heavily toward putting offenders out of office, while Northern magistrates showed a preference for banishment (early on especially) and disfranchisement. In New York, exclusion penalties of all kinds constituted a total of 10.8 percent of punished seditious speech cases. The chart shows a relatively high number (40 percent) in the colony's first decade. Most of these came as we have seen, from a short-term bulge in exclusion from office penalties in that decade. Because of that, the precipitous drop from the 1660s to the 1670s is somewhat misleading. Yet the overall decline continued in less dramatic fashion. From 1670 through 1700, the average was 4.4 percent with a notable decrease through the 1680s followed by a mild rebound in the final decade.

As sanctions like banishment and humiliation fell into disuse, imprisonment as a punishment in its own right steadily gained ground in early modern Europe generally and in England particularly. Evidence suggests that it was becoming more common toward the end of the seventeenth century for serious offenses in the colonies as well.[27] But incarceration was unusual for seditious speech in the colonies, and—bucking the trend—it became even less so across the century. The reasons are not hard to see. Building dependable jails and holding colonists unable to supply their own fare were very expensive undertakings. Besides, leaving offenders to languish in prison prevented them from being productive members of the community and added in myriad ways to the burden people around them had to bear—a proposition largely unacceptable to colonial leaders. When officials used imprisonment, they did so almost invariably for brief periods. Terms of longer than a month were extremely rare.

The most common form of "incarceration" involved detaining an offender pending arraignment, trial, or punishment. This did not necessarily involve sitting in a formal prison cell. Such short-term confinement could mean simply being held in "the sheriff's hands" or in cages kept for the purpose. Even stocks, pillory, and bilboes offered convenient means to hold prisoners for brief periods. While such treatment may well have been uncomfortable and embarrassing to the defendant, it was a practical necessity, not a punishment. For reference, 11.1 percent of the seditious speech cases in this study clearly involved the use of "imprisonment" for these purposes. There was no significant distinction among the colonial regions, or over time, in this regard.

Sometimes the attempt to place an offender in custody pending arraignment proved difficult. The Virginia authorities did not appreciate Captain Thomas Wilson's response, for example, when the governor and Council sent the sheriff with a warrant for his arrest in 1653. Wilson stood on the deck of his ship and flatly rejected the authority of the warrant, "deriding it with laughter and scorn," as the sheriff noted with obvious frustration. The captain seems never to have been brought to justice for that offense, nor for denying the Council the right to collect castle duties. More often, offenders were in fact taken into custody. Colonel Peter Sayer went to jail pending trial in Maryland on April 8, 1693. The colonel had "lately uttered and divulged diverse false, scandalous, mutinous and seditious speeches and reports" about the colony government, "bespattering, reviling, abusing, affronting and scandalously reflecting upon the same." Some thought Sayer possessed Jacobite writings as well, so the Council had his home thoroughly searched for "mutinous, seditious, traitorous or treasonable papers, writings, or pamphlets." The officials empowered the searchers "to unlock and break open and search all chests, trunks, cabinets, tables, doors or other private and suspected places (where the keys shall be denied or refused you)." The record does not indicate the final disposition of the case, but numerous witnesses appeared against Sayer. His other statements included the rather prophetic idea that Francis Nicholson would soon replace Governor Lionel Copley (he did) and the imprudent hope that the "rogue" Copley would be hanged (he was not).[28]

John Heardman went to jail pending trial as well, and—typical in seditious speech prosecutions—went back to jail pending punishment. In 1659 someone reported that Heardman was drunk and disorderly and a magistrate ordered his arrest. When the marshall found him in a nearby pub, Heardman threw "his hat upon the ground and bid the marshall touch him if he durst." The official promptly knocked the drunken fellow to the ground, then stomped him some to stop his wild kicking. Before Magistrate Fenn, Heardman insisted he was sober even though he was "reeling and staggering" and "ill pronouncing of his words, the word justice in particular which he bid him express plainly but he could not." Fenn jailed Heardman pending his appearance at the Court of Magistrates.

There, in a more sober frame of mind, Heardman confessed to all the charges against him, including the allegation that he had seditiously denied the laws of the colony and the availability of justice within the jurisdiction. As his defense, he argued that he had been drunk for two days on liquor supplied by Sergeant Baldwin, a man who "had always given him good counsel." "Had he given him more good counsel and less liquors," the magistrates retorted, "it had been well." At that Heardman fell silent. But when the judges began discussing the need to make an example of him, Heardman broke in and pled for mercy, declaring "himself to be a son of Beliall, not subject to any yoke, and that if all men were of his frame, it would be a hell upon earth and no living among them." In the end, the magistrates "looked upon his miscarriages as exceedingly great and greatly aggravated," particularly his "trampling the magistrate (as it were) under his feet and the laws of the jurisdiction, saying they are the wills of men." The judges preferred harsh corporal punishment, but because Heardman was "not well," they softened and exacted a £10 fine instead, requiring him "to lie in prison at his own charge" until he provided security for the fine.[29]

Holding a defendant pending trial or punishment was one thing. Jailing an offender deliberately as a punishment was quite another. Such incarceration occurred but rarely and usually lasted only a short time. After "abusing and menacing the magistracy" of Pennsylvania in 1685, Abraham Effingall suffered "14 days imprisonment at hard labor." In 1638 the Massachusetts Court of Assistants whipped Katherine Finch an unspecified number of lashes, then had her "committed till the next General Court" for "speaking against the magistrates, against the churches, and against the Elders." Richard Crocker faced a similar fate in 1626. As he and two others walked in the Virginia woods, Henry Elliot said that over in Martin's Hundred, one thousand nails could be had from John Day for a "barrel of ears." But Day no longer sold them because Captain Hamer was getting a barrel of corn and an additional ten pounds of tobacco. Hamer, a member of the Council, seems to have been eliminating the competition even though his price was higher. Crocker agreed with Elliot, adding "aye, there are two of them that are not fit to sit at the Council table, which is Captain Hamer and

Mr. Persey the merchant, for they deal upon nothing but extortion." Thomas Ward, the third man in the group, testified to the conversation in court and the Council ordered Crocker to "suffer one months imprisonment" for his words.[30]

Sometimes seditious speakers faced longer jail terms. After Maryland's Somerset County court sentenced John Pope to three months in prison in 1699, he appealed to the Council. There he admitted to having spoken "scandalous words" against Somerset County magistrate Matthew Scarborough, but revealed extenuating circumstances the county court judges had refused to consider. It turned out that Pope had a bit too much to drink one evening, and as he tried to make his way home, "Scarborough maliciously followed him from house to house and teased him so that he swore very much, for which he is heartily sorry." The Council agreed that Pope's treatment had not been fair and suspended his sentence pending a full investigation. The longest prison sentence handed out to a seditious speaker in the seventeenth century fell upon John Philpot. In 1694, on the testimony of four witnesses, a North Carolina jury convicted Philpot of speaking seditious words against the king. The Council sentenced him to "suffer imprisonment of his body for and during one whole year and a day without bail or mainprise." They may have rescinded Philpot's incarceration "in consideration of his weakness and age," but the record is unclear.[31]

Seventeenth-century colonial prison conditions were anything but comfortable. Prisoners had to provide for their own fare through personal resources and family support when possible. Sometimes they carried on their trades while imprisoned to provide for their needs. Prisoners without such resources lived miserably, forced as they were to survive on the largess of the government or, worse, the keeper. In such circumstances, bread and water ("prisoner's fare") remained the staple. Lashings for transgressions were common. Especially serious offenders and others thought likely to attempt escape were typically kept "close prisoner"—heavily chained to a post or wall. In general, sanitary conditions were abysmal and the common lack of even basic protection from the elements created great hardship, especially "during the winter season." Ill-compensated jailers had precious little concern for the comforts of prison-

Chart 4

Imprisonment (n = 50) as a Percentage of All Punished Cases

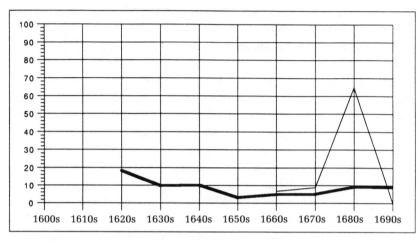

— New England and the South   — New York

ers, and even less incentive for developing any. Considering the general conditions of incarceration, it is not surprising that escapes were frequent.[32]

On the whole, imprisonment was not a common penalty in the seventeenth-century colonies. Only about one of fifteen punished seditious speech cases involved imprisonment as a specific, deliberate punishment. Southern authorities were more likely than New Englanders to pronounce this sanction against speakers of sedition. Roughly one in twelve Southern seditious speakers suffered imprisonment, while only one in seventeen New Englanders went to jail. In New York, about one in six (16.9 percent) colonists convicted of seditious speech went to jail as all or part of their punishment. But that figure is misleading, inflated, as Chart 4 indicates, by a huge bulge in the 1680s. The chart also shows that, across the century, imprisonment became even less common for seditious speech in New England and the South, though not dramatically so. The 1690s may represent a slow recovery from the aberrational increase of the 1680s, or they may reflect an inclination toward increased use of imprisonment as the eighteenth century came on. Without information from the first decades of the 1700s, it is impossible to say which.

In punishing seditious speech, colonial officials relied less and less on various penalties as the century progressed. Declining use of some sanctions, including humiliation and banishment, followed broader trends in colonial and European punishment. In other ways, including reduced rather than increased use of imprisonment, colonial practice went against those trends. Yet authorities still prosecuted colonists for speaking seditious words in the seventeenth century. Offenders still faced punishment. If these sanctions declined in severity and significance, what took their place?

A Growing Leniency

Across the seventeenth century, colonial officials increasingly abandoned a variety of harsher sanctions in punishing seditious words, adopting in the process milder penalties as replacements. Here we examine those expanding penalties, then explore in turn the decline of multiple sanctions, the rise of remittances, and the growing inclination to either forgo prosecutions or abandon them once begun. Each of these developments contributed substantially to an unmistakable pattern of growing leniency toward seditious speech in the early colonies.

Fines were by far the most common punishments pronounced against offenders in the seventeenth century. That was true not just for seditious speech, but also for most crimes, in Europe generally and in England and her colonies in particular. Fines tended to be relatively small, partly to reduce the likelihood of appeals. Colonial authorities used fines as a form of punishment in a remarkably wide variety of cases. Illegal voting, fishing on the Sabbath, swearing, failure to keep stock penned, trade violations, nightwalking—all of these offenses and many others commonly brought offenders fines from colonial courts. Sometimes the crime could be quite serious, as when John Burton killed an Indian chief in 1640, incurring the wrath of the Virginia authorities. The General Court fined him £20 sterling. Often the offense was less significant. In 1686 two boys were caught stealing watermelons, "last Thursday in the night about the going down of the moon," from Benjamin Lewis's yard in Fairfield County, Connecticut. The county court ordered the boys to pay fines of 11 shillings each—or else suffer the embarrassment of the stocks.[1]

In seditious speech cases, as in others, judges commonly levied fines in pounds, shillings, and pence, while offenders paid "in kind." New Englanders typically satisfied amercements in peas, corn, wheat, rye, or barley at exchange rates established by colony officials. Contemporaries called that "country pay." Chesapeake authorities usually specified fines in pounds of tobacco. The Middle Colonies used both tobacco and "country pay." Sugar passed as currency in the West Indies, naval stores in North Carolina, and, later, rice in South Carolina. For purposes of analysis, I convert amounts levied in goods to pounds, shillings, and pence at prices current when comparing punishments involving money.

Authorities sometimes required that fines be paid in unusual but appropriate forms. The Virginia General Court, for example, unabashedly used seditious speech prosecutions as a means of providing supplies to the soldiers fighting Indians in the 1670s. In 1674 the court ordered Marmaduke Newton to pay "two barrels of powder, one to James City fort and another to Nanzemond fort" for verbally abusing a member of the Council. On March 15, 1676/77, the court convicted William Hatcher of uttering seditious words and ordered him to "pay with all expedition eight thousand pounds of dressed pork unto his Majesty's Commander of his forces in Henrico County, for the supply of the soldiers."[2]

Specie was uncommon and much valued in the colonies, so requiring payment in it constituted an exceptional added imposition. The aftermath of Bacon's Rebellion saw a peculiar instance of this in the case of Colonel William Kendall. In 1676/77, Kendall spoke "diverse scandalous and mutinous words tending to the dishonor of the right honorable the Governor," which the court considered a "great crime." Perhaps sensing their ire, he made the unusual move of suggesting his own penalty, "the said Col. Kendall submitting himself, and offering fifty pounds sterling as a fine." The court accepted the very large sum, and later made a gift of it to the governor. More often than not, court records do not specifically indicate the form of payment. Two typical Pennsylvania cases illustrate the point. In 1687 Richard Crosby paid a fine of £7 "for being drunk and abusing the magistracy" of Chester County. Two years later, John Maddocke, "of the township of Ridley," appeared before the same county court "for speaking and uttering scandalous and dishonorable words against the life, person, and government" of William Penn and his governor, John Blackwell. The jaundiced judges fined Maddocke £5 after he confessed and put himself at their mercy. In such cases, we must assume that specie was not required.[3]

Whether expected in silver or commodities, fines rarely had to be paid immediately. Authorities ordinarily allowed offenders months and even years to pay off fines so long as they posted security or accepted a property lien to guarantee payment.[4] Just under 42 percent of all seditious speakers for whom a punishment was recorded paid a fine of some kind in the seventeenth century. And though fines had declined in usage somewhat by the 1690s, they remained the single most widely pronounced penalty for seditious speech in the seventeenth century. That is not surprising. It is revealing, however, that in fining offenders for seditious words, colonial authorities increasingly abandoned larger amercements as the century progressed.

Chart 5 traces the use of fines of £5 or more in seditious speech cases involving fines. For New England and the South, after climbing a bit in the 1650s, the larger amercements resumed a steady decline, falling particularly in the last two decades of the century. By the 1690s, only 25 percent of offenders paying fines for seditious speech paid £5 or more. (And of the very large proportion paying under £5, one in five faced amercements of less than 40 shillings.) When compared to the 75 percent paying larger fines in the 1620s, the decline over seven decades is especially dramatic. The New York trend is less clear. The strong and steady rise in larger amercements from the 1660s through the 1680s is graphically offset by a precipitous decline in the 1690s, again making it difficult to fix and analyze a pattern (particularly because the number of cases is small).

In any event, the general trend toward using smaller fines to punish seditious speech is unmistakable. Defendants did not increasingly come from the ranks of the poor, so that cannot explain the trend. Nor did the price of goods decline across the seventeenth

Chart 5
Fines of £5 and Over (n = 140) as a Percentage of All Fines

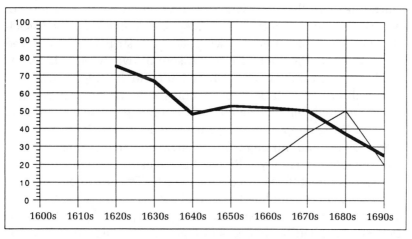

Legend: ▬ New England and the South ▬ New York

century in the colonies, so deflation cannot explain it either. Indeed, the century witnessed moderate inflation. Officials simply came to treat seditious words with greater leniency as the seventeenth century progressed.

That growing leniency showed itself in other areas as well. Colonial authorities not only relied increasingly on small fines when amercing seditious speakers, but they also increasingly employed other sanctions that were inherently mild. Bonds were particularly important. Bonds of various types were a common aspect of colonial life. Authorities used them, for example, to ensure that merchants paid appropriate customs duties, that the fathers rather than government bore the expense of raising bastard children, that masters trained apprentices as agreed, and that sheriffs properly handled taxes they collected. Within the judicial system, bonds enjoyed varied uses as well. They were often required to ensure appearance at trial, not just of defendants, but of all involved parties. Authorities commonly used bonds as a way of guaranteeing offenders' future good behavior. When strongly suspicious of defendants, judges occasionally placed them under behavior bonds after prosecutions had been dropped, or even following acquittals. Authorities sometimes required bonds to assure that a court order would be obeyed or to prevent some anticipated action, including flight to avoid obligations and the like. Courts regularly used bonds as a form of intervention to stop recurring incidents. A Maine Court of Associates ordered James Hermon whipped "ten stripes on the naked back" in 1669, then bound him "in sum of twenty pounds for his good behavior until the next County Court" for beating his wife.[5]

In seditious speech cases, as in others, colonial authorities sometimes required behavior bonds as the only punishment. In 1663 Thomas Durfee appeared before the Rhode Island Court of Trials, "for speaking and uttering words of great contempt against the government of this colony." Rather than make a fight of it, Durfee confessed and let the bench decide his fate. The judges ordered him to post a £20 behavior bond to stand in effect until the next meeting of the Court of Trials, "and not to depart without leave." Thomas Duckett, Jonathan Songhurst and Jonathan Parsons, among others, found themselves in trouble in 1683 for subscribing to a seditious petition against the Pennsylvania government. The subscribers were bound to their good behavior toward the government in "a single recognizance of fifty pounds" until the next meeting of the General Assembly. Frances Sturgeon appeared before the Albemarle County court in North Carolina "for speaking several scandalous words against the right honorable [Governor] Seth Sothell, Esquire" in 1685. The court discharged Sturgeon after her husband provided "sufficient security" for her good behavior.[6]

Sometimes behavior bonds came in conjunction with other penalties. Daniel Browne, jailed by New York authorities in 1672 after "contemning the authority" of the Whorekill court, proved to be very pliant when he appeared before the Council. He confessed his transgression and begged for clemency, adding that "it will be his ruin if he not return speedily to his habitation, both in regard of a crop of tobacco he hath, and some corn, which will be all lost without his attendance on it." The placated Council released Browne after forcing him to post a £20 bond and ordering him "to acknowledge his fault and ask pardon of the magistrates at Whorekill for his misdemeanor."[7]

A large bond could keep a man perpetually in jail. Authorities knew that, of course, and as a rule merely required that an offender pledge to forfeit the amount of the bond if convicted of the same offense again within the time specified. Because bonds were pledges and not actual payments, and because they often reflected less the malefactor's ability to pay than the degree of fear authorities wished to instill, they were normally larger than fines. Bonds of less than £5, for example, were unknown in seditious speech cases, and almost half (46.5 percent) were for amounts in excess of £100. Bonds, especially large ones, thus theoretically kept colonists in constant dread that a misstep could bring ruin. Indeed, that was just their purpose—to ensure good behavior through fear of forfeiture. But in practice various factors mitigated that fear. Most importantly, bond forfeitures in seditious speech cases were virtually unknown. That could mean that offenders stood in such terror that they rarely misbehaved, or that officials were not very watchful after ordering such bonds. More likely, it was a combination of a healthy consciousness on the part of the offender and a reasonable flexibility on the part of authorities. In addition, behavior bonds were normally required for a relatively brief and specified period, not levied for life or an indeterminate time. The most common approach was to place an offender under a behavior bond until the next quarterly court, then if no one came to object against him, to release the bond obligation. Authorities occasionally continued bonds through one or more courts after the first, but that was unusual. Toward the end of the seventeenth century, placing offenders under behavior bonds for a year seems to have become a standardized practice. Finally, offenders under behavior bonds could petition authorities to be released of the bond before the specified time. Courts often granted such petitions, presumably because offenders who went to the trouble of filing a formal petition usually had a good case and reasonable hope of success.

Behavior bonds were less severe than many penalties exacted for seditious speech in the seventeenth-century colonies. The same must be said of sureties. Though designed to accomplish the same ends as bonds, they took a somewhat different approach. Rather than merely posting a behavior bond, offenders had to find others willing to post such bonds in their behalf. In effect, these "sureties" pledged to forfeit given amounts of money if the offender misbehaved. That effectively made sureties watchdogs, giving them a personal stake in the offender's behavior.[8]

Colonial authorities used sureties, like bonds, to punish seditious speech among a wide range of offenses. On rare occasion, they required only a single surety. In 1654 the Connecticut General Court convicted Thomas Baxter of "insufferable, reproachful speeches" uttered "against the Chief of this jurisdiction." The judges ordered Baxter to find "some able person" willing to pledge £200 as security for his good behavior for one year. More often, authorities required two or more sureties. These sometimes went unspecified in the records. In 1624 the Virginia General Court ordered William Tyler to find "two sufficient sureties" to guarantee his good behavior after he spoke seditiously about the governor and Council. Had the words not been "mentioned occasionally and accidentally," Tyler might have lost his ears. Nor did New York officials specify the amount of Simon Smith's sureties when he appeared in 1700 to be discharged of a behavior bond he had previously posted for seditious words. The Quarter Sessions judges ordered him discharged after he paid the fees of court. Smith balked at this, giving "the court very abusive language, telling them he would pay none, that they had no authority to compel him, that he would find a law for them," adding the superfluous comment "that he cared no more for the Mayor than another man." The court ordered Smith to find unspecified but "sufficient" sureties for his good behavior and future appearances, then jailed him until he did so. Officials usually specified the amount of the sureties, and these covered a wide range. A few were quite small. In 1672 Dr. Robert Couch appeared before the Massachusetts Suffolk County court "for making verses tending to the reproach of the late Governor Richard Bellingham." The judges ordered Couch to find two sureties of "five pounds apiece." Others were quite large. When Henry Jowles appeared before the Maryland Council in 1693 for seditious words against Governor Blackiston, the body required him to find "two sufficient sureties in the sum of two hundred and fifty pounds sterling each" for his future good behavior.[9]

Sometimes authorities used sureties, like bonds, to guarantee appearance for trial. William Hatch found himself in trouble for seditious words in Plymouth Colony on September 4, 1641. The magistrates ordered him to find two sureties worth £20 each to assure that he "shall personally appear at the next General Court." That Hatch also posted a personal bond highlights another notable characteristic of sureties. They almost always accompanied one or more other punishments. Officials mixed sureties with behavior bonds, appearance bonds, and other punishments in various combinations. Bay Colony magistrates fined Richard Scott £50 for possessing a seditious letter in 1675, for example, then required him to post a behavior bond of £20 and to find two sureties of £10 each. After a Maryland jury convicted James Lewis of spreading false reports in 1672, the provincial court ordered that he "receive immediately thirty nine lashes on the bare back" and find "such sureties as two of the Justices shall approve" to guarantee his good behavior.[10]

When offenders appeared as ordered or had behaved themselves properly during the prescribed period, the terms of the surety obligation had been fulfilled. At that point, the guarantors were legally freed of their obligation, normally following a petition to that effect. If an offender did not meet the stipulations outlined by the court, the sureties forfeited the pledged amount. As with bonds, such forfeitures were rare, but people did sometimes go to jail if unable or unwilling to pay a surety forfeiture in full.[11]

Colonial authorities also used admonishment as a form of punishment in the seventeenth century. Though undoubtedly uncomfortable, even embarrassing, for the offender, this was certainly the mildest of available sanctions. In practice "admonishment" meant that the presiding judge formally reprimanded the offender in open court. Rebukes and warnings often came from the bench during trial and sentencing, but our concern here is with admonition as a specific punishment. Sometimes authorities combined admonition with other penalties, and sometimes they used admonishments alone. On November 7, 1668, the Massachusetts Court of Assistants sentenced Joshua Atwater and Benjamin Switzer to be admonished as well as fined (£10 and £5 respectively) for their leading roles in circulating a seditious petition. Thomas Gilbert stood trial before the Bay Colony's General Court two years earlier for seditious words. To deter such "unsafe and extravagant expressions," the court ordered only that he "be solemnly admonished publicly in open court, by the honored Governor." In 1683 Nicholas Moore appeared before the Pennsylvania Council for "words against the proceedings of the Governor, Provincial Council and Assembly." "They have this day broken the Charter," Moore had said in a pub in the presence of some Council members, adding that "hundreds in England will curse you for what you have done, and their children after them." The Council released the indiscreet Moore with an admonition.[12]

Use of smaller bonds and sureties (both of less than £50) and admonition as punishments for seditious speech grew substantially in New England and the South during the first part of the seventeenth century, reaching a high of 32.1 percent in the 1660s. Then their use fell off sharply during the turbulent 1670s before beginning a climb back up. By the end of the century, better than one in five cases (21.1 percent) ended with an admonition or a moderate recognizance. New York stood in stark contrast. Authorities there pronounced these penalties in only four cases between 1664 and 1700.

In handling seditious speech in the seventeenth century then, colonial authorities turned away from harsher sanctions, increasingly pronounced milder versions of long-used punishments, and exhibited a growing reliance on inherently milder penalties. Two related elements contributed significantly to that pattern of growing leniency—the increase in single sanctions on the one hand and remittances on the other.

Colonial officials exacted multiple sanctions throughout the century and in all colonial regions. Thomas Dexter appeared before the Bay Colony's Court of Assistants in 1632/33 "for speaking reproachful and seditious words against the Government here established." He had insisted that "this captious government will bring all to naught," then let fly a stinging insult by "adding that the best of them was but an attorney." The court fined Dexter £40, disfranchised him, and ordered him set in bilboes for an undisclosed time. In 1674/75 New York officials took exception when John Burroughs wrote a seditious letter in the name of the town of Newtown. Before the Council could complete its investigation, Burroughs wrote "another letter of the like nature." The Council ordered him "forthwith committed to the custody of the Sheriff of this city, to remain in prison until some time on Monday next." On that day, "for signing seditious letters in the name of the town of Newtown, against the government and Court of Assizes," he was to "be brought to the whipping post before the City Hall, and being fastened thereunto, to stand an hour, with a paper on his breast" announcing his crime. After this ignominy, they rendered Burroughs, the Newtown town clerk, "incapable of bearing any office or trust in the government for the future." Jonathan Clapper appeared before the North Carolina General Court "holden at the House of Thomas White," on February 25, 1694/95. Arrested by warrant from the Grand Council for seditious words against Deputy Governor Harvey, Clapper received a mild sentence upon conviction. The court ordered him to ask forgiveness for his offense and to "give bond for his good abearing" until the next General Court. Clapper's "abearing" must have been acceptable, for he was later appointed "Constable for the north side of Piquemons River."[13]

Through the 1630s nearly two out of every three colonists in New England and the South (65.2 percent) received more than one sanction when convicted of seditious speech, many of those suffering three or more penalties. But the following decades saw a dramatic decline in multiple sanctions against seditious speakers, to about 20 percent by the end of the century. The same basic pattern obtained in New England and the Southern colonies, and authorities in both regions exacted multiple penalties in about the same percentage of their seditious speech prosecutions. New York exhibited a similar pattern. Officials there readily exacted multiple sanctions early on (60 percent of seditious speakers in the 1660s) but became significantly less inclined to as the decades passed (just 28.6 percent by the 1690s).

A clear trend is evident here. Greater emphasis on multiple sanctions in a colony's early years followed by a move away from them was normal, regardless of when those years fell in the century. Officials' perceived need for the severity of multiple sanctions declined as colonies became more settled and stable. Conversely, all the colonies witnessed a precipitous decline in the use of multiple punishments in the 1680s followed by a resumption of the milder decline in the 1690s. Times of extreme danger and uncertainty, like the years surrounding the Glorious Revolution, tended to produce temporary abeyances to avoid the risk of inflaming tensions. Equally noteworthy, when authorities did order multiple punishments for speakers of sedition toward the end of the century, they usually pronounced only two, and those combinations were most often of less severe penalties. Fines, exclusion penalties, humiliation, corporal punishment, imprisonment—all declined in severity and usage. Offenders facing multiple sanctions at the end of the century most often endured small fines combined with moderate behavior bonds or judicial admonitions.

Besides their growing use of inherently milder penalties against speakers of sedition, and their move away from multiple sanctions, colonial officials also showed an increasing inclination to remit ordered punishments. That inclination contributed significantly to the growing leniency evident in seventeenth-century seditious speech prosecutions. The heading of "remittance" includes not only technical remittance, but also pardons, suspensions of sentences, and reduction of a pronounced sentence to something milder.

Often remittances were only partial. When a Maine jury convicted Abel Molton "of speaking abusive words against authority" in 1696, York County magistrates fined him £3, which he immediately paid. Later, his father petitioned the court for clemency, and the judges remitted half the fine in hopes that mercy would encourage Abel's "good deportment for the future." In 1680 Robert Willen appeared before Delaware's Kent County court for speaking seditiously against the justices of the peace. Willen had said "that he did wonder that the Duke of York was such a fool as to make such inconsiderable sons of whores to be justices." The only wonder at the trial was that the scowling judges did not exact a sterner retribution. They fined Willen five hundred pounds of tobacco (a bit over £3) and placed him under an unspecified behavior bond "for the space of one year and a day." Willen paid the fine, then later petitioned for a remission of the bond—a request the justices granted. Sometimes, penalties were entirely remitted. In 1669 George Wood appeared before New York's Newtown town court "for his protesting against the Court of Sessions and this town court's proceedings." Ordered to enter security in an amount unspecified for his good behavior for one year, Wood reconsidered his comments and later "expressed himself very sorry for his folly and abusive behavior." Already fined for seditious speech the previous July and obviously no friend of the court, he may have reasonably feared forfeiting the bond for another outburst before a year passed. Whatever Wood's motivation, the court accepted his humble apology and released him of the bond obligation.[14]

Full remittances sometimes accompanied unusual circumstances. Martha Wearing and Robert Drummer appeared before the Burlington Court of Quarter Sessions and Pleas held on November 4, 1699, charged with unlawfully living together. The West Jersey court gave them a choice: "marry or part within one month." The judges also fined Wearing five pieces of eight for speaking "abusively and contemptibly" of a magistrate. Whether the words flowed from the cohabitation altercation is unclear, but "in consideration of her poverty" the fine "was remitted unto her." In 1650 the Bay Colony's Ipswich County court fined Thomas Cooke £5 "for his abusive speeches against authority." He died soon after, and Rachel, his widow, petitioned the General Court for an "abatement and remitment" of the fine. "Being informed of the miserable estate the widow is left in," the court remitted the fine. In October 1659 Plymouth Colony officials ordered Thomas Ewer "to lie neck and heels during the pleasure of the court" for his "tumultuous and seditious carriages and speeches." Ewer "was an infirm man, and was troubled with a rupture," so the court somewhat grudgingly "suspended the sentence so as not to execute it," but not without warning him if in the future he failed to "rule his tongue, they will take a course to rid him out of the colony."[15]

Such suspended sentences, though uncommon, amounted to full remittances. As in the Plymouth example, they had the character of a second-chance offer. In 1684 the Maryland Council convicted John Saxon "for having in most scurrilous language, and behavior, mocked and abused the honorable Colonel William Stevens, a member of this Board." Saxon "had nothing to say in his defense" but "humbly begs pardon" for "his inadvertency and folly therein." Upon Saxon's humble supplication, the Council ordered that "his offense for this time be passed by, and the punishment thereof suspended." But, they carefully added, the suspension stood only "until such time as he offer further occasion" for reprimand.[16]

Sometimes authorities pardoned offenders outright. A Maryland jury convicted William Seely in 1661 for "certain words scattered from him which passes as mutinous." After he apologized for the "passionate expressions," the provincial court pardoned him. In 1688 Pennsylvania authorities summoned a group of colonists to answer for subscribing "to what was endorsed on the back of" a "contemptuous printed advertisement against keeping a fair at the center." The deputy governor and Council pardoned each of them. A "pardon" did not always bring remittance of punishment, however. Abel Hardenbroek learned that in 1673 after being fined 25 florins for derogating some New York magistrates and using "very foul and unseemly language" to the Schout in New York City. When Hardenbroek petitioned the court for clemency, the judges pardoned the offense itself, but they refused to reduce the fine, "it being not so much by half as ought to have been imposed upon him for his great crime."[17]

The growing use of remittance in colonial seditious speech cases across the seventeenth century is noteworthy. For New England and the South, the propensity to remit all or part of a pronounced sentence in such prosecutions climbed from a low of 8.5 percent in the 1630s to a high of 32 percent in the 1690s. That climb was slow and steady except for a short-term surge in the 1650s. New York fluctuated more wildly, beginning with 50 percent remissions in the 1660s, dropping dramatically in the following two decades, then jumping up to 57.1 percent in the 1690s.

Colonial officials not only showed themselves increasingly inclined to remit punishments in seditious speech cases, but they also revealed a growing inclination not to prosecute seditious words fully as the century progressed. Sometimes authorities failed to press charges when they knew of seditious words, even after formally hearing testimony and investigating or discussing the incident. In 1689, according to a bricklayer named Thomas Masters, James Emott was traveling through East Jersey when he stopped for a moment's conversation. Mrs. Masters asked "from whence he came, whereupon the said Emott replied, he came from New York." He "had been on board the ship Beaver," Emott volunteered, "and had taken before Father Smith the Oath of Allegiance to be true to the King." This being 1689, Mrs. Masters's next question was only to be expected. Which king? "The said Emott answered King

James," adding that Thomas Stevens, Daniel Whitehead, and others had "taken the like oath at the same time." Neither Emott nor the men he named were prosecuted, though the deposition was formally sworn and recorded by the authorities.[18]

Sometimes, formal charges were filed but no trial followed. Though rare, this did happen when a grand jury made the charge. Maine officials ignored such presentments in three seditious speech cases in successive years in the 1660s. In 1663 a York County grand jury presented Robert Jordan "for saying the governor of Boston was a rogue and all the rest thereof were traitors and rebels against the King." In 1664 another York County grand jury presented Edward Colcord "for saying that York men were a company of pitiful rogues and rascals, naming Mr. Rishworth and Captain Raynes and all the Associates that acted in the case about Jeremiah Sheers [another speaker of sedition]." The grand jury at the November 1665 Saco Court of Pleas presented John Breame, of Cascoe, for slighting Henry Jocelyn, a magistrate. All three offenders went unprosecuted. Such cases occurred in other colonies, though usually later in the century. In 1692 Peter DeMilt, a baker and onetime Leislerian Assembly member, was presented by a New York grand jury "for misdemeanor in uttering malicious and scandalous words against the government." Jarvis Marshall testified against DeMilt, and the sheriff was ordered to take him into custody. Whether that occurred or not is uncertain, but DeMilt was not tried.[19]

Slightly more often, prosecutions were dropped after an official had preferred the charge. Robert Snead got off easy after appearing before the Pennsylvania Council on May 19, 1698. Snead had written to England that "though the governor knew of and had the proclamation to seize pirates, yet he had refused to seize several of the pirates of Avery's crew." When finally captured, they escaped because the governor "bailed them after seizure and denied and refused guards to watch them, the gaol being insufficient." Snead denied the seditious speech charge, but admitted that he had "complained home of abuses he had received" in the colony. It was "his duty, first to have complained here for redress of the said abuses," the deputy governor rejoined, "and when it was denied him here, it was then time enough to have complained home." The Council released Snead with that admonition, letting the words about pirates pass. When Mathias Nicolls, secretary to the governor of New York, complained in 1675 against Jonas Wood and several others for spreading it about that he had falsified official records, the complaint was duly noted, but no action taken. Ship captain Francis Harbin objected to having his men impressed in Maryland in 1698, declaring that "he did not know of any authority the Governor had to command men from on board ships and that he did not know whether the King could do so much." Harbin went unprosecuted, though John Young, an official who heard the words, filed a sworn deposition against him.[20]

More commonly, failure to bring an offender to trial for seditious words followed charges made by individual colonists. Some came very early in the century. John Martin, for example, went unprosecuted in Virginia after casting "some aspersion upon the present government" in a letter to another colonist in 1619. But most occurred later. Though charged in 1681 with saying the magistrates of Albany, New York, "were not promoters of the welfare of the community," William Teller never went to trial. William Furber went untried in 1693 even though the New Hampshire Council considered his reported words "a great affront put on not only his Honor [the Governor] but the whole House" and commented that "he ought to be severely punished and made an example to deter others from doing the same." The Maryland Council used even stronger words to describe Thomas Johnson's offense in 1694. They ordered him to post a huge bond of £500 sterling and find two sureties of £250 sterling each to assure his appearance for prosecution for the "rebellious and treasonable words spoken and uttered by him" to Doctor Symon Wotton. Johnson never stood trial.[21]

Once a trial had run its course, the disposition was sometimes left unrecorded. Interestingly, considering the uncertainties inherent in the sources, this was extremely unusual in seditious speech cases. Such instances cannot be classified as dropped prosecutions, or even as decisions not to punish offenders. They most likely resulted from the recorders' oversight. The plausibility of carelessness as an explanation is strengthened by the occasional "after the fact" reference to a seditious speech prosecution without any record of the charges or trial. Richard Webber, for example, petitioned New Hampshire's Governor Cranfield on July 10, 1683, seeking "pity and pardon" for his seditious words against Nathanial Fryer, the deputy governor. That was the first and only reference to the case in the records.[22]

Such cases point to an important reality. One traverses difficult ground in trying to extrapolate authorities' intentions from what does not appear in the records. The mere failure to record a prosecution, after all, does not prove that one never occurred. Yet certain kinds of prosecutions, including seditious speech cases, tended to be more or less fully recorded. Moreover, as the century wore on, records tended to be more complete. This was due in part, no doubt, to the gradual increase in appeals and the demands they placed on accurate documentation, and to a growing interest in "procedural niceties" as the century progressed. A greater degree of social and legal development accompanying the firmer establishment of settled government probably contributed as well. Yet the incidence of seditious speech cases disappearing from the records increased over time, even as the propensity to keep more complete records grew.

Cases that were clearly dropped, not merely disappearing, offer a less speculative landscape. On very rare occasion, authorities dropped seditious speech charges for known reasons completely unrelated to their view of the offense. New York authorities did just that in 1678. Johannes de Peyster faced seditious speech charges at the Albany Court of Sessions on April 13 after losing a civil suit and then his temper. He "was very much dissatisfied with" the outcome of the suit, "saying he intended to drag all the commissaries before the great Court of Assizes" for their "unjust judgment." The muddied magistrates ordered de Peyster to post an appearance bond of £100 sterling pending trial "to answer for the words." But the charge was dropped a few weeks later because de Peyster "is now completely bereft of his senses." Going insane saved him from punishment for seditious speech.[23]

Prosecutions were more often dropped for legal reasons. George Puddington escaped trouble in 1640 when a Maine grand jury returned "ignoramus," even after "the whole bench" had charged him with speaking seditious words. That was unusual, if only because grand juries rarely were called upon to indict colonists for seditious speech. Legal limitations involving the failure to prosecute were more common. In 1660 John Easton, Rhode Island's "General Attorney," brought charges against Samuel Gorton at the Court of Trials for speaking against the court. Easton failed to appear at the time appointed for the trial. Gorton claimed the statutory protection and "according to the liberty of the law, none being there to prosecute," the justices dismissed the case. Peter Clock went free in 1695 for the same reason. Obligated under a £20 personal bond with an additional £20 surety, Clock appeared before the New York Supreme Court for having "lately spoken several seditious words to the disturbance of his Majesty's government." Attorney General James Graham failed to appear, so Clock was discharged, "no prosecution being made against him."[24]

Sometimes authorities dropped seditious speech charges because of insufficient evidence. An interesting instance of this came with proceedings against Giles Porter, Philip Bergen, Ralph Chiffem, and Francis Child. In 1686 Maryland officials proceeded against the men for "libelous and scandalous words spoken against" James II which dishonored "the King and his Crown and Kingdom." The prosecution nearly ended before it began when the star witness failed to appear at the initial proceedings. After a "diligent search," Constable Thomas Yerbury finally found Peter Dermott "not far from the court house behind a shady bush," napping pleasantly. Yerbury awakened Dermott, none too gently we may suppose, and escorted him into court. Dermott testified that "coming by a mischance having a sore leg and being in a very bad condition," he was resting "upon a bed in a kind of kitchen" at Philip Bergen's house. There he overheard the four men sitting at a table "with a bowl of punch discoursing about the Duke of Monmouth." Giles Porter drank to Monmouth's health, announcing that the "bloody rogue" James had "poisoned his brother the late King Charles and began the first invention of burning of London." The judges ordered all four men arrested for seditious speech. After some wrangling, they dropped the charges against Bergen, Chiffem, and Child because of insufficient evidence, and decided to prosecute Porter for treason instead—using the others as witnesses. But they denied hearing any words spoken against James, and in the end, after fourteen long months of investigation, tedious questioning, letters back and forth between colony officials and Lord Baltimore, and Baltimore's own conferences with "several lawyers" in England, the prosecution fell.

One witness was not enough in law to convict of seditious speech in any event, and Dermott was "not of good repute" sufficient to carry a treason prosecution in this instance.[25]

The propensity to drop charges specifically for some legal reason became much more common later in the seventeenth century. The numbers are small, but of twenty-six such cases, twenty-three occurred after the 1660s. Others were dropped when the offender quickly apologized to authorities. This was more common at the beginning of the century, and amounted to an informal conviction upon confession. Out of fifty-two such cases, forty (76.9 percent) occurred before 1660. This followed the general pattern noted in the last chapter of a move away from affirmation/humiliation type of penalties. Interestingly, the century saw a marked increase in prosecutions being stopped either because the offender escaped, or because officials decided instead to refer the case to England for disposition. Of the seventeen speakers of sedition fleeing justice, only four escaped in all the years before 1682. And of all seditious speech cases referred to England for disposition, only two came before the 1690s.

Overall, then, colonial authorities became significantly more lenient in dealing with seditious speech during the seventeenth century. That growing leniency manifested itself in various ways, from gentler application of long-used punishments and greater reliance on milder penalties to reduced use of multiple sanctions and increasing propensity to remit sentences. Particularly when this is combined with the growing inclination not to prosecute offenders fully and the clear decline in harsher penalties outlined in the previous chapter, the case that colonists tried for seditious speech faced dramatically less severe retribution at the end of the seventeenth century than at the beginning is compelling. The growing leniency colonial authorities revealed in their treatment of speakers of sedition was a manifestation of a changing attitude toward the offense. With that change came a substantial broadening of colonists' freedom to criticize government and its officials by the end of the century. In the next and final chapter, we will consider how and why that attitude changed.

SEVEN

Fruits of Circumstance

Across the seventeenth century, colonial authorities came to punish seditious speech much more mildly, abandoning humiliation, exclusion, and bodily injury in favor of milder sanctions including small fines and admonition. They also abandoned the older propensity for multiple punishments of a single seditious speech offense, remitted penalties they had pronounced, and increasingly left unprosecuted clear and known instances of the crime. As this softening process continued, colonial officials also gradually changed in the kinds of words they chose to prosecute as seditious. *Scandalum magnatum* cases increasingly centered on misprision issues; false news prosecutions for words against leaders faded in favor of controls on rumors about events. Defendants accused of seditious speech turned in growing numbers to juries to decide their cases, and juries acquitted in growing numbers of those cases. Magistrates increasingly let those acquittals stand without interference, and increasingly granted appeals to convicted offenders.

In the midst of these important changes, authorities' basic rationale for punishing seditious speech changed, as did their attitude toward the offense. The fundamental justification for defining and punishing some kinds of speech as "seditious" remains today what it has always been: to preserve the state. That essential view lay behind England's seditious speech laws from her earliest days and continued in her colonies through the seventeenth century. Yet the logic behind that fundamental, enduring justification underwent significant changes in the seventeenth-century colonies.

The most ancient English manifestation of the "security of the state" justification for punishing seditious speech, established at least as early as 1275, was that words which impugned the honor and dignity of great men in the realm scandalized and weakened the government generally. Justice Coke explained the reasoning with a rhetorical question in his 1606 *de Libellis Famosis* ruling. "What greater scandal of government can there be," he asked, "than to have corrupt or wicked magistrates to be appointed and constituted by the King to govern his subjects under him?" Based on this reasoning, England and her colonies for centuries punished as seditious words which charged "great men" with wrongs. Gradually, the idea came to be applied to government officials rather than to nobles, per se, but the basic logic prevailed. Impugning the integrity of such men undermined the state.[1] Maintaining officials' honor and dignity, and by implication the honor and dignity of the state, remained a part of the rhetoric surrounding seditious speech matters throughout the seventeenth century. But in practice that rationale fell into virtual disuse in the actual prosecution and punishment of seditious speech in the colonies. By 1700 the "honor and dignity" language accompanying seditious speech legislation, presentments for seditious words, and pronouncements of sentence had largely become pro forma.

A second, equally ancient and widespread manifestation of the "security of the state" justification for controlling seditious speech was that such words encouraged a "breach of the public peace." The reasoning was rooted partly in the early development of seditious speech law. Libel and slander had long been punishable because they tended to provoke a violent response in their recipient, producing a breach of the peace. In developing seditious speech law, English authorities borrowed from existing slander and libel statutes. Defaming a great man in the realm (or later a government official) not only provoked him, but also called the government as a whole into disrepute and encouraged disobedience to it, thus in two ways encouraging breaches of the peace. Punishing words "which have a pernicious tendency," Blackstone explained, was "necessary for the preservation of peace and good order, of government and religion." English authorities maintained this view at least from Edward III through the end of the Stuart line. Yet, like the "dignity and honor" language, it had largely become a pro forma rationale in seditious speech cases on both sides of the Atlantic by 1700. "Words damaging to the government that tended, however remotely, to cause a breach of the peace constituted seditious libel according to the courts," Leonard Levy has observed. "But such reasoning explained nothing," he added, "because every crime theoretically breached the King's peace. Criticism of the government that went too far, not the tendency of the words to breach the peace, distinguished the crime of seditious libel" by the eighteenth century.[2]

In practice, colonial officials moved increasingly away from these ancient theoretical justifications for punishing seditious speech and toward a much more practical approach. With "dignity" and "peace" rapidly becoming little more than standardized catchwords, danger to the state became the compelling concern—not the theoretical danger implied by the two older justifications, but real, immediate danger. Genuine danger had always played a role in matters related to seditious speech in the colonies. From the beginning of the seventeenth century on, times of crisis had produced brief surges not only in prosecutions for seditious speech, but in the severity both of seditious speech laws and punishments meted out for the offense. This pattern continued through the 1690s and at first glance seems to have remained largely unchanged. But a closer examination of the types of "dangerous words" officials increasingly singled out for prosecution is revealing.

Throughout the century, officials gave immediate attention to seditious words spoken in dangerous contexts. Those spoken in favor of recently settled rebellions and revolutions were a favorite in this regard. The cases of John Forgisson and John Windower were typical. On March 20, 1682/83, the Maine Court of Sessions ordered Forgisson "to receive nine stripes at the post upon his bare skin, and to pay all charges of court," for "giving too much cause of suspicion by his speeches of his approbation of Gove's Rebellion." Forgisson appealed the case, and in the appeal his actual words came out. "Gove was an honest man," Forgisson had said, "and he would die for his cause." The way the secretary recorded that last phrase makes it impossible to tell if Forgisson pledged his own life, or merely admired Gove's willingness to forfeit his own. Either way, he lost the appeal and, presumably, took his nine lashes.[3]

The words of John Windower, a New York goldsmith, contained not an ounce of ambiguity. "At seven or eight of the clock" at night on May 11, 1694, his business dispute with Jarvis Marshall at Edward Buckmaster's inn got out of hand. Windower tossed a piece of eight onto the table and said to Marshall "there is your money." When Marshall disputed the amount, Windower angrily threw down another piece of eight and then hit him in the face. At that, innkeeper Buckmaster, who also happened to be the High Constable, "came into the room and commanded the peace." During the ensuing argument, Windower said "that Leisler and Milbourne were murdered," and "that he would stand up for Jacob Leisler while he had a drop of blood in his body and that there should be others hanged in a short time to balance the said Leisler and Milbourne." What became of the case is unclear. Indeed, Windower seems to have escaped prosecution not only on this occasion, but on at least one other in 1695 because the attorney general pressed no formal indictment.[4]

Dangerous contexts did not have to accompany revolutions to earn the special attention of authorities. Consider the cases of Thomas Breden and Robert Vaughan. Captain Thomas Breden found himself in trouble in 1662 when he disputed the terms of his commission with members of the Massachusetts General Court. Reasonable disagreement was one thing, but "contemptuous carriage" that smacked of "usurping authority," especially when done "in the face of the country," could not be tolerated. His words, "tending to mutiny, sedition, and subversion of the government here established," earned Breden a very stiff fine of £200, and an additional £200 as a behavior bond. Vaughan's troubles came on Kent Island—a territory bitterly disputed between Virginia and Maryland, and a hotbed of unrest throughout Maryland's early years. The island had already been inhabited by Virginia colonists when the Marylanders arrived in 1634. The Virginians' leader, William Claiborne, kept a running battle of words and swords going for years before finally losing legal control to the Calverts. In 1648 Captain Robert Vaughan, commander of the island for Maryland, found himself in serious trouble for uttering "diverse reviling, scoffing speeches" against the newly appointed governor, Thomas Greene. Accusing Greene of partiality in administering justice on the island and poking fun at him in front of the inhabitants, Vaughan was hardly encouraging the people to be obedient. He was "inciting rather, and animating thereby those people committed to his charge to sedition and rebellion." Vaughan escaped punishment for his offense after an especially slobbery apology, though Greene may have found mercy a useful alternative to further exciting the Kent Islanders by punishing their commander.[5]

Such cases continued to appear throughout the century. Interestingly, however, even as "dangerous words" came to occupy a growing proportion of seditious speech cases, one particular type came to predominate among them—words actually encouraging others to disobey or rebel. John Crandall and Samuel Carter offer two examples. In 1671 John Crandall went to jail at the order of Connecticut's New London County court for being "a mover of sedition or endeavors that way," leading to "open rebellion." This for opposing Connecticut's exercise of authority east of the Pawcatuck River. Refusing to post bond, Crandall remained in custody six months until he came to trial before the Court of Assistants meeting at Hartford. Crandall refused to plead, but the court heard the evidence against him and fined him £10 and costs of prosecution. Samuel Carter appeared before the county court of Essex in East New Jersey on March 12, 1699/1700, "in behalf (as he said) of himself and his neighbors." Stepping forward, Carter "in an insolent and contemptuous manner railed and disowned the authority and power of the court and of the President and Justices there sitting." He called President William Sandford "William Rascall," and had challenged "him and the rest of the Justices out of the court several times, often giving the President the lie and bidding him to kiss his arse." In this instance, Carter became so unruly that the court "could not proceed in the hearing, trying and determining of matters before them." His words and actions were such that if not punished, might "turn to a convulsion in government to the ruin of the colony." The court ordered Carter jailed pending his appearance before the provincial court, then quickly adjourned as the people there began making "a general noise and hollowing with unseemly actions and insolent gestures, which seemed rather to look like a rebellion than otherwise." Whatever the provincial court did to Carter, it did not long deter him. Six months later, he appeared at the court again, this time among a "rabble" of some sixty men. Passing from words to actions, they forcibly ejected the justices, pulling the wigs from their heads and beating them with sticks.[6]

In the growing role of these kinds of "dangerous words" in seditious speech cases, not only did the rationale for punishing seditious speech become more practical overall, but the role of danger itself moved from the theoretical to the actual, and from context to intention. And not only did dangerous words occupy a growing portion of seditious speech prosecutions, but punishments for them were harsher than for other seditious words. Indeed, punishments betray a two-tiered pattern. Harsher penalties came by the end of the century to be reserved for words that posed a genuine rather than merely potential danger to the government. On the other side, those forms of seditious speech which posed no such threat brought milder punishment, if any at all.

Colonial authorities, then, evinced a growing practicality in their prosecution and punishment of seditious speech, and increasingly abandoned ideas of potential danger to the state in favor of actual danger as their essential rationale. In real terms, that meant that colonists came, in the seventeenth century, to experience a dramatically broadened liberty to criticize their government and its officials.

This development occurred because authorities became, in a word, more tolerant of criticism. Toleration does not mean approval. Rather, to become more tolerant is to increasingly leave unmolested that which remains unapproved. This is just what was happening to most forms of seditious speech by the end of the seventeenth century. Colonial officials did not like criticism of themselves or the governments they ran in 1700 any more than they had in 1607 (government officials seldom do). That they retained statutes proscribing seditious speech stands as a clear reminder of that. That they continued to punish seditious words at all, however mildly and uncertainly, is also a reminder. Yet by the end of the century, officials' growing tolerance for criticism that did not immediately threaten the government had created a situation in which the degree of freedom of speech had broadened substantially.

Why did that happen? It happened as the result of a confluence of various more or less unrelated historical developments occurring in the seventeenth century. Each of these developments, in its own time and in its own way, encouraged the growth of free speech in the early colonies. That encouragement found expression in two simultaneous outlets. On the one hand, colonists themselves became more outspoken and less respectful as authority in general became less sacrosanct. On the other, officials were pushed by events beyond their control into a growing practicality in dealing with seditious speech.

Among the fundamental developments or changes occurring through the seventeenth century that encouraged the growth of free speech, the vicissitudes of stability made a major contribution. On the whole, colonial governments simply became more settled and stable over time. With that growing stability, officials could allow more criticism without endangering their governments. Authorities occasionally demonstrated this reality in a left-handed way by lapsing into brief surges of prosecution, harsher laws, and stiffer punishment when their governments temporarily faced more dangerous times. Ironically, however, those periods of instability pushed in the opposite direction when they reached crisis proportions, actually encouraging greater tolerance. Precisely when government faced its greatest dangers, authorities rejected strict enforcement and severe punishment in order to avoid further inflaming tensions.

A wide range of other changes occurred in England and her colonies during the seventeenth century. These accompanied the general backdrop of growing stability, and themselves encouraged the growth of free speech. In the political realm, entire governments fell in revolutions. In the mother country, lawful kings twice lost their thrones in the seventeenth century, not replaced by royal pretenders or deposed by an overweening nobility, but cast out by commoners. Inevitably such doings encouraged a gradual change in the relationship between government and the governed, leading—however haltingly and uncertainly—toward more responsive government. It led also to a decline in the ancient awe of kingship, and of government generally, upon which the Tudor dynasty had been based. As awe of political authority declined and perceptions of governmental responsibility gathered strength, both the willingness to criticize government and the acceptability of doing so grew.

Simultaneously and intimately related with that process, battles for supremacy within government itself raged. The legislative won out over the executive. By the end of the seventeenth century, Parliament occupied a position of indisputable dominance over the monarchy. This same basic process occurred in the colonies as colonial assemblies battled governors for supremacy within government. Like Parliament, those provincial assemblies won out to a large extent. At the same time, other battles "within government" continued throughout the period in the colonies. Towns and counties fought among themselves over various issues and struggled for more autonomy from centralized control within colonies. Colonies competed among themselves for hegemony over disputed areas. Colonial authorities, especially in New England, deliberately worked to thwart and undermine the imposition of centralized authority from London. As elements of government fought among themselves in these various ways, that infighting encouraged the taking of sides among ordinary colonists. That in turn undermined their sense of "authority" as a single, unified entity deserving of respect and reverence and made government less unassailable, less immune to criticism.

Important changes were occurring in the area of religion as well as in politics. England witnessed a decline in ecclesiastical authority from the Reformation through the seventeenth century which in general terms lessened instinctive respect and awe for the church. The great fracturing of the Catholic monolith during the Reformation set in motion a descending spiral of reduced respect for church authority, especially in England, where altogether secular purposes lay behind the spiritual reform. And the rise of Protestant sects— particularly in the aftermath of the Civil War—forced a move toward toleration of religious diversity. This diversity encouraged the decline of centralized religious authority, battle as the Anglican hierarchy might to prevent it. Various dissenting groups arose to challenge the authority of an offending Erastianism, and in the process reduced its power, whether in their victories or defeats.

In the colonies, religious developments spelled a decline in authority as well. Puritan persecution first of the Hutchinsonians and Williams, later of the Quakers, eroded respect among some for both secular and spiritual authority. Within the independent church itself, bitter controversies over church membership and choices of ministers divided and embroiled the congregations. Growing strife among the clergy diminished their influence and prestige. In Virginia, settlers scattered along the estuaries to grow tobacco on isolated plantations, making spiritual authority difficult to maintain. Ministers were poorly paid, so the area did not generally attract capable clerics. Their lesser abilities and dedication only served to erode further the colonists' respect for them and, by implication, the church they represented. Battles between Catholics and Protestants marred Maryland's early years, leading to a declaration of religious toleration necessary to preserve the government itself. But those battles nevertheless eroded respect for authority, particularly when it was wielded by a hated faction. In the Middle Colonies, battles between Quakers and others eroded respect for authority. And religion and ethnicity became intertwined in the struggle between the Dutch and the English in New York and the Jerseys. Again, as government increasingly became the province of alternating factions, respect for authority declined.

At the same time, the increasing diversity of religious groups in the colonies encouraged growing toleration there as it had in England. This occurred sometimes as a matter of necessity, as in Maryland in the 1630s, other times by command of the home government, as in orders to New England regarding Quakers. But whatever the initial impetus, men learned that on issues of most fundamental importance to them in their lives they could tolerate different views from neighbors without undermining their own. Though the precise effect cannot be measured, it is reasonable to suppose that the growth of religious toleration encouraged growing tolerance of free expression on matters political.

Even as broad developments in religion and politics undermined respect for the authority of church and government within the colonies, changes in the family undermined that locus of authority as well. New England in particular witnessed a decline in family authority wrought over time by the sheer availability of land. An ever-present and expansive frontier, in simple terms, made it increasingly difficult for parents to dominate children by controlling access to dwindling amounts of family property. The Chesapeake pattern centered more on the lack of cohesive family units in the seventeenth century. Parents died early and spouses remarried often enough to create considerable instability in family life. That instability and the independence it bred undermined the establishment of family authority.

Other demographic factors contributed to reduced respect for authority, especially in the Southern colonies. There, large numbers of single men, lacking the settling effects of wife and family, made for instability. Life expectancy was low and mortality rates high, producing the need for a constant influx of immigrants to maintain the population and refresh the labor pool. People new to a colony were less tied to it and less automatically respectful of its leaders (who, after all, were certainly not the country gentlemen or nobility known in England). This basic problem remained throughout the seventeenth century, for not until the eighteenth did the population of the Southern colonies become self-sustaining.

Economic changes encouraged a decline in respect for authority as well. Among tobacco farmers in the South, periods of boom and bust and a growing enslavement to the international market eroded colonists' confidence in governments seemingly unable and unwilling to protect them. In the New England and Middle colonies, where trade played a dominant economic role, ever-tightening mercantile regulations from 1651 to 1696 and beyond placed colonists in growing conflict with the interests of the mother country. And the colonists increasingly involved themselves in illegal trade and deliberate circumvention of maritime regulations, commonly with the support of colonial authorities. This often produced open opposition to English trade officials, and brought corruption into the justice system as juries increasingly refused to convict merchants and seamen obviously guilty of trade violations.

Some colonies, especially New York and Pennsylvania, even became notorious by the end of the century for harboring pirates who preyed on trading ships from the Caribbean to the Mediterranean. These seagoing outlaws brought their plundered riches to be melted down and coined, sold, or otherwise disposed of in the Middle Colonies and Massachusetts, often with the open participation of colony officials. Even governors sometimes took a cut. Such official participation in and sanctioning of illegal activity inevitably undermined respect for governmental authority.

On the whole, these political, religious, demographic, and economic trends coalesced in the seventeenth century to make authority less sacrosanct than it had been. In doing so, they eroded the basic boundaries which had so long proscribed criticism of leaders and authority in the family, the church, and the government. The result was a practical expansion of the acceptability of such criticism among colonists. When the alternating contributions of growing stability and periodic crisis combined with this expanding acceptability of criticism, they created both a milieu amenable to the growth of free speech and conditions which encouraged that growth.

Colonists thus came to experience a much greater degree of political free speech across the seventeenth century as a result of a coalescence of historical trends. Yet the growth of free speech before 1700 was largely unexpected and unwanted by colonial authorities, and probably only semiconsciously enjoyed and appreciated by ordinary colonists at the time. The growth of free speech in the seventeenth century, the expansion of freedom to criticize, to challenge verbally, to hold government accountable—these were not the progeny of volition. They were, rather, the fruits of circumstance. The call to restore freedoms under attack, the deliberate defense of the right to criticize government, these would not arise until the eve of the Revolution in the next century. There, nurtured for decades by a continuation of the circumstances that had encouraged the growth of free speech in the seventeenth century, the cry for freedom would flower. That would not have happened so easily, if indeed at all, had it not been for the foundation laid deep and firm in colonial experience in the century before Paine and others arose. For all the schooled leaders' talk of precedents and political theory, of tyrants not to be tolerated and such, the colonists at large drew upon something more solid—a tradition of freedom passed down from the time of their parents' grandparents.

Notes

Introduction: Leaving the Shadow

1. Leonard W. Levy, *Emergence of a Free Press* (New York: Oxford University Press, 1985), 20–28 *passim*.
2. See VA/GCR:14 (1625) for the Barnes prosecution.
3. In addition, using Noel W. Sainsbury and others, eds., *Calendar of State Papers, Colonial Series, Preserved in the State Paper Department of Her Majesty's Public Record Office* (London: Her Majesty's Stationary Office, 1860–1910), I have found abstracts of prosecutions from Surinam, Barbados, Jamaica, Providence Island (Bahamas), and Bermuda. The West Indian cases serve, like those from the Middle Colonies other than New York, as points of comparison and illustrations of typical characteristics. But the close, long-term analysis of prosecutions that forms the heart of this study centers on the South, New York, and New England. Colonies which began in the 1680s and later do not allow measurement of long-term trends, hence the exclusion of the Jerseys, Pennsylvania, and Delaware from that aspect of the analysis. Exclusion of the West Indian cases is a mere matter of practicality. Time and space force limitations on the breadth of the work. Of the twenty-one colonies contributing cases, then, the twelve mainland colonies existing before 1682 form the central core.
4. A standard caveat should be entered here. Any study of crime (seditious speech in this instance) involves special problems. The path from actual to recorded crime is long and uncertain. Myriad factors mitigate against reporting crimes, and overworked, disinterested, doubtful, or dishonest authorities might not prosecute reported offenses. Even if prosecuted, cases often went partially or entirely unrecorded. Curiously, that might offer an advantage in a study of seditious speech. Marking the boundaries of political expression involves measuring of-

ficial toleration and extrapolating the practical limitations of freedom from that. Recorded incidents of seditious speech may not represent all occurrences of the offense, but they do reveal how officials perceived and handled the transgression. If one can discover a sufficient number of cases covering a long span of time, and if enough of those cases provide information on prosecution and punishment adequate to allow analysis, one can draw dependable conclusions about the parameters of political expression in early America. That is just what I have done here.

1. The Boundaries of Colonial Speech

1. PLY/CR-2:449 (1642). Until 1752 officials in England and its colonies used the Old Style (Julian) calendar to date government documents. Under it the new year began on March 25 rather than on January 1 as is now the case under the New Style (Gregorian) calendar (based on the calendar ordained by Gregory XIII in 1582). Dates in this study are rendered Old Style, as they appear in the records. That means that ordinarily January 1 through March 24 dates appear with dual years, as in 1681/82. Also, spelling and punctuation have been modernized in quotations except in occasional obvious instances.

2. Virginia and New Jersey laws—VA/BR-2:350 (1691) and NJ/A-2:206 (1698). For a discussion of similar Virginia statutes promulgated in 1619, 1631, 1657–58, and 1674–75, see Philip Alexander Bruce, *Institutional History of Virginia in the Seventeenth Century: An Inquiry into the Religious, Moral, Educational, Legal, Military, and Political Condition of the People, Based on Original and Contemporaneous Records*, 2 vols. (New York: G. P. Putnam's Sons, 1910), 1:42–44. New York had its share, as did the Caribbean colonies. See, for examples, NY/DRCH-4:288 (1697), CSP-5:640 (1668—Antigua), CSP-7:352 (1672—Barbados), and CSP-7:332 (1672—Jamaica).

3. Sherlot—MA/CAR-1:197 (1681). Washburn—MA/PlyCo:247 (1700). For two other cross-dressing examples, see CSP-12:413 (1687—Jamaica) and PA/CCD-2:27 (1698).

4. Massachusetts law—MA/GCR-1:126 (1634). Weed—MA/ECC-2:409 (1674). Virginia tax regulation—VA/BR-1:10 (1619). For more on early Massachusetts sumptuary laws, see Samuel Eliot Morison, *Builders of the Bay Colony* (Boston: Houghton Mifflin, 1930), 162–63, and John Winthrop's own useful discussion at MA/JWJ-1:132 (1634).

5. Winthrop—MA/WP-2:282. Woodward—NC/R-1:100 (1665).

6. Jones—VA/GCR:119 (1626). See John Winthrop for the classic characterization of the status of women in marriage—MA/JWJ-2:239. For an example of a servant punished, see John Pope's whipping at MA/CAR-2:92 (1640). For a law against children abusing their parents, see Rhode

Island's 1647 statute at RI/R-1:162. For a child severely punished after abusing his parents, see the Porter case at MA/GCR-4/2:216 and MA/CAR-3:139. Colonial laws did protect servants, children, and wives from abuse. See, for example, NH/CHS-8:236.

7. Sir William Blackstone, *Commentaries on the Laws of England in Four Books*, ed. William Draper Lewis, 4 vols. (Philadelphia: Rees, Welsh, and Company, 1902), 4:150. For practical colonial examples, see cases at ME/PCR-1:135 and ME/PCR-1:239, 409.

8. For some slander cases, see PLY/CR-1:128; HAVEN-1:419; CT/CR-1:126; CSP-5:86 (1662—Jamaica); ME/PCR-2:147 (1664); NY/NAR-5:287 (1665); PA/PUC:101 (1678); DE/RSC:59 (1681); NJ/CCRC:209 (1686); NC/R-1:522; VA/CSP-1:21 (1688); MD/A-54:78. Rhode Island preamble—RI/R-1:184 (1647). In 1673 William Pynchon ordered Goodwife Hunter to be "gagged, and so to stand half an hour in the open street" for railing and scolding "and other exhorbitancies of the tongue" against another woman. See MA/PCR:278 (1673).

9. Ford—ME/PCR-1:236 (1665). Nason—ME/PCR-3:257 (1687). Matthews—MA/PCR:243 (1659). New York incident—NY/ARS-3:540–41 (1685). For other examples of threats and affronts to lower officials, see PLY/CR-3:125 (1657); NY/ARS-2:278 (1677); NJ/BCB:32 (1684); MA/DR:275 (1686); PA/PQS:90 (1694/95). For some other actual attacks, see VA/BR-2:19 (1661/62); ME/PCR-2:391 (1663/64); MD/A-57:453 (1669); MA/SCC-2:1066 (1679); PA/UCC:180 (1680); NJ/A-2:328 (1700).

10. Abbee—MA/PCR:307 (1684). Colonial laws made contempt a specific offense. For some examples, see RI/R-1:232 (1650); CT/CR-1:539 (1650); HAVEN-2:585–86 (1656); NY/NTC:209 (1677); MD/A-67:446 (1678); NH/PP-1:389 (1679/80); NJ/A-2:364–66 (1700/01). For examples of contemptuous actions, see CT/CR-1:155 (1647); MD/A-57:568 (1670); MA/SCC-2:601 (1675); PA/CCD-1:56 (1685); NC/R-1:409 (1694); NH/PP-2:129 (1694); ME/PCR-4:50 (1695). For some verbal contempts, see MD/A-54:655; MA/SCC-1:232, 488; MA/DSS-1:429; HAVEN-2:72, 333; PLY/CR-2:8; 4:190; CT/CR-1:111, 394; NC/R-1:409, 533.

11. Mitchell—MD/A-10:173 (1652). For similar examples, see MA/CAR-2:105 (1641); PLY/CR-3:150 (1658); HAVEN-1:39, 257; PLY/CR-4:152; MA/SCC-2:1019; MA/GCR-4/2:307; VA/SAL-1:156.

12. Randolph—NH/SP-19:665 (1679/80). See also Robert N. Toppan, ed., *Edward Randolph: Including His Letters and Official Papers from the New England, Middle, and Southern Colonies in America, with Other Documents Relating Chiefly to the Vacating of the Royal Charter of the Colony of Massachusetts Bay, 1676–1703*, 7 vols. (Boston: The Prince Society, 1898), 6:97. The Earl of Danby (Thomas Osborne) had been Charles II's chief minister until his fall in 1678 at the height of the anti-Catholic hysteria in England. Though the phrase *scandalum magnatum* was not used by colonial officials, I have adopted it as a convenient means of description.

13. Starr—PLY/CR-5:27 (1669). Van Amersfoort—NY/KP-1:251 (1665). Jones—ME/PCR-3:257 (1687). English authorities used similar characterizations. See Sir William S. Holdsworth, *A History of English Law*, 16 vols. (London: Methuen, 1922–52), 8:341.
14. Vaughan—MD/A-4:440, 459 (1648). See CT/CR-2:306–7 (1677) for a similar case.
15. Thing—ME/PCR-2:41–42 (1655). Norman—MA/SCC-1:554 (1672).
16. Winthrop—MA/JWJ-2:237 (1645). On the statutory standing of slander, see Holdsworth, *A History of English Law*, 6:628. For some examples of authorities mixing civil and criminal elements in seditious speech cases, see VA/BR-2:115 (1677) and HAVEN-1:257–59 (1646). English authorities did not clearly distinguish between the person and the office, at least in the early seventeenth century. See Holdsworth, *A History of English Law*, 5:208–9.
17. Tomlinson—HAVEN-2:309–11, 367–69. Other New England colonies made the same distinction in practice. For some examples see—MA/GCR-5:153; MA/SCC-2:992–93; PLY/CR-2:152; CT/CR-1:117, 242.
18. VA/EJC-1:69, 470, 477. For a Middle Colony example, see Mary Lawrenson's prosecution at NY/NTC:211 (1668/69). A Barbados Council debate about the oath required of councillors in 1683 produced an instructive exchange on this subject. Henry Walrond, a Council member, had argued "for separating the person from authority, saying for instance that he would give faithful advice to Sir Richard Dutton as governor, but not perhaps to Sir Richard Dutton as Sir Richard Dutton." "I told him," acting Governor John Witham wrote, "that I did not expect to hear such old and exploded arguments from him." Not everyone, it seems, accepted the idea of separating the office from the person holding it, particularly when it was being turned to personal advantage by a dishonest man. CSP-11:437 (1683—Barbados).
19. MD/A-19:516 (1697). A Maryland constable failed to post a list of titheables in his county in 1677 not because he was unwilling, but because, as he admitted, he was illiterate. MD/A-67:9 (1677). "The better sort" shunned such posts, and even less respected men sometimes endured punishment rather than accept appointments. For some examples, see MD/A-41:418 (1660) and MD/A-54:220 (1661), 36 (1670). Refusal to serve was a growing problem in early New York as well. See Michael Kammen, *Colonial New York: A History* (New York: Charles Scribner's Sons, 1975), 151. For concurring assessments of lower officials in North Carolina, see Paul McCain, *The County Court in North Carolina Before 1750* (Durham, N.C.: Duke University Press, 1954), 148, and Donna J. Spindel and Stuart W. Thomas, Jr., "Crime and Society in North Carolina, 1663–1740," *Journal of Southern History* 56, no. 2 (1983):227. For a comparison with contemporary English officials, see J. A. Sharpe, "Crime and Delinquency in an Essex Parish, 1600–1640,"

in J. S. Cockburn, ed., *Crime in England, 1550–1800* (Princeton, N.J.: Princeton University Press, 1977), 96.

20. Mason—MA/CAR-3:187–88; MA/GCR-4/2:340–41 (1666). Prosecutions for seditious words against the king were rare in the colonies, and usually accompanied revolutionary changes of government in England. For two examples, see MA/GCR-4/2:5 and NC/R-1:430–31. For a useful comparison of treason and seditious speech, see the discussion at CSP-12:158 (1686—Jamaica). For examples of clear treason cases, see RI/CT-1:16 (1655/56); VA/GCR:511 (1663); CSP-5:133–34 (1663—Barbados); NY/DRCH-2:612 (1678); PA/CCD-1:64 (1685); MA/DSS-1:119 (1686); MD/A-8:191 (1690); CSP-14:102 (1693—Carolina). As early as 1534, treason in England could include words or actions. See Philip A. Hamburger, "The Development of the Law of Seditious Libel and the Control of the Press," *Stanford Law Review* 37 (1985):667.

21. Fletcher—NY/JLC-1:48 (1693).

22. Sprague—MA/SCC-1:424 (1674). Smith—NY/SAR:173–74 (1699). For similar examples, see MA/CAR-2:76 (1638); PLY/CR-2:140 (1649); HAVEN-2:242, 247 (1658); MA/GCR-4/2:307 (1666); ME/PCR-3:212–13 (1684/85). See also the Barbados law of 1652 in this regard. It allowed "that no minister be deprived except on scandalous living, seditious preaching, or unsound doctrine proved against him." CSP-9:85 (1652—Barbados).

23. Virginia law—VA/BR-2:308 (1688). North Carolina law—NC/R-1:xix (1709). Ledra—MA/CAR-3:93, 109 (1660/61). For other Quaker trials, see PLY/CR-3:183; MA/CAR-3:68–69; HAVEN-2:233, 238, 291; CSP-7:506 (1673—Barbados). For examples of legislation dealing with Quakers, see HAVEN-2:241 (1658); CSP-10:37 (1676/77—Barbados); MA/GCR-5:198–99 (1678). Exasperated Massachusetts authorities hanged Quakers returning from banishment because no other way of dealing with them "prooved effectual." See MA/GCR-5:198–99 (1678).

24. Crab—HAVEN-2:242 (1658). For some other examples, see MA/GCR-4/2:291 (1665) and MA/DSS-1:95 (1685). In the latter case, Zechariah Roads insisted that the Massachusetts authorities "had not to do with matters of religion." Roads was ahead of his time.

25. Hull—HAVEN-2:26–28 (1653). For a similar case, see the Raynes prosecution at ME/PCR-2:24 (1653). For some contempt cases, see MA/CAR-2:68 (1637); PLY/CR-3:22 (1652/53); MA/SCC-1:147 (1672); CSP-10:246–47 (1678—Barbados); DE/KC:154; PA/PCC-1:441 (1693/94); NJ/BCB:207 8 (1698).

26. Wells—MD/A-17:279–80, 438 (1684).

27. Wheeler—CT/CR-3:18 (1678). Dexter—MA/CAR-2:24, 30 (1632). For examples of seditious criticism of colonial legislation, see CT/CR-1:33 (1639); CSP-9:485 (1676—Barbados); MA/CAR-1:201 (1681). For more general words, see ME/PCR-2:81; PLY/CR-5:25; CT/CR-4:34. For some

words against taxes, see NC/R-1:296–97 (1679) and PLY/CR-2:17 (1641). If Edward Randolph can be trusted, the complaints were sometimes well founded. In 1681 he claimed that the New Hampshire Council had "raised great sums upon the inhabitants and it doth not appear how expended, the only visible expense being in eating and drinking, the Council always meeting in an Ordinary." Toppan, *Edward Randolph,* 3:107.

28. Bennett—MA/CAR-3:74–75 (1659/60). Griffin—MA/ECC-5:269 (1673).
29. VA/BR-2:204, 228–29 (1684). A desire to strengthen royal authority lay behind crown support for such appeals generally. See Julius Goebel, Jr., and T. Raymond Naughton, *Law Enforcement in Colonial New York: A Study in Criminal Procedure (1664–1776)* (New York: Commonwealth Fund, 1944), 225. For an example of the kind of trouble Mrs. Bland caused, see VA/EJC-1:1 (1680).
30. Merchant—VA/EJC-1:438 (1699). For an interesting case of a death penalty clemency petition leading to seditious speech, see PA/PCR-1:378 (1693). For a Caribbean law specifically allowing petitions to the king, see CSP-7:22 (1669—Barbados).
31. Sothell—NC/R-1:370 (1691). In 1661, Parliament revised the English law regulating petitions because they had "been used to serve the ends of factious and seditious persons . . . and have been a great means of the late unhappy wars, confusions, and calamities." See Holdsworth, *A History of English Law,* 6:167, 304, 426. For examples of colonial restrictions on the right to petition, see RI/R-1:255–56 (1652); PA/PCR-1:263; VA/BR-2:339–40; MA/HSC-8:217; NJ/A-1:265; MD/A-22:55 (1698).
32. Springfield and Suffield—MA/GCR-5:483 (1685). Virginia comments—VA/SAL-2:482 (1680). For similar examples, see MD/A-10:424 (1655); CSP-7:357, 384 (1672—Barbados); MA/GCR-4/2:577 (1673/74). In 1684, the Massachusetts General Court decided that complaints against juries for their decisions would be uniformly seditious unless presented in a formal, legal petition. See MA/GCR-5:449–50 (1684).
33. NC/R-1:9 (1665). The issue had not been decided in England until late in the century. See Frederick S. Siebert, *Freedom of the Press in England, 1476–1776* (Urbana: University of Illinois Press, 1952), 116. Though dated and centered in the eighteenth century, Mary Patterson Clarke's *Parliamentary Privilege in the American Colonies* (New Haven: Yale University Press, 1943) remains a valuable study of the subject.
34. MD/A-20:87, 91, 92–94; MD/A-22:193 (1697/98).
35. MD/A-22:182, 334 (1698).
36. NC/R-1:256, 259 (1680).

2. Seditious Speech Law

1. As quoted in James F. Stephen, *A History of the Criminal Law of England*, 3 vols. (London: Macmillan, 1883), 2:301–2. This chapter's discussion of the development of English seditious speech law relies heavily on Stephen, *A History of the Criminal Law of England;* Sir William S. Holdsworth, *A History of English Law*, 16 vols. (London: Methuen, 1922–52); John G. Bellamy, *The Tudor Law of Treason: An Introduction* (London: Routledge and Kegan Paul, 1979); and Philip A. Hamburger, "The Development of the Law of Seditious Libel and the Control of the Press," *Stanford Law Review* 37 (1985):661–775.
2. Bellamy, *The Tudor Law of Treason*, 45. These statutes were intended less to protect the reputation of magnates (that could be accomplished with slander laws) than "to safeguard the peace of the kingdom." See Holdsworth, *A History of English Law*, 3:409. Even so, they could be used as a basis for private action as well as criminal prosecution. See Hamburger, "Development of the Law of Seditious Libel," 661.
3. See Bellamy, *The Tudor Law of Treason*, 45. J. A. Sharpe, *Crime in Seventeenth Century England: A County Study* (Cambridge, U.K.: Cambridge University Press, 1983), 82.
4. Bellamy, *The Tudor Law of Treason*, 14, 78, 84, 183–84.
5. See Holdsworth, *A History of English Law*, 4:499, and Bellamy, *The Tudor Law of Treason*, 46. In 1579 one fellow lost a hand for writing seditious words about Elizabeth I. The man's name, even before the macabre penalty, was "Stubbe." For a discussion of the case, see Frederick S. Siebert, *Freedom of the Press in England, 1476–1776* (Urbana: University of Illinois Press, 1952), 91–92.
6. See Holdsworth, *A History of English Law*, 4:495, 511–12, and Sharpe, *Crime in Seventeenth Century England*, 82. The passing years did not dampen the Virgin Queen's interest in this area. In 1585 the crown introduced a bill in Parliament that would have made printed slander of the government (not just officials) a felony, and "a slander of a member of the Council" punishable by "imprisonment at the Queen's pleasure." The bill never became law. See Hamburger, "Development of the Law of Seditious Libel," 676.
7. Hamburger, "Development of the Law of Seditious Libel," 671. The Tudors still considered sedition as part of treason. As William Conklin has noted, "sedition did not appear as a separate legal crime until 1606." See "Origins of the Law of Sedition," *Criminal Law Quarterly* 15 (1973):277.
8. Coke as quoted in Hamburger, "Development of the Law of Seditious Libel," 694. See also Holdsworth, *A History of English Law*, 8:336, 340. For other discussions of the *de Libellis Famosis* case, see Stephen, *A History of the Criminal Law of England*, 2:304–5; Holdsworth,

A History of English Law, 5:208; Siebert, Freedom of the Press in England, 119; Jeffery A. Smith, Printers and Press Freedom: The Ideology of Early American Journalism (New York: Oxford University Press, 1988), 60, 81; Julius Goebel, Jr., and T. Raymond Naughton, Law Enforcement in Colonial New York: A Study in Criminal Procedure, 1664–1776 (New York: Commonwealth Fund, 1944), 152; and Leonard W. Levy, Emergence of a Free Press (New York: Oxford University Press, 1985), 7.

9. The Star Chamber punished seditious speech, to borrow Julius Goebel's arresting phrase, "with a malignant ferocity." After its demise in 1641, the common law courts handled seditious speech. But "even at the end of the eighteenth century," Holdsworth observed, the common law courts "were hardly less strict than the Star Chamber" had been in punishing the offense. Indeed, English authorities prosecuted seditious speech with great frequency and considerable severity throughout the century, and even the Glorious Revolution did not significantly alter the law. See Goebel and Naughton, Law Enforcement in Colonial New York, 556, and Holdsworth, A History of English Law, 8:340. Others agree with his harsh assessment. See Stephen, A History of the Criminal Law of England, 2:308–9 for one example. Regarding the frequency of prosecutions later in the century, see Holdsworth, A History of English Law, 8:341, and Stephen, A History of the Criminal Law of England, 2:313. The general observation about frequent prosecutions later in the century is Holdsworth's, and it is widely shared. Philip Hamburger has challenged this (see the entire Hamburger article, "Development of the Law of Seditious Libel," esp. 758–62), arguing that most of these cases were actually prosecutions for violating licensing acts. For our purposes, that distinction is needlessly technical. English officials worked to control seditious speech. Such acts merely offered a convenient tool for accomplishing that end.

Treason proved more elusive. Not until 1629 was it firmly established, for example, that merely speaking (or privately writing) words against the king did not constitute treason without an overt act. See Stephen, A History of the Criminal Law of England, 2:308; Holdsworth, A History of English Law, 8:312; and Bellamy, The Tudor Law of Treason, 3. Still, words could sometimes be treasonous if they sufficiently implied an overt act, and offenders were prosecuted in such circumstances. See Holdsworth, A History of English Law, 6:399; Hamburger, "Development of the Law of Seditious Libel," 684. Such exceptions dated back to the Tudors (see Bellamy, The Tudor Law of Treason, 183–84) and were well known in the colonies. For examples, see MA/GCR-5:194 (1678); MA/AAR-1:55 (1692/93), 255 (1696). Some limitations existed, and those came to fruition after 1720 when "treason as a purely verbal crime, unconnected with some overt act beyond the words themselves, died out." See Levy, Emergence of a Free Press, 9.

10. For examples of colonial laws prohibiting seditious words in the military, or in a military context, see NC/R-1:1 (1629); ME/PCR-1:20 (1639); MD/A-3:543 (1665/66); NY/DRCH-3:380 (1686); PA/PCR-1:361 (1693/94). The 1670s brought a spate of military "seditious speech" regulations. For some examples, see MD/A-15:82; MA/GCR-5:50; CT/CR-2:393; MA/CLM:343. Virginia's infamous 1611 "Dale Code" ordered three successive whippings for words spoken against the Council. But that was only for the first offense. For the second, offenders spent three years in the galleys at hard labor. Colonists persistent enough to repeat the offense a third time faced death. See W. Keith Kavenaugh, ed., *Foundations of Colonial America: A Documentary History* (New York: Chelsea House, 1983), 3:1871. New Netherland also established the death penalty for "words tending to sedition" in the militia. See NY/DRCH-2:623 (1673).

11. Instructions—VA/SAL-1:69 (1606). General Court ruling—VA/GCR:480 (1631). On the same day, December 6, 1631, "one was whipped and lost his fine for concealing such slander." These are the words of Conway Robinson paraphrasing now lost records. Whether the careless use of the word "slander" was his or those of the original court secretary is unclear.

12. See VA/EJC-1:468 (1677) and VA/SAL-2:386.

13. VA/SAL-2:463–64 (1680).

14. Commission—MD/A-3:50 (1637). Law—MD/A-1:73 (1638/39). Grand Inquest—MD/A-15:129–30 (1676).

15. Law of 1647—RI/R-1:163 (1647). For the 1663 law, see John D. Cushing, ed., *The Earliest Acts and Laws of the Colony of Rhode Island and Providence Plantations, 1647–1719* (Wilmington, Del.: Glazier, 1977), 59. For a prosecution under this statute, see John Havens's trial at RI/CT-2:39–40 (1664).

16. The first quotation is from HAVEN-1:21 (1639). Blatchley—HAVEN-1:271–72 (1646). The 1656 Code—HAVEN-2:568 (1656). For an especially instructive additional case, see Jeremiah Jagger's prosecution at HAVEN-2:63–65, 141, 216 (1653/54). Some scholars minimize the influence of biblical law in early New England. See, for example, George E. Woodbine, "The Suffolk County Court, 1671–1680," in David H. Flaherty, ed., *Essays in the History of Early American Law* (Chapel Hill: University of North Carolina Press, 1969), 202. Few, however, would disagree that such influence was particularly strong in the New Haven colony. For other examples of this principle being clearly established, see HAVEN-1:69 (1642), 1:130 (1644), and 1:191 (1644/45).

17. Ludlow Code—CT/CR-1:525 (1650). For a seditious speech prosecution ending in banishment under this code, see the John Dawes case at CT/CR-1:242 (1653). For the 1672 revision of this code, see John D. Cushing, ed., *The Earliest Laws of the New Haven and Connecticut Colonies, 1639–1673* (Wilmington, Del.: Glazier, 1977), 115.

18. Thomas Hutchinson, *The History of the Colony and Province of Massa-chusetts Bay*, ed. Lawrence Shaw Mayo (Cambridge, Mass.: Harvard University Press, 1936), 1:373. See also George L. Haskins, *Law and Authority in Early Massachusetts: A Study in Tradition and Design* (New York: Macmillan, 1960), 125. The biblical orientation of Bay Colony law was humorously illustrated in a nonseditious speech case when Puritan authorities spared a man's life not because he could read scripture, but because "we read otherwise in scripture." See George A. Billias, ed., *Law and Authority in Colonial America: Selected Essays* (Barre, Mass.: Barre Publishers, 1965), 10. Useful discussions of the relationship between scripture and law in early Massachusetts may be found in Haskins, *Law and Authority in Early Massachusetts*, 145–52, and Barbara A. Black, "Community and Law in Seventeenth Century Massachusetts," *The Yale Law Review* 19 (1980):232–46. For a discussion of post-1661 laws, see Edwin Powers, *Crime and Punishment in Early Massachusetts, 1620–1692: A Documentary History* (Boston: Beacon Press, 1966), 61.
19. PA/SAL-1:131 (1682), 194 (1693). See also PA/PCR-1:427. The Caribbean colonies followed suit as well. Montserrat officials, for example, outlawed "scandalous speeches against members of the Council and Assembly." See CSP-5:641 (1668).
20. VA/SAL-1:106–8 (1611/12).
21. Oaths—PLY/CR-11:8 (1636), 80 (1658). Interestingly, the 1664 oath required of nonfreemen (both resident and stranger) proscribed actions against the colony, but made no mention of words. See PLY/CR-11:191 (1664). Statute—PLY/CR-3:167 (1659). Robinson case—PLY/CR-3:183, 189 (1659/60).
22. Virginia law—VA/SAL-2:501–2 (1664). Maryland law—MD/A-67:446 (1678). Rhode Island law—RI/R-1:438–39 (1672). The editor of Roger Williams's letters calls this "a repressive act" in discussing its background. See Glenn W. LaFantasie, ed., *The Correspondence of Roger Williams*, 2 vols. (Providence: Brown University Press/University Press of New England, 1988), 2:639. For additional Virginia examples, see VA/LJC-1:44, 54 (1682) and VA/EJC-1:524 (1690). For a similar 1672 Connecticut statute and a significant prosecution following it, see Cushing, *Earliest Laws of the New Haven and Connecticut Colonies*, 89, and CT/CR-2:258–59, 310, 577–78 (1675).
23. Massachusetts law—MA/GCR-1:213 (1637). New Haven law—HAVEN-2:585–86 (1656). New Hampshire law—NH/PP-1:389 (1679/80). For a prosecution under Plymouth law, see Timothy White's case at PLY/CR-6:41 (1680). Virginia pardon—VA/BR-2:148 (1680).
24. Slye—MD/A-23:408, 520, 525 (1698). Constant difficulty marked Governor Nicholson's rule in Maryland. "I have had," he wrote in a letter to the Board of Trade on August 20, 1698, "a continual very troublesome and chargeable government in all respects." The real reason was

not the peculiar contumacy of Marylanders. Instead, Nicholson wrote, "I have observed that a great many people in all these provinces and colonies, especially those under Proprietors, and the two others of Connecticut and Rhode Island, think that no law of England ought to be in force and binding to them without their own consent. For they foolishly say they have no representatives sent from themselves to the Parliaments in England." John Locke, an active member of the Board of Trade and a correspondent of Nicholson's, received the letter. One wonders what went through his mind as he read this passage. See MD/A-23:492 (1698).

25. South Carolina law—John D. Cushing, ed., *The Earliest Printed Laws of South Carolina, 1692–1734* (Wilmington, Del.: Glazier, 1978), 89. Maryland law—MD/A-2:273–74 (1671). Maryland law—MD/A-13:17 (1684). Maryland proclamation—MD/A-5:391–92 (1681).

26. For one such Maryland prosecution, see the John Tyrling trial at MD/A-15:386–87, 392–93 (1681). Virginia laws—VA/LJC-1:198, 202 (1693) and VA/BR-2:472, 473, 475 (1693). For a Virginia case of this type, see Charles Scarburgh's prosecution at VA/EJC-1:519 (1688), with additional testimony at VA/CSP-1:21–22.

27. Massachusetts law—MA/GCR-2:104–5 (1645). Plymouth laws—PLY/CR-1:63, 95–96 (1653) and PLY/CR-11:128, 138 (1660). Later Massachusetts law—MA/AAR-1:53 (1692/93).

28. New York laws—John D. Cushing, ed., *The Earliest Printed Laws of New York, 1665–1693* (Wilmington, Del.: Glazier, 1978), 78, 79. Pennsylvania law—PA/PCR-1:40 (1682). For Pennsylvania reaffirmations, see PA/SAL-1:96–97, 123, 173, 182, and PA/PCR-1:411–13.

29. Virginia laws—VA/SAL-1:361 (1649), 434–35 (1657/58), and 2:109 (1661/62). The 1702 law indicated that colonial authorities clearly continued to separate false news and *scandalum magnatum* into the eighteenth century. See VA/EJC-2:262–64 (1702).

30. Maryland laws—MD/A-2:273–74 (1671), MD/A-17:363–64 (1684/85), MD/A-5:497 (1686), and MD/A-20:328–29 (1695). For later reaffirmations of the general false news laws, see MD/A-22:103 (1697/98) and MD/A-25:202 (1706). South Carolina law—SC/CCR:66 (1692). Just how often South Carolina authorities revived this specific act in the following years is unclear, but it did appear again in 1711.

31. For some examples of such investigations, see MD/A-15:129–30 (1676); MA/GCR-5:185 (1678); MD/A-8:94 (1698).

32. MA/GCR-4/2:187. The problem proved to be persistent. John Pynchon, in writing to Connecticut's Governor John Winthrop, Jr., in 1674, observed that "it is strange to think how some men will enlarge when they have got a story though false." Carl Bridenbaugh, ed., *The Pynchon Papers: Volume I, Letters of John Pynchon, 1654–1700* (Boston: Colonial Society of Massachusetts, 1982), 131.

33. VA/EJC-1:75 (1685).

34. MA/ECC-4:351 (1671).
35. Gardenier—NY/ARS-3:435, 439 (1684).
36. Holdsworth, *A History of English Law,* 4:493–94, 495; Hamburger, "The Development of the Law of Seditious Libel," 719.
37. Stephen, *A History of the Criminal Law of England,* 2:313. In 1684 alone, for example, authorities prosecuted at least sixteen such cases. Before James II was ousted, many others faced prosecution for seditious words in England, including Baxter in 1685, Johnson and Dr. Eades in 1686, and the Seven Bishops in 1688. See Holdsworth, *A History of English Law,* 8:340–41, and Hamburger, "The Development of the Law of Seditious Libel," 698–99.
38. Virginia laws—VA/SAL-1:361 (1649), 434–35 (1657), 2:109 (1661/62), and VA/EJC-2:262–64 (1673).
39. VA/SAL-2:385 (1676/77). Under a 1677 companion statute, colonists could be disabled from holding office if they spoke words which tended to cause the people to dislike the colony's government. Charles II thought this too mild and ordered it toughened in 1680 after fully reviewing the events and explanations of Bacon's Rebellion. The burgesses complied, making the penalties up to a year in jail and a fine of up to £500 sterling. See VA/EJC-1:468 (1677); VA/SAL-2:463–64 (1680). The false news and *scandalum magnatum* statutes of the 1670s remained in force through the century in Virginia, and authorities continued both under a single 1702 statute. See VA/EJC-2:259, 260, 262–64 (1702).
40. Rhode Island laws—RI/R-1:63 (1647); RI/R-1:246 (1652); Cushing, *Earliest Acts and Laws of the Colony of Rhode Island,* 59 (1663); and RI/R-1:438–39 (1672). Responses to changing circumstances did not end with the seventeenth century in any colony. For an example of its continuation in North Carolina, see the preamble to their 1711 law in John D. Cushing, ed., *The Earliest Printed Laws of North Carolina, 1669–1751* (Wilmington, Del.: Glazier, 1977), 167.
41. The following discussion of the Maryland seditious speech bill is taken from the assembly minutes in MD/A-13:301, 316, 320, 322, 328, 333, 404, and 439–40 (1692).
42. MD/A-23:513 (1698).
43. Repeat offenders further inflated the number of trials. Among the Coode faction, Philip Clarke appeared once for seditious speech in 1697, then twice in 1698. Benjamin Hall appeared twice and Thomas Johnson the second time in 1698. Old John Coode himself, one-time leader of the Glorious Revolution in Maryland, appeared twice. See MD/A-20:72; MD/A-23:178–80, 415, 419, 444, 448, 450–55, 468, 470, 475–76, 479–88, 510, 511. For Governor Nicholson's background, see Stephen Saunders Webb, *The Governors-General: The English Army and the Definition of Empire, 1569–1681* (Chapel Hill: University of North Carolina Press, 1979), 491, 498–99.

44. Assembly—MD/A-22:352 (1699). Blackiston—MD/A-22:351 (1699).
45. VA/EJC-2:35–36 (1699).

3. The Nature of the Words

1. Whitman—MD/A-65:36 (1672). Matthews—NJ/A-1:416–17, 420, 422–23 (1683). Greene—RI/CT-2:65 (1668). For similar cases, see VA/BR-1:84 (1652); NC/R-1:296–97 (1676); ME/PCR-3:292 (1690); NY/CCM:68 (1691).
2. Van Dyke—NY/ARS-3:364–67 (1683). Virginia petition—VA/BR-2:114–15 (1677).
3. Adams and Cock—NC/HC:346 (1684). Webber—NH/CHS-8:138 (1683). Waters—CT/CR-4:71 (1692). For similar cases, see ME/PCR-1:87 (1645); PLY/CR-3:4 (1651/52); MD/A-54:286 (1669/70); VA/EJC-1:490 (1682); NY/DH-2:44, 74, 188 (1689).
4. Lee—MA/CAR-2:49, 50 (1634).
5. Roberts—RI/CT-1:51, 55–56 (1658/59). Hog—NH/CHS-8:177 (1684).
6. Wright—NJ/BCB:54–55 (1686). For his theft, the Burlington court ordered Wright whipped thirty-nine stripes "upon his bare back" while being slowly dragged behind a cart "from the house of John Crips in Burlington to Henry Grubb's at the town's landing." Barnes—PA/CCD-2:38 (1699). Avery—NY/DRCH-12:603–4 (1678). For a similar case, see NY/KP-2:487 (1672).
7. Jowles—MD/A-8:558–59 (1693). Thomas Carvile narrowly escaped punishment in Maryland in 1683. He wisely fled the colony after calling the proprietor "an old Papist Rogue" who was "not fit to govern the people of this Province," adding that "the Tower of London was a more fit place for him than the place he was." See MD/A-17:184–86 (1683).
8. Bland—VA/GCR:390, 399, 518 (1674). A year and a half later, Bland's mother and father each petitioned the king in their son's behalf. On April 22, 1676, Mrs. Bland asked that the fine be abated because the Virginia Council had "proceeded arbitrarily, violently, and injuriously against the petitioner's son." See CSP-9:379, 404. The following month, Mr. Bland clarified the original incident. Apparently Giles Bland grew angry after "gloves were exchanged" and Ludwell never showed up for the fight. See CSP-9:392.
9. Ferris—CT/CR-1:44 (1639). Scott—CT/CR-1:422, 424, 436 (1663/64).
10. Briggs—RI/CT-2:22–23, 28 (1663). Read—VA/BR-1:xliv, 86–87 (1653). Billings—NC/HC:362 (1685). For similar cases, see MD/A-2:247–69 *passim* (1670/71); NY/DRCH-14:701 (1675); PA/PCR-1:550–51 (1698). The answer to Abraham Read's petition is nowhere to be found, prompting us to agree with the editor's comment on this prosecution: "having commenced with the case of Captain Read, the compiler [of

the Bland manuscripts from which the case is taken] should have been careful to give the whole story."

11. Lucase—PLY/CR-5:182 (1675). Buttler—MD/A-17:135, 139–40 (1683).
12. Dawes—CT/CR-1:242 (1653). Munsey—ME/PCR-3:278 (1688). Walton—NH/PP-2:322 (1699).
13. Wilson—MD/A-23:466.
14. Cowin—PLY/CR-5:54, 61 (1670/71). Broome—VA/CSP-1:23 (1689). For similar cases, see RI/R-2:41–42 (1664); NC/HC:19, 60 (1693/94); NJ/A-2:331 (1700); and Phillip Alexander Bruce, *Institutional History of Virginia in the Seventeenth Century: An Inquiry into the Religious, Moral, Educational, Legal, Military, and Political Condition of the People, Based on Original and Contemporaneous Records*, 2 vols. (New York: G. P. Putnam's Sons, 1910), 1:268–69 (1680s). For similar words against Oliver Cromwell when he was Lord Protector, see William Randall's case at PLY/CR-3:223 (1656/57), and the prosecution of five drunken revelers at RI/CT-1:36–37 (1657/58).
15. Grey—VA/EJC-1:447; VA/BR-3:183–84, 197–200 *passim* (1699).
16. Lloyd—PA/PCR-1:602–4 (1700).
17. Gentleman—CSP-9:153 (1674—Virginia). Fletcher—CSP-14:169 (1693—New York).
18. Jennison—MA/CAR-2:48, 52 (1634). Charles—HAVEN-1:298 (1646).
19. Ogle—NY/DRCH-12:530, 531, 537–38; NY/CCM:23 (1675).
20. Jones—PA/PQS:237–38 (1695).
21. Ellis—MD/A-8:20–21 (1688).
22. Denison and company—CT/CR-2:258–59, 310 (1675). The complete text of the original Stonington petition is provided in CT/CR-2:577–78. The court secretary's description is taken directly from the first paragraph. For other examples, see MA/CAR-2:73 (1637/38); PLY/CR-3:185–86 (1660); PA/PCR-1:371 (1693).
23. Carroll—MD/COA:31–34 (1696).
24. Gyndall—ME/PCR-2:199 (1670). Four men—NH/SP-17:618 (1684).
25. Utie—MD/A-49:398–99, 489–90 (1664/65). Utie soon suffered a devastating personal loss. On September 30, 1665, "Jacob, a negro slave and servant" of Utie's, entered the colonel's house with "a drawn knife of two pence value," and there several times "did strike and stab" Mary Utie, Nathaniel's wife, "giving her a mortal wound four fingers broad, in the upper part of her right arm." She died four days later. Jacob went to the gallows soon after.
26. Bellemont—NY/DRCH-4:524–25 (1699).
27. Dyer—RI/R-2:108–9 (1665). For a similar case, see William Furber's prosecution at NH/SP-17:632 (1693).
28. French—NJ/BCB:57–58 (1686).
29. Nason—ME/PCR-3:212 (1684/85). Drink sometimes led offenders to speak a bit too freely, about taxes as about other things. New York's Hendrick Koster found himself before the Albany judges on October 17,

1672, for speaking against their court "when the farming of the excise took place." When questioned about his words, he "answers that he knows nothing about it, as he was very intoxicated at the time, and requests that he may be excused." Instead, the court fined him five beaver hides (equivalent to £3 at the prevailing exchange rate). Koster—NY/ARS-1:315 (1672).

30. Martin—VA/BR-1:12 (1619). Captain John Pegro and two other ship-masters created a stir in 1653 with their response when ordered to pay the customary castle duties. They rejected the order and slighted the authority from which it came, "deriding it with laughter and scorn." Pegro—VA/BR-1:88 (1653). For some other examples, see VA/GCR:501 (1644); VA/BR-2:87, 88, 104 (1680s); VA/BR-3:184 (1699).

31. Lynn—MA/CAR-2:19 (1631). Stockbridge—PLY/CR-1:87, 97 (1638). Rendell—ME/PCR-1:160–61 (1650/51).

32. Donaldson and Wood—PA/PCR-1:569, 570 (1699).

33. Scott and Fogg—MA/CAR-1:61 (1675). Edminson and Darvall—PA/PCR-1:114, 116 (1684).

34. Covill—MD/A-15:233–34 (1678/79).

35. Jennings—VA/EJC-1:179–82 (1691).

36. London—CT/CR-2:396, 399 (1675/76).

37. Clock—NY/SAR:68–69 (1695).

38. Whitpain—PA/PCR-1:246 (1688/89). Governor Nicholson forbade Andries Greveraet to tell anyone when he arrived in New York with the news of William of Orange's landing. See CSP-13:198 (1688).

39. Diggs—VA/EJC-1:281–83, 302 (1693). For another Virginia instance, see VA/EJC-1:491 (1682). Virginia authorities sometimes endured great frustration in attempting to limit the spread of false tales about their colony through London. See the Jones affair, for example, at VA/CSP-1:39–40 (1692).

40. Popell—SC/CCR:65 (1692). Sothell arrived as governor in 1683 after escaping years of Algerian captivity at the hands of pirates (see CSP-10:326 for documents relating to this episode). Albemarle colonists ousted him in 1689. He went to Charleston and ousted Governor Colleton in 1690. Sothell ruled in Colleton's place until the Palatine court suspended him in 1691, charging him with treason. The controversy did not end until his death in 1694.

41. Sollers—MD/A-8:47 (1688). Randolph—VA/EJC-1:287 (1693).

42. Burdett and others—MD/A-15:227–31 *passim* (1678/79). For other Maryland searches for false report authors see MD/A-15:129–30 (1676); MD/A-15:357–58 (1681); MD/A-8:94 (1689). For Henry VIII's 1515 London search, see James F. Stephen, *A History of the Criminal Law of England*, 3 vols. (London: Macmillan, 1883), 2:306.

43. Turner search—PA/PCR-1:210 (1687). For a similarly unsuccessful search in Virginia, see VA/BR-2:114–15 (1677). Searching for the author of false reports, as well as those posting pasquinades, was the normal

approach among the Dutch at New Netherland. See, for example, NY/
DRCH-1:511 (1652). For a New York search long after the English took
over, see CSP-14:112 (1693).

44. Maryland practice—CSP-15:2 (1696). Nicholson letter—CSP-13:321
(1690). New York—NY/DH-2:82 (1689). New Jersey—NJ/NJCD-13:217
(1695). Investigations sometimes went outside the immediate bounds
of a given colony. In 1690, the Virginia government sent Colonel Cuth-
bert Potter as "a messenger to ascertain the truth of matters in New
England and New York." See CSP-13:278 (1690).

45. English proclamations—CSP-14:652 (1695/96); CSP-12:60 (1685). Effingham—CSP-12:117, 151 (1685).

46. Proclamation—PA/PCR-1:297 (1689). Council meeting—PA/PCR-
1:299–300 (1689).

47. Brightwell—MD/A-23:177 (1697). For examples of false rumors causing
trouble, see CSP-12:579 (1688—Jamaica); CSP-13:559 (1691—Bahamas); MD/A-19:258, 462, 495 (1695).

48. Governor's statement—CSP-14:464–65 (1695—New York). For some
examples of proclamations issued in lieu of prosecutions, see VA/BR-
2:114–15 (1677); CSP-12:561 (1688—Jamaica); NY/DH-2:323 (1690/91);
CSP-14:305 (1694—New York). In 1693, the New York Council minutes noted that "in consequence of scandalous reports in the town
that there were not ten men in a company in the troops at Albany, the
Governor produced the latest returns showing 261 effective men in the
four companies, 39 having deserted." No prosecutions occurred. See
CSP-14:208 (1693).

4. Between the Millstones

1. Hoskins—NH/PP-1:54 (1680).
2. Colcord—NH/PP-1:237–38 (1661).
3. Blackleich—CT/CR-1:376, 377–78 (1661/62). Seith—PA/PCR-1:378
(1693).
4. White—PA/PCR-1:109 (1684). Pinhorne—CSP-16:242, 270 (1698—
New York). For similar cases, see NY/SC-3:161; MD/A-15:227 (1678);
VA/CSP-1:23 (1689).
5. Fendall—MD/A-15:388 (1681). George and Saintloe—Robert N. Toppan, ed., *Edward Randolph: Including His Letters and Official Papers
from the New England, Middle, and Southern Colonies in America,
with Other Documents Relating Chiefly to the Vacating of the Royal
Charter of the Colony of Massachusetts Bay, 1676–1703.* 7 vols. (Boston: The Prince Society, 1898), 6:202–4 (1686).
6. Cloet—NY/ARS-3:416–19 (1683/84).
7. Taylor and Curtis—NJ/A-1:313–14, 322 (1680). The pubs' potential for
troubles did not escape colonial officials, particularly when conniving

rivals found creative ways to use them. Such was the case in 1638 when men seeking to discredit the government of Virginia sent "spies" through "all parts of London" to seek out planters returning from the colony and invite them "into taverns, and after working upon their weakness with the advantage of wine, 'drain from them some matter of grievance, which is straightly written down,' and the party thus ensnared to justify a complaint without cause." See CSP-1:288 (1638/39).

8. Dorsey—MD/A-8:375 (1692).

9. Nicarson—PLY/CR-4:134, 155–56, 168 (1666).

10. Burdett—CSP-1:284 (1638). New York Council—CSP-13:757 (1689). Leisler—NY/DH-2:55 (1689/90). West—CSP-7:186 (1670/71). On May 10, 1632, the Providence Company ordered Governor Bell to allow the Bahamas planters "free liberty to send letters without being opened," except "in such particular cases wherein your reasons so to do may give us good content." Colonists angered over Bell's liberal use of that exception got the letter-opening authority revoked just over a year later, but company officials soon regretted the rescission. They were "unable at present to complete his portion of servants," they told Bell in 1634, "the reputation of the island having been weakened by discouraging letters from thence." See CSP-1:149 (1632), 167 (1633), 187 (1634).

11. Child—MA/GCR-2:162 (1646). Such searches had to be properly authorized. For an example of an official punished for an illegal search, see the James Satterthwait case at NJ/BCB:217 (1698/99). Pennsylvania Council—PA/PCR-1:271 (1689).

12. Virginia defendants—VA/EJC-1:112–14 (1690). Maryland Council order—MD/A-20:517 (1696). The failure of witnesses to appear did not always delay a trial. For one example, see NY/MC:655–56 (1683). Lack of a quorum of judges and inclement weather, especially in "the winter season," were common causes of trial postponements. See DE/RSC:61 (1681/82), 116 (1684); PA/PCR-1:312 (1689/90); NJ/CCRC:268 (1694). Sometimes court was delayed for more unusual reasons. The Middlesex County court could not meet on time on March 3, 1699/1700, because the people in the town had nailed the doors of the courthouse shut. See NJ/A-2:315–17 (1699/1700). Measles forced a suspension of the New York Council years later. See NY/CCM:307 (1728/29).

13. RI/R-1:204 (1647).

14. For the Connecticut order restricting noise, see CT/CR-1:13–14 (1637). Higgs—MD/A-17:283, 382 (1684). Virginia colonists' request—VA/BR-2:100 (1677). For examples of tardiness, absenteeism, leaving court prematurely, and a physical assault from the bench, see ME/PCR-2:157 (1664); NJ/BCB:12 (1682); DE/RSC:55 (1681); RI/R-1:333–34 (1655/56); and VA/EJC-1:319 (1694). For examples of other kinds of courtroom misbehavior, see RI/R-1:360, 365 (1657); ME/PCR-3:64 (1680); MD/A-70:290 (1682); NJ/BCB:164–65 (1693/94); PA/CCD-2:19 (1698); DE/KC:139 (1699).

15. Duty—NJ/A-13:167–68 (1686). For another example of the rules being bent, note Samuel Hanson's treatment on Barbados. Under close questioning about his seditious words in 1682/83, Hanson insisted that it was "illegal that he should be compelled to swear against himself." Angered by the response, the island's governor jailed Hanson for five weeks. See CSP-11:377 (1682/83). Other cases, though not involving outright violations of procedural rights, betray an attitude leaning that direction. John Palmer, for example, appeared in court for uttering words "in defamation of the government and of the late Queen Mary" on Antigua in 1696. The Assembly preferred the charge. Palmer went unpunished not simply because the words had been spoken years before, but because he had in the meantime committed no similar offense. See CSP-15:28, 93, 169, 174–75 (1696). In some (nonseditious speech) cases, procedural protections were clearly upheld. For some examples, see the following. Self incrimination—MD/A-53:308 (1662); PA/PCR-1:278–79 (1689). Double jeopardy—NC/R-1:428 (1694). Statutes of limitation—ME/PCR-1:320 (1666); MD/A-57:369–70 (1668).

16. Ransome—PLY/CR-5:32 (1669/70).

17. Hinson—MD/A-54:197 (1660). For examples of the two-witness rule used in seditious speech cases in other colonies, see PA/PCR-1:107 (1684); NJ/BCB:105 (1690); VA/EJC-1:302 (1693). The inclination to hedge in applying this rule, as Gail Marcus has observed, must have been very strong, particularly when a credible witness appeared against a defendant with a history of transgressions. She also notes that this brought increased pressure on defendants to confess. These observations could apply equally well to the other procedural protections discussed above. See Gail Sussman Marcus, "'Due Execution of the General Rules of Righteousness': Criminal Procedure in New Haven Town and Colony, 1638–1658," in David D. Hall, John M. Murrin, and Thad W. Tate, eds., Saints and Revolutionaries: Essays on Early American History (New York: W. W. Norton, 1984), 116–17.

18. Berry—NJ/CCRC:194 (1685). Armitage—Toppan, Edward Randolph, 3:212–13.

19. Johnson—MD/A-15:348, 419 (1678/79). See also MD/A-15:327 and MD/A-17:380.

20. David T. Konig, Law and Society in Puritan Massachusetts: Essex County, 1629–1692 (Chapel Hill: University of North Carolina Press, 1979), 165.

21. Maine court day—ME/PCR-2:146–62 (1664).

22. See, for example, John M. Beattie, Crime and the Courts in England, 1660–1800 (Princeton, N.J.: Princeton University Press, 1986), 403.

23. Wearing—NJ/BCB:226 (1699). Conflicting court meetings occurred in all of the colonies except Plymouth and New Haven, where most matters were handled in a single court. See Bradley Chapin, Criminal Justice in Colonial America, 1606–1660 (Athens: University of Georgia

Press, 1983), 97. For other examples of conflict of interest and regulations regarding them, see MA/GCR-3:89 (1646); ME/PCR-1:215 (1665); MD/A-54:350 (1676); PLY-11:257 (1680); PA/PCR-1:81, 82 (1683); NJ/A-1:514–16 (1686); CSP-14:381 (1694—Barbados); NC/HC:238 (1695); MD/A-22:323 (1699); NY/SAR:176, 190 (1700).

24. Julius Goebel, Jr., and T. Raymond Naughton, *Law Enforcement in Colonial New York: A Study in Criminal Procedure (1664–1776)* (New York: Commonwealth Fund, 1904), 573. Chapin, *Criminal Justice in Colonial America, 1606–1660*, 41. Beattie on Surrey, England, in J. S. Cockburn, ed., *Crime in England, 1550–1800* (Princeton, N.J.: Princeton University Press, 1977), 166. For Beattie on lawyers in seditious speech trials, see his *Crime and the Courts in England, 1660–1800*, 357. The growing use of lawyers generally late in the century in England fits Edwin Powers's observation that although a 1673 Massachusetts statute allowed attorneys to sue in the client's name (unlike in England), a legal bar did not become established in the Bay Colony until 1686. At that time, lawyers were officially admitted to practice and required to take formal oaths. See Edwin Powers, *Crime and Punishment in Early Massachusetts, 1620–1692: A Documentary History* (Boston: Beacon Press, 1966), 438–39. The 1680s also saw the Maine Court of Common Pleas take a keener interest in supplying attorneys to conduct business, "there being a deficiency therein" (presumably in the number rather than the quality). See ME/PCR-3:262 (1687). The increasing presence of lawyers may have contributed to the growing attention to legal technicalities David Konig observed in Essex County, Massachusetts, in the 1680s. Konig, *Law and Society in Puritan Massachusetts*, 165.

25. Rhode Island law—RI/R-2:239 (1668/69). Pennsylvania Council order—PA/PCR-1:172–73 (1686). Randolph's comment—MA/HSC-62:xxi. For examples of colonial laws regarding attorneys, see VA/SAL-1:303 (1645); CSP-7:53 (1669/70—Jamaica); CSP-7:149 (1670—Barbados); NJ/A-1:407 (1683); NY/SAR:186 (1695).

26. MD/A-22:179 (1698). NC/R-1:299 (1676). Rombouts—NY/SAR:13 (1681).

27. Plymouth law—PLY/CR-2:3 (1623). New Jersey Concessions—NJ/A-1:228 (1678). Pennsylvania law—PA/PQS:175 (1694/95). Virginia law—VA/LJC-1:196, 203, 204 (1693). Wyatt—VA/SAL-1:110, 111 (1621). For other examples, see VA/SAL-2:73; RI/R-1:157 (1647), 246 (1652); CT/CR-1:535 (1650); NY/NAR-5:330 (1666). The right had limitations. See, for examples, PA/UCC:40 (1676); CSP-7:188 (1670/71—Antigua); CSP-5:641 (1668—Montserrat). For colonists avoiding jury duty, see MA/CAR-2:76 (1638); PLY/CR-3:223 (1656); MD/A-49:319 (1664); MA/ECC-4:215 (1669/70); RI/R-2:525 (1674); PA/PCR-1:95 (1683); DE/RSC:113 (1684/85); NJ/CCRC:223 (1687); NY/SAR:77, 79 (1695); DE/KC:146 (1699); NC/R-1:533 (1700). For examples of relevant statutes, see VA/EJC-2:36 (1677) and CT/CR-4:99 (1693). For jurors pun-

ished for neglecting their duty in other ways, see MA/ECC-7:290 (1679);
NJ/BCB:9 (1681); MD/A-8:527 (1693).

28. For some coroner's juries, see MA/CAR-2:6 (1630); NY/NAR-6:228
(1670); PA/PCR-1:94 (1683); NC/HC:430 (1688/89); NJ/CMC:271–72
(1693). For some presenting juries, see MD/A-57:597, 617 (1669/70);
NY/SAR:43, 49 (1693); PA/CCD-2:13 (1697); DE/KC:169 (1700).

29. See CT/CR-3:52; PA/PCR-1:467, 556; NJ/BCB:60–61 (1686), 143 (1692),
182 (1695). The size and procedures of grand juries varied widely
among colonies. For some examples, see ME/PCR-2:154 (1664); CT/
CR-3:52 (1680); NY/SAR:122 (1697); MD/A-65:9. Useful discussions of
grand juries can be found in Goebel, *Law Enforcement in Colonial New
York*, 334, and in Peter C. Hoffer, *Criminal Proceedings in Colonial
Virginia* (Athens: University of Georgia Press, 1984), xxvi.

30. Maine consent—ME/PCR-1:244 (1665). Duke's Laws—PA/SAL-1:95
(1664). For typical jury numbers, see CSP-7:165 (1670/71—St. Kitts);
PA/PCR-1:38 (1682), 412–13 (1693). One man denounced a Delaware
jury's ruling because the jury numbered less than twelve. "The verdict
of seven men," he argued, "was and is contrary to the known laws
of England." See DE/RSC:91 (1682/83). For typical jury constituency
stipulations, see CT/CR-1:138 (1646); MD/A-57:147 (1666); NY/WC:48
(1687); NC/HC:269 (1696); VA/BR-3:137 (1699). Jury selection procedures varied widely. For some ethnic restrictions on jury membership,
see RI/R-2:509 (1673) and MD/A-20:570 (1696). For a female coroner's
jury, see DE/RSC:103 (1683). When selecting a jury in East Jersey, the
names of adult freemen were "written on equal pieces of parchment
and put into a box," from which "the number of the jury shall be drawn
out by a child under ten years of age." See NJ/A-1:404, 407 (1683).

31. For English practice, see Beattie, *Crime and the Courts in England,
1660–1800,* 390. For colonial practice near the end of the century, the
lengthy description at CT/CR-4:98 (1693) is instructive. I have found
juries typically hearing from one to two dozen cases a day in the
colonies. That squares with the findings of other researchers. See, for
example, Erwin C. Surrency, "The Courts in the American Colonies,"
American Journal of Legal History 11 (1967):258. English juries followed the same pattern well into the eighteenth century. See Cockburn,
Crime in England, 1550–1800, 165.

32. French—NJ/BCB:57–58 (1686). For examples of laws protecting the
right of challenge, see NJ/A-1:253 (1677); PA/PCR-1:38 (1682); NJ/A-
1:406 (1683). For typical examples of challenges see NY/SAR:10 (1681);
NJ/CCRC:58 (1683); NJ/BCB:136–37 (1686—an entire jury set aside);
NY/SAR:193 (1700). For two examples of no challenges made when
defendants were given the chance, see NY/ARS-2:443 (1679) and NY/
ARS-3:192–93 (1681/82). For some examples of offenders seditiously
criticizing juries, see MA/CAR-2:97 (1640); MA/PCR:207 (1640); NH/
CHS-8:139 (1683); ME/PCR-3:133 (1686).

33. Monroe—NJ/BCB:166 (1694). For an equally instructive example, see Theunis Gysbert's case at NY/SAR:78 (1695). Colonial authorities worked to prevent tampering with juries once they had been selected. For some examples, see MA/CAR-2:87 (1639); NY/DRCH-2:712 (1674); MA/CAR-2:78 (1674); PA/PCR-1:336–37 (1690).

34. John M. Murrin, "Magistrates, Sinners, and a Precarious Liberty: Trial by Jury in Seventeenth-Century New England," in David D. Hall, John M. Murrin, and Thad W. Tate, eds., *Saints and Revolutionaries: Essays on Early American History* (New York: W. W. Norton, 1984), 154, 160, 162. For concurring views, see Paul McCain, *The County Court in North Carolina before 1750* (Durham, N.C.: Duke University Press, 1954), 43; Chapin, *Criminal Justice in Colonial America, 1606–1660*, 30, 41, 88; Goebel and Naughton, *Law Enforcement in Colonial New York*, 379–83; Hoffer, *Criminal Proceedings in Colonial Virginia*, xxx–xxxi; Surrency, "The Courts in the American Colonies," 258; Philip Alexander Bruce, *Institutional History of Virginia in the Seventeenth Century: An Inquiry into the Religious, Moral, Educational, Legal, Military, and Political Condition of the People, Based on Original and Contemporaneous Records*, 2 vols. (New York: G. P. Putnam's Sons, 1910), 1:554; and Roger Thompson, *Sex in Middlesex: Popular Mores in a Massachusetts County, 1649–1699* (Amherst: University of Massachusetts Press, 1986), 7. Commenting on Henry Greenland's 1671 Maine prosecution, the editor of the records observed: "Here we see the Englishman's primeval right to trial by a jury of his peers, seldom availed of but always in the background." See ME/PCR-2:432 (1671).

35. Nevell—MD/A-53:515 (1664). For a similar incident, see MD/A-53:543 (1664/65). Connecticut costs—CT/CR-4:312–14 (1699). For examples of provisions for jurors, see MD/A-53:515 (1660); ME/PCR-2:101 (1661); CSP-5:194 (1663—Nevis); NY/HTR-1:121 (1664); NH/CNNH-8:122 (1682); MA/ECC-4:232 (1694).

36. Rhode Island quote—RI/R-2:348 (1670). For a useful example of the kinds of costs involved, see MD/A-65:60–61 (1672). Sometimes witnesses attempted to overcharge people for whom they had testified, and that prompted legislation on occasion. See, for example, MD/A-57:365 (1668).

37. Hoffer, *Criminal Proceedings in Colonial Virginia*, xxx–xxxi, lxvii. Murrin, "Magistrates, Sinners, and a Precarious Liberty," 164. Cockburn, *Crime in England, 1550–1800*, 183. These figures include guilty pleas.

38. Arnold—RI/CT-1:80 (1669). Maryland question—MD/A-20:439 (1696). For a protestation similar to Arnold's, see Paul Batt's argument at MA/SCC-1:540–41 (1674). For typical examples of judges empowered to modify or set aside jury verdicts, see CT/CR-1:138 (1646); ME/PCR-2:148, 154 (1664); MA/GCR-4/2:308 (1666—overturned on appeal). Only West New Jersey made jury verdicts sacrosanct in law. See NJ/A-

1:225 (1676/77). For examples of judges improperly interfering with juries, see PA/PCR-1:136 and CSP-1:473 (1658/59—St. Kitts).

39. Fendall—MD/A-5:327–28 (1681). For examples of judges acting to save colonists from juries, see NY/CCM:11 (1670—witchcraft); PA/PCR-1:438–39 (1693/94—horse stealing). For instances of juries chastised for trying to determine matters of law rather than fact, see MD/A-66:349–50 (1676); NJ/A-1:255 (1676/77); NY/ARS-2:207 (1676/77); NY/ARS-3:155 (1681); NJ/CCRC:307 (1697). Maryland's governor revealed much about juries when in 1697 he instructed the Chief Justice to charge every jury "to find the matter of fact according to evidence and not (as usually they do) to consider the poverty of the person, by thinking the party will be ruined if he loses the cause." MD/A-23:253 (1697). For the role of the law versus fact in seditious libel cases, see the useful discussions in Sir William S. Holdsworth, *A History of English Law*, 16 vols. (London: Methuen, 1922–52), 8:345, and Frederick S. Siebert, *Freedom of the Press in England, 1476–1776* (Urbana: University of Illinois Press, 1952), 274.

40. Goebel and Naughton, *Law Enforcement in Colonial New York*, 555–56. Jesson—MA/CAR-1:55, MA/SCC-2:588–92 (1675). The editors of the Suffolk County court records offer the following comment: "This case is an interesting parallel to Bushell's case, in England, which established the juror's right to independent judgment almost contemporaneously. Bushell's case grew out of the trial of William Mead and William Penn . . . in which expressions at times strikingly similar to those of Jesson were employed to greater effect." Punishment of jurors did not end in 1675 with Jacob Jesson. See similar examples at NH/SP-17:618 (1686) and MD/A-22:179–80, 182 (1698). Disagreements between judge and jury did not always end with jurors being punished. For examples in which jurors prevailed, see RI/CT-2:20 (1663) and MD/A-15:261 (1679). For useful discussions of juries being punished, see R. H. Helmholz and Thomas A. Greene, *Juries, Libel and Justice: The Role of English Juries in Seventeenth- and Eighteenth-Century Trials for Libel and Slander* (Pasadena, Calif.: Castle Press, 1984), 78, 80–81, and J. S. Cockburn, *A History of the English Assizes, 1558–1714* (Cambridge, U.K.: Cambridge University Press, 1972), 123. Note Brad Chapin's observation that by 1700 jury verdicts in England were sacrosanct in law, and had been in practice well before that, with some exceptions. See Chapin, *Criminal Justice in Colonial America, 1606–1660*, 47.

41. Rhode Islanders were more likely than any other colonists to seek juries when tried for seditious speech, doing so in almost one in ten cases across the century. Colonists in New York, New Hampshire, Connecticut, and New Haven were least likely to use juries; I found no jury trials for seditious speech in any of these colonies. This follows the known patterns for crime more generally.

42. For examples of wrongs righted on appeal, see NY/SAR:6 (1680); MD/ COA:11–12 (1694); MD/A-25:74–75 (1699); PA/PCR-1:579 (1700). For some appealed cases where judges and juries disagreed, see MA/GCR-3:179–80, 4/1:73, 212–13.

43. Andros fees—NH/CHS-8:283–84 (1686). For previous New Hampshire fees, see NH/CHS-8:123 (1682). A typical Rhode Island law formally upheld the right of all freemen to challenge a court decision so long as a fee of 2s.6d accompanied the appeal. See RI/R-1:255–56 (1652). Virginia stipulation—VA/BR-2:519 (1678). Massachusetts county court limitation—MA/DR:231 (1686). New Jersey allowance—NJ/A-1:284 (1678). By 1677, limiting the size of appealable awards had become a significant grievance among Old Dominion colonists. See, for example, the Northampton petition at VA/BR-2:100 (1677). See also VA/BR-3:137 (1699). Such limits hurt the poor in civil matters, for their cases inevitably involved smaller amounts. Colonial authorities sometimes tried to help, as when New York's Council decided in 1692 to allow appeals even "for the smallest sum." See NY/JLC-1:30 (1692). But most colonies found that only restricting appealable amounts could curb abuses and reduce difficulties endemic to the right of appeal. Massachusetts 1645 statute—MA/GCR-2:105 (1645). New York refusals—NY/DRCH-3:829–30 (1691/92) and NY/NAR-7:372 (1666). Pennsylvania requirement—PA/PCR-1:76 (1683). Before Pennsylvania was a year old, the Council fined the Philadelphia County Court £40 for violating this law in judging a case that should have been heard in Bucks County. See PA/PCR-1:76 (1683). The New Haven quotation is from Marcus, "'Due Execution of the General Rules of Righteousness': Criminal Procedure in New Haven Town and Colony, 1638–1658," 108. For some examples of appeal bonds, see DE/KC:139 (1699); NY/SAR:20 (1681); MA/ECC-8:43 (1680); NJ/A-1:106 (1672); NY/DRCH-12:569 (1670s), and NY/SAR:23 (1670s). For restrictions on appeals to England, see NY/DRCH-4:550 (1699); Goebel and Naughton, *Law Enforcement in Colonial New York,* 225, 230; Powers, *Crime and Punishment in Early Massachusetts,* 57, 68; MA/DR:233 (1686); NY/DRCH-4:71 (1693); NJ/A-2:359 (1700/01). On Barbados, every colonist leaving the island had publicly to post his name and the purpose of the voyage well in advance of departure (to ensure he was not fleeing obligations). Authorities there watched those postings and sometimes jailed those announcing intended appeals to England. Barbados—CSP-7:55 (1669/70). With the gradual strengthening of royal administration toward the end of the century, appeals to England became increasingly available. For some examples, see MD/A-15:75 (1676); VA/EJC-1:516 (1688); MD/A-8:279 (1691). Yet colonists rarely exercised their right of appeal to England even when colonial law did not forbid or limit it. The expense alone proved an enormous discouragement when stretched across the sea. Establishing the right was far more important to the king in spreading and affirming his

authority in principle than to colonial subjects availing themselves of his justice and mercy in practice.

44. Surrency, "The Courts in the American Colonies," 270. Chapin, *Criminal Justice in Colonial America, 1606–1660*, 74. For some examples of appeals to abate or reduce fines, see MA/GCR-2:227, 3:167, 235, 304, 428.

45. Waldron—NH/CHS-8:202–3, 339, 341 (1683). For decades off and on, Waldron had been a deputy to the General Court from Dover. He also sat as a magistrate in New Hampshire and Maine for many years, even serving as governor of New Hampshire from Cutt's death on March 27, 1681, until Cranfield's arrival the following October 4. Waldron was killed one June evening in 1689 at the full age of seventy-three years by some Indians who broke into his home and overcame him. After a stiff fight, they sliced open his chest with knives, then cut off his ears and nose, stuffing them into his mouth, before pushing him upon a sword to end his life. Wilkinson—VA/GCR:469–70 (1640). Cutler—MA/CAR-1:355 (1691).

46. Hunt—MA/GCR-4/2:138 (1664). Richards—CT/CR-2:78–79 (1667).

5. Sanctions in Decline

1. Endicott—MA/GCR-1:297 (1639). For one offender whipping another, see RI/CT-2:39 (1664). Colonial and English laws prohibited inflicting corporal punishment on gentlemen, "because the loss of honor they would incur would be a greater punishment than the law intended." John M. Beattie, *Crime and the Courts in England, 1660–1800* (Princeton, N.J.: Princeton University Press, 1986), 463. Edwin Powers says this was later changed in New England. See Edwin Powers, *Crime and Punishment in Early Massachusetts, 1620–1692: A Documentary History* (Boston: Beacon Press, 1966), 168. For a colonial law prohibiting corporal punishment for gentlemen, see MD/A-1:184. Blackstone observed that seditious words could be punished in England with "fine and such corporal punishment as the court in its discretion shall inflict," always "regarding the quantity of the offense," he added, "and the quality of the offender." Sir William Blackstone, *Commentaries on the Laws of England in Four Books*, ed. William Draper Lewis, 4 vols. (Philadelphia: Rees, Welsh, and Company, 1902), 4:151.

2. Bussaker—MA/CAR-2:64 (1636). Colonial authorities used the "special severity" language frequently for a wide variety of offenses. Phrases like "stripes well laid on" appeared regularly in colonial court records. For some examples, see VA/GCR:330 (1670); VA/GCR:228 (1670); NJ/BCB:43–44 (1685). English judges favored "until his back be bloody" and "till the blood come." For some examples, see Beattie, *Crime and the Courts in England, 1660–1800*, 462. In 1681, the Cecil County

court ordered Sheriff Edward Inglish to whip a man thirty-nine lashes. Inglish tied his "hands into the whipping post, and some small peach tree switches was brought to whip the said person." When officials objected to the small size of the switches, "Inglish went himself to cut more that might give content." In the meantime, someone in the watching crowd freed the offender. Inglish pursued the fleeing man, but returned emptyhanded. Adding to his humiliation and anger, "William Howell at that time stood in the Court house porch making laughter thereat." Such vignettes aside, whippings were no laughing matter. See MD/A-17:59 (1681).

3. Erbery—MD/A-2:55–57, 120–22 (1666).
4. Weston—PA/PCR-1:92 (1683). Moline—NC/HC:208, 220, 236 (1695). For other examples of whippings, see CSP-5:55 (1661—Jamaica); NY/MC:741 (1675); PA/PCR-1:241 (1688/89).
5. Colonial authorities, following the biblical injunction, normally limited whippings to no more than thirty-nine lashes "for one fact at one time." For examples, see MA/CLM:129 (1672); Powers, *Crime and Punishment in Early Massachusetts, 1620–1692*, 166–67; PA/PCR-1:97 (1684). Though rare, lashings as high as 150 stripes (administered in batches of thirty-nine or less) were recorded. For examples, see NY/SAR:34 (1682); Phillip Alexander Bruce, *Institutional History of Virginia in the Seventeenth Century: An Inquiry into the Religious, Moral, Educational, Legal, Military, and Political Condition of the People, Based on Original and Contemporaneous Records*, 2 vols. (New York: G. P. Putnam's Sons, 1910), 1:624–25; and Julius Goebel, Jr., and T. Raymond Naughton, *Law Enforcement in Colonial New York: A Study in Criminal Procedure (1664–1776)* (New York: Commonwealth Fund, 1944), 705.
6. For examples of women being whipped, see PLY/CR-1:132; NY/NAR-5:272 (1665); NY/ARS-2:280 (1677); NJ/BCB:73; and Bruce, *Institutional History of Virginia in the Seventeenth Century*, 1:622–23. New Haven authorities convicted Bethiah Hawes, "a loose, vaine wench," of fornication and being with child in 1659 after John Baldwin "had the use of her three times, one time at the stable end, and twice against the rails." The judges ordered Hawes whipped, "as may suit her sex," but there is no indication that this phrase brought any special treatment. See HAVEN-2:290, 291 (1659). For examples of pregnant women receiving special leniency, see MD/A-57:199 (1667) and PA/PCR-1:184 (1694/95). For a law allowing women to choose a fine, see VA/SAL-2:385 (1677). For some examples of offenders being given a choice, see MA/PCR:255 and RI/R-1:350.
7. The Pott case is discussed in John G. Bellamy, *The Tudor Law of Treason: An Introduction* (London: Routledge and Kegan Paul, 1979), 184.
8. Bruce, *Institutional History of Virginia in the Seventeenth Century*,

1:629. Quaile—VA/GCR:12 (1624). Ratcliff—MA/GCR-1:88 (1631). Winthrop—MA/JWJ-1:67. Whether Carpenter Quaile purchased his ears is not recorded, but he did write a contrite letter to Virginia Company officials indicating that his punishment had left him "plentiful in nothing but want and wanting nothing but plenty." See S. M. Kingsbury, ed., *The Records of the Virginia Company of London: The Court Book, from Manuscripts in the Library of Congress*, 4 vols. (Washington, D.C.: U.S. Government Printing Office, 1933), 4:468. For other examples of seditious speakers having ears cut, see VA/GCR:93 (1625); VA/GCR:81, 85 (1625); CSP-5:642 (1668); and MD/A-54:531–32 (1672). Colonial officials cut ears for various other crimes. For some examples, see MA/GCR-1:295 (1640); MA/CAR-1:57 (1675); MD/A-70:384–86 (1683—later proven innocent); NJ/BCB:75 (1687/88); MD/A-54:531–32. See also George Francis Dow, *Every Day Life in the Massachusetts Bay Colony* (Boston: Society for the Preservation of Antiquities, 1935); reprint edition (New York: Dover, 1988), 213.

9. Barnes—VA/GCR:14 (1625). Officials used tongue boring against various offenses, including bigamy in New York and blasphemy more generally. See Goebel and Naughton, *Law Enforcement in Colonial New York*, 63; and Alice Morse Earle, *Curious Punishments of Bygone Days* (New York: Macmillan, 1896); reprint edition (New York: Book League of America, 1929), 142. See CSP-1:340 (1650) for a Barbados case. This was a harsher variant of the tongue-pinching sometimes pronounced against gossips. New Englanders used a partially split board which they spread apart, placing the offender's tongue in the crevice for a short period of time. For an example of this numbing experience, see Elizabeth Applegate's punishment at MA/CAR-2:64 (1636). For an example of boring through the tongue with a hot iron, see HAVEN-2:240.

10. For a useful discussion of branding, see Earle, *Curious Punishments of Bygone Days*, 138–49. In 1679, officials at Albany, New York, branded a black thief on the back rather than the cheek at the special request of his master. See NY/ARS-2:437 (1679).

11. Warran—CSP-5:621 (1668—Jamaica). For New Netherland use of the wooden horse, see NY/DRCH-2:624 (1673).

12. Pidcock—PLY/CR-3:4 (1651/52).

13. Virginia order—VA/BR-2:467 (1693). Duke's Laws—PA/SAL-1:104 (1664). For other examples, see ME/PCR-1:137 (1649); ME/PCR-2:197 (1670); MA/ECC-7:113 (1679); RI/ARB:60 (1681). For some English background of the pillory, see Bellamy, *The Tudor Law of Treason*, 184.

14. Munsey—ME-3:278 (1688).

15. Eden—VA/GCR:57 (1625). Ewer—PLY/CR-3:175 (1659). Conell and Bradt—NY/ARS-2:181–82 (1676).

16. Humphry—DE/KC:3 (1680). Johnson—DE/RSC:116 (1684).

17. Knower—MA/CAR-2:21 (1632). Dexter—MA/CAR-2:30 (1632/33).

Shorthouse—MA/CAR-2:81 (1638). The "prison cell" quote is from Earle, *Curious Punishments of Bygone Days*, 10. For other offenses punished with bilboes, see MA/CAR-2:4, 32, 53, 65, and CSP-5:1–5 (1662—Barbados). For a rare instance of a woman set in the bilboes, see Mrs. Weston's case at MA/CAR-2:75 (1638). For a typical law requiring construction of bilboes, see ME/PCR-1:137 (1649).

18. Willis—VA/GCR:476, 483 (1640). Smith—RI/CT-2:6–7 (1662). Bowers—MA/GCR-5:153 (1677). For "his mutinous and seditious speeches at Point Cagua" in 1663, Jamaica's Council ordered Francis Willson to "stand near the gallows at St. Jago de la Vega for two hours" with "a gag in his mouth for half an hour, and a drum beating the remaining time, with his transgressions written on paper and pinned to his back." Willson—CSP-5:132 (1663—Jamaica). For a similar punishment, see Isaac Brickshaw's prosecution at PA/CCD-1:192 (1689).

19. Starr—MA/CAR-2:73 (1637/38). Hatcher—VA/BR-1:93; VA/SAL-1:387 (1654).

20. Lawrence—NY/ECM-1:77 (1666). Wood—NY/NTC:234, 235 (1669). For the common use of this sanction generally in New York, see Goebel and Naughton, *Law Enforcement in Colonial New York*, 689.

21. Rooke—VA/BR-2:476–77 (1693). For a rare Pennsylvania case late in the century, see Allen Robinett's punishment at PA/CCD-1:176–77 (1689). For some 1670s prosecutions, see MA/GCR-5:68, 69 (1675), and VA/GCR:532 (1676/77). In that last case, Charles Blanckeville appeared in one of Governor Berkeley's Green Spring courts for "stirring up the people to mutiny, by speaking diverse mutinous words in the county of Elizabeth City." He had to acknowledge his crime at the next Elizabeth City County court and ask forgiveness "upon his knees, with a rope about his neck."

22. John Beattie has made a similar point. Noting that use of the pillory declined in England from the late seventeenth to the early nineteenth centuries, he observed that the trend was encouraged during the first decade of the nineteenth century "by several examples . . . of men whom the government wanted to expose as traitors and seditious speakers being honored by the crowd rather than despised." Beattie, *Crime and the Courts in England, 1660–1800*, 616. For the decline of humiliation punishments in England and Europe generally, see J. A. Sharpe, *Crime in Early Modern England, 1550–1750* (London: Longman, 1984), 178–79, and Michael R. Weisser, *Crime and Punishment in Early Modern Europe (1350–1850)* (Sussex, U.K.: Harvester Press, 1979), 162–63.

23. Catchmey—MD/A-10:286 (1653). Councillors—VA/GCR:500 (1643). Lloyd—PA/PCR-1:245 (1688). Officials were put out of office for offenses other than seditious speech. For some examples, see VA/GCR:380 (1674) and MD/A-23:459 (1698).

24. Corbett—MA/GCR-4/2:304–5 (1666). Corbett had managed for some

time to conceal his bigamy by living under two different names. To those in New Hampshire, he was Abraham Corbett. In Maine, he was Abraham Baker. See NH/PP-1:280, 286–87, and ME/PCR-3:199.

25. Phillips—CT/CR-2:306–7 (1677).
26. Ship's crew—MD/A-41:310 (1659). North—PLY/CR-2:70 (1643/44). Collet—MD/A-10:414 (1655).
27. See Weisser, *Crime and Punishment in Early Modern Europe*, 164; Sharpe, *Crime in Early Modern England*, 180; and Joseph H. Smith, ed., *Colonial Justice in Western Massachusetts (1639–1702): The Pynchon Court Record* (Cambridge, Mass.: Harvard University Press, 1961), 150.
28. Wilson—VA/BR-1:88 (1653). Sayer—MD/A-8:503–4, 560–61, 563 (1693). For an equally interesting case, see MD/A-8:495–516 *passim* (1693).
29. Heardman—HAVEN-2:271–74 (1659).
30. Effingall—PA/CCD-1:56 (1685). Crocker—VA/GCR:135, 136 (1626). Finch—MA/CAR-2:76 (1638). For similar cases, see VA/GCR:476 (1640); HAVEN-1:123 (1643); MD/A-17:53–54, 87–88 (1681); NH/CHS-8:74, 75–76, 77 (1681); MA/CAR-1:201 (1681). In that last case, William King went to jail in Massachusetts for seditious words, and later stood trial for blasphemy—an offense he vehemently denied in court, all the while claiming to be "the eternal son of God."
31. Pope—MD/A-25:74–5 (1699). Philpot—NC/HC:93–94, 109–12 (1694).
32. For cases highlighting conditions and hardships of imprisonment, see MD/A-57:154–71 *passim* (1666/67); NH/PP-1:42 (1680); NH/SP-17:618 (1686); MD/A-5:478–79 (1686); CT/CR-4:100 (1693). For bread and water ordered as a special form of severity, see CT/CR-1:82 (1642/43). For confinement in chains, see MD/A-4:183 (1642); NH/PP-1:136 (1682/83); MD/A-5:494–95 (1686); Bruce, *Institutional History of Virginia in the Seventeenth Century*, 1:269. For jails exposing prisoners to the elements, see ME/PCR-1:304 (1667); CSP-7:34 (1670—Barbados); NH/DRP-3:87 (1699); MD/A-24:87, 119 (1700). For typical escapes, see ME/PCR-3:133 (1686); MD/A-8:345 (1692); RI/R-3:334 (1698). For an illuminating example of how escapes and seditious speech could become intertwined, see Edward Commins's prosecution at MD/A-4:435–38 *passim* (1648).

6. A Growing Leniency

1. Burton—VA/GCR:478 (1640). Boys—CT/CR-3:197 (1686). For some interesting examples of fined offenses, see MD/A-54:166 (1659); CSP-5:55 (1661—Jamaica); RI/R-2:190 (1667); MA/SCC-1:485–86 (1674); NY/MC:745 (1680/81); ME/PCR-4:77 (1696). For valuable discussions of the use of fines in the seventeenth century, see Julius Goebel, Jr., and T. Raymond Naughton, *Law Enforcement in Colonial New York: A Study*

in *Criminal Procedure (1664–1776)* (New York: Commonwealth Fund, 1944), 710; Bradley Chapin, *Criminal Justice in Colonial America, 1606–1660* (Athens: University of Georgia Press, 1983), 51; and Michael R. Weisser, *Crime and Punishment in Early Modern Europe (1350–1850)* (Sussex, U.K.: Harvester Press, 1979), 63.

2. Newton—VA/GCR:371 (1674). Hatcher—VA/GCR:530 (1676/77). For similar examples, see VA/GCR:460, 461, 532, 533 (all in 1676/77).

3. Kendall—VA/GCR:529 (1676/77). Crosby—PA/CCD-1:91 (1687). Maddocke—PA/CCD-1:161 (1689). Specie was so valuable that payments in it meant a significant reduction in the amount owed. Abatements ranged from as little as one-fourth to as much as one-half, one-third being most common. For some examples, see MA/GCR-5:121 (1676); NH/PP-1:94 (1682); CT/CR-3:189 (1685); CT/CR-4:212 (1697). Specie could mean Spanish pieces of eight, reales (coins worth one-fourth of a peseta each), English pounds sterling (usually called "hard money"), or colonial coins. "Boston money" would have meant Pine Tree (and other) shillings, minted in Boston from 1652 until the abrogation of the Bay Colony charter in 1684. These contained slightly less silver than English shillings to keep them circulating in the colonies rather than going to England as English money tended to.

4. Pennsylvania's practice, for example, was typical. See PA/PCR-1:172 (1686).

5. Hermon—ME/PCR-2:412 (1669). For some examples of bonds outside the judicial system, see MD/A-53:414 (1663); NC/HC:434 (1677); VA/EJC-1:51 (1683); VA/EJC-1:424–25 (1699); NJ/A-2:333 (1700). For a useful discussion of appearance bonds, see Goebel and Naughton, *Law Enforcement in Colonial New York*, 723. Such bonds could sometimes work a substantial hardship. William Hofmeyer had to mortgage his home for bond money in 1669, for example. See NY/NAR-6:155, 161 (1669). For some typical appearance bonds, see ME/PCR-1:262 (1666); MD/A-54:394–95 (1666); DE/RSC:68 (1681/82); NC/HC:193 (1695); NY/SAR:141, 143, 164 (1698). For an example of a behavior bond following acquittal, see the John Laine bestiality case at NJ/CCRC:234 (1688). For some bonds requiring obedience of court orders, see ME/PCR-1:316 (1666) and NC/HC:412 (c. 1692). A Maine woman, convicted as a "tale bearer, from house to house, setting differences between neighbors," had to post a £5 bond to discourage that in the future. See ME/PCR-1:333 (1667).

6. Durfee—RI/CT-2:27 (1663). Ducket et al.—PA/PQS-1:92 (1683). Sturgeon—NC/HC:364 (1685). For two other interesting cases where seditious speakers posted bonds, see HAVEN-2:65 (1653) and MD/A-54:350 (1676).

7. Browne—NY/ECM-1:140–41 (1672). For another example, see PA/CCD-2:1 (1697).

8. Sureties were rooted in the medieval "frankpledge." Under that system,

authorities divided male inhabitants into groups of ten. When one erred, the others either made sure he appeared for justice or suffered in his stead. This system worked best in a communal setting with a relatively stable population, so it fell into disuse as European society gradually changed. A modified version evolved in the form of the surety. For a useful discussion of the "frankpledge," see Weisser, *Crime and Punishment in Early Modern Europe*, 90.

9. Baxter—CT/CR-1:253 (1653). Tyler—VA/GCR:20 (1624). Smith—Goebel and Naughton, *Law Enforcement in Colonial New York*, 606. Couch—MA/SCC-1:235 (1672). Jowles—MD/A-8:559 (1693). For some interesting additional examples of sureties required, see PLY/CR-1:162 (1640); MA/SCC-2:1066 (1679); PA/CCD-1:192 (1689); NC/HC:89 (1694); MD/A-20:72 (1694).

10. Hatch—PLY/CR-2:24, 25 (1641). Scott—MA/CAR-1:61 (1675). Lewis—MD/A-65:40 (1672).

11. For an example of a guarantor being freed of further surety obligation, see NY/NAR-6:302 (1671). See Goebel and Naughton, *Law Enforcement in Colonial New York*, 485, for a useful discussion of surety forfeitures.

12. Atwater and Switzer—MA/CAR-3:177–78 (1668). Gilbert—MA/GCR-4/2:307 (1666). Moore—PA/PQS-1:58–59 (1683). For two examples of admonition in other kinds of cases, see MA/CAR-1:12 (1673—listening to Quaker preaching) and MA/CAR-1:144–45 (1679—"for enticing others to steal a boat and turn pirate"). For some other seditious speech admonitions, see ME/PCR-2:84 (1659); HAVEN-2:412–15 (1661); NY/DRCH-2:644 (1673); VA/EJC-1:507 (1686); MA/DSS-1:398 (1698); MD/A-24:26 (1700).

13. Dexter—MA/CAR-2:30–31 (1632/33). Burroughs—NY/DRCH-14:685–86 (1674/75). Clapper—NC/R-1:453, 524 (1694/95). For more on the Burroughs case, see NY/CCM:20, 21, and Jessica Kross's lengthy discussion in *The Evolution of an American Town: Newtown, New York, 1642–1775* (Philadelphia: Temple University Press, 1983), 118–19.

14. Molton—ME/PCR-4:84 (1696). Willen—DE/KC:3, 6 (1680). Wood—NY/NTC:252, 254 (1669). For Wood's previous conviction, see NY/NTC:234, 235. For other examples of remittances and sentence reductions, see PLY/CR-2:85 (1645); MA/GCR-4/1:156–57, 313 (1653); CT/CR-2:259, 310 (1675); MD/A-5:333–34 (1681); MD/A-15:402–4; CT/CR-4:305 (1699). When Goody Greene asked Marshal James Wiggin whether he "would carry in a dish of meat to the Bay magistrates," in 1663, he replied "by god if it were poison he would carry it to them." Judges ordered Wiggin whipped and bound in £20, then reduced the sentence to a £10 fine at his humble request. See ME/PCR-2:140–41 (1663).

15. Wearing—NJ/BCB:226 (1699). Cooke—MA/GCR-4/1:12 (1650). Ewer—PLY/CR-3:175 (1659).

16. Saxon—MD/A-17:288–89 (1684).

17. Seely—MD/A-41:523–24 (1661). Pennsylvania group—PA/PCR-1:224 (1688). Hardenbroek—NY/NAR-7:9–10, 14–15 (1673).
18. Emott—NY/DRCH-3:747 (1689).
19. Jordan—ME/PCR-2:142 (1663). Colcord—ME/PCR-2:153 (1664). Breame—ME/PCR-1:235 (1665). DeMilt—NY/SC-2:26 (1692).
20. Snead—PA/PCR-1:550–51 (1698). Wood—NY/DRCH-14:701 (1675). Harbin—MD/A-23:467 (1698).
21. Martin—VA/BR-1:12 (1619). Teller—NY/ARS-3:187 (1681). Furber— NH/SP-17:632 (1693). Johnson—MD/A-20:72 (1694).
22. Webber—NH/CHS-8:138 (1683).
23. de Peyster—NY/ARS-2:313, 323 (1678).
24. Puddington—ME/PCR-1:75 (1640). Gorton—RI/CT-1:76 (1660). Clock—NY/SC-3:49–50 (1695).
25. Porter, Bergen, Chiffem, and Child—MD/A-5:490–91, 532–33; MD/A-8:14–15 (1686).

7. Fruits of Circumstance

1. Coke as quoted in Philip A. Hamburger, "The Development of the Law of Seditious Libel and the Control of the Press," *Stanford Law Review* 37 (1985):668.
2. Sir William Blackstone, *Commentaries on the Laws of England in Four Books*, ed. William Draper Lewis, 4 vols. (Philadelphia: Rees, Welsh, and Company, 1902), 4:152. Leonard W. Levy, *Emergence of a Free Press* (New York: Oxford University Press, 1985), 8.
3. Forgisson—ME/PCR-3:178–79, 101 (1682/83).
4. Windower—NY/DH-2:418 (1694). See also, NY/SC-1:167.
5. Breden—MA/GCR-4/2:69 (1662). Vaughan—MD/A-4:439–40, 459 (1648).
6. Crandall—CT/CR-2:160–61 (1671). Carter—NJ/A-2:313–15, 333–35 (1699/1700).

Bibliography

Primary Sources

The Acts and Resolves, Public and Private, of the Province of the Massachusetts Bay: To Which Are Prefixed the Charters of the Province with Historical and Explanatory Notes, and an Appendix. Boston: Wright and Potter, Printers to the State, 1869.

Ames, Suzie M., ed. County Court Records of Accomack-Northampton, Virginia, 1632–1640. Washington, D.C.: American Historical Association, 1954. Reprint edition, Millwood, N.Y.: Kraus Reprint Company, 1975.

————, ed. County Court Records of Accomack-Northampton, Virginia, 1640–1645. Published for the Virginia Historical Society. Charlottesville: University Press of Virginia, 1973.

Arber, Edward, ed. The Story of the Pilgrim Fathers, 1606–1623 A.D.: As Told by Themselves, Their Friends, and Their Enemies. London: Ward and Downey, 1897.

Armstrong, Edward, ed. "Records of the Court at Upland, in Pennsylvania, 1676–1681." Historical Society of Pennsylvania, Memoirs 7 (1860):9–203. Philadelphia: J. B. Lippincott and Co., 1860.

Bartlett, John Russell, ed. Records of the Colony of Rhode Island and Providence Plantations in New England, 1636–1792. 10 vols. Providence: A. Crawford Greene and Brother, State Printers, 1856–65.

————, ed. Rhode Island Court Records. 2 vols. Providence: Rhode Island Historical Society, 1920–22.

Batchellor, A. S., and H. H. Metcalf, eds. Laws of New Hampshire, Including Public and Private Acts and Resolves and Royal Commissions and Instructions. Manchester and Bristol, 1904–22.

Beckman, Gail Mcknight, comp. The Statutes at Large of Pennsylvania in the Time of William Penn. New York: Vantage Press, 1976.

Bond, Carroll T., and Richard B. Morris, eds. *Proceedings of the Maryland Court of Appeals, 1695–1729.* Washington, D.C.: American Historical Association, 1933.

Bouton, Nathaniel, and others, eds. *Documents and Records Relating to the Province, [State and Towns] of New Hampshire, from the Earliest Period of Its Settlement.* 49 vols. Concord: George E. Jenks, State Printer, 1867–1943.

———. *[New Hampshire] Province Records and Court Papers from 1680 to 1692.* New Hampshire Historical Society, *Collections* 8 (1866). Concord: Printed for the Society by McFarland and Jenks, 1866.

Bowden, William H., comp. "Marblehead Town Records [1648–1683]." *Essex Institute Historical Collections* 69 (1933):207–329.

Bradford, William. *Of Plymouth Plantation, 1620–1647.* Edited by Samuel Eliot Morison. New York: Alfred A. Knopf, 1953.

Bridenbaugh, Carl, ed. *The Pynchon Papers.* 2 vols. Boston: Colonial Society of Massachusetts, 1982–85.

Brigham, Clarence S., ed. *The Early Records of the Town of Portsmouth.* Providence: E. L. Freeman and Sons, State Printers, 1901.

Bronner, Edwin B., ed. "Philadelphia County Court of Quarter Sessions and Common Pleas, 1695." *American Journal of Legal History* 1 (1957): 79–95, 175–90, 236–50.

Browne, William Hand, and others, eds. *Archives of Maryland.* 72 vols. to date. Baltimore: Maryland Historical Society, 1884–.

Buckenham, J. E. B., ed. *Records of the Courts of Quarter Sessions and Common Pleas of Bucks County, Pennsylvania, 1684–1700.* Meadville, Penn.: Printed by the Tribune Publishing Company for the Colonial Society of Pennsylvania, 1943.

Byrd, William, et al. *The Correspondence of the Three William Byrds of Westover, Virginia, 1684–1776.* Edited by Marion Tinling. 2 vols. Charlottesville: University of Virginia Press, 1977.

Capwell, Helen, ed. *Records of the Court of Trials of the Town of Warwick, Rhode Island, 1659–1674.* Providence: Shepley Press, 1922.

Chapin, Howard Miller, ed. *Documentary History of Rhode Island.* 2 vols. Providence, 1916–19.

———, ed. *The Early Records of the Town of Warwick.* Providence: E. A. Johnson Company, 1926.

Christoph, Peter R., Kenneth Scott, and Kenn Stryker-Rodda, eds. *New York Historical Manuscripts: Dutch, Kingston Papers.* 2 vols. Baltimore: Genealogical Publishing Co., Inc., published under the direction of the Holland Society of New York, 1976.

Colonial Records of Pennsylvania, 1683–1790. 16 vols. Philadelphia: Printed by Joseph Severns & Co., 1852–53.

Connecticut Historical Society. *Records of the Particular Court of Connecticut, 1639–1663.* Connecticut Historical Society, *Collections* 22 (1928). Hartford, 1928.

————. The Wyllys Papers: Correspondence and Documents Chiefly of Descendants of Governor George Wyllys of Connecticut, 1590–1796. Connecticut Historical Society, Collections 21 (1924). Hartford, 1924.

Crozier, William, ed. Virginia County Records. 11 vols. Baltimore: Genealogical Publishing Company, 1971.

Currer-Briggs, Noel, ed. Virginia Settlers and Adventurers: Abstracts of Wills, 1484–1789, and Legal Proceedings, 1560–1700, Relating to Early Virginia Families. Baltimore: Genealogical Publishing Company, 1970.

Cushing, John D., ed. Acts and Laws of New Hampshire, 1680–1726. Wilmington, Del.: Glazier, 1978.

————. The Earliest Acts and Laws of the Colony of Rhode Island and Providence Plantations, 1647–1719. Wilmington, Del.: Glazier, 1977.

————. The Earliest Laws of the New Haven and Connecticut Colonies, 1639–1673. Wilmington, Del.: Glazier, 1977.

————. The Earliest Printed Laws of New York, 1665–1693. Wilmington, Del.: Glazier, 1978.

————. The Earliest Printed Laws of North Carolina, 1669–1751. Wilmington, Del.: Glazier, 1977.

————. The Earliest Printed Laws of Pennsylvania, 1681–1713. Wilmington, Del.: Glazier, 1978.

————. The Earliest Printed Laws of South Carolina, 1692–1734. Wilmington, Del.: Glazier, 1978.

————. The Laws of the Province of Maryland. Wilmington, Del.: Glazier, 1978.

de Valinger, Leon, Jr., ed. Court Records of Kent County, Delaware, 1680–1705. Washington, D.C.: American Historical Association, 1959.

Dow, George F., ed. Records and Files of the Quarterly Courts of Essex County, Massachusetts, 1636–1683. 7 vols. Salem, Mass.: Published by the Essex Institute, 1911–21.

Early Records of the Town of Providence. 21 vols. Printed under the Authority of the City Council of Providence by the Record Commissioners. Providence: Snow and Farnham, City Printers, 1892–1915.

Edsall, Preston W., ed. Journal of the Courts of Common Right and Chancery of East New Jersey, 1683–1702. Philadelphia: American Legal History Society, 1937.

Fernow, Berthold, comp. Calendar of Council Minutes, 1668–1783. New York State Library Bulletin 58 (History 6) [1902]. Reprint edition, Harrison, N.Y.: Harbor Hill Books, 1987.

————, ed. The Records of New Amsterdam from 1653 to 1674, anno domini. 7 vols. New York: Knickerbocker Press, 1897.

"First Public Records of Cape May County [New Jersey]." The Cape May County Magazine of History and Genealogy 1 (1937–38):269–85.

Ford, Worthington Chauncy, ed. Diary of Cotton Mather, 1681–1724. 7 vols. Boston: Massachusetts Historical Society, 1911–12.

Fox, D. R., ed. Minutes of the Court of Sessions (1657–1696), Westchester

County, New York. White Plains, N.Y.: Westchester County Historical Society, 1924.

"Governour Bradford's Letter Book." Massachusetts Historical Society, *Collections* 3 (1794): 27–84. Boston: Printed in the Year 1794. Reprint edition, Boston: Munroe & Francis, Printers to the Massachusetts Historical Society, 1810.

Grant, W. L., and James Munro, eds. *Acts of the Privy Council of England, Colonial Series.* London: His Majesty's Stationary Office, 1908. Reprint edition, Nenbeln, Liechtenstein: Kraus Reprint, Ltd., 1966.

Greene, C. A., comp. "Gleanings from the Ancient Records of Bristol, R. I." *Narragansett Historical Register* 3 (1884):59–66.

Greene, Jack P., ed. *Settlements to Society: 1584–1763.* New York: McGraw-Hill, 1966.

Gregorie, Anne K., ed. *Records of the Court of Chancery of South Carolina, 1671–1779.* Washington, D.C.: American Historical Association, 1950.

Hall, Clayton C., ed. *Narratives of Early Maryland, 1633–1684.* New York: Charles Scribner's Sons, 1910.

Hamlin, Paul M., and Charles E. Baker, eds. *Supreme Court of Judicature of the Province of New York, 1691–1704.* 3 vols. New York Historical Society, *Collections* 78–80. Baltimore: Waverley Press, 1959.

Hening, William W., ed. *The Statutes at Large, Being a Collection of all the Laws of Virginia, from the First Session of the Legislature in the Year 1619.* 13 vols. New York: Printed for the Editor by R. & W. & G. Bartow, 1823.

Historical Society of Pennsylvania. "Extracts from the Records of the Courts Held in Germantown, from 1691 to 1707." Historical Society of Pennsylvania, *Collections* 1 (n.d.):243–58. Philadelphia: John Pennington, n.d.

Hoadly, Charles J., ed. *Records of the Colony and Plantation of New Haven [1638–1665].* 2 vols. Hartford: Printed by Case, Tiffany and Company, 1857.

Hoadly, Charles J., and J. H. Trumbull, eds. *Public Records of the Colony of Connecticut, 1636–1776.* 15 vols. Hartford: Brown and Parsons, 1850–90.

Hoffer, Peter C., ed. *Criminal Proceedings in Colonial Virginia.* Athens: University of Georgia Press, 1984.

Horle, Craig W., ed. *Records of the Courts of Sussex County Delaware, 1677–1710.* 2 vols. Philadelphia: University of Pennsylvania Press, 1991.

Hutchinson, Thomas. *The History of the Colony and Province of Massachusetts Bay.* Edited by Lawrence Shaw Mayo. Cambridge, Mass.: Harvard University Press, 1936.

Jameson, J. Franklin, ed. *Johnson's Wonder-Working Providence, 1628–1651.* New York: Charles Scribner's Sons, 1910.

Kavenaugh, W. Keith, ed. *Foundations of Colonial America: A Documentary History.* 6 vols. New York: Chelsea House, 1983.

Kingsbury, S. M., ed. *The Records of the Virginia Company of London:*

The Court Book, from Manuscripts in the Library of Congress. 4 vols. Washington, D.C.: U.S. Government Printing Office, 1933.

Konig, David Thomas, ed. *Plymouth Court Records, 1686–1859.* 3 vols. to date. Wilmington, Del.: Glazier, 1978.

Labaree, Leonard W., ed. *Royal Instructions to British Colonial Governors, 1670–1776.* New York: D. Appleton Century Company, 1935.

LaFantasie, Glenn W., ed. *The Correspondence of Roger Williams.* 2 vols. Published for the Rhode Island Historical Society. Providence: Brown University Press/University Press of New England, 1988.

Lapp, Dorothy, comp. *Records of the Courts of Chester County, Pennsylvania.* Danboro, Penn.: Published by Richard T. and Mildred C. Williams, 1972.

Libby, Charles T., Neal W. Allen, and Robert E. Moody, eds. *Province and Court Records of Maine, 1636–1692.* 4 vols. Portland: Maine Historical Society, 1928–47.

McDonald, William, ed. *Select Charters and Other Documents Illustrative of American History, 1606–1775.* New York: Macmillan, 1899.

McIlwaine, H. R., ed. *Executive Journals of the Council of Colonial Virginia, 1680–1721.* 3 vols. Richmond: Davis Bottom, Superintendent of Public Printing, 1925–27.

———, ed. *Legislative Journals of the Council of Colonial Virginia.* 3 vols. Richmond: Virginia State Library, 1918–19.

———, ed. *Minutes of the Council and General Court of Colonial Virginia, 1622–1632, 1670–1676, with Notes and Excerpts from Original Council and General Court Records, into 1683, Now Lost.* Richmond: Virginia State Library, 1924.

McIlwaine, H. R., and John P. Kennedy, eds. *Journals of the House of Burgesses of Virginia, 1619–1776.* 13 vols. Richmond: Virginia State Library, 1924.

Maryland Historical Society. *The Calvert Papers.* 3 vols. Baltimore: John Murphy and Company, 1889–99.

Massachusetts Historical Society. "Extracts from the Records of the Province of Maine." *Collections of the Massachusetts Historical Society for the Year 1792,* vol. 1. Boston, 1792.

———. *The Winthrop Papers, 1498–1649.* 5 vols. Boston: Massachusetts Historical Society, 1929–47.

Minutes of the Board of Proprietors of the Eastern Division of New Jersey from 1685 to 1705. Perth Amboy, N.J.: Published by the Board of Proprietors of the Eastern Division of New Jersey, 1949.

Mitchell, James T., and Henry Flanders, comps. *The Statutes at Large of Pennsylvania from 1682 to 1801.* 9 vols. Harrisburg, 1896–1915.

Moody, Robert E., ed. *The Saltonstall Papers, 1607–1815; Volume I: 1607–1789.* Boston: Massachusetts Historical Society, 1972.

Morris, Richard B., ed. *Select Cases of the Mayor's Court of New York City, 1674–1784.* Washington, D.C.: American Historical Association, 1935.

New York Historical Society. "Proceedings of the General Court of Assizes Held in the City of New York, Oct. 6, 1680 to Oct. 6, 1682," and "Minutes of the Superior Court of Judicature, April 4, 1693 to April 1, 1701." New York Historical Society, *Collections* 45 (1912). New York: Printed for the Society, 1913.

Noble, John, and John F. Cronin, eds. *Records of the Court of Assistants of the Colony of Massachusetts Bay, 1630–1692.* 3 vols. Boston: Published by the County of Suffolk, 1901–28.

O'Callaghan, Edmund B., ed. *Journal of the Legislative Council of the Colony of New York, Began the 9th Day of April, 1691; and Ended the 27 of September, 1743.* Albany: Weed, Parsons, and Company, Printers, 1861.

———, ed. *The Documentary History of New York; Arranged under the Direction of the Hon. Christopher Morgan, Secretary of State.* 4 vols. Albany: Weed, Parsons, and Co., Public Printers, 1849–51.

O'Callaghan, Edmund B., and Berthold Fernow, eds. *Documents Relative to the Colonial History of the State of New York; Procured in Holland, England and France by John Romeyn Brodhead, Esq., Agent.* 15 vols. Albany, 1853–71.

Palmer, William P., ed. *Calendar of Virginia State Papers and Other Manuscripts, 1652–1781, Preserved in the Capitol at Richmond.* 11 vols. Richmond: R. F. Walker, Superintendent of Public Printing, 1875.

Paltsits, Victor Hugo, ed. *Minutes of the Executive Council of the Province of New York, Administration of Francis Lovelace, 1668–1673.* 2 vols. Albany: Published by the State of New York, 1910.

Parker, Mattie Erma Edwards, ed. *North Carolina Charters and Constitutions, 1578–1698.* Raleigh: State Department of Archives and History, 1963.

Parker, Mattie Erma Edwards, William S. Price, and Robert Cain, eds. *North Carolina Higher-Court Records, 1670–1696.* 5 vols. Raleigh: State Department of Archives and History, 1963–81.

Records of the Court of Newcastle on Delaware, 1676–1681. Genealogical Society of Pennsylvania, *Collections* 68, 69 (1904).

Records of the Court of New Castle on Delaware, 1681–1699. Philadelphia: Colonial Society of Pennsylvania, 1935.

"Records of the Suffolk County Court, 1671–1680." Colonial Society of Massachusetts, *Collections* 29, 30 (1933). 2 vols. Boston: Published for the Society, 1933.

Reed, H. Clay, and George J. Miller, eds. *The Burlington Court Book: A Record of Quaker Jurisprudence in West New Jersey, 1680–1709.* Washington, D.C.: American Historical Association, 1944.

Rhys, Ernest, ed. *Chronicles of the Pilgrim Fathers.* New York: E. P. Dutton, 1910.

Sainsbury, W. Noel, and others, eds. *Calendar of State Papers, Colonial Series, Preserved in the State Paper Department of Her Majesty's Public Record Office.* London: Her Majesty's Stationary Office, 1860–1910.

Salley, Alexander S., Jr., ed. *Narratives of Early Carolina, 1650–1708*. New York: Charles Scribner's Sons, 1911.

Saunders, W. I., ed. *Colonial Records of North Carolina (1662–1776)*. 10 vols. Raleigh: P. M. Hale, Printer to the State, 1886–90.

Shurtleff, Nathaniel B., ed. *Records of the Governor and Company of Massachusetts Bay in New England, 1628–1686*. 5 vols. in 6. Boston: William White, Printer to the Commonwealth, 1853–54.

Shurtleff, Nathaniel B., and David Pulsifer, eds. *Records of the Colony of New Plymouth in New England, 1620–1692*. 12 vols. Boston: From the Press of William White, Printer to the Commonwealth, 1855–61.

Silverman, Kenneth, comp. *Selected Letters of Cotton Mather*. Baton Rouge: Louisiana University Press, 1971.

Smith, Joseph H., ed. *Colonial Justice in Western Massachusetts (1639–1702): The Pynchon Court Record, An Original Judge's Diary of the Administration of Justice in the Springfield Courts in the Massachusetts Bay Colony*. Cambridge, Mass.: Harvard University Press, 1961.

Smith, Joseph H., and Philip A. Crowl, eds. *The Court Records of Prince George's County, Maryland, 1696–1699*. Washington, D.C.: American Historical Association, 1964.

Street, Charles R., comp. *Huntington Town Records, Including Babylon, Long Island, N.Y., 1653–1688*. 2 vols. Huntington and Babylon: Published by Authority and at the Expense of the Two Towns, 1887.

Sweeny, William K. "Gleanings from the Records of (Old) Rappahannock County and Essex County, Virginia." *William and Mary Quarterly*, 2d ser., 18 (1938): 297–313.

Thomas, M. Halsey, ed. *The Diary of Samuel Sewall, 1674–1729*. 2 vols. New York: Farrar, Straus and Giroux, 1973.

Toppan, Robert N., comp. "Dudley Records." Massachusetts Historical Society, *Proceedings*. 2d ser., 13 (1899):226–86. Boston: Massachusetts Historical Society, 1900.

——, ed. *Edward Randolph: Including His Letters and Official Papers from the New England, Middle, and Southern Colonies in America, with Other Documents Relating Chiefly to the Vacating of the Royal Charter of the Colony of Massachusetts Bay, 1676–1703*. 7 vols. Boston: Prince Society, 1898.

Town Clerk, comp. *Records [of the] Town of Brookhaven up to 1800*. Patchogue, N.Y.: Printed at the Office of the Advance, 1880.

Trumbull, Annie E., ed. *Records of the Particular Court of the Colony of Connecticut, Administration of Sir Edmund Andros, Royal Governor, 1687–1688*. Hartford: Case, Lockwood, and Brainard, 1935.

Turner, Charles H. B., comp. *Some Records of Sussex County, Delaware*. Philadelphia: Allen, Lane, and Scott, 1909.

Tyler, Lyon G., ed. *Narratives of Early Virginia, 1606–1625*. New York: Charles Scribner's Sons, 1907.

van Laer, A.J.F., ed. *Court Minutes of Albany, Rensselaerswyck, and Sche-*

nectady, 1668–1685. 3 vols. Albany: University Press of New York, 1926–32.

Virginia Historical Society. *Journal of the London Company (1619–1624).* Virginia Historical Society, *Collections,* n.s., 7 (1888), 1 and 2.

———. "Virginia Council and General Court Records, 1640–1641," from "Robinson's Notes." Virginia Historical Society, *Collections* 2:277–84.

Whitehead, William A., Frederick W. Ricord, William Nelson, and others, eds. *Archives of the State of New Jersey.* 1st ser., *Documents Relating to the Colonial History of the State of New Jersey.* 27 vols. Newark: Printed at the Daily Journal Establishment, 1880–1906.

Whitmore, William H., ed. *The Colonial Laws of Massachusetts.* Reprinted from the edition of 1672, with supplements through 1686. Boston: Rockwell and Churchill, City Printers, 1890.

Wingfield, Edward Maria. "A Discourse of Virginia." *Transactions and Collections of the American Antiquarian Society* 4 (1859):77–98. Boston: John Williams and Son, 1860.

Winthrop, John. *Winthrop's Journal: "History of New England," 1630–1649.* Edited by James Kendall Hosmer. 2 vols. New York: Barnes and Noble, 1946.

Winthrop, Robert C., ed. *Life and Letters of John Winthrop.* 2 vols. Boston: Little, Brown, and Company, 1869.

Young, Alexander, ed. *Chronicles of the First Planters of Massachusetts Bay, 1623–1636.* Boston: C. C. Little and J. Brown, 1846.

Secondary Sources

Adkins, E. Dale. "Early Courts of General Jurisdiction and the Eastern Shore of Maryland." *Maryland State Bar Association* 60 (1955):182.

Allen, David Grayson. *In English Ways: The Movement of Societies and the Transferal of English Local Law and Custom to Massachusetts Bay in the Seventeenth Century.* Chapel Hill: University of North Carolina Press, 1981.

Ames, Suzie M. "Law in Action: The Court Records of Virginia's Eastern Shore." *William and Mary Quarterly,* 3d ser., 4 (1947):177–91.

Anderson, David A. "The Origin of the Free Press Clause." *UCLA Law Review* 30 (1983):455–541.

Andrews, Charles M. *The Colonial Period of American History.* 4 vols. London: Oxford University Press, 1934. Reprint edition, New Haven: Yale University Press, 1964.

Andrews, Kenneth R., N. P. Canny, and P. E. H. Hair, eds. *The Westward Enterprise: English Activities in Ireland, the Atlantic and America, 1480–1650.* Detroit: Wayne State University Press, 1979.

Andrews, William. *Old Time Punishments.* New York, 1890. Reprint edition, Williamstown, Mass.: Corner House Publishers, 1977.

Archdeacon, Thomas F. *New York City, 1664–1710: Conquest and Change.* Ithaca, N.Y.: Cornell University Press, 1976.

Bassett, John S. *The Constitutional Beginnings of North Carolina (1663–1729).* Baltimore: Johns Hopkins University Press, 1894.

Baumgartner, M. P. "Law and Social Status in Colonial New Haven, 1639–1665." *Research in Law and Sociology* 1 (1978):153–74.

Beattie, John M. *Crime and the Courts in England, 1660–1800.* Princeton, N.J.: Princeton University Press, 1986.

———. "The Pattern of Crime in England, 1660–1800." *Past and Present,* no. 62 (1974):47–95.

Bellamy, John G. *The Tudor Law of Treason: An Introduction.* London: Routledge and Kegan Paul, 1979.

Bender, Thomas. *Community and Social Change in America.* New Brunswick, N.J.: Rutgers University Press, 1978.

Bergen, James. "Colonial Courts of Somerset County." *New Jersey Law Journal* 29 (1906):358.

Bigelow, John O. "A Chapter in Chancery of New Jersey." *New Jersey Law Journal* 59 (1936):193–97 passim.

Billias, George A., ed. *Law and Authority in Colonial America: Selected Essays.* Barre, Mass.: Barre Publishers, 1965.

Billings, Warren M. "English Legal Literature as a Source of Law and Legal Practice for Seventeenth-Century Virginia." *Virginia Magazine of History and Biography* 87 (1979):403–16.

———. "The Growth of Political Institutions in Virginia, 1634–1676." *William and Mary Quarterly,* 3d ser., 31 (1974):225–42.

Billings, Warren M., John E. Selby, and Thad W. Tate. *Colonial Virginia: A History.* White Plains, N.Y.: KTO Press, 1986.

Black, Barbara A. "Community and Law in Seventeenth Century Massachusetts," *Yale Law Review* 19 (1980):232–46.

Blackstone, Sir William. *Commentaries on the Laws of England in Four Books.* 4 vols. Edited by William Draper Lewis. Philadelphia: Rees, Welsh, and Company, 1902.

Blume, William W., and Elizabeth G. Brown. "Territorial Courts and Law: Unifying Factors in the Development of American Legal Institutions." *Michigan Law Review* 39 (1962–63):467.

Bonomi, Patricia U. *A Factious People: Politics and Society in Colonial New York.* New York: Columbia University Press, 1971.

Botein, Stephen. *Early American Law and Society.* New York: Alfred A. Knopf, 1983.

Boyer, Paul, and Stephen Nissenbaum. *Salem Possessed: The Social Origins of Witchcraft.* Cambridge, Mass.: Harvard University Press, 1974.

Brant, Irving. "Seditious Libel: Myth and Reality." *NYU Law Review* 39 (1964):1–8.

Breen, T. H. *The Character of a Good Ruler: A Study of Puritan Political*

Ideas in New England, 1630–1730. New Haven: Yale University Press, 1970.

———. "Looking Out for Number One: Conflicting Cultural Values in Early Seventeenth-Century Virginia." *South Atlantic Quarterly* 78 (1979): 342–60.

Brewer, John, and John Styles. *An Ungovernable People: The English and Their Law in the Seventeenth and Eighteenth Centuries.* New Brunswick, N.J.: Rutgers University Press, 1980.

Bridenbaugh, Carl. *Fat Mutton and Liberty of Conscience: Society in Rhode Island, 1636–1690.* Providence: Brown University Press, 1974.

———. *Jamestown, 1544–1699.* New York: Oxford University Press, 1980.

Bronner, Edwin B. *William Penn's Holy Experiment: The Founding of Pennsylvania, 1681–1701.* New York: Temple University Publications, 1962.

Brown, Katherine B. "Freemanship in Puritan Massachusetts." *American Historical Review* 54 (1954):865–83.

Bruce, Philip Alexander. *Economic History of Virginia in the Seventeenth Century: An Inquiry into the Material Condition of the People, Based upon Original and Contemporaneous Records.* New York: Macmillan, 1896.

———. *Institutional History of Virginia in the Seventeenth Century: An Inquiry into the Religious, Moral, Educational, Legal, Military, and Political Condition of the People, Based on Original and Contemporaneous Records.* 2 vols. New York: G. P. Putnam's Sons, 1910.

Burney, Eugenia. *Colonial North Carolina.* New York: Thomas Nelson, 1975.

Bushman, Richard L. *From Puritan to Yankee: Character and the Social Order in Connecticut, 1690–1765.* Cambridge, Mass.: Harvard University Press, 1967.

Butler, Lindley S. "The Early Settlement of Carolina." *Virginia Magazine of History and Biography* 79 (1971):20.

Cahn, Mark D. "Punishment, Discretion, and the Codification of Proscribed Penalties in Colonial Massachusetts." *American Journal of Legal History* 33 (1989):101–36.

Carr, Lois Green, and David William Jordan. *Maryland's Revolution in Government, 1689–92.* Ithaca, N.Y.: Cornell University Press, 1974.

Carr, Lois Green, Phillip D. Morgan, and Jean B. Russo, eds. *Colonial Chesapeake Society.* Chapel Hill: University of North Carolina Press, 1988.

Chafee, Zechariah, Jr. "Colonial Courts and the Common Law." *Massachusetts Historical Society, Proceedings* 68 (1952):132–59.

———. *Free Speech in the United States.* Cambridge, Mass.: Harvard University Press, 1964.

———. *Freedom of Speech.* New York: Harcourt, Brace and Howe, 1920.

Chapin, Bradley. *Criminal Justice in Colonial America, 1606–1660.* Athens: University of Georgia Press, 1983.

Chitwood, Oliver P. *Justice in Colonial Virginia*. Baltimore: Johns Hopkins University Press, 1905. Reprint edition, New York: De Capo Press, 1971.

——. "Justice in Colonial Virginia." *West Virginia Law Quarterly* 32 (1926):83–269 passim.

Chumbley, George L. *Colonial Justice in Virginia: The Development of a Judicial System, Typical Laws and Cases of the Period*. Richmond: Deitz Press, 1938.

Clarke, Mary Patterson. *Parliamentary Privilege in the American Colonies*. New Haven: Yale University Press, 1943.

Cockburn, J. S. *A History of the English Assizes, 1558–1714*. Cambridge, U.K.: Cambridge University Press, 1972.

——, ed. *Crime in England, 1550–1800*. Princeton, N.J.: Princeton University Press, 1977.

Cockburn, J. S., and Thomas A. Green, eds. *Twelve Good Men and True: The Criminal Trial Jury in England, 1200–1800*. Princeton, N.J.: Princeton University Press, 1988.

Colonial Society of Massachusetts. *Law in Colonial Massachusetts, 1630–1800*. Colonial Society of Massachusetts, Collections 62. Boston, 1984.

Condon, Thomas J. *New York Beginnings: The Commercial Origins of New Netherland*. New York: New York University Press, 1968.

Conklin, W. E. "Origins of the Law of Sedition." *Criminal Law Quarterly* 15 (1973):277.

Cook, Edward M. *The Fathers of the Towns: Leadership and Community Structure in Eighteenth-Century New England*. Baltimore: Johns Hopkins University Press, 1976.

"The Courts of New York and the Reports of Their Decisions." *Abbott New York Digest* 6 (1942):143–75.

Craven, Wesley F. *The Colonies in Transition, 1660–1713*. New York: Harper and Row, 1967.

——. *The Southern Colonies in the Seventeenth Century, 1607–1689*. Baton Rouge: Louisiana State University Press, 1949.

——. *White, Red and Black: The Seventeenth-Century Virginian*. Charlottesville: University Press of Virginia,1971.

Daniell, Jere R. *Colonial New Hampshire: A History*. Millwood, N.Y.: KTO Press, 1981.

Daniels, Bruce C. *The Connecticut Town*. Middletown, Conn.: Wesleyan University Press, 1979.

——. *Dissent and Conformity on Narragansett Bay: The Colonial Rhode Island Town*. Middletown, Conn.: Wesleyan University Press, 1983.

——, ed. *Town and Country: Essays on the Structure of Local Government in the American Colonies*. Middletown, Conn.: Wesleyan University Press, 1978.

Davies, Kenneth G. *The North Atlantic World in the Seventeenth Century*. Minneapolis: University of Minnesota Press, 1974.

Dawes, Norman H. "Titles as Symbols of Prestige in Seventeenth-Century New England." *William and Mary Quarterly*, 3d ser., 6 (1949):69–83.

Demos, John. *A Little Commonwealth: Family Life in Plymouth Colony.* New York: Oxford University Press, 1970.

Dow, George Francis. *Everyday Life in the Massachusetts Bay Colony.* Boston: Society for the Preservation of New England Antiquities, 1935. Reprint edition, New York: Dover, 1988.

Dowdel, E. G. *A Hundred Years of Quarter Sessions: The Government of Middlesex from 1660 to 1760.* Cambridge, U.K.: Cambridge University Press, 1932.

Duniway, Clyde Augustus. *The Development of Freedom of the Press in Massachusetts.* Cambridge, Mass.: Harvard University Press, 1906.

Eades, Ronald W. "Control of Seditious Libel as a Basis for the Development of the Law of Obscenity." *Akron Law Review* 11 (1977):29–58.

Earle, Alice Morse. *Colonial Days in Old New York.* New York: Charles Scribner's Sons, 1896. Reprint edition, New York: Empire State Book Co., 1926.

———. *Curious Punishments of Bygone Days.* New York: Macmillan, 1896. Reprint edition, New York: Book League of America, 1929.

Earle, Carville V. *The Evolution of a Tidewater Settlement System: All Hallow's Parish, Maryland, 1650–1783.* Chicago: University of Chicago, Department of Geography, 1975.

Erikson, Kai T. *Wayward Puritans: A Study in the Sociology of Deviance.* New York: John Wiley and Sons, 1966.

Faber, Eli. "Puritan Criminals: The Economic, Social and Intellectual Background to Crime in Seventeenth-Century Massachusetts." *Perspectives in American History* 11 (1977–78):81–144.

Faught, Albert S. "Early Rules of Court in Pennsylvania." *Dickinson Law Review* 44 (1940):273–89.

Fitzroy, H. W. K. "The Punishment of Crime in Provincial Pennsylvania." *The Pennsylvania Magazine of History and Biography* 60 (1936):242–69.

Flaherty, David H. *Privacy in Colonial New England.* Charlottesville: University of Virginia Press, 1972.

———. "A Select Guide to the Manuscript Court Records of Colonial New England." *American Journal of Legal History* 11 (1967):107.

———. "A Select Guide to the Manuscript Court Records of Colonial Virginia." *American Journal of Legal History* 19 (1975):112–37.

———, ed. *Essays in the History of Early American Law.* Chapel Hill: University of North Carolina Press, 1969.

Frank, John P. Review of *Records of the Court of Chancery of South Carolina, 1671–1779. William and Mary Quarterly*, 3d ser., 8 (1951):155–57.

Friedman, Lawrence M. *A History of American Law.* New York: Simon and Schuster, 1973.

Geiger, Marilyn L. *The Administration of Justice in Colonial Maryland, 1632–1689.* New York: Garland, 1987.

Goebel, Julius, Jr. "King's Law and Custom in Seventeenth-Century New England." *Columbia Law Review* 31 (1931):416–48.

Goebel, Julius, Jr., and T. Raymond Naughton. *Law Enforcement in Colonial New York: A Study in Criminal Procedure (1664–1776).* New York: Commonwealth Fund, 1944.

Grant, Charles S. *Democracy in the Connecticut Frontier Town of Kent.* New York: Columbia University Press, 1961.

Green, Thomas A. *Verdict According to Conscience: Perspectives on the English Trial Jury, 1200–1800.* Chicago: University of Chicago Press, 1980.

Greenberg, Douglas. *Crime and Law Enforcement in the Colony of New York, 1691–1776.* Ithaca, N.Y.: Cornell University Press, 1976.

———. "Crime, Law Enforcement, and Social Control in Colonial America." *American Journal of Legal History* 26 (1982):293–325.

Greene, Evarts B., and Virginia D. Harrington. *American Population before the Federal Census of 1790.* New York: Columbia University Press, 1932.

Greene, Jack P. *Pursuits of Happiness: The Social Development of Early Modern British Colonies and the Formation of American Culture.* Chapel Hill: University of North Carolina Press, 1988.

———. *The Quest for Power: The Lower House of Assembly in the Southern Royal Colonies, 1689–1776.* New York: W. W. Norton, 1972.

———, ed. *Great Britain and the American Colonies, 1606–1763.* Columbia: University of South Carolina Press, 1970.

Greene, Jack P., and J. R. Pole, eds. *Colonial British America: Essays in the New History of the Early Modern Era.* Baltimore: Johns Hopkins University Press, 1984.

Greven, Philip J. *Four Generations: Population, Land, and Family in Colonial Andover, Massachusetts.* Ithaca, N.Y.: Cornell University Press, 1970.

Haight, Elizabeth S. "The Northampton Protest of 1652: A Petition to the General Assembly from the Inhabitants of Virginia's Eastern Shore." *American Journal of Legal History* 28 (1984):364–75.

Hall, David D., John M. Murrin, and Thad W. Tate, eds. *Saints and Revolutionaries: Essays on Early American History.* New York: W. W. Norton, 1984.

Hall, Kermit. *The Magic Mirror: Law in American History.* New York: Oxford University Press, 1989.

Hamburger, Philip A. "The Development of the Law of Seditious Libel and the Control of the Press." *Stanford Law Review* 37 (1985):661–765.

Hamlin, Elbert B. "The Court of Common Pleas." *Connecticut Bar Journal* 9 (1935):202–5.

Hanley, Thomas O. *Their Rights and Liberties: The Beginnings of Religious and Political Freedom in Maryland.* Westminster, Md.: Newman Press, 1959.

Haskins, George L. "Codification of the Law in Colonial Massachusetts: A Study in Comparative Law." *Indiana Law Journal* 30 (1954):1–17.

———. *Law and Authority in Early Massachusetts: A Study in Tradition and Design*. New York: Macmillan, 1960.

Haskins, George L., and Samuel E. Ewing. "The Spread of Massachusetts Law in the Seventeenth Century." *University of Pennsylvania Law Review* 106 (1958):413.

Helmholz, R. H., and Thomas A. Greene. *Juries, Libel and Justice: The Role of English Juries in Seventeenth- and Eighteenth-Century Trials for Libel and Slander*. Pasadena, Calif.: Castle Press, 1984.

Henretta, James, Michael Kammen, and Stanley N. Katz, eds. *The Transformation of Early American History: Society, Authority, and Ideology*. New York: Alfred A. Knopf, 1991.

Hentoff, Nat. *The First Freedom: The Tumultuous History of Free Speech in America*. New York: Delacorte Press, 1980.

Herring, R. W. "The Judicial System of the Proprietary and Royal Governments in North Carolina." *North Carolina Journal of Law* 1 (1904):286–359.

Herrup, Cynthia B. *The Common Peace: Participation and the Criminal Law in Seventeenth-Century England*. Cambridge, U.K.: Cambridge University Press, 1987.

Hirst, Derek. *Authority and Conflict: England, 1603–1658*. Cambridge, Mass.: Harvard University Press, 1986.

Hoffer, Peter C. *Law and People in Colonial America*. Baltimore: Johns Hopkins University Press, 1992.

Hoffer, Peter C., and N. E. H. Hull. *Impeachment in America, 1635–1805*. New Haven: Yale University Press, 1984.

Holdsworth, Sir William S. *A History of English Law*. 16 vols. London: Methuen, 1922–52.

Howe, Mark DeWolf. "Records of the Suffolk County Court." *The New England Quarterly* 7 (1934):307–14.

———, ed. *Readings in American Legal History*. Cambridge, Mass.: Harvard University Press, 1949. Reprint edition, New York: De Capo Press, 1971.

Howe, Mark DeWolf, and Louis F. Eaton. "The Supreme Judicial Power in the Colony of Massachusetts Bay." *New England Quarterly* 20 (1947):291–316.

Hudon, Edward G. *Freedom of Speech and Press in America*. Washington, D.C.: Public Affairs Press, 1970.

Hurst, J. Willard. "Treason in the United States." *Harvard Law Review* 58 (1944):226–72.

———. *The Law of Treason in the United States: Collected Essays*. Westport, Conn.: Greenwood, 1945.

Illick, Joseph E. *Colonial Pennsylvania: A History*. New York: Charles Scribner's Sons, 1976.

Isaac, Rhys. "Order and Growth, Authority and Meaning in Colonial New England." *American Historical Review* 76 (1971):728–37.

Ives, Joseph M. *The Ark and the Dove: The Beginning of Civil and Religious Liberties in America.* New York: Cooper Square, 1969.

James, Sydney V. *Colonial Rhode Island: A History.* New York: Charles Scribner's Sons, 1975.

Jeffrey, William, Jr. "Early American Court Records—A Bibliography of Printed Materials: The Middle Colonies." *University of Cincinnati Law Review* 39 (1970):685–710.

———. "Early New England Court Records—A Bibliography of Published Materials." *American Journal of Legal History* 1 (1957):119–47.

Johnson, Herbert A. *Essays on New York Colonial Legal History.* Westport, Conn.: Greenwood Press, 1981.

———, ed. *South Carolina Legal History.* Spartansburg: University of South Carolina Press, 1980.

Jones, Alice Hanson. *The Wealth of a Nation to Be: The American Colonies on the Eve of the Revolution.* New York: Columbia University Press, 1980.

Kammen, Michael. "Colonial Court Records and American History." *American Historical Review* 70 (1965):732–39.

———. *Colonial New York: A History.* New York: Charles Scribner's Sons, 1975.

———. *Spheres of Liberty: Changing Perceptions of Liberty in American Culture.* Madison: University of Wisconsin Press, 1986.

Katz, Stanley N., and John M. Murrin, eds. *Colonial America: Essays in Politics and Social Development.* 3d ed. New York: Alfred A. Knopf, 1983.

Koestler, Samuel. "History and Development of Chancery Court of New Jersey." *New Jersey Law Journal* 59 (1936):17–18, 21–23.

Konig, David T. *Law and Society in Puritan Massachusetts: Essex County, 1629–1692.* Chapel Hill: University of North Carolina Press, 1979.

Konvitz, Milton R., and Clinton Rossiter, eds. *Aspects of Liberty: Essays Presented to Robert E. Cushman.* Ithaca, N.Y.: Cornell University Press, 1958.

Kross, Jessica. *The Evolution of an American Town: Newtown, New York, 1642–1775.* Philadelphia: Temple University Press, 1983.

Labaree, Benjamin W. *Colonial Massachusetts: A History.* Millwood, N.Y.: KTO Press, 1979.

Land, Aubrey C. *Colonial Maryland: A History.* Millwood, N.Y.: KTO Press, 1981.

Land, Aubrey C., Lois Green Carr, and Edward C. Papenfuse, eds. *Law, Society, and Politics in Early Maryland.* Baltimore: Johns Hopkins University Press, 1977.

Langbein, John H. "The Criminal Trial before the Lawyers." *University of Chicago Law Review* 45 (1978):263–316.

Lawhorne, Clifton O. *Defamation and Public Officials: The Evolving Law of Libel.* Carbondale: University of Southern Illinois Press, 1971.

Leach, Douglas E. *The Northern Colonial Frontier, 1607–1763.* New York: Holt, Rinehart and Winston, 1966.

Leder, Lawrence H. *Liberty and Authority: Early American Political Ideology, 1689–1763.* Chicago: Quadrangle Books, 1968.

Lee, Carol F. "Discretionary Justice in Early Massachusetts." *Essex Institute Historical Collections* 112 (1976):120–39.

Lee, Francis B. "An Outline Sketch of Some of the Early West Jersey Courts." *New Jersey Law Journal* 14 (1891):357, and 15 (1892):4.

Lefler, Hugh T., and William S. Powell. *Colonial North Carolina: A History.* New York: Charles Scribner's Sons, 1973.

Lemon, James T. *The Best Poor Man's Country: A Geographical Study of Early Southeastern Pennsylvania.* Baltimore: Johns Hopkins University Press, 1972.

Levy, Leonard W. *Emergence of A Free Press.* New York: Oxford University Press, 1985.

———. *Legacy of Suppression: Freedom of Speech and Press in Early American History.* New York: Oxford University Press, 1960.

———. "On the Origins of the Free Press Clause." *UCLA Law Review* 32 (1984):177–218.

Lockridge, Kenneth A. *A New England Town: The First Hundred Years.* New York: W. W. Norton, 1970.

Lovejoy, David S. *The Glorious Revolution in America.* New York: Harper and Row, 1972.

Lubasz, H. M. "Public Opinion Comes of Age: Reform of the Libel Law in the Eighteenth Century." *History Today* 8 (1958):453–61.

McCain, Paul M. *The County Court in North Carolina before 1750.* Durham, N.C.: Duke University Press, 1954.

———. "Magistrates Courts in Early North Carolina." *North Carolina Historical Review* 48 (1971):23–30.

McConnell, Edward B. "A Brief History of the New Jersey Courts." *West's New Jersey Digest* 7 (1954):349–58.

McCormick, Charles H. *Leisler's Rebellion.* Ann Arbor, Mich.: University Microfilms, 1971.

McCusker, John J. *Money and Exchange in Europe and America, 1600–1775: A Handbook.* Chapel Hill: University of North Carolina Press, 1978.

McGuire, F. H. "The General Court of Virginia." *Virginia State Bar Association* 7 (1895):197.

Mann, Bruce H. *Neighbors and Strangers: Law and Community in Early Connecticut.* Chapel Hill: University of North Carolina Press, 1987.

Mayton, William T. "Seditious Libel and the Lost Guarantee of Freedom of Expression." *Columbia Law Review* 84 (1984):91–142.

Melvoin, Richard I. *New England Outpost: War and Society in Colonial Deerfield.* New York: W. W. Norton, 1989.

Miller, George J. "The Courts of Chancery in New Jersey, 1684–1696." *New Jersey Law Journal* 58 (1935):1, 3–5.

Morgan, Edmund S. *American Slavery—American Freedom: The Ordeal of Colonial Virginia.* New York: W. W. Norton, 1975.

Morison, Samuel Eliot. *Builders of the Bay Colony.* Boston: Houghton Mifflin, 1930.

Morris, Richard B. "Massachusetts and the Common Law: The Declaration of 1646." *American Historical Review* 31 (1926):443–53.

———. "The Sources of Early American Law: Colonial Period." *West Virginia Law Quarterly* (1934):212–23.

———. *Studies in the History of American Law: With Special Reference to the Seventeenth and Eighteenth Centuries.* New York: Columbia University Press, 1930.

Munroe, John A. *Colonial Delaware: A History.* Millwood, N.Y.: KTO Press, 1978.

Neill, Edward D. *Terra Mariae, or Threads of Maryland Colonial History.* Philadelphia: J. B. Lippincott, 1867.

Nelson, Harold L. "Seditious Libel in Colonial America." *American Journal of Legal History* 3 (1959):160–72.

Noel, Dix W. "Defamation of Public Officers and Candidates." *Columbia Law Review* 49 (1949):875–903.

Ogilvie, Sir Charles. *The King's Government and the Common Law, 1471–1641.* Oxford: Basil Blackwell, 1958.

Page, Elwin L. *Judicial Beginnings in New Hampshire, 1640–1700.* Concord: New Hampshire Historical Society, 1959.

Pencak, William. *War, Politics, and Revolution in Provincial Massachusetts.* Boston: Northeastern University Press, 1981.

Pencak, William, and Wythe Holt, Jr., eds. *The Law in America, 1607–1861.* New York: New York Historical Society, 1989.

Perkins, Edwin J. *The Economy of Colonial America.* New York: Columbia University Press, 1980.

Pomfret, John E. *Colonial New Jersey: A History.* New York: Charles Scribner's Sons, 1973.

———. *The Province of East New Jersey, 1609–1702.* Princeton, N.J.: Princeton University Press, 1962.

———. *The Province of West New Jersey, 1609–1702: A History of the Origins of an American Colony.* Princeton, N.J.: Princeton University Press, 1956.

Pomfret, John E., and Floyd M. Shumway. *Founding the American Colonies, 1583–1660.* New York: Harper and Row, 1970.

Powe, Lucas A., Jr. *The Fourth Estate and the Constitution: Freedom of the Press in America.* Berkeley: University of California Press, 1991.

Powell, Sumner C. *Puritan Village: The Formation of a New England Town.* Middletown, Conn.: Wesleyan University Press, 1963.

Powers, Edwin. *Crime and Punishment in Early Massachusetts, 1620–1692: A Documentary History.* Boston: Beacon Press, 1966.

Prager, Herta, and William W. Price. "A Bibliography of the Courts of the Thirteen Original States, Maine, Ohio and Vermont." *American Journal of Legal History* 1 (1957):336–62. This is part one. Part two appears in *American Journal of Legal History* 2 (1958):35–52 and 148–54.

Preyer, Kathryn. "Penal Measures in the American Colonies: An Overview." *American Journal of Legal History* 26 (1982):326–53.

Prince, W. F. "The First Criminal Code of Virginia." *Annual Report of the American Historical Association* 1 (1899).

Proctor, L. B. "Court of Chancery of New York. Opening of First Trial Term with Scenes and Anecdotes." *Albany Law Journal* 49 (1894):236.

Rankin, Hugh F. *Criminal Trial Proceedings in the General Court of Colonial Virginia.* Charlottesville: University Press of Virginia, 1965.

Reed, Clay H. "The Court Records of the Delaware Valley." *William and Mary Quarterly,* 3d ser., 4 (1947):192–202.

Reid, John G. *Acadia, Maine, and New Scotland: Marginal Colonies in the Seventeenth Century.* Toronto: University of Toronto Press, 1981.

Ritchie, Robert C. *The Duke's Province: A Study of New York Politics and Society, 1664–1691.* Chapel Hill: University of North Carolina Press, 1977.

Robinson, Conway. "Virginia Courts and Reports." *Virginia Reports* 40 (1843):iii–x.

Roeber, A. G. *Faithful Magistrates and Republican Lawyers: Creators of Virginia Legal Culture, 1680–1810.* Chapel Hill: University of North Carolina Press, 1981.

Rutman, Darrett B. *Winthrop's Boston: A Portrait of a Puritan Town, 1630–1649.* New York: W. W. Norton, 1965.

Rutman, Darrett B., and Anita H. Rutman. *A Place in Time: Middlesex County, Virginia, 1650–1750.* New York: W. W. Norton, 1984.

Samaha, Joel. "Gleanings from Local Criminal-Court Records: Sedition amongst the 'Inarticulate' in Elizabethan Essex." *Journal of Social History* 8 (1975):61–79.

———. *Law and Order in Historical Perspective: The Case of Elizabethan Essex.* New York: Academic Press, 1973.

Scott, Arthur P. *Criminal Law in Colonial Virginia.* Chicago: University of Chicago Press, 1930.

Semmes, Raphael. *Captains and Mariners of Early Maryland.* Baltimore: Johns Hopkins University Press, 1937.

———. *Crime and Punishment in Early Maryland.* Baltimore: Johns Hopkins University Press, 1938.

Sharpe, J. A. *Crime in Early Modern England, 1550–1750.* London: Longman, 1984.

———. *Crime in Seventeenth Century England: A County Study.* Cambridge, U.K.: Cambridge University Press, 1983.

Shoemaker, Robert Brink. *Prosecution and Punishment: Petty Crime and the Law in London and Rural Middlesex, 1660–1725.* Cambridge, U.K.: Cambridge University Press, 1991.

Siebert, Frederick S. *Freedom of the Press in England, 1476–1776.* Urbana: University of Illinois Press, 1952.

Smith, James Morton, ed. *Seventeenth-Century America: Essays in Colonial History.* Chapel Hill: University of North Carolina Press, 1960.

Smith, Jeffrey A. *Printers and Press Freedom: The Ideology of Early American Journalism.* New York: Oxford University Press, 1988.

Smith, Joseph H. *Appeals to the Privy Council from the American Plantations.* New York: Columbia University Press, 1950.

Sosin, J. M. *English America and Imperial Inconstancy: The Rise of Provincial Autonomy, 1696–1715.* Lincoln: University of Nebraska Press, 1985.

Spindel, Donna J. *Crime and Society in North Carolina, 1663–1776.* Baton Rouge: Louisiana State University Press, 1989.

Spindel, Donna J., and Stuart W. Thomas, Jr. "Crime and Society in North Carolina, 1663–1740." *Journal of Southern History* 56, no. 2 (1983): 223–44.

Stephen, James F. *A History of the Criminal Law of England.* 3 vols. London: Macmillan, 1883.

Surrency, Erwin C. "The Courts in the American Colonies." *American Journal of Legal History* 11 (1966):253–76.

Sutherland, Stella H. *Population Distribution in Colonial America.* New York: Columbia University Press, 1936.

Tate, Thad, and David Ammerman, eds. *The Chesapeake in the Seventeenth Century: Essays on Anglo-American Society.* Chapel Hill: University of North Carolina Press, 1979.

Taylor, Robert J. *Colonial Connecticut: A History.* Millwood, N.Y.: KTO Press, 1979.

Thompson, Roger. "'Hold Watchfulness' and Communal Conformism: The Functions of Defamation in Early New England Communities." *New England Quarterly* 56(4) (1983):504–22.

———. *Sex in Middlesex: Popular Mores in a Massachusetts County, 1649–1699.* Amherst: University of Massachusetts Press, 1986.

Van Deventer, David E. *The Emergence of Provincial New Hampshire, 1623–1741.* Baltimore: Johns Hopkins University Press, 1976.

Van Veeder, Vechten. "The History and Theory of the Law of Defamation." *Columbia Law Review* 8 (1903):546–73.

Vaughan, Alden T. *American Genesis: Captain John Smith and the Founding of Virginia.* Boston: Little, Brown and Company, 1975.

Vaughan, Alden T., and George A. Billias, eds. *Perspectives on Early American History: Essays in Honor of Richard B. Morris.* New York: Harper and Row, 1973.

Wall, Robert E., Jr. *Massachusetts Bay: The Crucial Decade, 1640–1650.* New Haven: Yale University Press, 1972.

Walsh, Lorena S., and Russell R. Menard. "Death in the Chesapeake: Two Life Tables for Men in Early Colonial Maryland." *Maryland Historical Magazine* 69 (1974):211–27.

Warden, Robert. "Law Reform in England and New England, 1620 to 1660." *William and Mary Quarterly*, 3d ser., 35 (1978):668–90.

Watson, Alan D. "The Constable in Colonial North Carolina." *North Carolina Historical Review* 68 (1991):1–16.

Webb, Stephen Saunders. *The Governors-General: The English Army and the Definition of the Empire, 1569–1681.* Chapel Hill: University of North Carolina Press, 1979.

Weir, Robert W. *Colonial South Carolina: A History.* Millwood, N.Y.: KTO Press, 1983.

Weiss, Harry B., and Grace M. Weiss. *An Introduction to Crime and Punishment in Colonial New Jersey.* Trenton: Past Time Press, 1960.

Weisser, Michael R. *Crime and Punishment in Early Modern Europe (1350–1850).* Sussex, U.K.: Harvester Press, 1979.

Wells, Robert V. *The Population of the British Colonies in America Before 1776: A Survey of Census Data.* Princeton, N.J.: Princeton University Press, 1975.

Wolf, Stephanie G. *Urban Village: Population, Community, and Family Structure in Germantown, Pennsylvania, 1683–1800.* Princeton, N.J.: Princeton University Press, 1976.

Wright, Louis B. *The Atlantic Frontier: Colonial American Civilization, 1607–1763.* New York: Alfred A. Knopf, 1947. Reprint edition, Ithaca, N.Y.: Cornell University Press, 1964.

———. *The Cultural Life of the American Colonies, 1607–1763.* New York: Harper and Row, 1957.

Zanger, Jules. "Crime and Punishment in Early Massachusetts." *William and Mary Quarterly*, 3d ser., 22 (1965):471–77.

Index

Acquittal rates, 83; in jury trials, 86
Admonition: as a form of punishment,
121–22
Alcohol: as an excuse for seditious
words, 44, 156–57 n. 29; false
accusation of judges drinking, 58;
seditious words spoken while
drinking, 44, 92–93, 109–10, 111,
115–16, 156 n. 14; used to extract
complaints against the government,
158–59 n. 7
Appeals, 86–89; in civil compared to
criminal cases, 87; to England, 87,
165–66 n. 43; English practice, 148 n.
31; less likely when fines were small,
114; as a legitimate mechanism for
criticizing courts, 15–16; rarity of in
general, 87; restrictions on, 86–87,
165 n. 43; basic role of, 86; use of in
seditious speech cases grows, 89
Attorney(s): attitudes toward, 44, 78–79,
122; availability of, 78; debate over a
statute regarding, 18; contribution to
growth of legal "technicalities," 161 n.
24; examples of laws regulating, 161 n.
25; a woman serving as, 16; use of
grows, 161 n. 24

Bacon's Rebellion: mentioned, 12;
punishment following, 102, 115;
seditious speech law following, 24, 29,
36, 154 n. 39
Bonds: in appeals, 87; characteristics of,
119; as punishment, 117–19; use of
smaller ones in seditious speech
prosecutions grows, 122; uses in
colonial life, 117–18

Civil War, English, 49, 75
Conflict of interest: in the court system
generally, 77–78; and juries, 81–82
Contempt: compared to seditious
speech, 14–15, 99; examples of cases
involving, 45, 51, 145 n. 10, 147 n. 25;
punished to protect the court system,
8–9; laws regulating, 145 n. 10
Corporal punishments, 91–97; none
allowed for gentlemen, 104, 166 n. 1;
arms broken, 2, 94–95; branding, 96;
dragging behind a boat, 7; ear cutting,
94–95; ear nailing, 95; riding the
wooden horse, 96; running a gauntlet,
95; tongue bored through, 2, 95; use of
in seditious speech prosecutions
declines, 97; whipping, 91–94
Courts: efforts to preserve the integrity
of, 8–9; volume of business normally
done, 77; what they were like, 74
Crime, problems analyzing, 143–44 n.
4

Crimes and offenses, references to: abusing officials, 8; adultery, 6; bastardy, 80; bestiality, 5, 171 n. 5; blasphemy, 9, 170 n. 30; burglary, 96; cross-dressing, 6; drunkenness, 6, 70, 92, 109; fighting, 80; forgery, 96; fornication, 6, 55, 167 n. 6; hog stealing, 44; illegal voting, 114; infanticide, 81–82; killing a horse, 15; lying, 51, 55; manslaughter, 96; murder, 114; nightwalking, 114; piracy, 73, 172 n. 12; religious dissent, 91; Sabbath breaking, 6, 114; stealing watermelons, 114; stock left unpenned, 114; threatening others, 55; trade violations, 114; wife abuse, 10, 91, 118; witchcraft, 164 n. 39. *See also* Contempt; Seditious speech; Slander; Treason

Culpepper's Rebellion, 19

Danger, role of in seditious speech law and prosecutions, 35–37, 124, 134–37

Death penalty: in seditious speech cases, 95, 151 n. 10

de Libellis Famosis (Star Chamber case), 23, 35, 133, 149–50 n. 8

Deterrence, as a rationale for punishment, 128

Dominion of New England: excessive court fees under, 87; mentioned, 10, 39; and growing role of legal "technicalities," 77

Exclusion penalties, 104–8; banishment, 106–7; disfranchisement, 105–6; put out of office, 104–5; use of in seditious speech prosecutions declines, 107–8

False news, 57–65; colonial laws regarding, 30–34; definition of, 18–19; efforts to counter spread of, 62–64; "new" type, 58–60; why "new" type predominated, 64–65; "old" type, 57–58; proclamations and declarations refuting, 58, 62–64

Fendall's Rebellion, 53

Fines, 114–17; normally paid "in kind," 115; use of smaller ones in seditious speech cases grows, 116–17

Frankpledge, 171–72 n. 8. *See also* Sureties

Glorious Revolution: and English seditious speech law, 150 n. 9; mentioned, 37, 154 n. 43; news of reaches the colonies, 60; surge of prosecutions during, 49; milder punishment during, 123–24

Government, words against, 50–57, 65; colonial laws regarding, 27–29; definition of, 14–18; derogating courts, 50–52; derogating legislation, 52; derogating taxes, 54

Gove's Rebellion, 134–35

Humiliation punishments, 98–104; acknowledgment of wrongdoing, 101–3; bilboes, 100; paper announcing offense, 100–101; pillory, 98–99; stocks, 99–100; sword broken, 95; use of declines, 103–4

Imprisonment, 108–13; escapes from, 112; pending process, 72, 108–10; as a specific penalty, 110–11; prison conditions, 111–12, 170 n. 32; use of as a punishment declines, 112–13

Indians: colonists pretending to be, 98; chief killed by a colonist, 114; man grotesquely murdered by, 88, 166 n. 45; rumor of attack upon, 99; rumor of attacks by, 63; rumors of Catholic conspiracy with, 30; supplies for fighting paid for by seditious speech fines, 115; woman mutilated by, 63. *See also* King Philip's War

Ingle Rebellion, 36

Juries, 79–86; increasing acquittals by in seditious speech cases, 85–86; deciding facts but not law, 84; expense of, 82–83; kinds of, 80–81; reverence for right to trial by, 79–80; use of in seditious speech cases grows, 85–86; why not widely used in criminal

prosecutions, 82–85; verdicts set aside by judges, 83–84. *See also* Jurors
Jurors: punished for verdicts, 84–85; defendant's right to challenge, 81–82

King Philip's War: seditious speech fine remitted for distinguished service during, 52; mentioned, 57; upsurge in some kinds of punishments during, 102
King, words against, 48–50; usually accompanied revolutionary changes in England, 147 n. 20; compared to treason, 12–13; examples of, 69, 75, 88, 111, 127, 128, 130

Law, seditious speech, 20–41; changes in response to circumstances, 35–40; consistency of in the colonies, 34–35; English development of, 20–23
Levy, Leonard: as leading authority on colonial free speech, 1; and the evolving rationale for punishing seditious words, 134

Mental illness: grand jury determines status of man accused of, 80; man accused of complains to authorities, 68; seditious speech charge dropped because of, 129
Money: beaver hides as, 157 n. 29; "country pay," 115; fines smaller when paid in specie, 171 n. 3; forms of specie, 171 n. 3; rice as, 115; specie uncommon in the colonies, 115; sugar as, 115; tobacco as, 115; unusual forms of, 115
Monmouth's Rebellion, 62, 130

Parliamentary privilege, as an avenue of legitimate criticism of the government, 17–18
Peasant's Revolt of 1381, 21
Petitions: as an avenue of legitimate criticism of the government, 16–17; restrictions on, 17
Pickering, Lewis, 23. See also de *Libellis Famosis*

Poor people, how the justice system worked against, 83, 165 n. 43
Procedure: during trial, 73–74; pre-trial, 72–73; protections upheld, 160 n. 15; "technicalities" in, 76–77, 129. *See also* Self incrimination, protection against; Statutes of limitation; Two-witness rule
Punishment, 91–126; changes in, 137; choice of given to offenders, 11, 52, 94, 96, 102, 125, 167 n. 6; gender differences in, 36–37, 94, 167 n. 6, 169 n. 17; multiple sanctions in seditious speech cases decline, 122–24; remittances of grow in seditious speech cases, 124–26; special severity ordered, 92; suspended because of offender's illness, 125. *See also* Admonition; Bonds; Corporal punishments; Death penalty; Exclusion penalties; Fines; Humiliation punishments; Imprisonment; Sureties

Quakers: and banishment in New England, 106; a crime to attend their preaching, 172 n. 12; hanging of, 147 n. 23; legislation regarding, 147 n. 23; and political factionalism in the Middle Colonies, 140; and the growth of religious toleration in the colonies, 140; their reviling of magistrates not considered seditious in this study, 13–14

Religion: influence of on growing toleration of seditious speech, 139–40; punishment of religious offenses to preserve the church, 9; and seditious speech, 13–14. *See also* Quakers

Scandalum magnatum, 43–50, 65; a convenient means of description, 145 n. 12; colonial laws regarding, 24–27; against dead people, 23, 46; definition of, 10–14; insult types, 43–45; misprision types, 45–46; threats, 46–47

Search for author of seditious reports, 61–62, 157 n. 42; among the Dutch at New Netherland, 157–58 n. 43; no prosecutions resulting from, 33

Seditious speech: how discovered, 67–72; dual (personal and general) prosecutions of, 56, 65; English cases, 94, 149 n. 5, 150 n. 9, 154 n. 37; false accusations of, 51–52, 68; groups accused of, 52; in the military, 23–24, 35, 96, 151 n. 10; misdemeanor status of, 23, 35, 72; not prosecuted, 126–31; rationale for controlling changes, 132–37; religious elements in, 13–14; compared to slander, 11–12; examples of written, 55, 57, 71, 81, 93, 106, 109 (a search for), 118, 121, 122–23, 126, 127. *See also* False news; Government, words against; King, words against; *Scandalum magnatum*; Treason

Self incrimination, protection against, 160 n. 15

Slander, compared to seditious speech, 11–12

Social hierarchy, attitude toward and attempts to uphold, 6–8

Statutes of limitation, ignored in seditious speech cases, 69, 75

Sumptuary laws, 6

Sureties: as a form of punishment, 119–21; use of smaller ones in seditious speech cases grows, 122

Toleration of seditious speech, why it developed, 137–42

Treason: examples of cases involving, 12, 75, 78, 130–31, 147 n. 20; difficulty of separating from seditious speech, 12–13; and seditious speech in English law, 21–22, 35, 150 n. 9

Two-witness rule: avoided by the Tudors, 21–22; forces release of seditious speakers, 60, 75–76, 131; null if the single witness is a magistrate, 72

Winthrop, John: impugned while governor of Massachusetts, 43–44; on Philip Ratcliff (a seditious speaker), 95; on the role of women in marriage, 144 n. 6; on the social hierarchy, 7

Women: abused by husbands, 10, 91, 118; abusing a constable, 8; one attacked by Indians, 63; an attorney, 16; a husband abuser, 7; as jurors, 81; examples of as seditious speakers, 44, 47, 55, 78, 93, 110, 118, 125; in the sexual hierarchy, 7; as witnesses, 69, 75. *See also* Punishment, gender differences in

Zenger, John Peter, 65

THE PRIVATE LIFE OF HENRY VIII

THE PRIVATE LIFE
OF HENRY VIII

by

N. BRYSSON MORRISON
Author of "Mary, Queen of Scots"

Illustrated

NEW YORK
THE VANGUARD PRESS, INC.

89585

To
SIR GEORGE MIDDLETON, K.C.V.O.
Physician and Friend

Their story . . . abides everywhere . . .
woven into the stuff of other men's lives.

Contents

1   The Small Colossus   11
2   The King is Dead   21
3   Long Live the King   29
4   First Victory   35
5   The New Rival   43
6   The Quality of Mercy   51
7   Defender of the Faith   59
8   Diplomatic Reversal   69
9   Lady-in-Waiting   78
10 Trial of a Queen   89
11 Death of the Cardinal   99
12 Matters of Conscience   108
13 A King Bewitched   118
14 "Commend Me to His Majesty"   132
15 Trumpets for a Prince   146
16 Rose Without a Thorn   157
17 Backstairs Scandal   172
18 The Last Bargain   184
    A Chronology of Henry VIII   198
    Index   201

Illustrations

facing page

Henry VIII, aged forty-nine, painted by Holbein in the year he married Anne of Cleves. In the Corsini Gallery, Rome 48

Henry VII, father of Henry VIII, holding the red rose of Lancaster. Painting by an unknown artist, reproduced by permission of the National Portrait Gallery 49

Elizabeth, wife of Henry VII and mother of Henry VIII, holding the white rose of York. Painting by an unknown artist, reproduced by permission of the National Portrait Gallery 49

Prince Arthur, the elder son, who married Katherine of Aragon and died at sixteen. After the painting in the Royal Collection, Windsor 64

Prince Henry, the younger son, when he was a child. From the painting in the collection of Sir Edmund and Lady Verney at Rhianva, Anglesey 64

Princess Margaret (identity uncertain), the elder daughter, headstrong and dominant. Painting by an unknown artist, reproduced by permission of the National Portrait Gallery 64

Princess Mary, Henry's favourite sister, the loveliest woman of her day. A painting of the French School, sixteenth century 64

Katherine of Aragon, Henry's first wife, mother of Mary Tudor. A painting by Michael Sittow, reproduced by permission of the Kunsthistorischen Museum, Vienna 65

Anne Boleyn, Henry's second wife whom he described as "my great folly"; mother of Elizabeth Tudor. Painting by an unknown artist, reproduced by permission of the National Portrait Gallery 65

Jane Seymour, Henry's third wife, mother of his only legitimate son, Edward Tudor. A drawing after Holbein   65

Anne of Cleves, Henry's fourth wife. A painting in St. John's College, Oxford   144

Katherine Howard, Henry's fifth and youngest wife, said to be the loveliest of all his brides. After a miniature by Holbein in the Royal Collection   144

Katherine Parr, Henry's sixth and last wife. An engraving from a painting by Adrian van der Werff   144

Henry VIII arriving at the Field of the Cloth of Gold. After a contemporary painting at Hampton Court   145

Henry with his three children, Edward, Mary and Elizabeth, all of whom reigned. An engraving by F. Bartolozzi from the original by Holbein at Ditton Park   160

Edward, Henry's beloved son, known as England's Treasure. A chalk and watercolour drawing by Holbein, reproduced by permission of the Kupferstichkabinett, Basel   160

Charles Brandon, Henry's closest lifelong friend who married Princess Mary   161

Thomas Wolsey, Cardinal of York, with the college he founded at Oxford in the background. From the original by Holbein in the collection at Christ Church, Oxford   161

CHAPTER ONE

THE SMALL COLOSSUS

"Our King, he is the rose so red,
That now does flourish fresh and gay:
Confound his foes, Lord, we beseech,
And love His Grace both night and day!"

HE WAS born, this second son and third child, on the 28th June,
1491, and something of the shine and splendour of summer at its
zenith accompanied him throughout his fifty-five years of life. Even
his baby face with its broad brow and robust cheeks looked as though
the sun were full upon it, and his hair when it began to grow was
seen to gloss his head with gold. He was christened Henry after his
father, the founder of the House of Tudor, but it was principally
from his mother's side that he inherited his handsome looks.

Since the child is father to the man he, big for his age from
infancy, prefigured he would grow more than life size. He stood
sturdily, his legs apart, a small colossus equally distributing his
weight. He had not been premature like his delicate brother but
exuberant with health, learning with precocious ease, quick at
mathematics, mastering Latin, picking up their language from his
French tutors as they taught him to write in a script that was a
mixture of the new simple Italian style and the old-fashioned involved English.

A second son, no crown or throne awaited him as they awaited
his brother Arthur, so he was destined for the Church, which meant
he was grounded and educated to fill high clerical office. From his
earliest days he loved music and had his own band of minstrels to
delight him, quite apart from those of his kingly father or Prince
Arthur. He loved not only to listen to music but to play it, and learnt
the lute, organ and harpsichord until he had the skill of the master—
not only to play it but to create it, so that in the days to come

his songs and instrumental pieces soar amongst the finest productions of his times.

Honours were heaped on him before he was a year old. The baby cradled by his nurse Ann Luke was appointed Warden of the Cinque Ports and Constable of Dover Castle, received the honourable office of Earl Marshal, was created Duke of York, dubbed a Knight of the Bath, made Warden of the Scottish Marches, that turbulent neighbour over the border, so grievous a thorn in England's side, and invested with the Garter. Thus his painstaking father, by appropriating for his children great offices of state, channelled their fees, emoluments, perquisites, tributes, into the royal coffers. Better to keep high administrative posts in the family, under his direct supervision, than grant them to nobles who could become mischievous with power.

His children never noticed their father's thin hair and careworn face, and his subjects were unaware he was neither handsome nor distinguished. To his children, the King was their father, and he was the first sovereign in England to be referred to by his subjects as His Majesty.

He had the countenance of an ascetic, long-faced and pale, yet his thin tight mouth could twitch unexpectedly into a smile and his grey eyes suddenly quicken that shrewd hard face. He walked the earth carefully, as befitted one who had been captive or fugitive since the age of five until he had knelt on the ground of Bosworth Moor to thank God for giving him victory in battle. They had carried the plundered naked body of the defeated king from the field and placed his battered crown, found hidden in a hawthorn bush, on the head of the Welshman who had little hereditary right to it, while his victorious army, half the size of that it had vanquished, sang the *Te Deum*.

He had prayed that day for grace to rule in justice and in peace the people God, by giving him victory, had committed and assigned to him, and they were content to be governed by his resolute hand. For thirty years their country had been laid waste as two Houses warred for the crown. The ding-dong of battle had favoured now the white rose of York, now the red rose of Lancaster, and the impoverished land had shuddered to its roots while the long-drawn-out contest waged. It mattered little to his subjects that the man who now sat on the throne was there because his royal Lancaster grandmother had had a clandestine union with her Welsh clerk of the wardrobe. He grasped the sceptre with a strong hand, was establishing peace within the realm, and with peace came prosperity to the people.

No more disputed successions now a Prince of Wales was born to inherit from his father. Little wonder that his subjects called his consort "the good Queen", providing the royal nurseries with princes and princesses in goodly number. Her two young brothers had been murdered by the king her husband had defeated, and there were those who said she, Elizabeth of York, a king's daughter, had better right to the crown than her husband. But England had never been ruled by a queen, and they prayed God never would be. On the 22nd August, 1485, within an hour, the Welshman had won victory, crown and bride. His people needed no surer sign that Providence had arranged the union of their sovereign with Elizabeth of York when they flocked in their hundreds to see what had never been seen before: red and white roses, the rival colours of York and Lancaster, miraculously produced by the one bush.

On the rare occasions they saw her, borne in her litter or barge from castle to palace, they noticed more the gems that encrusted her coif than the face it framed. But to her children she was as heavenly-looking as an angel, fair-skinned, her hair pale gold banded on her smooth brow, her face still with a serenity that made it shine even when she did not smile.

The colourful feasts of Easter, Pentecost and Christmas lit the year with mirth and gaiety that followed the solemn religious services. Both the parents were devout, and the court stirred with divines, scholars and poets. Skelton, one of Prince Henry's teachers, was poet and priest; neither of his royal patrons could have been aware of his immorality, or read the coarsest of his satires. Christenings and birthdays, any family event that called for rejoicing, were celebrated with feasting and revelry. Favourite Greenwich House, the palace at Richmond, stately Westminster linked to the heart of London by the artery of the River Thames, towering Windsor—all were home to the royal children: parkland, hunting forest, gilded ceilings, costly tapestries, rich clothing, processions and pageantry the order of their common day.

Babies came and went in the royal nurseries, their lives a short passage from christening to catafalque, but the three eldest, Arthur,

Margaret and Henry, survived the shocks of early infancy, as did Mary, a younger girl. Garbed in miniature adult clothes, they held their receptions with a majesty that was not make-believe. Each had his own household, which circled round him like constellations round the sun. This tended to separate members of a family one from another, yet their very uniqueness drew them together in bonds that were as taken for granted as the air they breathed.

Prince Arthur as eldest and heir was naturally the brightest luminary in these nursery days, the centre of the most brilliant galaxy. Henry never thought to envy or covet his brother's position, for that would mean to call in question the immutable decree of omnipotent God.

The extreme fairness of the heir to the throne enchanted the dark Spanish ambassadors when they were shown him as a lively baby with a view to his marriage with their Infanta. That was a betrothal upon which the father of the prospective bridegroom had set his heart. The Infanta's parents, King of Aragon and Queen of Castile, were wealthy, which meant the bride's dowry would be substantial. They were powerful, and England had need of a strong ally with France lying across a strip of water, ruled by a king who dreamed of making himself not only sovereign of England but of the world. Also such a glittering match would consolidate and add prestige to his position at home, with impostors and pretenders rising in the unlikeliest places to claim the throne in the Yorkist cause. But all was going well; little Katherine of Aragon was now betrothed by proxy to Prince Arthur, who was so far ahead with his Latin that soon he could write love letters to her learned highness since she could speak no English as he could speak no Spanish.

A sister Margaret divided the two brothers. Like all her parents' children, she received an advanced education; unlike them, it availed her not one whit. Headstrong and dominant, she was too like her younger brother for them to pull together when they grew up, but she supplied something the delicate Arthur lacked, and meant much to him.

Mary was to be Henry's favourite sister, the prettiest little thing imaginable, with sportive winning ways, but his life was too full to feel the need of her companionship. He had his strenuous male comrades to hunt with and tilt against, chief amongst whom was Charles Brandon, some years his senior. King Henry had him brought up with his younger son in memory of the boy's father who had saved his life at the expense of his own. To Mary, big Charles Brandon, from the humble ranks of the county gentry, was to become the knight of knights.

All the royal children were blond and had bright colouring, and Mary was to grow in beauty until she became the loveliest woman of her day. There is a portrait of the three eldest which shows them sitting at a plain table with two apples and three cherries. Prince Arthur is in the middle, as is proper for the eldest, his fair curls covered by a flat hat, a handsome child with an uncaptivating expression. Henry, on his right, might be a grown woman, his hair frizzed into tight wig-like curls. Margaret is the pleasantest of the trio, a little Eve in ermine sleeves, smiling as she grasps one of the two apples. All three, being so fair, have been depicted without lashes,which gives their eyes the round look of a sea-bird's.

All the children are shown as plump. The food in their century was strong and stimulating, the only drink to be had alcoholic, tea and coffee as yet unknown. Sugar or honey was taken with every-thing, even with roast meat, and the sweetmeats which followed a meal were its most important part and called the banquet. Even the English commons fed well on light-coloured bread and beer and quantities of meat, unlike the half-starved French peasantry. Such a diet tended to make a people swift on the draw with both tongue and hand. There were no half measures where their passions were concerned.

And the royal children had the best of everything. In Henry's case, the rich food, the strong meats, the heady wines and sweet cakes, the herbs, fruits and vegetables, went into what country folk call "a good skin". He was not puffy like his elder brother but grew strong-boned and straight, self-reliant, smooth of skin and steady of eye, working off his energies learning to shoot and wrestle and cast the bar.

He was the guest of London when he was seven, the year his sister Mary was born. In anticipation of his visit, the civic authorities turned all vagabonds and anyone suffering from infectious disease out of the city. The unpocked citizens gave him a rousing welcome and the Mayor, on their behalf, presented him with a pair of gilt goblets, promising as he made the presentation of this "little and poor" gift, to remember him with a better one at some future time.

On his part, the self-possessed young Prince made a charming speech, thanking Father Mayor and his Brethren for their great and kind remembrance of him which he trusted in time coming to deserve.

He saw them then, his father's subjects, lining the streets to watch him go by, the women as rough and full of animal spirits as the men. And there tossed like communication between these Londoners and him, the cynosure of their gaze, the shared excitement of the moment—they the beholders, he the beholden.

The subjects their father ruled were a lusty folk, who came of healthy stock, bold, hardy and keen to do business. With the stability of the new reign, trade increased and their far-sighted King negotiated a favourable commercial treaty with the Netherlands. Instead of shipping wool to feed foreign looms, the cloth itself was now woven in England and exported, and the clothier flourished where the weaver had waxed and waned.

They gathered to watch hangings and floggings, shouldering each other for a better view, feeding their eyes on spectacles such as a royal progress, at one with the clamour of life that filled street and market-place; but not quite at one with the ecclesiastical processions that wended to or from cathedral or abbey. They were unaware of that themselves as they stood there looking on with speculative eyes. It was not the crucifix, the crosier, the canopy they were to deride; it was the men who bore them, "Pope's men".

The assiduous columns of figures, each initialled by the royal H, were mounting into a fortune of millions. The greying face that bent over them had begun to age perceptibly, as though his forty-odd years had soured on him. He looked like a nut whose shell has shrivelled instead of decayed, and now enclosed no seeds to release. Always pious, his devotion became more intensified. It was rumoured he had consulted a soothsayer who warned him his life was in danger.

One grim November day his subjects learnt that the young Earl of Warwick, royal Yorkist and best qualified pretender to the throne, had been executed for treason. As the Tower, where he had been incarcerated at the age of ten, had been his home since Bosworth, his opportunities for treason were few and far between; but that he had been allowed to grow to manhood proved that the first Tudor king preferred imprisoning his competitors to murdering them. His

execution now was said to be at the instigation of Ferdinand and
Isabella of Spain, who did not wish their daughter to marry the
Prince of Wales if one day he might be deposed by a rival.

The over-sanguine Spanish ambassador assured his master and
mistress that his death left not a doubtful drop of royal blood in the
kingdom, but many years later the sensitive bride was to remember
her marriage had been sealed by the spilling of innocent blood.

She sailed from her sunny home of myrtles and pomegranates in
the spring, arriving in England that blustering October with her
retinue of prelates, governess—for she was only sixteen, a year older
than her groom—duenna, donnas and grandees. But her welcome
at Plymouth made up for the inhospitable weather. The Spaniards
noted to their satisfaction that she could not have been received with
greater rejoicings if she had been the Saviour of the world.

She was brought towards London in easy stages, the nobility and
gentry of the counties she passed through entertaining her on her
way. Her arrival in England had the effect of a stone splashed into
a pool, causing currents that swirled across the whole country. Each
destination she reached on her way swelled more waves and ripples,
so that as she neared London accompanied by a train of four
hundred English knights and gentlemen, all mounted and dressed
in scarlet and black, she and the capital became like the vortex.

Some of the difficulty of travelling and communication can be
gauged when we learn it was not until a month after her arrival that
the King himself set out with the bridegroom to greet his daughter-
in-law. It was now November, and pelting rain made the going hard
over bad roads.

Young Henry learnt before the news percolated throughout the
court that Spanish cavaliers had sent forward a message stipulating
their Infanta could not be seen by either her bridegroom or his father
until her wedding day. The English King's reply had the force of
an ultimatum: as the Spanish Infanta was now in the heart of the
realm of which he was master, he might look at her if he so desired.

And he did so desire, for his suspicions were thoroughly aroused
that a so-called Spanish custom was a pretext to cloak some defor-
mity of the bride. He arrived in his wet riding-clothes at the entrance
of her apartment, where a Spanish archbishop, a bishop and a count
blocked his entry. Every English heart beat higher when it was
known what short shrift was made of their protestations as they were

brusquely informed that even if she were in her bed, he meant to see and speak with her.

There was nothing wrong with the Infanta. She could understand neither her father-in-law nor her groom as they could not understand her, but so courteous in their own language was each to the other, so great the pleasure had they in what they saw, that the air was gladdened with welcome.

She entered the city by London Bridge, one of the wonders of the world with its span of nineteen arches and white pillars. To the approaching traveller, London presented a forest-like picture, with branching masts and rigging of the vessels on its river, countless spires rising above the huddle of roofs, and garden trees spreading their leafless limbs like ship tackle. On that November day every bell rang out clamorous and jubilant, vying with the citizenry who, man, woman and child, roared their welcome at the bride from across the seas.

Young Henry was her escort and rode at her right side. His sister-in-law had come as a surprise to him. He knew his father was greatly taken not only with her appearance but her manners, which were so beautiful they made her beautiful. Here was someone who could not be other than she appeared, like a well-strung instrument that could only play in tune. But she was not dark as one imagined a Spaniard would be; instead her hair was a rich auburn, and she was fair-skinned as either Margaret or Mary. Her lively face lit and kindled in response to all she saw around her.

She rode a mule after the fashion of Spain, sitting on it on what looked like a small arm-chair. She wore a broad round hat tied under her chin with lace of gold to keep it on her head in that wild English weather. Under it was a coif of carnation colour and her copper hair streamed over her shoulders.

Her face eager as she looked at them, the Londoners took her to their hearts the moment they saw her, bellowing their appreciation as though loudness would convey to her what might be unintelligible in words. This was she who had come from far-away Spain to make her home amongst them, to wed their Prince and bear his sons and so make secure for ever the throne of England.

That was the young Duke of York, Prince Henry, who rode on her right side—a big lad with his bold brow for one not much older than ten, a prince every inch of him. They had a good laugh at the

Spanish ladies-in-waiting who followed their mistress, each riding a mule as she did, each led by an English maid-of-honour on a palfrey. But the Spanish women did not sit on the same side as the English, so that each pair rode back to back and looked as though they were quarrelling.

This was the wedding of their Prince, the hope of England, taking place in the heart of their city, and they who witnessed it were the pulse of London. They saw Prince Arthur on his wedding day, clothed in white satin, endow his bride at the great door of St. Paul's Cathedral with one-third of his property. The bride was all in white too, her face half veiled with the outlandish foreign head-dress she wore. Prince Henry led her to the bishop's palace where the nuptial dinner was to take place in the grand banqueting-hall: it was said the gold plate she would eat from was embedded with precious stones and pearls and worth twenty thousand pounds.

The people were there a few days later at Westminster Hall where a tilt had been set up from the west gate to King Street. There they could feast their eyes on a stage hung with cloth of gold where the King and his lords sat on one side, and the Queen, the bride and their ladies on the other. There was no end to the sights to be seen, and when the tilting began the enthusiasm reached its peak as a wager-loving nation shouted its encouragement or howled its rating.

That night, in winter dark, the lurking streets were restless with people slipping past one another, featureless and without bulk until a torch flared, when faces leapt into being and a tangle of shadows separated into bodies. The King's palace of Westminster rode the darkness like some fantastic ship, an impression confirmed by the river on whose bank it stood.

Inside all was magnificence, splendour and majesty, feasting and cheer. The treasure of solid gold plate was on show, a sight to dazzle any Spaniard's eyes. Tapestry, arras and cloth of gold hid walls green with river damp and age. Trumpet notes, song and music lent the permanence of eternity to the passing moment.

The bridegroom sat at his father's right hand on the royal dais, with the nobility ranged in their degrees. At the King's left sat the Queen, the bride, princesses and ladies. This division of the sexes made it appear as though the packs of many cards had been shuffled with the kings all arranged on one side and the queens on the other.

Prince Henry watched his brother and their aunt dance together a stately figure before the company. He saw the bride and one of her ladies leave the dais. They wore their strange hooped Spanish dresses never before seen in England, which as they performed a slow and gliding movement swayed from their waists like bells. Now it was his turn.

He took his sister Margaret by the hand and together they danced two dances, quick and nimble, smiling to each other as they span and whirled. They made an enchanting pair: the boy tall as his elder sister, strong, gallant and gay; she bright-haired, bright-faced at being the centre of attention.

So delighted were the King and Queen and the assembled company at their display that they took the floor once more. But finding his robe interfered with the leaping and cavorting of the dance, the young prince suddenly threw it aside and finished the figure in his jacket.

Already he had learnt to trip to his own measure.

CHAPTER TWO

THE KING IS DEAD

"The earth goeth on the earth glistring like gold,
The earth goes to earth sooner than it wold.
The earth builds on the earth castles and towers.
The earth says to the earth, 'All shall be ours'."

KING HENRY did not look to the English peerage for brides or grooms for his children: for one thing, there were few of the old aristocracy left after thirty despoiling years of the Roses War. He had surrounded himself with new men whose blood was anything but blue, lawyers and churchmen he could pay with judgeships and bishoprics instead of with grants of land. He accumulated and amassed; least of all did not part with land, bringing back to the crown estates that had passed to subjects, and adding to them the wide domains of his beaten opponents.

His children were royal, and royalty was a caste apart; it must marry royalty. His belief in marriage as an insurance of political union was implicit. Thus his son Henry and his small daughter Mary were proposed as the groom and bride of Eleanor, the granddaughter, and Charles, the grandson, of Ferdinand and Isabella. Charles was barely a year old but already King Henry had his eye on one who, heir to Castile and Aragon, Burgundy and Austria, grasped in his baby fist the political sceptre of Caesar.

Twice, when she was an infant, the hand of his eldest daughter Margaret was offered to James IV of Scotland. Surely such a marriage would stop for all time these running battles on the open seas between English and Scots captains, each calling the other pirate, these invasions over the borders from Scotland and costly incursions in retaliation from the English side, the harbouring and honouring of pretenders to the King of England's throne by his Scottish counterpart.

James was some fourteen years older than the child her father proposed as his bride, a handsome man with the Stewart red hair, a passionate lover and so nimble he could leap on his horse without touching his stirrup. His ambition was to marry a Spanish princess, and it was not until Ferdinand and Isabella told him they had no more single daughters that Scots ambassadors were sent over the border to discuss the marriage of their Stewart king with the Tudor princess.

They arrived for the betrothal, or engagement, ceremony not long after the bells of London had rung out the wedding of the Infanta and the Prince of Wales. Even hard-headed Scots could not wring from King Henry any more than a miserly dowry for his daughter, which the prospective bridegroom disdained to haggle over, and the twelve-year-old Margaret, his favourite child, signed in her square handwriting the marriage contract, binding herself to marry the right Excellent, right High and Mighty Prince James, King of Scotland.

She was called Queen of Scotland when she plighted her troth, but her father had stipulated he would not send her north for a further eighteen months. The ceremony, and jousting and ballets to celebrate it, took place at Richmond where the King had erected a new palace from a burnt-out old one. It was a favourite place of his which he had renamed Richmond after his own name before he was crowned. Standing on a hill-top, it commanded a view so far flung that one felt the whole of England was pent within one's sight, that the whole of England was arched by a high blue sky below which the shining Thames wound between green meadows, dipping sunny uplands and woodlands that feathered the landscape.

All Margaret's family were at her betrothment and took part in the gaieties except her favourite brother, the Prince of Wales. Soon after their marriage King Henry had dispatched his son and bride to Ludlow Castle in Shropshire to keep court, govern the principality of Wales and live as man and wife. This was against the advice of his council: the bride was only sixteen, the bridegroom little more than fifteen.

Neither could speak the other's language; what converse they held together had to be in stilted Latin, and there does not appear to have been any mutual attraction between the youthful pair, or any degree of familiarity in a marriage that was doomed not to survive six months of growing pains. To the day of her death Katherine contended that her union with Arthur, Prince of Wales, had never been consummated.

Some historians state that he died of a decline, others of the plague prevalent that wet spring in the Ludlow district. His health had always been precarious and the bright colouring which betokened robust good health in his brother Henry was probably in him the sign of consumption. He had time to make his will, leaving all his personal property, jewels, plate and wearing apparel to his sister Margaret. His bride of less than six months is not mentioned.

The dire news was broken to the King by his confessor. It was the Queen who sustained him, summoning up all the comfort she could from her deep fount of religion, reminding him he had been an only child, yet God had ever preserved him and brought him where he was now. "God is where He was," she told him, "and we are both young." But at the memory of her best beloved child, her heart fainted within her: together husband and wife took their "painful sorrows".

Young Henry now found himself heir apparent at the age of ten, the focus of his grave father's solicitude, the centre of ever-increasing attention as he grew to potent manhood in exact ratio as his parent's years diminished.

Everything was different now. Beamed on him was the hope of a nation. God in His unsearchable wisdom had cut off Arthur in his prime and decreed Henry should take his place. Their father was God's anointed and ruled only by His grace, the crown could not be separated from the cross. That was why the *mystique* between subject and monarch was much the same as the *mystique* between worshipper and deity.

Henry felt it, although he was his father's son. Children of those days paid their parents unquestioning unremitting obedience; it was not the tribe with which their roots were bound, it was the family. And King Henry was not only his father, he was his sovereign.

The boy's mind did not choose to vault into the future, when he might be called upon to fill not a brother's but a parent's place. To let such a thought flicker across his mind was like blasphemy, but he grew up in the certain knowledge that when and if that time did come it would be by God's edict and God's alone.

He saw his sister-in-law when his mother sent for the young

widow to come to her. Katherine's entry into London could not have been more different from her bridal triumph so short a time ago. Now she was boxed in a vehicle like a hearse covered with black, a widow who had lost both potential and actual position, amongst strangers whose language she neither spoke nor understood.

She wore her auburn hair smooth, parted in the centre above a face alive with intelligence. He would see her serious gaze upon him. Both knew her parents were negotiating for a marriage between them, but the prospect of a boy more than six years her junior as a husband cannot have appealed to her. Nevertheless what her father bade her, she would do.

A dispensation for a woman to marry her deceased husband's brother would be necessary, but the Pope would be only too willing to provide what a powerful prince asked. King Henry received the suggestion coldly. What touched him to the quick was the question of Katherine's dowry. Only part of the vast sum had been paid, and the wily Ferdinand, now his daughter was a widow, not only refused to pay any more but demanded the refund of his previous instalments. He met his match, however, in the tenacious King of England.

Chaffering and bargaining ceased if only temporarily when death stalked again into the royal household. Some ten months after her son, the mother died. On Candlemas Day, when good weather foretold a long winter and a bad crop and ill weather was lucky, Queen Elizabeth bore her seventh child, a daughter. She died unexpectedly nine days later on her birthday, and her baby did not long survive her.

Her death made a hole in the lives of all her children. It was not only they had lost their mother; an angel had departed and left them. The heavens were never quite the same when a star one had thought was fixed in its course was blotted out, never to reappear.

The King, always a solitary figure, retired by himself to nurse his grief. Something went out of his life at his consort's death; unconsciously he had walked in her light, and when that was snuffed, what was unlovely and unamiable in his character was revealed.

He gave her a magnificent funeral, as though these thousands of torches, these crosses of white damask and of gold, mourning-hoods, tapers and cloth of majesty were in some dumb way to make up to one he had always kept carefully in the background, to avoid all appearance of ruling by her right.

When the eighteen months were spent he said good-bye to his

elder daughter Margaret, giving her a prayer handbook on which he wrote, "Pray for your loving fader, that gave you thys book, and I gyve you at all tymes God's blessyng and myne. Henry R." Margaret's husband was the handsomest sovereign in Europe, who treated his small bride with the gentleness and consideration of an elder brother. Nevertheless she wrote home pettedly, in her atrocious handwriting, referring slightingly to her husband as "this King here" and lamenting she was not with her father.

Alive to the matrimonial, political and dowry advantages of a Spanish match, King Henry now proposed to marry his daughter-in-law himself, which so shocked her mother she commanded him to return Katherine straightway to Spain. Katherine's reaction to such a union was instantaneous: from that moment there was never any confidence between her and her father-in-law. He did not send her to Spain as her mother demanded, and when her father reduced his terms, agreed for a marriage treaty to be signed between his second son Henry and his first son's widow.

At the age of twelve young Henry was betrothed with great solemnity to his sister-in-law. The actual marriage was to take place two years later when he came of age at fourteen. The betrothal ceremony was performed in the Bishop of Salisbury's house in Fleet Street—it was December, not long after Katherine had celebrated her eighteenth birthday, although celebrate was not quite the word to use for a landmark she reached in an existence that was a kind of hiatus while she waited for her fate to be decided for her. Through the vacillating eight years that followed she never knew whether she was widow or bride. Certainly she felt more the first than the second, subjected as she was to every deprivation by her shrewd father-in-law while he argued with her parent over the terms of her portion.

The Archbishop of Canterbury, the highest church dignitary in England, opposed the marriage as absolutely unlawful. Did not the law of Moses forbid a man to take his brother's wife, calling it an unclean thing, and warning those who broke the law they would be childless? There were other prelates, however, who countered Leviticus with Deuteronomy, where a man was actually enjoined as his duty to take his dead brother's wife and raise seed. All that was needed to smooth away any difficulties was the Pope's dispensation which was tardy in coming and arrived after the betrothment, just in time to comfort Katherine's mother on her death-bed.

It was a new Pope who sat on St. Peter's throne in Rome, a swarthy buccaneer of a pontiff, and his dispensation did little to allay the Archbishop's scruples. He doubted very much whether it or the documents accompanying it were valid, and so influenced old Henry that young Henry found himself, on his coming of age when his marriage to Katherine was to take place, making formal protest that the contract between them was null and void. The occasion was all the more impressive because it was secret.

King Henry thus enhanced his son's value as a negotiable asset on the marriage market which the father had entered himself. There were other as, if not more, desirable brides than Katherine of Aragon for Henry minor, and more than one provocative prospect for Henry major. Also Charles was no longer a baby and had another grandfather as well as Ferdinand, the Emperor Maximilian, with whom King Henry could scheme and bargain, using his child Mary as premium. No longer was he the subservient partner in any alliance with the King of Aragon. Now he was his rival.

His patience was rewarded at long last by the signing of a treaty of marriage between the ten-year-old Princess Mary and the eight-year-old Charles. With characteristic caution he demanded surety for the adequate dowry he paid to the Emperor Maximilian, and Princess Mary received a cluster of magnificent diamonds of the first water valued at twice that sum. Parsimonious by nature, her father was careful even after he had accrued great wealth, but he had ever known what became him as a king, and on an occasion such as this the entertainment of the foreign dignitaries and ambassadors was sumptuous and without parallel.

From this union would stem not only political but commercial benefits to the country he had long served as father-king. Perhaps he was aware that this was the last of his worldly triumphs as he sat there in the seat he could not share and from which only death would make him abdicate, a little apart from it all, a ghost at his own feast, just beyond the pale of the sun. He had after all turned the half century, but it was not years that had broken and bowed his health. For over two decades his rule had brought order out of chaos, peace in the place of arms, profit, not loss. He was leaving his son a consolidated kingdom, an undisputed title and an over-flowing treasury.

His son and heir—his eye gladdened every time it rested upon him. All that was best in his ancestors made splendid the figure of young Henry, now approaching his eighteenth year. Tall as his royal grandfather, Edward IV, he inherited his handsomeness from him and his maternal grandmother. There was no one his match for prowess at the athletic pursuits of his day; yet the hands that could draw a bow, tame a steed and shiver a lance could play the flute and virginals, write songs and ballads and set them to music. His love of learning and of the fine arts was a direct legacy from his father, and he had, because of the fortune of his birth and upbringing and person, what his father could never claim, the magnetism that attracts popularity.

In the few short months granted King Henry, tentative spring loosened the grip of winter. Turned in upon himself, the dying man began to settle his account with God by writing off men's liabilities. He issued pardons, and paid the fees of prisoners thrown into gaol for debt. This was not the violent death of his predecessors, but a withdrawal in good order from the field of action. Not a horse-trampled battle-ground but a hushed room in his beloved palace at Richmond. When his eyes closed for the last time, he knew the crown would not be thrown into the cockpit of civil war but would pass without division to the son kneeling at his bedside.

With his failing breath he commended to his heir his faithful counsellors. He adjured him to complete his marriage with Katherine, to defend the Church and make war on the infidel. Thus he died, the first and the greatest of the Tudors, leaving his wasted body in the big bed. Perhaps his most fitting epitaph were five words of the contemporary historian: "What he minded he compassed."

They bore him between hedges and trees pricked with spring green and bright with blossom. In London the cortège was met by the mayor and aldermen, not clad in their violet gowns but clothed in black from head to foot, to accompany to his final resting-place the King who had always paid back his debts to them in full and in record time.

From St. Paul's to Westminster the procession wended down the Strand, through streets lined with members of companies and crafts, to rest in the soaring vaulted chapel with its matchless altar, the crowning glory of the buildings the dead man had raised. There he was laid beside his queen, dwelling "more richly dead than he did alive in Richmond or any of his palaces".

As the coffin was lowered into the vault, the heralds took their tabards from their shoulders, hung them on the railing round the catafalque and lamented, "The noble King Henry the Seventh is dead!" Then they put their tabards on again and with one voice shouted the cry loud with joy, "Long live the noble King Henry the Eighth!" The new reign had begun.

CHAPTER THREE

LONG LIVE THE KING

"Pastime with good company
I love and shall until I die.
Grudge who will, but none deny,
So God be pleased this life will I
    For my pastime,
    Hunt, sing, and dance,
    My heart is set;
    All goodly sport
    To my comfort
    Who shall me let?"
              —*Henry VIII*

THE new reign burst upon the country with the force of explosion when the people woke up to find they had not only a new king but a young one. There was a feeling of release, a quickening, the stimulus of change, as though the long-tended soil had suddenly blossomed and burgeoned. This was not so much a new beginning as transformation. Carving lost its medieval stiffness and became floreate and free, garments were slashed to show contrasting colours that flaunted with the arrogance of youth, hats brave with feathers took the place of the old king's monk-like hood. Instead of sober formality, there was ebullience and the excitement of exaggeration. It was as though everything had burst into song.

No longer did distance separate sovereign from his subjects; yet when they saw their new king, and he delighted to be seen, he seemed to them like someone with the shine of heaven upon him, everything about him golden, without peer, standing head and shoulders above lesser men. Open-handed and liberal, his very presence seemed to spread largesse, so forthcoming was he, the embodiment of what the nation desired their prince and king to be, who would rule over them as they wanted to be ruled.

Yes, they were due a change; the old sovereign had reigned for close on twenty-four years, and even those who remembered him when he came to the throne did not remember him as young. There are some born old, and he was one of them; maybe it was his coming into the world after the death of his father had something to do with it. Enshrined in his own chapel, embalmed by stone, was a fitting place to think of him—and leave him. God would rest his soul, for he had been a good and devout man. So was his son devout. He heard Mass three times a day, but as well he could draw a bow with greater strength than any man in England.

When he sent to the block two of his father's tax-gatherers, his popularity was enhanced even more. The people did not reason that after all the two councillors were simply tools for carrying out the old king's policy; by the time the axe had fallen, the victims had received only their deserts, the memory of the King's father was not defaced, and he had proved himself a lover of justice and wisdom.

He was to marry the Infanta, she who had been Prince Arthur's bride. Scarcely had the stir of the old king's funeral settled when the news was made public. It was common talk that the father in his death agony had urged his son to fulfil the marriage treaty. And it was only right that he should. Eight years if it was a day since she had sailed from far-away Spain to marry their prince, and now he was dead, she deserved King Henry after her long wake. There were some who spoke behind their hands, saying it was not right to marry your brother's widow, but royalty was a law unto itself or it wouldn't be royalty, and a good man like old King Henry would never have told his son to do what was wrong. He must have known that both Prince Arthur and his bride were so young when they married and they had so short a time to be abed before he died, it was not like a marriage at all.

The people only heard about the wedding after it had taken place on Barnaby Bright day in June, so early in the morning no one was afoot, privately in Greenwich Palace. It had to be private because their king who could do no wrong was still in mourning. The whole of London knew before the day was spent that the bride had been clad all in white to show she was a virgin. When they spoke about it amongst themselves, they told each other that hadn't they said so all along.

They saw her first as their Queen not a fortnight later when she and the King progressed in state to Westminster to be crowned. The streets of London were hung with tapestry for the occasion; Cornhill always did better than anywhere else and displayed cloth of gold.

Carried in a golden litter swung between white palfreys, there was not another woman in the realm to hold a candle to Katherine of Aragon, which was as it should be when she was bride and queen of such a king. Again the people marked she was clad in bridal white. The summer light made the jewelled crown on her head flash and glow, but nothing could eclipse her great beauty which was her long auburn hair that fell gloriously down her back, like a cloak above her embroidered white satin gown.

In the Abbey, when the people were asked if they would have Henry as their king, their "Yea, yea!" fierce with exultation sounded like the surge of oceans. They were witnesses of the festivities that followed, watched the goings to and fro of King and Queen. Never had they seen a groom more happy in and proud of his bride than their young lion of a king. This was no marriage he had been puffed into by a father's dying wish, but one he made of his own free choice and rejoiced in for all the world to see. As for the bride, her love for him made her at one with the people. They knew how she felt and held jubilee with her, she who was a king's daughter, worthy to be consort of theirs, fit mother for the sons she would bear him and England.

Within six weeks of his father's funeral, Henry was married, eight years of vacillation brushed aside in fewer weeks. He loved Katherine as a young and vigorous man loves for the first time, and his joy in her increased daily as he found her not only loving but with an intelligence that matched his own. She taught him Spanish to add to his list of languages, and for the first time since she had arrived in her adopted country she put her mind to learn English. She wrote to her father, asking him to send the King her lord three steeds on which he had set his heart, one a jennet, the second a Neapolitan, the third a Sicilian. Henry gave her one of his most beloved possessions, his mother's missal, in which he wrote in French, "If your remembrance is according to *my* affection, I shall not be forgotten in your prayers, for I am yours, Henry R. for ever."

Katherine on her part found herself lifted from a tedious anxiety-ridden existence, so poor she had to sell bracelets to buy a dress, to

become the centre of a gay and lively court, every luxury at her finger-
tips. Married life was one continual feasting, music day and night,
summer and winter. Henry was the leading spirit in all the romps
and revels that made short the winter evenings, Katherine the
audience so ready with her praise and to be surprised. Spanish
women were not brought up to follow hawk and hound like her
sisters-in-law, but she was always waiting for him on his return,
and there was no one with whom he would rather be.

These glad free days, with husband and wife both joyous and
festive, whose chief delight was to please and honour the other,
spending lavishly the wealthy patrimony the old king had so carefully garnered and guarded. Time hummed by merrily in a round
of good company. The days were not long enough for all the pastimes
and pursuits to be crowded into them; the nights, in which to love
your wife.

Henry at eighteen had grown to full manhood but he was little
more than a highly educated boy. The iron of his will, character and
powerful mind were still malleable with youth, and he was unaware
of his strength other than physical. The older he grew the more
remarkable he was to become. He kept his father's councillors
around him, except for the two he was advised to sacrifice on the
block, but he had more to divert him than the council table, and
they came to the conclusion he cared only for the pleasures of his
age.

His chief adviser was his wife's father, Ferdinand, King of Aragon,
who had made Katherine his ambassador at her husband's court.
Henry would certainly have been startled had he looked over his
wife's shoulder when she wrote to her father, "These kingdoms of
your highness are in great tranquillity," but there is no doubt that
for the first few years of his reign he was subservient to the powerful
Spanish King, as his father had been before him. Henry's antipathy,
generated by centuries and shared by every Englishman, was
directed against France. A hundred years of war had left England
only Calais as its remaining foothold in that country, and little more
than a strip of water divided them. In the tug-of-war for world
domination that pulled between Spain and France, Henry was
bound to throw England's might behind Spain.

The young King entered the arena of Europe like a knight entering the lists, bearing the standard of the Pope, the Vicar of Christ.

Henry's religion was that of his parents, stoutly orthodox. His counterparts in the various nerve centres of power were all old enough to be his grandfather, campaigners seasoned in intrigue, weathered by years of cynical scheming, deceit as native to them as the air they breathed between lips that spoke of God. Ferdinand of Spain heard he was accused by a rival of cheating him twice. "He lies," he contradicted, "I cheated him three times." Louis XII of France was not so decrepit and worn out that he could not still turn a political somersault whenever it suited him, and that swarthy soldier of a Pope, arch prince of the church, marched in step with whichever side opportunism dictated.

Before the end of the year Henry was able to write to Ferdinand that Katherine was pregnant. Heaven indeed was blessing him. He saw that every care was taken of his wife and that she did not run any risks with her health, but at the end of January, after days and nights protracted by cruel labour, the seven-month baby was still-born. The fact it was a daughter made its death easier for Henry to bear. Katherine wrote her father that the stillbirth was considered an evil omen in England, but that Henry took it cheerfully. She thanked God for having given her such a husband.

Her confessor noted that the King adored her, and she him. Shortly she was pregnant again and on the first day of the new year she bore a son.

Henry's cup of happiness was full to overflowing. In a crescendo of triumph the christening took place of the tiny son, a small wan thing to support so much magnificence. He was named Henry, and given the style Prince of Wales.

His father made a pilgrimage of Walsingham to thank God for His bounty, and an elaborate tourney was staged at Westminster to commemorate what was of such portent to both King and people.

Despite his sense of kingship, Henry was always approachable; and even when his dignity increased with the burden of years, never inaccessible. Today he was young and big with affability, father of a son and heir. He responded to the frenzy of joy with which the London citizens greeted him. This was as much their hour as his. And when they put out their dirty grasping hands to touch him, he did not recoil.

Bystanders were allowed into the royal palaces on special occasions, and a horde of them waited at the lower end of the great hall when the King and his lords appeared. He was dressed in purple satin, his garments encrusted with gold. A large man, his puffed garb made him appear enormous, and he had the effect on his audience, unaccustomed to such richness, of superabundance.

A delirium of adoration seized them. They pressed forward and began to pluck his clothes from the King, greedy to possess at least a particle of something he had worn. Like jackdaws, they fastened on his lords to strip them bare of their glittering ornaments, monograms of H and K in solid gold. The divested King, who sat down to the banquet that night in his doublet and drawers, treated it all as gaily as a game, advising his courtiers to do as he did, consider their losses as largesse to the commonalty.

Three days later the child was dead. God, who had given Henry and Katherine a son and heir, granted him only seven weeks of life.

CHAPTER FOUR

FIRST VICTORY

"O then we marched into the French land,
With drums and trumpets so merrily;
And then bespoke the King of France,
'Lo, yonder comes proud King Henry.' "

THE uproarious christening celebrations were stilled and silenced as the King's baby son was buried in Westminster Abbey at the cost of ten thousand pounds. The elaborate funeral was mocked by any traces of the festivity and gladness that had preceded it. So grief-stricken was the King, ambassadors dared not offer their condolences.

But Henry had all the resilience of a well-trimmed bow. He recovered his natural buoyancy long before Katherine regained her composure, persuading her at last not to take their loss so to heart, and to cease her lamentations. That she was always in his thoughts even when they were not together was revealed by the many times he was heard to remark, "This will please the Queen," and "The Queen must hear of this."

Court life swirled round them once more, Henry the heart of it, the momentum that sent the days spinning. When he was not hunting, there was archery and tennis. When they were not singing, there was dancing, masques and comedies. He was the handsomest man in the country, well above the usual height, fair-skinned, bright-complexioned, the stamp of nobility upon his unlined brow. And the only thing he hated was to do anything he did not choose; so he did not do it, for after all he was king.

Members of his council, accustomed to the authority of his father, complained amongst themselves that the sovereign should be present when important decisions were made. Only one disagreed, with smiling urbanity. "Let the King hawk and hunt," he said, "and not intermeddle with old men's cares."

He was a newcomer to the council chamber but already he was listened to, for he spoke with the voice of the leader. A man of commanding height with quick perceptive sight, he gravitated towards the centre as by natural law, and filled every position he attained to the manner born. His grace of bearing and eloquent tongue betrayed no trace of the Ipswich butcher's son. He had reached where he had through his own wit, learning and indefatigability, and an instinct for influential patrons.

There was nothing of the parvenu about Thomas Wolsey. He had long ago outstripped his beginnings, and was at home amongst the great and noble. There was no precariousness in his foothold on the ladder: every rung he climbed was tested and made secure as a spring-board for the next ascent.

The priest who had become one of the King's chaplains in Henry VII's reign began to move about the court in Henry VIII's, accomplished and diligent in his self-imposed task to serve Church and State. His love of music and the arts made play of the years that stretched between him and his sovereign lord and lady; they met on common ground. Warmed by his discretion and compassion, the Queen turned to him as friend, and he would be seen kneeling before his young king in that manner characteristic of him, attentive and deferential, listening with his whole head.

Religion was a very real part of Henry's life, not a worn-out convention to which he paid lip service. He needed no urging from an ecclesiastic when he heard France was besieging the Pope. His mind and Wolsey's moved as one in this as in so much else. He wrote he was prepared to sacrifice goods, life and kingdom for the Vicar of Christ and the Church, and joined his father-in-law King Ferdinand in uniting against Spain's arch rival and England's ancestral enemy. War was declared on France.

He travelled to Southampton to speed his departing army on its great enterprise. It was setting out to fight not the infidel Turk but the Most Christian Louis, who was prepared to lay sacrilegious hands on His Holiness.

It was May, and the further south the cavalcade journeyed, the milder it became. As they approached the coast, sea-gulls flew up from the ground like a sheet being waved. The sight of ships always set Henry's heart dancing; these galleys with their beak-heads used for ramming, lofty galleons and sturdy galleases were his pride and passion; the flap of sail, the tug of rigging, the stir of departure, music in his ears.

The army was to take ship for Spain, where it was to be joined by King Ferdinand's in the concerted invasion of France. Henry wished he could have sailed with his men: he did not take kindly to being left behind. His boundless energy, his matchless health, urged him to be in the thick of the battle. And all he could do was wish his army God-speed as it embarked on its lofty crusade.

Katherine had now mastered the English language and could speak it fluently, but she never lost the attractive Spanish accent which made her most ordinary sentence sound charming. Together they and Wolsey waited throughout that summer for news of victory. God would surely prosper the high purpose of Spain and England banded in holy alliance to fight for the Supreme Head of His Church on earth.

By October news reached them there had been no battle and their troops, near to insubordination, were on the brink of embarking for home. Henry's wrath knew no bounds. He wrote to his father-in-law to stop the return of the army, telling him to cut every man's throat who dared to refuse obedience. But he was too late: already his dishonoured troops who had never fought were on the high seas, making for home. The first military expedition of Henry's reign had ended in ignominy and disaster.

Ferdinand's trickster mind excelled itself juggling with plausible reasons why his army had not reinforced that of his son-in-law's. Henry, with Katherine at his side, could not believe that her father was perfidious, unlike his men who had been on the spot. They knew Ferdinand had used the presence of his English allies on Spanish soil as a providential screen while he waged an independent war of his own not against France, but against Navarre. To conquer that independent kingdom had always been a pet scheme of his, for now all Spain beyond the Pyrenees was under his rule.

Throughout the torrid alien summer the untried English troops, forced to inactivity, had drunk Spanish wine as if it were home-brewed beer. Officers in the heat of the day had been heard to blame Wolsey, not the King, as the cause of all the mischief, calling it a war of his making. Autumn had added to the hazards of unhealthy inaction and dysentery decimated the ranks. What remained of Henry's army embarked for home.

Ferdinand, who in the past had urged his son-in-law to recover his lost possessions in France, began to counsel him to make peace with Louis. What could be better than that Henry should add his signature to the truce which had been arranged behind his back between the Spanish and French Kings? But England dare not do anything so craven: her honour had been dragged in the mire, and her King refused to let it lie there, the taunt of both friend and foe.

This time he would lead his army himself. No more costly expeditions to unfamiliar shores: Calais, England's remaining French possession, was to be the base for the invasion of France. Henry landed there one summer evening, and felt below his feet earth that had been flattened through the centuries by the tramp of English armies.

He was accompanied by the main body of his troops, and disembarked with his banner and guard of six hundred picked men. Nothing had been left undone to impress the French and soldiery. Every detail of his entourage had been planned by that prince of showmen, Thomas Wolsey, who had even chosen the shade of the satin for the King's doublet.

Priests and singers, secretaries and clerks, sewers, grooms and pages of the chamber were in the retinue; even the King's lutanist had not been forgotten or the Master of his Jewel-house. Fourteen magnificent horses for Henry's own use travelled with him, royal as their master in their coverings of gold and crimson velvet hung with precious bells. In all the wealth and colour of the pageantry only one muted note was struck when, in a plain cassock on an undecked mule, was seen to ride in priestly humility the King's Almoner, Thomas Wolsey.

They left Calais to join the spearhead of their army which had already advanced into French territory. A wooden house where he could lodge instead of bivouacking might follow Henry on fourteen wagons wherever he went, but he did not always take advantage of Wolsey's foresight. Heavy rains made the going arduous and one drenching night he refused to undress: instead, he rode about the camp encouraging the watch. "Now that we have suffered at the beginning," he cheered them, "fortune promises us better things, God willing." Never had his men known such a King as this, who called them comrades and joined his archers in archery practice, surpassing them all. When German mercenaries, who marched with the English troops, pillaged a church, their king promptly had three of them hanged.

Every courier who left the camp for England carried with him letters to the Queen from Wolsey and from the King, unless he was too preoccupied with war. He had made Katherine regent before he left home, a wise step although unusual because she was a woman, and her letters to him were full of the war she had on her hands.

What had happened before was happening again. Every Scots sovereign from Malcolm Canmore had made a point of invading England whenever his neighbour was either engaged in hostilities with France or confused with civil war. James IV of Scotland might be married to Henry's sister Margaret, he might be bound by treaty not to make war on England; nevertheless he behaved as his ancestors had done before him and prepared to lead an army over the border to aid his old ally France.

Katherine quietened her fears for her husband's safety by occupying herself with preparations to meet the invaders. She wrote she was horribly busy making standards, banners and badges. "My heart is very good to it," she penned in her quaint language. All Henry's subjects at home were very glad to be busy with the Scots too: they looked upon fighting with their neighbours over the border as a form of pastime.

Henry, besieging Therouanne in France, knew that England was threatened at her back door by bellicose Scotland. He had left Thomas Howard, Earl of Surrey, in charge of the retaining army at home. Howard was the family name of the great Duke of Norfolk, known as the Jockey, who had lost his life fighting on the losing side at the Battle of Bosworth. His oldest son, Thomas, wounded and taken prisoner on the field, had been attainted by Henry VII.

The only master Thomas Howard could serve was the master who had stripped him of everything that made life worth the living. Only a king had been powerful enough to do it, only a king could reinstate him to his father's glory. He submitted to the victor of Bosworth Moor.

He watched the new men nearest to the young King, as he had watched them round the old one, upstarts every one of them, filling posts that by hereditary right belonged to the nobility. But Henry VII had deflowered the aristocracy: in the whole of England there was only one duke and one marquis left, and that one duke was not the Duke of Norfolk.

He saw the same men round Henry VIII now he was king. Not a nobleman's son was the young sovereign's boon companion, but a big, blustering blockhead like Charles Brandon, adept only with lance and sword and renouncing the women he married when he wanted to take another wife. The progeny of a simple esquire (scratch the esquire and you find the yeoman) had been created Viscount Lisle since his master's succession, one remove below an earl, which it had taken patient years for Thomas Norfolk to regain.

Charles Brandon was very close to the King in the campaign in France, for he was marshal of the army. It was not all active service, siege and strategy. There were charming interludes, as when the Emperor Maximilian arrived in person to serve as a private at a hundred crowns a day under the English banners, and his daughter, Margaret of Savoy, joined her father. To entertain her Henry played the gitteron, lute and cornet, and danced and jousted before her. He "excelled every one as much in agility in breaking spears as in nobleness of stature". So close was Charles Brandon to the King, he even made suit to the emperor's daughter, when Henry obligingly helped him out with his French.

The ogre Louis, who had threatened the whole of Christendom only a short year ago, did not lead his men in person. Instead he drove out of Paris in a carriage, and the war in his country reached him like echoes and reverberations against old ear-drums.

This impression of unreality hung over the whole campaign. A large French force arrived to raise the siege but at the sight of the English troops panic seized it and the French cavalry wheeled their horses. Their trot broke into a canter, the canter became full gallop. It was a bloodless fray, with a roll of prisoners and no toll of dead, and was referred to ironically by the French as the Battle of the Spurs. Henry had the exhilarating experience of chasing the routed army as long as his horse would go, and of taking prisoner the noblest blood of France. He often relived that afternoon: he was never to know its like again.

He made his triumphal entry into the first French town captured by English arms since the days of Joan of Arc. Tournay, the richest city north of Paris, was besieged. Within a week it fell. The French towns were going down before the English like Jericho before the chosen children of Israel: God was on their side.

Word was brought him that the English had crushingly defeated the Scots at Flodden and killed their king. Katherine wrote with pardonable pride that this victory was the greatest honour that could be, and worth more than all the crown of France. She sent him a piece of the King of Scotland's coat to make banners out of. She wished she could have sent the King of Scots himself but "our Englishmen would not suffer it". "It should have been better for him to have been in peace than to have this reward. All that God sendeth is for the best." Her letter, in which she addressed him as My husband and My Henry, ends touchingly, "Your humble wife and true servant, Katherine." She asked him what Thomas Howard was to do with the dead King's body.

James IV had died like a king and a soldier, fighting to his last breath. That may be why Henry could feel regret for his vaulting brother-in-law. "He has paid," he said, "a heavier penalty for his perfidy than we would have wished." He wrote to the Pope for permission to bury him with royal honours in St. Paul's; papal permission was necessary as the Scots King had been excommunicated for breaking his treaty with England. It was granted, but the interment never took place; perhaps the magnanimity of victory wore thin, and no one knows what became of the Scots King's body, honourable with wounds.

For his victory at Flodden Field, the dukedom of Norfolk was restored to Thomas Howard. At the same time Charles Brandon was raised to spectacular heights when the dukedom of Suffolk was conferred on him by his friend the King.

It was impossible in the sixteenth century to victual an army on foreign soil during winter. The five summer months were the fighting ones and they had now passed. A triumphant Henry sailed for home with England's prestige higher than it had stood for a century, so high indeed that the Spanish King was said to be afraid of his son-in-law's ever-growing influence. Katherine believed her husband's success was all due to his zeal for religion. England was now a power to be reckoned with.

She had kept faith single-handed this year, but next year allies were essential, for wars were costly, and Henry VII's wealth was rapidly draining away with these inroads upon it. A treaty was drawn up binding Henry, Maximilian and Ferdinand to a combined invasion of France the following summer. At the same time the pledge for Henry's sister Mary to marry Ferdinand and Maximilian's grandson Charles was renewed.

Mary was a spirited girl of fifteen in 1513, her beauty was exquisite and every foreign ambassador voted her the loveliest princess in Europe. It was agreed the marriage should take place next year when the bridegroom-to-be came of age at fourteen. Meanwhile he wrote to her signing himself "Your husband", and she tactfully sighed with love for him whenever she looked at his portrait in the presence of the Spanish ambassadors.

The King's arrival home was quite different from his departure. He landed quietly at Dover and rode at once post-haste to surprise the Queen when "there was such a loving meeting between them that everyone rejoiced who witnessed it".

He never saw the baby son born to Katherine shortly before his return; either it was stillborn or it died immediately after birth. No one would have known of its abbreviated existence had the Venetian ambassador not scented it out and reported it to the world.

CHAPTER FIVE

THE NEW RIVAL

"Cloth of gold, do not despise,
Though thou hast wedded cloth of frieze.
Cloth of frieze, be not too bold,
Though thou hast wedded cloth of gold."

AFTER the giddy flights of victory, the alighting; after the stirring events of 1513, the disposing and maintaining. The year 1514 was a year of backwash; the currents that lapped it were far-reaching enough, nevertheless they were backwash.

Scotland at England's back door demanded urgent attention with its new king an infant in Margaret's arms. Henry claimed for himself the empty title "Protector of Scotland", and left his sister to strengthen the English influence in her adopted country, uphill work with such a nation, to whom independence was the breath of its existence.

Every country had its secret service and paid agents—priests, merchantmen and servants. No sooner had Ferdinand signed the treaty binding him, Maximilian and Henry to a joint invasion of France than his son-in-law and Wolsey learnt through informers of his allies' treachery. Maximilian and Ferdinand had entered into a secret pact to make war on England whenever Henry should renew hostilities on France. But their subtlety and double-dealing were outmatched by Wolsey's, who could play them at their own game and score hands down.

A nuncio was dispatched to France to mediate a peace between young Henry and old Louis, lately bereft of his wife. Henry was no longer intimidated by the French King; it was the French King's turn to be fearful of Henry, and he was prepared to pay him a high price in the form of pensions for peaceful settlement.

Wolsey was not only dexterously manipulating the reins of government until he was handling everything about the King but he was the royal family's confessor, confidant and friend. The one-time chaplain collected three bishoprics in the same year, was angling for the cardinal's hat and would not stop short at St. Peter's throne. His appetite for titles and aggrandisement was insatiable, as though the more he gained, the more successfully he obliterated his beginnings. Prince of the Church, he began to build a palace for himself with rose-red walls, near enough London to be con-venient, far enough removed to be safe when plague struck the city.

1514 was to be the year in which the long-covenanted marriage between Mary Tudor and Spanish Charles was to be fulfilled, not later than May as stipulated in a treaty not three months old. January, February, March, April passed with no sign of Maxi-milian's purpose to seal his grandson's betrothal of six years' stand-ing. It was repeated in England that the potential bridegroom had been heard to remark he wanted a wife, not a mother, referring to Mary's two years' seniority.

When May came and went with no move made to keep his word, Maximilian's breach of promise was proclaimed to the world. Imme-diately negotiations were concluded for the marriage of the sixteen-year-old Mary Tudor, jilted by Charles, to the aged, newly widowed Louis, King of France.

It was a brilliant coup on Henry's and Wolsey's part. England, now on equal footing with France and Spain, by aligning herself to one, dangerously outweighed the other. The marriage of an English Princess to the French King would cement the peace between the two countries and was calculated to affect adversely Henry's father-in-law who had played so false with him. What would Ferdinand feel at the prospect of his grandson's rejected bride producing an heir to the French throne?

Certainly his lovely sister had no desire to marry a decrepit old man, even though he was King of France. Henry knew perfectly well she was in love with his favourite, Charles Brandon, recently elevated Duke of Suffolk, who, bold and masculine, played havoc with women's hearts. But after all the widower was old, and sickly into the bargain; Mary was not, by the laws of nature, being asked to undergo a life sentence. If she furthered Henry's plans with her first marriage, her brother undertook to allow her to marry whom she chose when it came to her second.

It was not a happy year for Katherine, for her husband, not sur-

prisingly, visited on his wife the ill-faith and betrayal of her un-
scrupulous parent, even threatening to put her away. Spain was
anathema in her adopted country. The Spanish ambassador felt in
England like a bull at whom everyone threw darts, nor did he find
an ally in the Spanish-born Queen who was more English than the
English. As for the King, every time his father-in-law's name was
mentioned, he behaved in the most offensive manner possible. The
ambassador added with bitter prophecy that if the King of Spain
did not put a bridle on this young colt it would soon become
impossible to control him.

Meanwhile the young colt was informing with some truth an
attentive Venetian envoy that the only ruler in the world who kept
faith was himself. "Therefore," he said with royal unction, "God
Almighty, who knows this, prospers my affairs." If Katherine had
now completely identified herself with her husband and his subjects,
her husband was in the process of identifying his Maker with himself. The time was to come when Henry was to take the place of
God, but the transition was gradual and no one could say when it
actually occurred.

The King and Queen and their court progressed to Dover to see
Mary embark for France. The marriage of the young English
princess to the senile French King shocked all Europe; and Europe,
accustomed to the ways of her sovereign lords, was not easily
shocked. Mary was to be escorted by the Duke of Norfolk, her
chamberlain and household, attended by her governess (whom she
and her sister Margaret had called Mother Guildford from their
infant days), servants and ladies-in-waiting, highly born girls, one
of the youngest of whom was a Mary Boleyn.

It was September, and it must have seemed to the unwilling
bride that the very elements were conspiring to keep her in England,
for storm after storm came blustering across the narrow Channel,
making sailing impossible. In his strong towered castle, called the
Key of England, Henry passed the days with his court waiting for
the winds to subside. These storm-beaten wintry walls had stood
high on the white cliff for so long they had become part of the
landscape. From embrasure slit and crenelle he could sight the
coast of France. The expanse and might of the ocean did not overawe him: he wanted ships strong enough to ride the waves, however
high. Already, since coming to the throne, he had built *Mary Rose*

and *Peter Pomegranate*, and this very year the *Henry Grace de Dieu*, known colloquially as *The Great Harry*, had been launched, a wonder man-of-war the like of which England had never seen before.

Not until October did the winds drop, when the bride and her attendants were roused before dawn to take advantage of the fairer weather. The leave-takings were painful: Henry might wear in his hat Mary's magnificent Spanish jewel given to her as surety for a marriage that had not after all taken place, but family ties were strong in the enclosed Tudor circle and he loved his sprightly young sister. He tried to comfort the weeping girl by painting a picture for her of a happy widowhood. She clung piteously to Katherine, who gave her the assurance and support of an older generation yet was bound up in all the gaieties and joyousness of a young court, as proud of Mary's beauty as though she were her mother.

Soon after the bride's arrival in France, distressed letters reached "My good Brother" and Wolsey, whom she addressed as "Mine own good Lord", for she looked upon him as her spiritual father. Would to God, she wrote, my Lord of York (Wolsey) had come with her in the place of Norfolk, for then she was sure she should not have been left as she now was—with no one of her own about her except two or three of her youngest ladies-in-waiting. All had been sent back to England by her royal spouse, the Duke of Norfolk weakly acquiescing. He had not put up a fight even for Mother Guildford. Mary wrote Wolsey she would rather lose the whole of France as lose her counsel. But the homely King Louis had taken the strongest aversion to Mother Guildford. He was astute enough to see that the Englishwoman with her officious stewardship of her royal ward would cause trouble in the French court. He felt sure the King, his good and loving brother Henry, would understand that Louis could not be merry with his wife if a strange woman was with her the whole time. Mary was told it was unsuitable for the Queen of France to have anyone such as a governess dictating to one who should command.

Dispatches describing the wedding reached England from the Duke of Suffolk, for the man who loved Mary Tudor was appointed by Henry as one of his ambassadors to see her crowned. In the jousting that followed, the Englishman laid about him to such an extent that he shocked the hostess country and killed a French cavalier.

Much did the Parisians wonder at the beauty of their new Queen, tall as a nymph, sweet of face and manner, skin and hair very fair to their dark Gallic gaze. With her spring-like vitality the bride blossomed through all the elaborate ceremonies that welcomed her arrival and led up to the climax of the wedding and coronation; they sat on her elderly groom, who had attacks of gout, more heavily than the cares of state. But he was enchanted with his young bride and heaped on her jewels the like of which Mary, a king's daughter, had never seen before. He was, however, judicious in his giving, chuckling as he explained that she was not to have them all at once but at different times, that he might be repaid by as many thank-you kisses as possible.

Henry received a letter from his new brother-in-law telling him he could not sufficiently praise his wife, that daily he loved her more, honoured and held her dear. Mary came to believe she was better without Mother Guildford and settled down to life with her royal husband, doing her best to content him in every way. Certainly she changed one or two things to make them more English. The French, for instance, had the curious custom of dining at eight in the morning and the King was accustomed to retiring for the night at six in the evening. Mary altered his dinner hour to noon, and he stayed up with her until midnight, just like the English court. She could not understand why his doctors should shake their heads warningly over this so much more natural arrangement.

That November Katherine held once again a living son, bent to kiss his brow, but the baby was premature and died a day or two later. Some attributed its premature birth to her husband's harshness over her father's treachery, but there is little ground for such an assumption. It was Katherine's second pregnancy that year, sufficient reason for its weak hold on life, and Henry shared with her what was sorrow for them both.

That New Year's Day, because she was better, he staged a ballet to celebrate her recovery and to amuse her. As, dressed in cloth of silver and blue velvet, he performed by light of torches with Charles Brandon and six other dancers the intricate figures of the ballet, his brother-in-law in France, his Christian Majesty Louis, suddenly died, not three months after his wedding.

Wolsey was at once instructed to write to the young widow not to enter into any matrimonial engagement. The next marriage of the

King's sister must not be dictated by the policy of France. Mary's reply was that she was not a child. The English ambassade dispatched to take charge of her and her considerable property included Charles Brandon, Duke of Suffolk, who, before he left, swore the ambassador's oath that he would not abuse his trust to the young Queen consigned to his care.

The envoys were also charged to renew the league with France's new King. He was a young man, two years younger than his English counterpart, and the moment he joined the most exclusive club of Europe, that of crowned heads, Henry scented competition.

"The King of France, is he as tall as I am?" he wanted to know, and was told they were of a height. "What sort of leg has he?" came the anxious demand. "Spare," came the welcome answer. Then he opened his doublet and placed his hand on his thigh. "Look here," he invited, "I have a good calf to my leg." On learning Francis wore a beard, not to be outdone, he allowed his own to grow. It grew in reddish, so with his golden beard he outshone the French King.

Thus began a mutual rivalry that was to last for over thirty rankling years. Francis I had the same tall, broad-shouldered figure of the athlete as Henry, with an oval handsome face where Henry's was round. The King of England, with his golden hair, fair skin and bright colouring, looked celestial as a seraph; the King of France, like the devil.

He was married to the Princess Claude, daughter of King Louis, whose fate of a libertine husband was that which does befall some virtuous women. Marriage did not deter him from making advances to the lovely English widow. Every day that passed in France seemed like a thousand to Mary, racked with toothache and unable to stop weeping. She wrote that she desired to return to her beloved brother, from whom she never wanted to be parted again.

Never, Charles Brandon communicated to his kingly friend, had he seen a woman weep as she did. He discovered two English friars had visited her, telling her that if she left France she would never land in England, as the Duke of Suffolk had orders to take her to Flanders where she was to be given in marriage to the Prince who had rejected her, Charles of Spain. Rather than that fate, Mary told him, she would prefer to be torn in pieces.

Nothing her lover said would drive this fear from her mind. There was only one way he could prove he had not come to entice her to

ANNO · ÆTATIS · · SVÆ · XLIX

Henry VIII, aged 49, painted by Holbein in the year Henry married Anne of Cleves

Henry VII, father of Henry VIII, holding the red rose of Lancaster

Elizabeth, Henry VII's wife and mother of Henry VIII, holding the white rose of York

her doom and that was there and then to marry her himself. "So I granted thereto," he wrote, "and so she and I were married."

Henry was now besieged with letters from his sister, recalling with Tudor tenacity that she had always been of good mind to my Lord of Suffolk, and her brother's promise that if she married the aged and sickly monarch she would be allowed to choose her second husband herself. She took upon herself full responsibility for the marriage, knowing the executioner's axe gleamed for her husband who had broken his promise, not for her. Remembering her jewel in Henry's hat, she made over to him on her wedding day, St. Valentine's, all the plate and vessels her late husband had bestowed on her, and the choice of her special jewels. Henry's favourite jousting partner threw himself on his sovereign's mercy.

Terror seized them when they heard from Wolsey that the King had taken the news grievously and displeasantly. It was Francis who stepped into the breach by allowing her to keep her French revenue and riches, of which he could have deprived her when she married again. An Englishman of low degree suited France better as a husband for their Queen Dowager than Charles of rival Spain.

Mary, twice married within a matter of months, sailed for England with her promised dowry as a sop to her brother's anger. They were not quite sure what awaited them on the other side, but at least they were together. Mary had been spared separation and a desolate life in a foreign convent, which she felt sure would have been the death of her.

As it was, Henry received his sister and favourite with *bonhomie*, giving their marriage royal sanction by being present with the Queen in Grey Friar's Church when it was solemnized, and tournaments celebrated the event as though everything had been orderly and wonted. No one appears to have thought twice about the bridegroom's previous marital entanglements; Suffolk's procedure was to marry again and depend on a complaisant Pope to confirm the *fait accompli*.

Mary, as well as plate, jewels, gold and dowry, undertook to repay to her brother the expenses of her former marriage at the yearly rate of a thousand pounds for twenty-four years. Wolsey took the credit that the bridegroom lost neither life nor bride, but he possibly over-painted the King's displeasure to gain their gratitude. It used to be said there were two obstinate men about the King who governed everything, one Wolsey, the other Brandon. Now the Suffolks, and he was fond of display and cutting a figure, frequently had to retire from court into the country to recoup when the terms fell due. That left only Wolsey to do and undo.

Henry bounded with good spirits—Katherine was pregnant again and as ever hope rode high. Very merry were they that May Day when the King and his courtiers dressed themselves as Robin Hood and his outlaws, all in green even to their shoes. They entertained the Queen, Mary and their ladies to a breakfast feast of venison in a forest glade where elaborate bowers had been constructed from hawthorn, spring flowers and mosses.

When more than one were thinking that the King was but a youngling who cared for nothing but girls and hunting, and wasted his father's patrimony, Wolsey received a message from him. His minister was requested to send to him a certain Act newly passed by Parliament for his "examination and correction".

CHAPTER SIX

THE QUALITY OF MERCY

"God save our King, and bless this land
With plenty, joy and peace."

THE mayor and aldermen of London repaired to St. Paul's on the feast of St. Matthew to return thanks to Almighty God for the Queen, who was quick with child. Wolsey, who never left a stone unturned, instructed them to attend the service, and they turned out to a man.

The child was born in February and lived, but to the disappointment of the people it was a daughter. Henry, however, was inordinately proud of his offspring, assuring everyone in the most besotted fashion that she never cried. When an ambassador tactfully tempered his congratulations because it was not a son, her father replied cheerfully, "We are both young; if it is a daughter this time, by the grace of God the sons will follow."

"We are both young": we catch an echo of his mother's voice, ten months before she died, when she comforted his father after the death of their eldest son. Henry was not twenty-five when he spoke these words, magnificent with youth, lusty for life. But Katherine was six years older, and at thirty-one she had begun to age. She had never attempted to keep up with her strenuous husband,who could tire out ten horses in the one day but not himself. In seven years of marriage she had had six pregnancies, and her figure had broadened and solidified, her serious face with its calm brow grown heavier, her copper hair begun to fade.

The child was christened Mary after her entrancing aunt. During Katherine's confinement her father King Ferdinand was finally out-tricked by death, but the news was kept from her lest it have an adverse effect. He was succeeded by his grandson Charles, the nephew Katherine had never seen.

Instead of sceptres gripped in practised old hands, young men felt them now; instead of Henry the most youthful of the trio—France, Spain, England—he was now the senior. The newcomer Charles was the youngest at sixteen, but, self-contained as an oyster, he might have been the eldest, this new King of Spain who was never seen to smile.

Katherine, the youngest of a large family of girls, was always very much the friend of Henry's sisters. When word reached them that Margaret, Queen of Scotland, was waiting at the border for permission to enter her brother's realm, consent was at once sent, as well as everything in the way of comforts and conveniences, for Katherine knew what straits her sister-in-law was in.

She had married again, captivated by the fine figure of the youthful Earl of Angus, to the disquiet of her adopted country. The Scots reasoned that he, the "childish young" head of the powerful house of Douglas, was already great, and the Queen's marrying him made him greater still. They would not allow her to continue as regent, for that would make him too great for the peace and safety of Scotland. She had to surrender her infant son the King, since all her plans for smuggling him into England failed, and seek refuge in her brother's country.

Once over the border, in an inhospitable keep, she bore a baby daughter and nearly died. On the day her life was despaired of, her husband left both wife and daughter to return to Scotland. For that Margaret never forgave him, not so much for his defection but because he chose such a day.

At last she was well enough to travel. A nature such as hers had no half measures but swung sharply from trough to crest, crest to trough. It was thirteen years since music and bells had chimed her, a bride of fourteen, all the way into Scotland. Now her spirits rose the deeper she was carried into England and the further she left her adopted country behind. She wrote to her brother *en route* that next to God he was her only trust and confidence, and arrived by barge at Greenwich, at the palace that was so bound up with all their childhoods, to find her family waiting to welcome her with open arms.

Tournaments and pageants celebrated her home-coming, but all was not so splendid and joyous as it appeared; behind the spectacle and show could be felt the tug and strain of family ties. The first

question Henry asked his sister was, "And where is my Lord
Angus?" When told he had returned to Scotland, his brotherly
comment came out pat, "Done like a Scot!" The jousting and
festivals were on such a lavish scale, the Suffolks could not afford to
keep up with them and had to retreat into the country to retrench.
Margaret had never been good at lessons and time had taught her
none, only served to emphasize the dominant traits of her character:
her hot impatience and headstrong will that would brook no curb.

She quickly adapted herself to the procedure at her brother's
court and wrote to Wolsey, excluding God in these instances, that
next to the King's Grace her trust was in him. Although Henry
most generously provided for her while she remained in his realm,
although her clothes, furs and jewels were sent to her from Scotland,
her letters to her brother and Wolsey betray her as the born bor-
rower, each time promising this is the last, that if her request is
granted she will be beholden for ever, importunate for reply yet
refusing to take No, however emphatic, for answer. "I am loth to
speak to the King my brother," she wrote, unabashed, to Wolsey,
"because I trust you will do it for me." Religion meant little to her
beyond a convenient patter; she had none of her parents' piety or
Henry's liberality in almsgiving, and appalled her Scots Council by
taking everything her husband left her in his will but leaving his
debts unpaid.

The court sports on May Day that year were spoiled by distur-
bances in London so violent that the 1st May, 1517, was remembered
ever afterwards as Evil May Day. Whenever there was trouble in
the city, you might be sure apprentices—a rough noisy quarrelsome
band ready to start a fray with or without provocation—would set
it afoot.

Now the King might employ foreign craftsmen and artists to
beautify his palaces, but his insular subjects detested all men not
"born of the land", and trade-conscious Londoners were more
envious of them than any. They muttered that foreign craftsmen
took the work out of their hands and so the bread from their mouths;
no one bought from them when foreign merchants were selling silks,
cloths of gold, wines and other wares; foreigners brought into the
country and sold cheaply the same goods that were made by honest
Englishmen.

On Evil May Day, a holiday when Satan found plenty of mischief for idle hands, the apprentices' battle-cry of "Clubs! Clubs!" was heard in the streets. They marched a thousand strong to Newgate and released some of their number who were held prisoner. They attacked Spanish, Venetian and Flemish traders, looting and destroying their homes and shops and lynching their masters. The terror lasted well into the night when they suddenly wearied and began to disband; then some three hundred were arrested and the following day another hundred were added to their ranks.

Henry swelled with disgust when he heard. Was London ruled by rascally apprentices, that strangers in their midst could not go about their lawful business without fear? What were the civic authorities doing, or not doing, to permit such things to happen? They put on mourning and hastened with gifts to Wolsey, craving his favour. Boys were hung on their masters' sign-posts before gibbets were set up.

Mothers streamed wailing to Greenwich to ask good Queen Katherine to intercede on behalf of their sons. Three queens pleaded for the prisoners, Katherine of England, Mary Dowager Queen of France, Margaret of Scotland.

Wolsey stage-managed a court scene where the prisoners were filed in, some four hundred of them. They had been in the Tower for days, crowded in narrow quarters, and each was as unkempt, dirty and tattered as his fellows. Each had a halter of rope round his neck, signifying the fate he deserved.

They blinked stupidly at the sight that met their gaze: the King himself, dazzling as the sun so that they dare not look lest they be blinded, his nobles and councillors, and the mayor and aldermen, out of their mourning and in their best robes as Wolsey had directed them to be.

Evidence was led so castigating and incriminating that each, stretching his neck in its rope collar, knew that condemnation was bound to follow. Judgement fell like the stroke of axe on block, but because they were mean fellows and not high-born, it would be the gibbet for them.

Then the man in the red coat—whom they knew to be Cardinal Wolsey from the times they had seen him ride through the city, second only to the King himself—the man in the red coat threw himself before the throne, pleading for them. And the King bestowed his pardon.

They could scarcely believe what they saw and heard, they felt it instead. It spread like wildfire through the city. By the King's favour they were free. Tears tracked paths down black faces, bumping from their cheeks and the stubble on young chins. The high almighty King on his throne deigned to have mercy on them, the most miserable of his creatures. It was said in every shop, house and home to which an apprentice returned with the fervour of an oath, "God save the King."

London might be unsafe because of the rioting apprentices and unwholesome because of so many bodies hanging from gibbets, but nothing would deter Margaret visiting it. She wrote Wolsey she would do as he thought best and in the same sentence prayed him as heartily as she could to let her come on the morrow, trusting to God no further trouble would interfere with her plans. She had made up her restless mind to return to Scotland where she had hopes of regaining the regency, and wanted to go to Baynard's Castle before she left to collect the gear she had accumulated during her year's stay at her brother's court.

Her father had rebuilt Baynard's Castle, transforming a battlemented fortress into a pleasant palace although it had no gardens, so close to the river it appeared to spring from it. Behind it the spire of St. Paul's soared above the city and all round were churches whose bells made the air vibrant with sound.

Margaret entered England in poverty and distress. She left it in style, with jewels, plate, tapestry, arras, coin, horses—all, the English onlooker noted, at "Our King's cost".

A curious pall hovered over London, like the torpor that precedes illness. People became increasingly aware of it, found themselves waiting and listening, looking over their shoulders, as though something they did not want was about to happen. When they saw wisps of straw hanging outside certain houses, they knew what it was—the dread sweating sickness.

You might be merry at dinner and dead at supper. They said if you could stand the heat and pain of it for the first twenty-four hours, you might recover. Few did. It forced its entry into the hovels huddling in back streets and walked unbidden into manor and palace.

Henry the lion-hearted retreated before it. This was something you could not shiver with a lance or quell with a look. He and the

Queen and the baby Princess moved from place to place. The pages who slept in the King's very bedchamber sickened and died; Henry stripped his household to a minimum and moved once more. He remained longest at Abingdon: there people were not continually coming to tell him about deaths as they did daily in London.

Wolsey nearly died of it, it took such toll of him that it made havoc of his appearance. His sovereign wrote to his chief minister to take every care of himself "that you may the longer endure to serve us". He could not visualize life without Wolsey who thought of everything, saw to everything, did everything. He told him the Queen his wife asked him to remember her to one she loved very well. "Both she and I will feign know when you will repair to us." That was the year Katherine had two miscarriages.

The epidemic subsided during the cold of winter, but revived the following year. Again Wolsey was struck down. His royal master concocted medicine himself to send him, christening it with a Latin name signifying Christ's Hand. He told him the good news that the Queen was pregnant.

One man in England transacted the business single-handed which occupied all the magistracies, offices and councils of Venice, civil, criminal, state and ecclesiastical. That one man was Thomas Wolsey. He distrusted parliament, never deputed, had neither party nor following, but was on a pinnacle by himself. The pinnacle was reared on his services to the King.

With gifts and benefactions, preferments and pensions, his wealth was boundless. He had grown tyrannical with power, and there were some who said his influence could not last, but it waxed, not waned. His temper became choleric and it was believed the Pope withheld the cardinal's hat a year because of his aggressiveness and ambition. He used to say, "His Majesty will do so and so." Now he said, "We shall do so and so." Very soon, as he reached the zenith of his power, he was to say, "I shall do so and so."

"Never," he was to write about this time, "was the kingdom in greater harmony and repose than now; such is the effect of my administration of justice and equity." He had sympathy with the poor and brought in decrees to help them, but he was never popular. The King was sacrosanct, and his chief minister received the redding-stroke whenever anything went wrong.

In the nine years since Henry's accession England had grown into a power to be reckoned with, due chiefly to Wolsey's skill. He was a past master at playing off the rivalry between Spain and France. The inconstant Maximilian had had an apoplectic stroke; when he died Charles would not only be King of Spain but Emperor of the Holy Roman Empire, a Caesar astride the world. Feverishly France courted England, and a treaty favourable to England, to Henry and to Wolsey was drawn up. It was handselled by the marriage alliance between the baby heir to the French throne and Henry's two-year-old daughter. The betrothal was not popular in England: the English disliked all foreigners in general and the French in particular.

Katherine missed the banquets and entertainments that followed, as it was one of her dangerous times. A month later, in November, her child was born. The people heard the news that it was another still-birth with the greatest vexation: no heir to the throne, and their princess trysted to a Frenchman. If someone didn't look sharp, the next thing to happen would be France would marry England's princess and swallow England as her dowry.

Half a year later, in early summer, Henry fathered an illegitimate son. The mother was a girl called Elizabeth Blount, who had taken gleeful part in all the revels and romps of the young court. She had beauty, for the child was said to be goodly, like his father and mother. He was christened Henry, and his godfather was Wolsey.

Henry ordered the affair with the greatest discretion. No ambassador or envoy knew of the liaison, or got wind of the birth. He was jealous of royal prestige, and to foreigners, innured to palace excesses and scandals, his court was a model of decorum.

He was outraged when he learnt that his sister Margaret was contemplating divorcing her young husband. Katherine sent one of her ecclesiastics north to plead with her not to take such a step; Henry dispatched a stern friar to tell her from him that Satan had put such wicked ideas into her head, and what an unnatural mother she would be thus to stigmatize her infant daughter. But gentle father or vehement friar, angry brother or pained sister-in-law had not the slightest effect on Margaret.

Henry insisted upon the attendance of sufficient councillors to enable him to transact business as he moved from place to place to circumvent the epidemic, and he arranged for a relay of posts every seven hours between him and Wolsey, whom business tied to London no matter how ill he was. In the enforced absence of his chief minister, were Henry's capable hands fingering the reins of government for the first time and liking the feel of them? He drew up a memorandum of twenty-one items he wished the Lord Chancellor to put into execution. Wolsey replied what a comfort it was for him to note the King's prudence, but he must have been dismayed at this royal poaching on his preserves.

The relationship between sovereign and prelate was warm and unstrained. There was friendly competition between the King's and the Cardinal's choirs. Should a jarring note be inadvertently sounded, Wolsey was adept at transmuting the discord into harmony. There was the occasion when he showed the King and Queen over his new palace of Hampton Court, with its two hundred and eighty guest rooms and rich tapestries that were changed every week before he could tire of them. He explained how spring water, recommended by his medical advisers, was brought all the way from Coombe Hill in lead pipes.

His Majesty as he looked round saw that this sumptuous place would take five hundred servants to run if it took a man. It was a king's residence, not the home of the King's servant, and he was provoked by what he saw into demanding what his Lord Chancellor meant by building for himself so magnificent a palace.

If Wolsey was taken aback, not for a moment did he reveal it. Never at a loss for the eloquent word, he explained at some length he meant it as a gift sufficiently worthy to be offered to His Majesty. With his father's acquisitiveness, Henry was not satisfied until he held the title deeds, but Wolsey continued to address his letters from "My Manor of Hampton Court".

Henry undertook to lead a crusade against the infidel Turk in person if only God would grant him an heir. Spanish physicians came to England to see what they could do, but the child born to Katherine in November was the last she was to bear. Never again was she to know the tremulous expectancy, the leaping joy and glad fulfilment of birth.

CHAPTER SEVEN

DEFENDER OF THE FAITH

"They hae gard fill up ae punch-bowl,
    And after it they maun hae anither,
And thus the night they a' hae spent,
    Just as they had been brither and brither."

THE treaty with France provided that the two kings should meet. It was broken to the English people that the meeting was to take place in France by stressing that although their king was crossing the water he was convening with his French counterpart on English soil.

Wherever Henry was he always filled the picture, not only because he was king but because he was Henry. Routine could not harness his flamboyant personality, so that even a practice hour at the butts or in the tilt-yard became a gala occasion for those who accompanied him. Now as he passed through the countryside on his way to the coast, every moment of his passage to those who watched him go by was a picked one. The approbation of the populace was so well justified by his person that his affability towards them surrounded him like a halo.

Never had they seen anything like this before: the procession winding through the vernal May landscape seemed endless. This would give these Frenchies something to stare at. And at the heart of the surge and sway and swirl of movement was the King himself, so eye-filling that after he had passed there was no sense of flatness, only pride that they had beheld one so worth the seeing. When they thought of him afterwards, he proceeded through their minds like a pageant, and when they saw a goldfinch, with its swelling coloured breast and wings barred with gold, they would wag their heads at it, addressing it as King Hal.

At Canterbury the King and Queen paused to keep holy Pentecost. It was there Henry heard that Spanish ships bringing Charles to England had been sighted off Dover. Charles was now King and Emperor. The man who ruled over one of the greatest accumulations of territories in history considered Henry important enough to visit, crossing continent and channel to do so, scrambling to get in before his meeting with the rival Francis. Well might Wolsey congratulate himself on the position England had attained. France and the Empire—whichever had not England as its ally was perilously outbalanced.

Wolsey put out in a small boat to meet their visitor, and conducted him to Dover Castle, where the Emperor, tired out after a stormy voyage, retired to bed. In the middle of the night he was disturbed by the stir of arrival—the King of England had ridden from Canterbury by torchlight to greet him. Emperor and King met at the top of the stairs, and nephew was embraced by his bounding uncle-in-law. Together they sat up half the night talking in the keep state-room.

So this was Charles, King of Spain and its South American colonies, of the Kingdoms of Sicily and Naples, Emperor of Austria and the Low Countries, which included the Netherlands, England's best foreign customer. He was not tall, neither was he small; his pale face, white after his sea journey, was made ugly by the protruding Hapsburg underlip, animated only by bright and intelligent eyes. His gravity was such that he might have been a grandfather instead of twenty, and he had as much charm as a lamp without a wick has light. Nothing here to pique Henry or challenge his competitive instincts. It was state business they talked as night winds drummed on old walls and whistled down the chimney.

It was state business they talked next day as they rode side by side to Canterbury, bridles ringing and jingling. Katherine met her unknown nephew joyfully, and for the first time Mary Tudor and the man to whom she had been betrothed came face to face. Every English pair of eyes was upon him, watching what he felt as he looked at the loveliest woman in the country. He appeared dejected, and refused to dance.

A few days later Charles took ship for Flanders, and Henry sailed in *The Great Harry* for France, but before parting they agreed to meet again at Calais after Henry's rendezvous with Francis. What they had been conferring must be bound and riveted by treaty.

Henry's former advent in France was like a dress rehearsal compared to this. In his retinue marched over four and a half thousand persons, including dukes, earls, marquises, bishops, barons, knights. The Queen was accompanied by a train of nearly thirteen hundred. Everything Wolsey's resourceful brain could invent materialized to impress the French with the wealth and power of England. A palace of art was one building to be erected which, although temporary, was so exquisite Italians declared it might have been designed by Leonardo da Vinci himself.

The ground where the kings were to meet lay between two castles still manned by English soldiers, so could be called English soil. So lavish was the display, the site became known as the Field of Cloth of Gold. In the vast courtyard of the English pavilion a fountain sprayed red, white and claret wine. Inside, the Tudor rose bloomed everywhere, flowering on hangings and curtains, entwining silver drinking vessels and plates, blossoming on the curious foreign glass in the windows. The French pavilion had to outmatch it if possible, no matter what it cost. Its motif was a midnight-blue ceiling of rich stuffs in which sparkled and glittered solid gold stars.

The King of England started from English-held Guisnes at the same time as the King of France started from Ardes, to meet in the valley between the two towns. As French and English converged, suspicion of French designs broke over the English ranks, but it was overcome.

Alone the two kings rode out to meet each other. A breathless silence hung over the waiting, watching multitudes, and a slight, almost imperceptible stir, like an escaped sigh, passed over both retinues. The sovereigns embraced on horseback, and then again on foot.

Everything here to rival and compete with the King of England. Francis was as tall, might even be taller (or perhaps it was only his long lean legs that gave that impression), as strong and as magnificently garbed, and he carried himself valorously, like a prince.

"I never saw Prince with my eyes that might of my heart be more loved," Henry told him. "And for your love I have crossed the seas, into the furthest frontier of my realm, to see you, which doing now gladdens me." Francis was as forthcoming in return, with a playful allusion to Henry as "my prisoner".

The French had to admit that King Henry was a very handsome

prince. They liked his manner, which struck them as gentle and gracious, and his becoming red beard. They noted their monarch was taller, but the English one undoubtedly had the better-looking face. Indeed beside his French counterpart, his fair skin made him appear to them almost womanly. It was like seraph meeting Lucifer.

For sixteen gilded days the two retinues remained together, entertaining each other, exchanging compliments. The two kings held the field against all comers, no one could say which outshone the other. They breakfasted together, gave gifts to one another, professed eternal amity, for all the world to see the fastest friends in Christendom. "These sovereigns," commented a penetrating Venetian, "hate each other very cordially."

There was no insincerity between the two queens; both devout and virtuous women, they were kindred spirits. Katherine considered no time so much wasted as that passed in dressing and adorning herself. Even if Queen Claude had not been pregnant, her nature was as retiring, and it was Mary, Dowager Queen of France, who rode between her brother and the King of France.

Only French memoirs record the incident when their king threw the English one. It was an unrehearsed occasion: Henry, hearty after beating Francis at archery, suddenly seized the tall Frenchman by the collar, saying, "Come, you shall wrestle with me." Francis was taken off his guard, but recovered quickly. The struggle that followed was over almost before it had begun. To the horror of the two queens and the watching courtiers they saw and heard the resounding thud as England's king was thrown to the ground.

Never had such a thing happened to him in his life before. Henry rose, his big face reddening until it flared scarlet. "Again!" he said in a voice of thunder. But the two queens fussed forward, courtiers flocked round. Everyone talked animatedly about nothing in particular, no one looked at anyone else, and the crisis passed by pretending it had not taken place.

The man responsible for the Field of Cloth of Gold had outgrown his humble cassock and uncaparisoned steed. Cardinal Wolsey was clad in crimson satin from head to foot, his mule's trappings were of gold, he was accompanied by two hundred gentlemen, and he had a bodyguard of two hundred archers. Francis, King of France, received him as his equal; when he celebrated mass on the last day bishops invested him with his robes and put sandals on his feet, and water to wash his hands was brought to him by some of the chief English nobles.

In air over-sweet with incense and flowers, with enormous golden candlesticks blazing like suns, with altars hung with cloth of gold tissue and golden images of the twelve Apostles looking blankly on, Thomas Wolsey reached the height of his splendour. This was what he had brought about, the meeting of two nations, hereditary enemies, in concord and love. Yet there was as little permanence in this peace as there was in the showy chapel, built in one night, in which he sang mass. Wolsey knew that in the war that was bound to break between France and Spain, England had already elected to side with Spain.

After the painted spectacle and parade of chivalry, transactions and acts. Henry, on his way back to England, met Charles at the Flemish town of Gravelines, and together they repaired to Calais. The Emperor was unlucky with weather; a great wind blew the roof of the conference hall away, but negotiations were satisfactorily completed. Henry bound himself to proceed no further in the marriage between Princess Mary and the Dauphin, and Charles bound himself to proceed no further in that between himself and Francis's little daughter. Not included but implicit in the treaty was the proviso that Charles should marry Henry's daughter himself. Wolsey's perquisite was the Emperor's promise to help him gain St. Peter's chair when it should fall vacant.

Once home, Henry for the remaining six months of the year spent his time hunting: from daybreak to sundown he was in the saddle. "He spares no pains to convert the sport of hunting into a martyrdom," remarked a sedentary bishop. Such exercise was excessive even for him, as though by thrashing his body tired he hoped to wear down a problem that threatened.

Katherine was not going to have another child. She was thirty-five now, and for two years there had been no quickening. Francis had said, "My brother of England has no son because, although a young and handsome man, he keeps an old and ugly wife." But Katherine had not always been old. The harvest of eight pregnancies was one small daughter, pale as an ear of wheat, and no heir. The humblest peasant in his realm took it as reproach if he had no male issue, and he, Henry King of England, had no heir to succeed him.

Yet his illegitimate son was growing in beauty and in strength. Only one Being was strong enough, powerful enough, omnipotent enough to lay this rod upon a sovereign He had favoured in every other way, and that one Being was God. The rod pointed at Henry's marriage to his brother's widow. Katherine's little waxen babies must be the token of His displeasure at their union.

Henry's loyal championship of the Pope did the religion in which he was cradled every credit. It did not matter whether he were the belligerent Julius or the peaceable Leo, Henry chivalrously defended him because he was the custodian of the Church, and in proof of this had taken up arms. His religion had a strong theological bent; he enjoyed discussing and amicably disputing with scholars and prelates. So incited was he on reading a heretical book by a pestilent German called Martin Luther that he wrote to Pope Leo he must defend the Church with his pen as well as his sword.

He took two years to write his book, dedicating to the Pope the first offerings of his intellect and his little erudition. The brilliant Wolsey was too wise to criticize or edit it, the author too shrewd to think it worthy of the Cardinal's high-flown praise; nevertheless he was proud of his brain child. It never, however, takes wings like his music and songs; instead it remains earth-bound, bogged down by long-winded rhetoric.

Of marriage Henry wrote sententiously: "The insipid water of concupiscence is turned by the hidden grace of God into the finest flavour. Whom God hath joined together let no man put asunder." Had God joined him and Katherine together? Not if the words in Leviticus were remembered: "And if a man shall take his brother's wife, it is an unclean thing . . . they shall be childless." He and Katherine were not childless, there was Mary of whom Henry was very fond, but they were sonless. It was of course impossible for Henry to do wrong, but he might in innocence have committed an illegal act by taking Arthur's widow. There was no such thing as an illegal marriage: a marriage that was not legal was not marriage. Supposing he and Katherine were not married at all, but had quite inadvertently–to neither could blame be imputed–been living in mortal sin all along? To neither could blame be imputed so long as they had been living together believing they were married. It was a different matter when doubts arose and conscience quirked.

A copy of Henry's book bound in cloth of gold was presented to

Prince Arthur, the elder son, who married Katherine of Aragon and died at sixteen

Prince Henry, the younger son, when he was a child

Princess Margaret (identity uncertain), the elder daughter, headstrong and dominant

Princess Mary, Henry's favourite sister, the loveliest woman of her day

Katherine of Aragon, Henry's first wife, mother of Mary Tudor

Anne Boleyn, Henry's second wife, whom h described as "my great folly"; mother o Elizabeth Tudor

Jane Seymour, Henry's thi wife, mother of his only legi mate son, Edward Tudor

Leo, patron of literature, who admired the binding and trim decking. He read five pages there and then, exclaiming at every second line. His Holiness remarked he was surprised at such a book coming from the King's grace, so necessarily occupied in other feats—men who had spent all their lives in study could not bring forth the like of this. He promulgated a bull which conferred on England's sovereign the superb title Defender of the Faith.

This distinction meant much to the diligent author, and the bull was received with great ceremonial. The new name rang the length of the hall as the heralds proclaimed it again and again. Patch, the King's fool, wanted to know why his master was so jocund. "Because of my new title," answered the King. "Prithee, good Harry," pattered the jester, "let thee and I defend one another and leave the Faith alone to defend itself."

The very diversity of Charles's far-flung empire made it difficult, if not impossible, to rule, for when there was peace in one quarter, there was trouble brewing and uprising elsewhere. It was in his realms too that men were beginning to dispute the indisputable, the Holy Roman Catholic Church, and heresy called for instantaneous suppression before it could run riot.

France, feeling herself encircled by her rival's spreading domains, took advantage of every opportunity that offered when Charles was hard pressed. The gnawing friction between them broke, as everyone knew was inevitable sooner or later, into open warfare, and each called on Henry to fulfil his treaty obligations by coming to his assistance.

For a stopgap measure Wolsey was dispatched to France to attempt to negotiate a truce between the two powers. Henry was not ready for war. His father's treasure was exhausted; money and an army would have to be raised. Time was essential, and it was time Wolsey played for on his mission, diplomatically falling ill when necessary. Henry could only maintain his balance between Charles and Francis so long as neither had the mastery; the longer, therefore, they were kept apart the better it suited him. When the breach came, he had no intention of standing aloof and letting the contenders fight it out to the death between them. It would be Charles's side, not Francis's, on which Henry would throw England's weight.

That had been arranged between king and minister before the

Cardinal crossed the Channel, and it was not a noble part for them to play. While Wolsey swore friendship to Francis, he was stroking the t's and dotting the i's of the treaty with Charles. The French with their logical minds could not credit the English were playing them false: surely England's policy would be to build up her strength and consolidate her reserves while the two rivals weakened themselves with war, leaving her in an unassailable position.

Henry's motive for aligning himself actively with Charles when he could have been neutral was that he was certain Charles would win, and he wanted to share in not only the defeat of Francis but the spoils. His minister's policy had been pro-French in the past. There are two schools of thought why Wolsey, the patriotic, skilled diplomatist, chose war rather than peace, to intrigue instead of to mediate. Either he took a gambler's risk, displaying before Henry the chance of recovering his rights to the crown of France to divert his attention from home affairs which were heading for ruin, or, and this is the more likely, he put himself first, and hitched England to Charles's star, because Charles, ruler of the Holy Catholic Empire, had promised him St. Peter's throne when it fell vacant.

While Wolsey was absent, Henry again handled state affairs. He was not like the Cardinal, who did everything himself and could not depute. Henry delegated, but he kept up his sleeve the master stroke of the last word. When his chief minister returned, King and Cardinal worked smoothly enough together in that Wolsey did the work and Henry retained the power of veto.

Three months after he had handled Henry's book, Pope Leo died. At once kings, princes, prelates, sprang into action to have the Holy See filled by their nominee. The lobbying, the pulling of wires, the jockeying for position, the heavy pressure brought to bear were intense as France tried for the election of a French delegate and the Empire an imperial one. In Rome the cardinals met to choose Leo's successor in an atmosphere that resembled a cockpit rather than conclave. Of them Charles's envoy wrote, "There cannot be so much hatred and so many devils in hell as among these cardinals."

Wolsey never had the ghost of a chance: for close on four centuries no Englishman had attained the Papacy, which had see-sawed between Spain and France. When his nominator arrived in Rome he learnt that Charles, not Francis, had won the papal stakes. The

new Vicar of Christ was a Netherlander who had been Charles's
tutor: such was the decayed condition of the Papacy, his honesty
made him one of the most unpopular pontiffs ever to be
enthroned.

As the days of the new year lengthened into spring, Wolsey busied
himself preparing for war with as many delaying tactics as he could
devise, for England was anything but ready. The lines running from
nose to mouth on his strong, once handsome face were becoming
more deeply etched. His temper was growing shorter, and there
were occasions when he would let fly a volley of abuse should he
be crossed. In an excess of fury, he even laid hands on an unfortunate nuncio who he believed was sending unfavourable reports of
him to France.

By this time Henry had had two known mistresses, the fair-haired
Elizabeth Blount and the current dark-haired Mistress Carey. His
morals were not unduly lax according to the standards of his day,
and he was no libertine like Francis.

Mistress Carey was one of Katherine's maids-in-waiting and until
lately, when she married, had been Mary Boleyn. Her father, Sir
Thomas Boleyn, had spent his time during the past few years posting
as envoy between France and England, but now war was imminent
he brought his younger daughter Anne home with him. Like her
sister Mary, she had been educated in France, one of three hundred
girls in Queen Claude's household, where she was taught to sing,
dance, work and pray.

She dances across the page for the first time at a court revel, very
young, light of heart, with more than one string to her bow. Her
blue-black hair and mirthful dark eyes betrayed her Irish ancestry.
She did not wear her very long hair smoothly coifed like the English
girls, but floating free after the French fashion, interlaced with
jewels since this was a special occasion. She was slight, and as alive
as a bird propelled by its own song, with a slender neck and the
flexible throat of the singer. She inspired the poet Wyatt to write
sonnets, and although he was married he paid advances to her, but
it was Henry Percy she favoured. So much in love were they, they
plighted their troth, the Earl's son and the merchant's granddaughter.

Mary was the King's mistress, and their father began to receive
honour after honour: every year a new benefaction filled the Boleyn

cornucopia. But Mary remained Mistress Carey. Henry kept the liaison very much in the background. He conceded not an iota of the deference due to the Queen as his consort and wife, but Katherine's face began to wear the sorrowful look of one who accepts that her prayers will go unanswered.

CHAPTER EIGHT

DIPLOMATIC REVERSAL

"The eagle's force subdues each bird that flies:
   What metal can resist the flaming fire?
Doth not the sun dazzle the fairest eyes,
   And melt the ice, and make the frost retire?
The hardest stones are pierced through with tools,
The wisest are with princes made but fools."
                                        —*Henry VIII*

HENRY played host to Charles again; this time the Emperor stayed some weeks instead of several days. He arrived with a large retinue of Spanish grandees and German nobles, and instead of flying spray salting their deliberations, Henry seized the opportunity to entertain his visitor in fitting manner. London fairly crackled with bonfires and flamed with torches; pageants and processions made lively the summer streets. A contemporary packed the six weeks of fête into a nutshell with the words, "Nothing lacked that could be gotten to cheer the Emperor and his lords, and all that came in his company were highly feasted." But Charles gives the impression of not being a very disportive guest, the one serious note in the fanfare.

Soon after his arrival Henry took him to Greenwich, to that favourite palace where the river wound. They landed by barge, climbing the water stairs. Waiting for them, framed in the principal doorway, stood Queen Katherine, holding by the hand Charles's future bride, the Princess Mary.

She was six years old, a tiny thing with brown eyes and hair the Tudor fairness. Already she could talk to foreigners in their own tongue and play the harpsichord with nimbleness. Henry thought the world of her. He was fond of children, and this clever little girl was his own daughter, not someone else's. Children for their part felt at home with his uninhibited personality. To Mary her father was the world; in his presence everything that was big, warm and splendid happened all at the one time.

She saw something of her future bridegroom during his stay, and the grave young man and small child drew together in a kind of mannered courtship. Already she was treated as Empress, and it was thus she, young as she was, deported herself. Charles signed the matrimonial treaty while he was in England, binding himself to marry her when she reached the age of twelve.

The agreement provided that if Henry had no son to succeed him, the eldest male child born to Charles and Mary should become King of England. It was a very full moment for Henry: his daughter to marry not a king's son but the Emperor himself, his grandson maybe not only to rule England but the Empire.

Charles was anxious for his bride to be sent to Spain where she could be educated as his wife, but every time the point was raised in the years to come Henry adroitly turned it aside. The Princess was too young as yet to stand a sea journey, or be moved from her native air, and where in all of Christendom could the Emperor find a more fit mistress to bring up his future wife after the manner of Spain than her own mother?

She was, however, subjected to a rigid education which excluded all idle books of chivalry and romance; the few stories allowed for her recreation were historical, sacred or classical. She had to concentrate on the Gospels night and morning, selected portions of the Old Testament, the Holy Fathers, and Latin and Greek masters. The "right merry and joyous" infant with her father's rosy cheeks grew into a pallid, spare, short-sighted scholar before she was twelve.

Henry, now irrevocably welded to Charles, declared war on Francis. It was pleasant to believe that the over-taxed French wanted to change their king and were crying, "*Vive le roi d'Angleterre!*" But nothing was more costly than war, and for the first time in his life Henry lacked money. Wolsey, who saw to everything, had to apply himself to the vital task of filling the emptied coffers. He as chief minister was responsible for the pro-Emperor policy, on which he and Henry had staked their all.

The rest of the country lacked their enthusiasm. War with France always meant war on two fronts: the moment an English army left its island base, the Scots would be across the border in their hordes to aid their French allies.

Wolsey began by instituting "voluntary" loans; his names for his various measures all turned out painful misnomers. The country responded handsomely enough, London alone supplying £20,000 with admirable promptitude, but the sums brought in, although large, were trifling to mount a full-scale invasion, and were swallowed up by some abortive naval engagements, the only attacks made that year. There was nothing else for it, or Wolsey would have done it: Parliament would have to be summoned and made to supply money for the war.

Parliament heard him in what the Cardinal himself described as a marvellous obstinate silence. Not a word could he extort from them, no matter how he railed and how shrilly he demanded some reasonable answer. Very humbly the Speaker intimated that the Members were refusing to speak except through him, their common mouth, and they would not give voice in the Cardinal's presence. Discomfited, Wolsey had to retire.

A delegation asked him to prevail upon the King to accept half of the enormous sum claimed. Wolsey spoke no more than the truth when he told them he would rather have his tongue plucked out of his head with red-hot pincers than induce the King to do any such thing. It took Parliament a hundred days before they granted appreciably less than two-thirds of the required sum.

As with all autocrats, the first step of his climb-down altered irretrievably Wolsey's direction. From that moment it was descent, not ascent. This was the first time he had failed the King, as he was to fail in his other attempts to raise money for an unpopular war. His position, alone on his pinnacle, was only tenable so long as the foundation on which it was reared did not move, and Wolsey's foundation was his master the King. The slightest shift in the substructure and fissure zigzagged from base to apex.

Nothing was going right for Henry. Gone were these halcyon days when life showered on him everything he could desire without the asking—save a son. He heard himself praised in Parliament as an ideal king of great judgement, learning, experience and diligence, yet its members only voted with the greatest reluctance part of the sum demanded. (Their sovereign noted that Parliament could not be browbeaten as Wolsey had attempted to do: Parliament should be handled as a means, not an end. The goose would not lay its golden eggs if it were badgered from its nest.) His subjects were complaining they shouldn't be asked to burn their fingers taking chestnuts out of the fire for the Emperor. Could they or would they not see that through war with France their all-wise king would recover his right to the French crown? Francis would receive from Henry's hand what King Richard had received from Henry's father on Bosworth Moor—defeat and death.

The largest army to leave England for a hundred years sailed for Calais before the end of August, delayed until autumn by the emptiness of the exchequer and the usual administrative hold-ups. It advanced to within forty miles of Paris, capturing all towns on the way, when it had to fall back on Calais as the Emperor's joint invasion did not materialize and winter was setting in. Only the dread of a second Flodden kept the Scots from pouring over the defenceless border.

Nothing was going right for Wolsey. The Pope died, his only popular act since he became pontiff less than two short years ago, and the citizens of Rome in their gratitude for his death erected a statue to his doctor. Wolsey told Henry he would rather continue in his service than be ten Popes, nevertheless he raised heaven and earth to be elected. Charles obligingly wrote a letter in his favour, but did not send it until after the election, when his own nominee was chosen.

The following year Charles made up for his inactivity and invaded France, laying siege to Marseilles. No attempt was made to help him from the English side. Henry had neither the heart nor the resources, and Wolsey was playing tit for tat with the Emperor. In the unpleasant hiatus between Henry's and Charles's invasions, the Cardinal had time to wonder if by aiding and abetting the Emperor England was not nourishing an ally who could overrun the world. Uneasily he watched the new Pope, in an effort to redress the imperial predominance, throw his weight on the opposite side. No longer was England the crucial balance between two forces: to keep any position at all she had to hop from side to side. Very tentative overtures were made to Francis.

It looked as though what was tentative would shortly be consolidated; the French defended Marseilles with spirited stubbornness. It did not fall and the imperial army were forced to retreat towards Italy before the onslaught of winter.

All would have been well for Francis had he been content to

defend his kingdom, but success went to his over-ambitious head. He had had victories and conquests in the past when he had taken the offensive; this time he would regain the glittering prize of Milan. He crossed the Alps with his army. As he sat down to besiege Pavia, astrologers foretold from the sky what any general knew, that his star was on the wane.

The English King was in bed when an excited courier arrived to tell him the startling news that imperial troops had annihilated the French army and taken their sovereign prisoner. Henry's joy knew no bounds. "You are as welcome as the Angel Gabriel was to the Virgin Mary," he declared lyrically to the messenger, and leapt out of bed to break the good news to Katherine himself.

The Queen began to smile again: she dreaded when English policy veered towards Francis, away from the nephew she longed to see her son-in-law. Henry ordered London to celebrate the capture of the French King, bonfires were lit and free wine dispensed to the citizens. The city rang with the music of minstrels and the songs of children, and the King and Queen attended a jubilant *Te Deum* in St. Paul's with the foreign ambassadors. To Henry the crown of France was near as touching.

The historic victory was won on the Emperor's birthday. Charles received the news of the complete defeat of the French and the capture of Francis with none of Henry's triumphant exuberance, but with a self-restraint that awed the world into admiration. At twenty-five years of age he was a Caesar astride the globe, in a position to dictate to Christian and infidel alike.

Henry, riding the crest of his ally's conquest, dispatched envoys to Spain proposing the Emperor should depose Francis and invade France with England to satisfy their just claims. Unhappily Wolsey had to fall in with his master's plans, which would inflate the Emperor's already dangerous influence to terrifying proportions.

An invasion of France meant money would have to be raised, and quickly. Wolsey dare not summon Parliament again so he proposed what he called an Amicable Grant, trying to soften the tax by explaining it was necessary for the King to invade France in person and he must go as a prince, which meant lavish supplies. But the old magic no longer worked. The Amicable Grant failed, as did the Benevolent one hastily instituted to take its place.

A nameless London councillor shot out at the great Cardinal that benevolences were illegal, giving chapter and verse for the statute. The men of Kent, who were always troublesome because they would not truckle, said darkly there would be no rest from such payments as long as *some one* was living, and openly refused to pay. So did East Anglia; the agitation in Norfolk and Suffolk reached violence. It was not only Wolsey who was blamed; no longer could the King do no wrong. He was compared most unfavourably to his father by the lieges. They pointed out to a startled Archbishop that King Henry had not one foot of land more in France than had his noble father, who lacked neither riches nor wisdom to win the kingdom of France if he had thought it expedient.

The situation was saved by Henry's denying any knowledge of Wolsey's demand for a sixth of every man's substance. He only wished to receive, he said, such money as his subjects would freely give him. As his subjects were obviously not in a mood to grant him a groat, the fatal taxes were dropped, a royal pardon issued to all who had been arrested for refusing to pay, and the country told their sovereign had given up all thoughts of his expedition to France. The people muttered amongst themselves that Wolsey for private gain and ambition had talked an unwilling king into going to war.

Rumour was darting and flickering like a snake's tongue, so scintillant it left no trace and one wondered if it had been, that Charles was going to repudiate his obligation to marry Henry's daughter. It forked to Princess Mary's ears, who wore Spanish dress to accustom herself to it. It was noticed she whitened when she heard her bridegroom was thinking of taking another cousin for his wife.

A beset Wolsey wrote an elaborate letter to the Emperor, enclosing an emerald ring from his small bride-elect, telling him it would prove how faithful she was to him, as she prayed he would keep constant to her. The Emperor stuck Mary's ring on his little finger as far as it would go, and said to the English ambassadors he would wear it for her sake.

They came no further speed with him. He had not defeated Francis to exalt his uncle-in-law, and showed no disposition to share a victory he had won alone with an ally who had stood idly by.

Home truths from the imperial side made the meeting uncomfortable. The Emperor knew all about the overtures to France, that Wolsey had called him a faithless liar and insulted his ambassador.

When he was asked by the envoys for the return of the five hundred thousand crowns their king claimed he had borrowed, they were told the Emperor was short of money too. The Englishmen saw it was needless to blow any longer at a dead coal, but reeled when they heard if they wanted him to marry their lady princess she must be brought to Spain at once with her dowry of £80,000.

Henry's pro-Emperor policy rattled in ruins about him; the dreams of his grandson succeeding to the English and Imperial throne dissolved into thin air, and the crown of France for himself proved delusion. Coldly he acquiesced when Charles asked to be freed from his engagement to Mary that he could marry Isabella of Portugal—first his sister, then his daughter. He made what capital he could out of his formal assent by demanding repayment of what his nephew owed him, but he did not recover a penny.

By the time Francis had bought his freedom at the price of promises he had no intention of keeping, England had negotiated a treaty of amity with France. Instead of an Emperor who held the corners of the earth in his hands, Henry had for his allies the Pope, a pontiff who trembled with irresolution, and a Lucifer who had fallen from heaven, cut down to the ground.

No longer was Mary, his daughter, called Empress. Her dark-eyed suitor was going to marry not a little girl of nine but a grown-up princess who was not only beautiful but had a dowry of one million crowns. Mary's small face tightened and her mouth compressed, bearing the unbearable.

The French Queen Claude had died, and there was talk of her marriage to the King of France: that was what her father desired above all else to revenge himself on the Emperor. To be Queen was not the same as Empress, the French King not the same as the darkling Spaniard, but it was second best and second best was better than nothing, particularly when her father had set his heart on it. Oh, if only she were more than nine, and such a small puny nine at that. What was the good of making herself old and wise with lessons when she looked so much younger than she even was?

She was sent to Ludlow Castle, on the marches of Wales, with a court of her own and state as befitted the King's daughter. In the same year her father's natural son, the child he had by Elizabeth Blount—terrible to think he was Mary's half brother—was created Duke of Richmond and Somerset and treated as heir apparent. It was said the six-year-old boy was to take precedence over all the nobility and over Princess Mary herself. All the church ceremonial that accompanied the investiture would not bless such a proceeding, not if they sprinkled the whole of the river Jordan on it. Her mother seemed very far away. If the King of France failed, Mary was to be affianced to his son, but what was a boy groom compared to the one she had lost, so nobly older than she?

No longer was Henry's favour curried and courted from every quarter of the globe; England was nothing compared to what she had been twelve years ago. That year it rained from November until the end of January: it was as though the land were accursed. The succession—the succession—the succession: persistent as the rain from leaden skies, thoughts of the succession dripped through Henry's mind.

If he died without a successor there would be anarchy, and he was not going to die without an heir, to toss the Tudor crown to be fought for by men who had no more claim to it than their common greed. Norfolk was one. Norfolk had to be ridden on a tighter rein than ever, now the son had succeeded the father; and there were plenty of others avid to stake their claim if Henry let them. But he was a man in his prime, as strong and able to have sons as he was to rule.

There was of course Mary. The people thought a woman could not come to the throne; Henry of course knew there was no law against it. But Mary did not secure the succession. She was delicate for one thing, always ailing, and might not reach maturity. If she did and married a subject, exactly the same conflicts would arise that had created the Wars of the Roses. If she married a foreign prince, her subjects would be jealous of foreign influence and the fear of foreign dominance would breed rebellion.

He had considered entailing the succession on his illegitimate son, which was why the boy had been created Duke of Richmond and Somerset and heaped with family titles. But the rights of a natural son to the throne could be disputed after the father was dead, so Henry's illegitimate child no more secured the succession than his legitimate daughter.

At last his sister Margaret, the Queen of Scotland, achieved what for eight years she had been working for, a divorce, and married for the third time. Henry boiled over with righteous anger that his sister, instead of behaving like a noble princess, could do anything so unnatural. When he learnt the annulment had been confirmed by the Pope, he wrote scathingly to her of the shameless sentence sent from Rome which plainly revealed how unlawfully it had been handled.

If the Pope could supply on the flimsiest pretexts possible an annulment for Margaret, who was a shame and disgrace to all her family, why should he not provide one for Henry, Defender of the Faith and ornament of rectitude, on lawful grounds? Never would Henry, unlike Margaret, stoop to do anything that was illegal or unorthodox. Every step he took must be sanctified by the Church and confirmed by law.

CHAPTER NINE

LADY-IN-WAITING

"Our King he has a secret to tell,
And ay well keepit it must be."

A SERIOUS drought followed the rains, which returned in April and continued for eight weeks. Grain rotted in the soaking soil, and there was no hay or straw for fodder. Animals died, and a plague attacked the remaining cattle. Their eyes sank back into their heads and their thin sides shuddered as they coughed themselves to death. The Hand of God lay heavily on the land, but the people did not place the blame at heaven's door. Soured with taxes at home and sullen with failure abroad, they held the Cardinal responsible for all their ills, while the King's name no longer roused them to patriotic ardour.

The first steps towards the annulment of his marriage to Katherine were taken before Anne Boleyn caught Henry's fancy. She had been dismissed from court and sent back to her father's house by Wolsey when he discovered she and Lord Percy had entered into a love troth. That was something for which Anne never forgave the Cardinal: she held him and him alone answerable when their contract was dissolved and her young lover married to the lord steward's daughter.

The Anne Boleyn who returned to court was not quite the same as the Anne Boleyn who had left it. Locked away for all time was the tremulous ecstasy of first love, and what took its place was neither tremulous nor ecstatic. Diamond bright, she scintillated where once she had sparkled. It is not known when the King's small eyes marked her out as his; probably it was her gaiety that attracted him. She had none of her mistress Queen Katherine's learning, but everything she did was characteristic and she was feminine to the core. She had no great beauty but she had the wit and charm to transform defects into attractions. She hid a strawberry mark on her neck with an ornamental collar band which her fellow maids of honour thought so beguiling they all began to wear collar bands. They copied too the long hanging sleeves she had brought from France, although they were not hiding as she was a tiny malformation on her left hand. She was very graceful dancing the leaping English dances, and when she sang, the oldest turned his head to listen.

If Henry ever thought to substitute Anne for his mistress, Mary Carey, he soon discovered that Anne was not so conformable as her sister. It has been said that her uncle, the Duke of Norfolk, primed her to set her sights for the highest dignity of all and not to become the King's mistress, but no amount of priming could have tutored a lady-in-waiting at Henry's court to hold His Majesty at arm's length.

Anne handled the situation to the manner born. She had the example of her own sister before her. To be the King's mistress had not advanced Mary in any way, while his earlier love, Elizabeth Blount, who had borne him a son, had been married off to an obscure knight. By the time she knew he was in love with her, all the cards were in Anne's hands, although it is unlikely they were the cards she would have chosen. "Wild for to hold, though I seem tame," she is described in a sonnet of Wyatt's. Henry became beglamoured of her before he knew where he was and he could not break from her spell. "My great folly" he describes it in one of his letters to her: his passion for her was his only folly in a life he mastered as he did a horse. The situation did not last for a year or two, but for at least six years before actual marriage. That it trailed on too long was Anne's tragedy; when marriage did come, Henry's passion was over-spent.

Katherine's unhappiness played on her health; she was like an instrument whose strings are broken or frayed. Her husband never came to her apartments now and there was no longer the communion between them of unspoken question and answer when they were apart. They had shared so much in the past that neither could say which was the giver and who the taker, only that they belonged to one another. No longer warmed by the sun of his presence, her life was emptied; and the occasions when she was at his side as his consort only served to heighten her loneliness without him.

No longer did she advise or was kept advised on state affairs. Spain was the enemy now, France the ally. She would have died content to think of Mary safe in her native land as Empress, but that would never be—her nephew had married Isabella of Portugal. She had not even her beloved little daughter beside her—Mary had been sent to luckless Ludlow Castle where Katherine had journeyed with her boy-husband after their marriage a lifetime ago, and where he had died. Mary had been provided with a more honourable court than had even Arthur, Prince of Wales. Her father wanted the King of France to marry her, so she must have the state befitting his daughter and the future French queen. Again the face of Francis I rose before Katherine as she had seen it at the Field of Cloth of Gold, beginning to lose its perfect oval, the strong nose beginning to thicken, the dissipated eyes under the drooped lids, the full lips smiling redly above the black beard.

It was Wolsey who had to be thanked for the rupture with Charles and strengthening friendship with France. Now Henry was not in the Spanish camp, he naturally felt safer on Francis's side; after all, France boasted four times the inhabitants that England had. But Wolsey—for long enough Katherine's communications with the Cardinal had been more and more distant. There were stirrings behind the scenes. She only heard faint whispers but enough to tell her something was afoot, something inimical to her.

A French bishop, over with a delegation to consider the alliance between the English princess and his king, questioned Henry about his marriage to Katherine of Aragon. If it were not valid (how could it be argued a marriage was not valid after eighteen years?), then his daughter Mary he wished to marry to their sovereign could not be legitimate. As though Henry's mind were not fecund enough with probings and findings without this further fertilization.

What was he discussing with all these doctors and divines, theologians and jurists who were stealthily finding their way to him? She heard of his very secret visit to Wolsey's house—Wolsey was at the foot of everything; the Archbishop of Canterbury was present. He was to whisper in Katherine's ear four Latin words which signified the wrath of a king meant death.

Footsteps on unknown errands, padding into silence, hurrying to the King with news, all were gathered into Henry's when he visited her in her apartments. He was a big man and they seemed to shake the foundations. When was the last time he had been here, and why had he come?

Did she really want to know when she heard him tell her that for the past eighteen years they had been cohabiting, unmarried? Katherine was Arthur's widow, not Henry's wife. That was why God had punished them by the deaths of all their male children. Katherine must now choose a place where she could retire, for Henry's conscience, reinforced with Holy Writ, would not permit him to continue living in mortal sin.

Henry took it for granted he could read Katherine like a book: a dutiful, devoted and faithful helpmeet who had always put him first and deferred to his slightest wish would accept the inevitable with a brave submissiveness. Above all she would be reasonable.

What happened was so unforeseen he found himself totally unprepared to cope with it. Katherine burst into tears. She lifted up her face and wept without restraint, as women have wept since Biblical times, when they were taken captive, mourning for their dead, forsaken in some alien land.

Anything he could have borne, so well accoutred he would have welcomed debate, but not this. For this he had neither weapon nor balm. Covered with confusion, he beat a hasty retreat. "All shall be done for the best," he told her hurriedly before he left, and found himself begging her not to divulge what he had told her.

He was under the quite mistaken impression that what was termed "the King's great matter" was known to no one but the prelates with whom he had discussed it. As a matter of fact all London knew of it. It was the burning topic discussed behind the painted lattices of inns, in the taverns in East Cheap, in the Grass, Fish and Meat Markets, by the sober merchants as they went in and out of their halls. It might have been proclaimed by the town crier instead of instilled and percolated through Spanish sources. The King had been told by some ferreting churchmen that the marriage between him and the Queen was damnable, and it was said he was going to put her aside. Only the people could not believe he would ever carry out so wicked a project. But the Spanish ambassador noted sadly they had no leader to guide them: "So this people will probably content themselves with only grumbling." He knew the English.

Henry's conscience might be arbitrary but it was none the less genuine. He did not think he was right, he knew he was. Twinges of conscience, stirrings of doubts or of remorse, never troubled him as they did those of lesser breed. It was not to justify himself to himself that he hounded the Pope and never yielded until he had achieved his ends. The supreme egotist who has never been countered feels no need of self-justification. It was to prove to the world he was right and anyone who thought the contrary was wrong.

Unlike Henry, Katherine refused to accept that they had been living in sin: they were bound as husband and wife in holy matrimony. To believe otherwise would imperil her immortal soul. And nothing would make her change her mind, even Henry. This lack of accommodation on her part came as an unpleasant surprise to him; he did not realize that Katherine might and did look upon him as her husband, king and lord, but never God.

She had not offended, but she believed the King's wish to separate from her was a judgement of God because her marriage to his elder brother had been sealed by innocent blood. Throughout the years she had been haunted by the memory of the young Earl of Warwick, and had always treated his sister tenderly. The sword had swept for him at her father's behest only because of his royal lineage: King Ferdinand had refused to fulfil her marriage contract until a potential rival of the Prince of Wales was removed—the dead could not usurp. There were some who believed Henry VIII's sonlessness was God's punishment for his father's action that November day on Tower Hill.

Only the Pope could grant a dispensation to annul their marriage; therefore everything depended on the Pope as far as the King and Queen of England were concerned. The new pontiff was an unknown quantity, but surely, Katherine prayed, no Vicar of Christ would annul a marriage a predecessor had legalized and blessed.

The lurid news that Rome had been sacked by the Emperor's troops who had taken the Pope prisoner spread like conflagration through Christendom. The very ground on which the Church stood crumbled beneath it. When horror reached saturation point and had to subside, one fact stood out stark as a solitary landmark on an otherwise riven landscape. No Pope would grant the King of England a divorce from his Spanish wife when he was a prisoner of the Spanish wife's nephew. Clement might be allowed to sit on

St. Peter's chair, but it would not be his voice that would pronounce edicts, mandates and dispensations. It would be the Emperor's.

More than ever was Katherine sure that Wolsey was at the foot of everything when she heard he was going to France. She blamed him in the first instance for sowing in Henry's mind the seeds of separation from her. Now he was going to promote the King's marriage with a French princess. He was the originator, author and founder of the alliance with France; but for him, she was certain Henry would still be aligned to her nephew, whom Wolsey blamed for losing him the papal throne. England itself had no friendly disposition towards its hereditary enemy, and the engagement of Princess Mary that year to the French King's son roused no popular enthusiasm. The French envoys appraised the Dauphin's future bride very much as a farmer appraises stock—they might admire her conversation and looks, but she was so thin, spare and small, they said with some irritation, it would be impossible for her to be married for at least three years.

It was imperative for Wolsey to go to France; the necessity was driven home to him—only he could achieve what was to be done. He had to enlist the aid of Francis to force Charles to release the Pope, otherwise the Pope could not supply the annulment for the King. And he had to prepare for the King's marriage, once he was free, to the Duchess of Alençon, sister of Francis.

He had no suspicion when he left England that the King intended to make Anne Boleyn his queen, no suspicion at all. How could he have, when her father was on a mission to France at the same time, to bring back the Duchess of Alençon's picture to show her future royal bridegroom? He never dreamt his expedition to France was a ruse by his enemies, headed by the Boleyn faction, to get him out of the country. That spring the hate between Norfolk and Wolsey had flashed into high words in front of the King himself. The aristocrat loathed the Cardinal not for what he was but for what he had sprung from. One day, he promised himself, he would eat that butcher's cur alive.

On his return, Wolsey rode post-haste to Richmond to tell the King he had brought back a firm alliance with France. He did not find his sovereign alone; Anne Boleyn was with him. It was she who spoke to his messenger, not the King: "Where else should the Cardinal come? Tell him to come here, where the King is."

As the tall Cardinal bowed his way backwards from their presence, he realized that if the King married Anne Boleyn exactly the same impediment stood between them as existed between him and Katherine. Katherine had been his brother's wife before she had been his; the King had been intimate with Anne Boleyn's sister, and the fact that it was illicit made it no less an impediment. That meant the Pope would have to be asked to make Katherine and the King's union unlawful and for the same reason make the King's union with Anne Boleyn lawful. It seemed a lot to ask, but Wolsey, who knew the ways of popes, did not doubt it could be done—once Clement was freed to do it.

Not a French princess to unite England and France for all time, their son and heir to be king of both countries, make them a power in the world strong enough, united enough to stand up to any emperor. The place of Katherine of Aragon, daughter of a Spanish king and Castilian queen, to be taken not by a princess of royal blood but an insignificant lady-in-waiting. To make her marriage lawful to England's king, the whole complicated machinery of the Church to be set in motion. Trumpery like Anne Boleyn to be England's queen!

Never again was the old warm rapport between king and minister to be re-established; there was an artificiality, a straining after effect in this trio that had never marred the duet. He might supply Anne Boleyn with delicacies from his table; she found them more delectable than even from the King's, but he knew there was more tooth than sweetness behind her honeyed blandishments. He might receive a letter from her assuring him she could never repay him for the great pains and troubles he was taking on her behalf except by loving him, next to the King's Grace, above all creatures living, but he knew such words were penned only because he was the means by which she hoped to be made queen. If confirmation were needed, he found it in the postscript added by the King, trusting by Wolsey's diligency and vigilancy (with the assistance of Almighty God) shortly to be eased out of trouble. Shortly! Wolsey tried to buy Anne's patience with rich and goodly presents, and assuage the King's impatience by writing still another petitioning letter to the Pope.

London was stolidly behind Katherine; they loved her, and sorrowed for her that she had not borne an heir to the throne. Providence, not she, was responsible for that. When they learnt that her place might be taken by Anne Boleyn, they seethed with indignation. It did not matter to them that her mother had been of noble birth; they thought of her as Nan Bullen, the granddaughter of a mayor, one of themselves, a lady-in-waiting to supplant her mistress and their queen—had the King taken leave of his senses?

The Pope was nominally free again, but everyone knew he was in the hollow of the Emperor's hand. At once two English bishops were dispatched to Italy, to obtain from him a commission empowering Wolsey to pronounce Katherine's marriage null and void. It was made as plain to the Supreme Pontiff as Wolsey could make it that if he refused the King of England's demands, he would involve Wolsey, the safety of the country and the papal cause in England in complete ruin.

The prelates found a cowed Pope in bad lodgings: his Holiness admitted that captivity in Rome was better than liberty here. He cried easily, sighed a great deal and escaped out of every corner he was hemmed into by saying he must consult his advisers. Day after day the Englishmen returned to assail the Holy Father for four or five hours at a stretch with their king's matrimonial troubles, their foreign voices rough and rude with plain speaking.

First of all they had to put Clement right on one or two points: they discovered he actually thought their sovereign wanted an annulment because he had fallen in love with a lady of doubtful virtue! Not for anything under the sun, they assured His Holiness, would Cardinal Wolsey have allowed himself to be influenced except by the conviction of the insufficiency of the King's present marriage. They dwelt at length on the purity of the lady Anne's life, her constant virginity, her maidenly and womanly modesty, her soberness, humility, wisdom, finishing with a flourish on her apparent aptness to procreate children.

On top of this shambles, on top of the sack of Rome, on top of horror, destruction and the total loss of all papal territories, the King of England's "great matter". Why were they bringing it to him who had so much else of so much more moment to despoil him? They must know the Emperor was breathing down his back. Why did the King of England not have two wives? A precedent could always be found in handy papal archives—dispensation granted to Henry IV of Castille to marry a second wife on condition that, if within a fixed time he had no issue by her, he should return to his first. Why could Queen Katherine not retire into a nunnery? That would involve injury to only one person, herself. When she refused to be agreeable, he wished her in her grave. Why, oh why, could the King of England not settle the matter for himself, as his brother-in-law Charles Brandon had done—obtain a divorce from the English courts and marry a second wife? All the Pope would be called upon to settle then would be validity of the second marriage, a comparatively easy matter after it was an accomplished fact.

Henry, however, was as determined to make the Pope shoulder his responsibilities as the Pope was anxious not to accept them. The King of England must have a sentence that would ensure the legitimacy of his children by the second marriage. The world must be shown the King of England's second marriage was unassailable. Only the Pope, whose decrees were the laws of the Church, could supply the necessary warrant.

It took more than one English commission to wring from him permission for Wolsey and (to give the proceedings an impartial air) the Italian Cardinal Campeggio to try the King's case in England and pronounce sentence. Either Cardinal might act by himself, and all appeals from their jurisdiction were forbidden. The Pope secretly bound himself not to revoke the case and gave a written promise he would confirm the Cardinals' decision.

The two English bishops returned to England with their good tidings, which they carried to Greenwich. Princess Mary and some of her attendants were ill with smallpox, so Anne Boleyn had found temporary lodging in the tiltyard to be out of infection's way. She was enraptured with the news, and as grateful as though they had brought the papal dispensation with them in their pockets. The King was as delighted, now things really were moving. Cardinal Campeggio was no stranger to England, a man after Henry's heart, a great canonist who knew the law. It was satisfactory to reflect that some years ago Henry had conferred upon him the bishopric of Salisbury, that the temporalities and revenues from the English diocese must mean a great deal to an Italian whose house had been looted and who had lost all his possessions in the sack of Rome.

The firm alliance Wolsey had brought back from France included a joint declaration against the Emperor. The people in England woke up one day in January to find they were at war with their best customer—Flanders. Bales of cloth deteriorated on London wharves waiting to be shipped abroad. Trade dried up as looms clacked to a standstill. Merchants would not buy wool they could not sell to clothiers who had lost their markets. Workmen were dismissed, shops closed. There was revolt in Norfolk, rising in Wiltshire, the clothiers of Kent were all for seizing Wolsey and turning him adrift in a boat with holes bored in it.

Because war spelt ruin to the most prosperous industry in both England and Flanders, Henry and Charles began to discuss peace before hostilities actually took place and between them they reached a unique gentlemen's agreement: trade with Flanders was to go on as if there were no war. Thus it petered into a truce, leaving in its trail on the English side a gathering hatred against the Cardinal.

The dismal weather that spring foreboded the return of the dread sweating sickness. Henry made will after will, shared her devotions with Katherine and wrote love letters to Anne. The epidemic took its doleful toll, snatching the King's twelve-year-old nephew, only son of his sister Mary.

It was a blow from which Mary never recovered. She retired with her two daughters into the country where she who signed herself Mary the French Queen reigned sweetly and simply as lady of the manor. Her days of dancing youth had long since passed: if one of her husband's previous wives was not making claims, the other one was sure to be. She saw little of him in the years to come, for he was always at court, taking a masterful hand in the affairs of state, bearing the sceptre at a new queen's coronation, escorting another one to the Tower. He long survived his royal bride, the big rugged body stoutly weathering the years, into which he seemed to shrink a little, like the occupant of a family house only tenanting a few rooms.

With the Italian Legate on his way from Rome to pronounce his marriage to Katherine null, Henry had deemed it wise to silence the tittle-tattle regarding his favourite by sending Anne from court. She took her demission hardly and "smoked" over it in her father's house, refusing to return when permission was granted. This absenting of herself and making herself precious had the effect of greatly increasing the King's ardour, and he rode to visit her through the summer days, sounding his bugle when he came to a certain hill-top to tell her of his approach. It was to be a further three years before she consented to give herself to him.

As spring in England that year wasted into a barren summer, Cardinal Lorenzo Campeggio was arduously making from Italy to England. Crippled with gout, his journey was slow and painful: it was a physical impossibility for him to come with the haste his fellow Cardinal kept importuning for, and every stage of the way took toll of the pain-ridden traveller. Not until October did he reach England, his mandate from the Holy See stamped on his upright mind: to do his utmost to restore mutual affection between the King and Queen, not to proceed to sentence, and—the Church's unfailing nostrum—to protract the matter as long as possible.

He had to be borne in a litter for he was too weak to ride. Gnarled with disease, he was like one of those old trees whose knurrs and knots make it look as though it is growing upside down, its roots uppermost. As he swayed by on the road to London, women sprang up in his path, hurling at him acclamations for Queen Katherine and shouting, their voices violent with warning, "No Nan Bullen for us!"

CHAPTER TEN

TRIAL OF A QUEEN

"Cold, alter'd friends, with cruel art,
Poisoning fell Misfortune's dart."

THE Italian found it impossible to impress the Pope's point of view on his fellow Cardinal; he had no more success in persuading Wolsey than if he had spoken to a rock. Wolsey's objections were founded on the invalidity of the marriage, the instability of the realm and the succession. It was driven home to Campeggio that the King would brook no procrastination; the affairs of the kingdom were at a standstill, and the cause dare not remain undetermined any longer.

The Englishman's vehemence startled the Italian: the King must have his annulment which the Pope must supply, otherwise where would Wolsey stand and what would happen to the Papacy in England? Industriously Campeggio reported to Rome that the Cardinal of York was certainly proving himself very zealous for the preservation of the See Apostolic in England, adding with one of those flashes of penetration of which the single-minded are capable, "because all his grandeur is connected with it".

Unable to ride or walk, he was carried to have audience with the King. Here was no English prelate eager to implement his sovereign's most difficult demand smoothly for him, but a fleshless Italian earnest with another opinion.

If Campeggio found himself against a rock when he spoke to Wolsey, he wrote that not even an angel in heaven could turn the King from his own interpretation of the facts. The English monarch listened patiently enough, but in reply trotted out all the arguments he had already heard from Wolsey. The King was word perfect as the dictums and axioms originated from him in the first place.

Only when Campeggio suggested the Queen might be persuaded

to enter a religious house did the atmosphere lighten. The King became cheerful at once: that would be the solution to everything. After all, Katherine had always been devout, and even when the court was at its gayest had denied herself and observed vigils. Now he had ceased cohabiting with her and would never return to her bed, a nunnery was surely the most appropriate place for her to end her days. If she agreed, he would be prepared to be most generous, would even settle the succession on her daughter should he fail to have sons by another marriage. No time must be lost, and it was arranged Wolsey and Campeggio should repair the very next day with this most fruitful suggestion to his consort.

Katherine had been born in camp when her mother's forces were beleaguering Granada. She had been brought up amidst battles and siege, and she did not succumb when faced by two Cardinals. In all the shabby business with its sordid dissembling and specious argument, she stands out with a nobility that still reaches and touches us.

Wolsey cannot have felt comfortable or happy in her presence, but he was at such a desperate pass that in all probability exigency forestalled every other emotion. We do know that Katherine concentrated on the Italian rather than the English Cardinal.

She nonplussed them both by saying she had heard they were to come to induce her to enter a religious house. Both pictured for her the advantages of a nunnery. She would have everything to gain and nothing to lose by taking such a step—her dower and the guardianship of her daughter. She was reminded of the first wife of Louis XII of France who still lived in the greatest honour and reputation with God and all that kingdom. Katherine listened with her customary courtesy, but they were talking to a woman who did not believe she could accommodate her immortal soul.

One dark winter's morning Wolsey wakened Campeggio at daybreak with the news the Queen was asking leave to confess to him. Gone like a summer day never to return were the times he, Wolsey, Archbishop of York, had acted as confessor and confidant to his sovereign lady. For a lifetime he had played second fiddle to one alone and that was the King; everyone else had had to dance to his tune. Now he found himself taking second place to an Italian twisted with pain, impoverished to beggary after being forced to redeem his life at a great sum by the vandals who sacked Rome.

Henry found Katherine indestructible as an adversary. She had nothing to hide, and the very simplicity of her case could stand the broad glare of daylight. That was why, like the Pope, he often wished her dead, not so much that death would silence her but that only death could bring his great matter to a conclusion no one could gainsay.

She came early that morning to the Italian Legate and spent a long time with him. What she told him was under the seal of confession but she granted him permission to repeat it and to write certain resolutions to the Pope. "She affirmed on her conscience that from her marriage with Prince Arthur on the 14th November, until his death on the 2nd April, she had not slept with him more than seven nights, and that he had left her as he had found her—a virgin." Instead of entering a religious house, she intended to live and die in the state of matrimony to which God had called her—"that she would always remain of that opinion and never change it." Her words had the ominous ring of an ultimatum, and ultimatums were the prerogatives of her husband, not his wife.

Campeggio received the Queen's statements on her union with the Prince of Wales gratefully: in his view they closed the door irrevocably on any marriage-suit case. Her husband must know if her words were true, as Campeggio was convinced they were. Then it did not matter whether the dispensation were valid or invalid; she was Henry VIII's wife and not the Prince of Wales's widow. Where was the point of holding an investigation when obviously there was nothing to investigate? But this Wolsey would not allow. Dexterously he elaborated argument after argument with his persuasive tongue. Rome was tired of the whole matter, but Wolsey dare not let Rome go. The King expected, the King had been led to believe the Pope would confirm the verdict the Legates reached in England: there must therefore be a court, a verdict and a confirmation.

The only way to deal with an indestructible adversary was to behave exactly as though she had no case, which, when Henry considered his own inviolate one, was a comparatively easy matter. Katherine could be spied on, mistreated, stripped of her interests and rights, her wishes ignored, all because the King knew his cause was just.

He summoned the Lord Mayor and his aldermen to his palace at Bridewell where he expounded to them, that they could declare it to the people of England, why there had to be a trial. Londoners had no love of or reverence for the Pope—Campeggio had seen ribald remarks about his master scrawled on the walls, and they had shrugged aside the sack of Rome with the comment that the Pope was a ruffian, unworthy of his place, who began the mischief and was well served.

Henry dwelt at length on the sores that vexed his mind. He harped back to the succession again and yet again—it must be ensured; compared the twenty years of peace and prosperity they had enjoyed during his reign with what their forebears had endured during the Wars of the Roses when the succession was in dispute. He extolled the Queen's many qualities—God's law and God's law alone stood in his way of continuing to live with so good a wife. He hoped the affair would be settled amicably—that was their affable monarch they knew so well who was speaking. But if he "found anyone, whoever he was, who spoke in any terms than he aught to do of his Prince, he would let him know that he was his master". His audience sighed and said nothing. "Never a head so dignified but that he would make it fly." He meant that, every word of it, bluff King Hal.

The curious thing was, despite being made the King's confidants, despite no heir to the throne, the people still backed the Queen. It was she London championed, not the King. Henry had never envisaged such a situation, and it outraged him. His council mirrored his hurt feelings by expressing as their own that the Queen was acting contrary to her temper and ordinary behaviour, showing herself much abroad, and by civilities and gracious bowings of her head (which was not her custom formerly) seeking to work upon the affections of the people. The Queen, however, had the affections of the people, particularly the women, without any working upon them. Throughout the whole proceedings she acted in character, and it was this endowment that lent her dignity sweetness and spiritual power.

Meanwhile the King had lodged her rival in a fine house near to his own, hoping in this way so to accustom his subjects to her they would begin to take her for granted. The French ambassador busily reported to his government the King was so infatuated God alone could abate his madness. He noted more homage was paid to her than *she* ever paid the Queen: she had her ladies-in-waiting, her train-bearer, her chaplains, and courtiers flocked round the favourite who dispensed patronage as though she already wore the crown. Anne had staked her claim; she must have all or nothing, and the King, who signed his letters to her "Your loyal and most assured servant," made no secret that she was to have all.

He wrote her a very short note before she was installed in her new house, found through the offices of the indefatigable Wolsey, in which he takes her to task very kindly. He remarks that what he was writing to her was being circulated in London, at which he marvelled not a little. Lack of discreet handling alone could be the cause: he meant Anne's overtalkative tongue. The note is signed, "Written with the hand of him that longeth to be yours, H.R." A volatile temperament such as hers readily betrayed her into indiscretions. That is why her cool and calculating handling of her royal lover proves that where he was concerned she was ruled by her head and not her heart.

The King was entering his thirty-eighth year and the new Venetian ambassador was as rapturous over his appearance as any of his predecessors had been when he was much younger. Such corporal and intellectual beauty in "this Eighth Henry" not merely surprised but astounded. "His face is angelic rather than handsome; his head imperial and bold." But for the first time Henry's magnificent physique revealed its human origin rather than the god-like immunity which had protected it heretofore. He began to suffer from incapacitating headaches: in one of his letters to Anne he mentions the pain in his head after spending more than four hours of that day writing his book in defence of the dissolution of his marriage. Henry was nothing if not literate.

The weeks of the new year teased themselves into months as new deputations were sent from England to the Pope. His Holiness was asked to declare as forgery a providential brief Katherine's party had unearthed which removed any doubts about the earlier dispensation. The Queen had suggested both she and her husband should take monastic vows—would Clement dispense with the vows in the King's case but not the Queen's?

His Holiness began to show every indication of irritation at the King's great matter not being allowed to settle on its lees. Henry was the two horns of his dilemma. At one meeting he forbade the English delegate to proceed and, growing more angry and more excited, said he would make no further concessions. Obviously the

Pope was prepared to do nothing for the King's Grace; indeed there was talk in Rome that the Emperor had commanded Clement to recall the Legatine commission. The delegation returned promptly to England—the trial must go forward with expedition before the Pope could interfere.

It opened in London, in the great hall of the Black Friars, on the last day of May, 1529, the trial to determine the validity of the marriage of Henry VIII to Katherine of Aragon, which the Legates were to decide and the Pope to confirm.

Every day the court sat the two Legates were there, sitting "in a solemn place", before an empty railed table covered with carpets and tapestry. They entered behind "crosses, pillars, axes, and all ceremonies belonging to their degree". On the right, under a cloth of estate, was a chair and cushions for the King when he was present, on the left a chair on a lower level for the Queen. Council for the King and Queen faced each other on opposite sides. The Archbishop of Canterbury and all the bishops of the realm sat in a semicircle before the Legates. Officers of the court, proctors, the lords temporal, ladies and friends of the court, witnesses filled the body of the great hall with restlessness like palpitation.

In his chair covered with cloth of gold sat Wolsey, Cardinal of York, next his fellow Legate. If ever there was a stickler for the law it was Cardinal Campeggio. Not one jot nor one tittle was allowed to pass, not that all should be fulfilled but, it seemed to his colleague, to protract the proceedings indefinitely. The only occasions the tedium of the sessions was broken were when the King graced the court with his presence.

Both he and the Queen were there on the 21st June, the first and only time they were present on the same day. She arrived first, then the King made his entrance. The atmosphere was charged to explosion point. The King rose and harangued the court, telling it he was determined to live no longer in sin with his wife the Queen. The legality of the marriage which pained his conscience must be decided speedily; therefore he required the Legates to proceed at once.

Wolsey reminded the court that the case had been committed to him and his colleague by the Pope. He promised he would render judgement to the best of his poor ability and "omit nothing that the justice of the case required".

Now it was the Queen's turn. She did not address the court as she had done previously, she addressed the King. She had to make her way amongst the crowded assemblage until she reached his chair, where she knelt at his feet.

"Sir," she began, "I beseech you for all the loves that hath been between us, and for the love of God, let me have justice and right, take of me some pity and compassion, for I am a poor woman and a stranger born out of your dominion. I have here no assured friend, and much less indifferent counsel. I flee to you as to the head of justice within this realm."

It was he who had taught her to speak English, but she had always spoken it with a broken accent. Today it made her sound very much a foreigner.

"I take God and all the world to witness, that I have been to you a true, humble and obedient wife, ever conformable to your will and pleasure; I loved all those you loved, only for your sake, whether they were my friends or mine enemies."

She had not always been as she was now, small, broad and moving like a column, but that was what she was now.

"This twenty years I have been your true wife, and by me ye have had divers children, although it hath pleased God to call them out of this world, which has been no fault of mine."

They rose before him, a ghostly small train, the first little dead daughter, the son he had held in his arms who was to secure the succession for all time, the boy he had never seen born to him between the victories in France and of Flodden, the baby fleetingly referred to as "the King's new son" who lived only long enough to be christened, the miscarriages, the premature births—every one proved the wrath of Omnipotent God. Only Mary had He allowed, Mary who was a daughter, not an heir.

"And when ye had me at the first, I take God to be my judge, I was a true maid without touch of man; and whether it be true or no, I put it to your conscience."

His conscience. God had turned His face from their union. Henry dare not fly in the teeth of His manifest displeasure any longer. That was what his conscience told him. The succession must be assured.

Twice he raised his kneeling wife. She questioned the validity of the court and on the words "To God I commit my cause!" she made a low obeisance to the King. Then leaning on the arm of her receiver-general, she left the court instead of resuming her seat.

"Madam," her attendant whispered to her, "you are called back."

"I hear it well enough," she answered as the crier's summons rang after her, "Katherine, Queen of England, come again into the court." "But on—on, go you on, for this is no court wherein I can have justice. Proceed, therefore." She had not gone more than a few steps before she said, more to herself than to him, "I never before disputed the will of my husband, and I shall take the first opportunity to ask pardon for my disobedience."

"She is, my lords," said her affected husband, "as true, as obedient, and as conformable a wife as I could, in my fantasy, wish or desire. She has all the virtuous qualities that ought to be in a woman of her dignity, or in any other of baser estate."

Outside, waiting for her, were the women of London. They shouted their encouragement to her, telling her to care for nothing and not to give in to her enemies. If the matter were to be decided by the women, the French ambassador reported, the King would lose the battle.

But the matter was to be decided by men, by two Legates hearing legal argument, and witnesses brought forward to substantiate the King's case that Queen Katherine was not a virgin when she came to his bed. Twenty-five years they went back to a boy bridegroom who boasted, "I have been this night in the midst of Spain." Fifteen was the Prince of Wales? The Earl of Shrewsbury attested he had known his wife before he was sixteen. The Duke of Norfolk remembered Prince Arthur was of good complexion and nature and above fifteen—of course he carnally knew his lady—did not the speaker himself at the same age know and carnally use a woman? "They may do whatever they like," Campeggio wrote to Rome, "and conduct the trial with all those arts which can influence the results in their favour."

Not quite as they liked. One man "stood stiff in the Queen's cause": John Fisher, Bishop of Rochester, whose robes hung on a body lean with abstinence and penance, upright and tall as a tree. There he stood, saying, since the King sought to know the truth, John Fisher would be glad to tell him. He presented himself before their reverend lordships to assert and demonstrate with cogent reasons that this marriage of the King and Queen could not be dissolved by any power, divine or human. In maintenance of this he was willing to lay down his life. As a gesture of confirmation of all he had spoken, he handed the Legates the copy of a book he had written on the subject.

His flailing words caught Wolsey on the raw, but he was never at a loss for a reply. In the stunned silence he protested against this attack on the Legates. The court had been called to hear the case and render judgement in whatever way divine wisdom should incline them so to do. How dare the Bishop of Rochester take upon himself by the positiveness and vigour of his utterance to pre-empt the prerogative of the court and pronounce judgement himself!

His fellow Legate said nothing, but from the moment John Fisher, like the knuckle-bone of God, made his stand, he, Lorenzo Campeggio, was different. The Cardinal of York—everyone—marked the change, wondering what it betokened. Instead of with precision, he acted now like a man who had the courage to come to decision.

On the 23rd July the King's Grace was present to hear the ruling in his favour. After the preliminary lengthy perorations his counsel at the bar called fast for judgement, and Cardinal Campeggio rose to pronounce it.

In the fluent Latin of the scholar which his audience could all understand, he said it was the custom of the court in Rome to suspend all legal proceedings from the end of July until the commencement of October. "I shall wade no further in this matter, unless I have the just opinion and judgement, with the assent of the Pope, of such other of his counsel as hath more experience and learning in such doubtful laws as I have. Wherefore I will adjourn this court for this time, according to the order of the court in Rome, from whence this court and jurisdiction is derived."

He had obeyed the secret instructions of his master to settle the case without pronouncing sentence. It was a moment or two before the full import of his words reached his hearers, as they adjusted themselves to believe the unbelievable. Instead of sentence adjournment, instead of pronouncement in the King's favour, nothing at all.

Noisily Henry rose. He and his cause had been held up to ridicule before England, before the world. In that hall, stale with reaction as if death had taken place, his every movement sounded as if he were an army in full battle array. He clattered from the court.

The scene was not played out. There was still another actor to say his part, a principal player who could redeem the piece. The commission wrung from the Pope provided either Cardinal could act by himself. Now was the turn of Campeggio's colleague to retrieve the situation and declare for his King.

He rose, his ageing face grey with fatigue, and seconded his fellow Legate. "We be but commissioners for a time, and can, or may not, by virtue of our commission, proceed to judgement without the knowledge and consent of the chief head of our authority, and having his consent to the same; which is the Pope."

At the end of the road, when it came to the parting of the ways, Thomas Cardinal Wolsey enlisted on the side of the Church and forsook his sovereign lord. He needed no archbishop to whisper in his ear that to provoke the wrath of a king spelt death.

CHAPTER ELEVEN

DEATH OF THE CARDINAL

"K was a King, so mighty and grand,
L was a Lady, who had a white hand."

HENRY had reached a watershed in his life; he had reigned for twenty years and was to reign for a further eighteen. The first twenty had been coloured by the brilliant personality of his chief minister, Thomas Wolsey, the latter eighteen were to be stamped by the character and will of the King himself. With Wolsey went spectacle and the spectacular, with the King came government and rule. The difference between the two men was the difference between personality and character: the King was what Wolsey was not, a realist. His development was not so much a matter of slow growth, rather a succession of gigantic starts that rounded themselves into finality, like the mounds a mole throws up. His continuity was a channelling more than roots, painful as these can be, and so finally he undermined himself as a man.

He used Parliament to shape his ends. Never before in the annals of England had Parliament met so often as it did in the latter half of Henry's reign, and it was this governing by consent that makes him great as a king. He did not distrust Parliament as Wolsey had done; he was not afraid of it as some of his predecessors had been. He might dominate it but he never attempted to intimidate it. Embedded in the statute-book for the last eighteen years of his reign are acts and laws which mark a turning point in English history and which have never been equalled.

He was learning also how to master himself, to curb a temper that could have betrayed a lesser man into bouts of violence. His passions were strong but he kept them well bridled, his manners were invariably good even under the most trying circumstances, and above all he knew how to keep himself to himself. "Three may keep counsel if two be away," he was wont to say; "and if I thought my cap knew my counsel, I would cast it in the fire and burn it." This concealment of his thoughts and intentions was what made him so terrifying as he grew older: no one knew until sentence fell how long one had been at the bar, and there was neither reprieve nor pity from the judge who sat in isolation in that uncapped head.

The difficulty of procuring an annulment, which he had thought would be simple, undoubtedly hardened him, and much of his pleasantness receded before the steeling and strengthening of his will. But that was in the years to come; the blood still ran warm in his veins, and he still had affection for the man who had been his chief minister. It was Anne Boleyn, made vindictive by disappointment, to whom Wolsey attributed his downfall. "I know there is a night crow that possesses the royal ear against me, and misrepresents all my actions."

The Duke of Norfolk had the exquisite pleasure of demanding from the butcher's cur the Great Seal of England, but this my lord of York refused to deliver until he saw the King's signature. Back next day rode Norfolk with the Master of the Rolls and letters from the King. The surrender of the seals, on St. Luke's Day, toppled the Cardinal from his lofty pinnacle. He was required to give up to the King the great palaces he had built at York Place and Hampton Court, his property and estates, and all his goods. Seldom had such an accumulation of riches been displayed: plate of silver and gold, cloths of all colours including a thousand pieces of fine holland, and vestments the like of which had never before been seen in England.

London assembled in its thousands at the water's edge and took boat to catch a nearer view, to watch the stricken Cardinal being taken to the Tower. The pomp, panoply and parade with which he used to ride through the city had all diminished to a barge, rocking on the tide. Here he came, with only a single cross borne before him this time, that of York.

That was not—that could not be the Cardinal. Had they not seen him often enough to tell him at a glance? But that was he, all right, the cross told you that, and the redness of his robes; only his face had dwindled to half its size, like a finger-nail it looked.

He must know what was awaiting him at the Tower, they all knew what was awaiting him. All that display of pride and power come to this. He must have been about the richest man in England

—that was one thing churchmen knew better than their paternoster, how to amass and keep wealth. They were all the same, every single one of the Pope's men, with the priest refusing to bury your dead until you had paid the last penny of what he claimed as his fee. Bare of bed and board the Cardinal would find the Tower after the opulence of his palaces. A great man he had been, firm with substance; and now you were going to watch him, old and shaken, slipping past you on the way to prison in his red robes, the only thing he had left.

But the barge was not heading for the Tower, it was moving in the other direction. What did that mean, think you? Only one thing: he wasn't being carried through Traitors' Gate, so you could wait here long enough for he was not going to pass. The King must still be behind him then, or it would have been the wind in his teeth for him.

The Cardinal went to Esher Palace, a subsidiary old house to new Hampton Court. Both had belonged to him in the past, both now were the King's like everything else in his one-time possession, but his royal master allowed his old servant to tenant it in the meantime.

Here Thomas Wolsey waited, feeding himself on secret messages from his sovereign to be patient. Others sat where he had sat, filled offices he had filled, handled affairs of state as he would not have handled them. The man praying in Esher for restoration to the King's favour did not realize his day was past, a day that encompassed an epoch. Never again would a cleric wield the power he had wielded; a lawyer now held the Great Seal in place of the priest. Never again would a servant of the crown, cleric or layman, possess the power he, Thomas Wolsey, had possessed.

He could not foresee in the shuffling of the cards, as posts were refilled and the insignia of authority changed hands, that there was one there who would become Pope in England with powers no Pope had ever possessed. He was not to know that the King with his boy's face had learnt from him the principle of one-man rule, and that the pupil was far to out-distance the master.

The first thing Henry did after the debacle of the Legates' court was to summon Parliament, which was the last thing his former minister would have done. It was an audacious move on his part, for the people, represented by Members of Parliament, were sympa-

thetic towards Katherine and actively hostile to the woman whom
he wished to supplant her. But nobody strengthened Henry's hand
more than the Pope, whose bungling irresolution galvanized itself
into the decisive step of maintaining that the King's case would not
only have to be decided by Rome but in Rome.

Every Englishman, whoever he was, noble or yeoman, thought
the same about that. Their King cited to appear in Rome! Who
did this Pope think he was to publish such a decree? They would
like to tell him if the King did go it would be at the head of an
army. They had never liked the idea to begin with of their monarch
summoned to plead in his own realm before an English and an
Italian papal representative; even Katherine's sympathizers expressed resentment at their sovereign subjected to such a procedure.
But cited to appear in person at a foreign court in a foreign land,
with the Emperor's foreign spears bristling behind the papal throne!
There was not a man in England who would have allowed such a
thing, far less King Hal himself, thank God for that.

This harmony between sovereign and subject was what made it
possible for Henry to achieve what he did. He understood the temper
of his people, and they acquiesced in what he did because he and
they were on the same side. For long a corrupt Church had lost its
hold, and secularization spreads in a thriving commonalty. It might
be a theological age, it was also an irreligious one. The Reformation
did not come in England as it came in neighbouring Scotland, as it
did to Germany and Switzerland, through men whose blazing heat
to redress wrongs forged Protestantism. There was no John Knox
in England, no Martin Luther or John Calvin. When the English
Reformation came it came through the State and not a counter
church, and the State was Henry VIII. Its impulse was not a matter
of conscience but a grievance about money. It would have come
about without the King's divorce; the wand of the arrow had been
fashioning for some time as men disparaged the Church for its
wealth, but the divorce was the goose's feather that winged it on
its way.

Word was brought to Wolsey at Esher how the new Lord Chancellor had spoken of the King, who was present at the opening of
Parliament, as the good, ever vigilant shepherd who, for the well-
being of his flock, had recently thrust out "the great wether". He
did not need to be told who was the great wether who had presumed

the shepherd had no wit to perceive his crafty doing. Pitiable indeed had been his mistake, for his Grace's sight was so quick and penetrable he not only saw but saw through him, both within and without.

The Lords, after mustering forty-four charges against him, brought in a bill of attainder to make the Cardinal's reinstatement impossible. Only one man spoke in his defence, Thomas Cromwell, his one-time secretary, and he persuaded the Commons to reject the bill. Wolsey knew he must have acted with the King's connivance, or it would have been passed. His one link with his royal master in the days to come was this Cromwell, an up-and-coming man, not a butcher's but a blacksmith's son, who had been a trooper, a merchant and a money-lender in the past, and who carried the rigour of the soldier, the perspicacity of the trader and the tenacity of the money-lender into the present.

Parliament was informed that their vigilant shepherd wished to be released from the obligation to repay a loan which the great wether had raised for him. His flock did not allow the bill to pass without some opposition and final amendment. A member of London, one John Petit, rose and spoke against releasing the King from his debts to his people. There was no question of Henry treating him as an offender or ordering his arrest; genially he would ask the next time he was there if Petit were on his side. He was too secure in the saddle not to give Parliament rein, or to resort to pack it. No go-between was allowed to come between him and either of the Houses; his relation to both was more like that of an acting prime minister than spectator sovereign.

Measures were passed for reforming the clergy in which old grievances were redressed. Clergy were forbidden to hold more than one living, a priest was prohibited to keep a benefice unless he lived in it, and could be fined if he absented himself for more than a month. The people felt well served by Parliament. Poetic justice had been meted out to clerics who could no longer extort exorbitant dues and fees and could be fined themselves if they did not behave.

Henry was not so successful in his domestic women's world as he was with that of a man's Parliament. Instead of well on the way to marriage with the King and crowned as his queen, Anne found herself as far away as ever from her aims. Frustration made her waspish.

She knew consciously now what she had always known unconsciously: that, despite his handsome presents and the flower of his
compliments, the Cardinal despised her. She and her party were
convinced it was not lack of skill that had failed to procure the Pope's
annulment, but lack of will. Wolsey could if he would, and he had
not.

She exacted full payment for her disappointment from Henry,
charging him with the passing of her youth, putting a price on her
honour and holding over his head the perpetual threat that she
would go away. Her tears had the effect that a woman's tears do
have on certain men. He felt he would go to almost any lengths to
mollify her, abjectly entreating her not to leave him.

Katherine remained at court, his nominal wife, his more than
nominal consort and queen, the woman whose life he had shared
for twenty years, whom he had once loved and would always respect.
She did not cry her eyes out in front of him, nonetheless he felt she
was due some consideration. Man-like, he tried to please both in
turn, and in his effort to make up to one for the other, heavily over-
played his hand with each.

That Christmas the thirteen-year-old Mary was at Greenwich to
join the festivities with her father and mother. His small flaxen-
haired daughter did not make the demands, tacit or otherwise, that
his love and helpmeet made. He could lavish on her all the tenderness he felt without any sense of guilt. One would really think his
bookworm of a daughter was the apple of his eye, not Anne.

Some contemporaries believed that Anne was Henry's mistress
by this time; Wolsey obviously did with his night crow remark.
They were certainly cohabiting eighteen months later. But in 1529,
the year of the Legates' court, Henry's almost slavish attitude to her
points to unfulfilled desire.

Anne Boleyn was small boned and this slenderness made her
appear less tall than she was. Very tiny and very precious she seemed
in the King's big arms, with her brown eyes and heart-shaped face.
She was sprightly with intelligence and her beautiful mouth could
say things that were clever and had an edge to them. She was not a
good husbandwoman like Katherine; the King, as well as gratuities
and costly gifts and an indulgent income, was forever paying
accounts for her from the privy purse for stuffs and furs, hunting
gear that she could join in his sport, including a shooting-glove,

wearing apparel, embroidery, everything a lady of fashion could desire.

The Cardinal was allowed to retain the rich archbishopric of York, and hopefully he set out for his See in spring. He had been appointed to it fifteen years ago but had never gone near it or taken the trouble to be installed. His enemies believed he, an absentee arch-priest, would be murdered by the people of his province, and were chagrined to learn he was quite well received. Their chagrin developed into distrust when they heard how humbly the Cardinal had entered on his pastoral duties, winning not only respect and praise from his flock but their love. Would York, a great way off, contain their old enemy? They did not believe it would.

Many men were administering what once one alone had controlled. The King burst forth at his council that the Cardinal was a better man than any of them at managing matters to his liking. They feared Wolsey more after his fall than they had in his pride. This man's goose would have to be cooked once and for all before it was too late.

On the 1st November, on the eve of his belated enthronement, when Wolsey was sitting at dinner with his chaplains, a strong party of horsemen rode into the courtyard. It was led by the young Earl of Northumberland whom the Cardinal knew well, for he had been in his service to be trained in the way he should go when he was Lord Percy. Was that only seven short years ago? How time slackened and contracted with the using of it. When the Earl had been Henry Percy, the Cardinal had broken at the King's command his love-troth with Anne Boleyn. A spirited defence he had put up of the girl with whom he had tangled and ensured himself. Even after his father had been brought from the north to tell him roundly to do as he was bid, he had argued and objected until forced to renounce his word.

Here he was, young Henry Percy, who had stepped into his father's shoes since then and one of the worthiest earldoms in the kingdom, being greeted by his old master on All Saints as though his visit at that hour with so many attendants was natural and expected.

Pretending not to notice his one-time pupil was trembling with agitation, the Cardinal took him into his bedchamber that he might put off his riding apparel, talking all the time like the good host he was to make his guest at ease. Immediately they were shut off from attendants, servants and chaplains, Wolsey snapped silent. In silence the young man and the old walked to the window, when the Cardinal felt his companion's hand placed lightly on his arm.

"My lord, I arrest you of high treason."

The gifts, messages and tokens from the King since his demission were all obliterated by words spoken faint as a whisper. The protection of the royal shadow no longer hovered over him. Wolsey knew what lay before him: the Tower, trial and certain death. He left York with the noise of his parishioners reverberating in his ears, "God save your Grace!" "God save your Grace!" "The foul evil take all them that take you from us!"

God did save his grace. Suffering from a cruel internal complaint, he died on his way to London in Leicester Abbey. The monks reverently clothed the long narrow bones in the full robes and regalia of his office, and laid him to rest. "If I had served God as diligently as I have done the King," he sighed on his death-bed, "He would not have given me over in my grey hairs."

After his death, Henry had neither the compunction nor regret for his former chancellor that he had felt during his lifetime. It was as though the memory of his old servant was not only sponged from his mind but must be ground from the records. He erected his own coats of arms wherever he could on Wolsey's palaces and renamed after himself Cardinal College, which had been the dead man's joy and pride to build at Oxford.

If the King had to come and go with Parliament, he found he could ride roughshod over the Lords spiritual. Except for Fisher, there was not one of the heroic mould that makes for martyrdom. The Archbishop of Canterbury, the highest dignitary in England, was a man mild to timidity, who would accept bad lest a worst thing befall him. In the past when Church and sovereign clashed, the Church had been stronger than king. Sure of its own ground, the line of demarcation across which royal prerogative dare not penetrate was jealously guarded. In Henry's time there was no line—as he found.

He demanded to be recognized as sole protector and "Supreme Head of the Church and clergy of England". The prelates were horrified at a title that diminished papal supremacy, but the Archbishop was even more horrified at the thought of the royal displeasure, and nothing is more contagious than fear. When he proposed the new title for their sovereign, with the meaningless rider "as far as the law of Christ allows", he added weakly, "Silence gives consent." "Then are we all silent," cried the clergy.

Henry had his way; whatever opposition he might have to encounter in the future, he knew it would not come from the Church in his own land.

Reinforced with new ammunition, he returned to his assault on the entrenched See of Rome. Politely he wrote to Clement, taking some pains to make it clear to the Vicar of Christ that he, the King of England, was only head of the Church in England. Once more the Pope was requested to annul his marriage. Should he fail to do so, Henry, using the royal we, pointed out, "Our condition will not be wholly irremediable. Extreme remedies are ever harsh of application; but he that is sick will by all means be rid of his distemper." His Holiness had been warned.

CHAPTER TWELVE

MATTERS OF CONSCIENCE

" 'Ye are my jewel, and only ane,
　　Nane's do you injury;
　For ere this-day-month come and gang
　　My wedded wife ye'se be.' "

KATHERINE and Anne were like two rival queen bees in the hive
of the court; when the elder woman took her customary place, the
younger did not appear, and when the younger queened it at a
banquet given by the King in her honour, the elder was absent.
There was no intermingling of their trains; only the dominant males
remained the same.

Henry did not open the divorce question directly with Katherine
after the first occasion when the ominous news was broken to her
they had been living in sin all their married lives. If she had to be
approached on the subject, a delegation prompted by the King was
appointed to put before her still another proposal amplified by his
views. So that when they met, and dined side by side, there appeared
on the face of things nothing different in the pattern of their
lives.

Yet to Henry nothing was the same. Instead of the one to exert
pressure, he for the first time in his life became the object feeling it.
Anne, now sure of her hold on him, became more and more tyrannical until he complained to her uncle Norfolk that she was not like
the Queen, who never in her life used ill words to him.

He could boast, and mean it, that if the Pope issued ten thousand
excommunications he would not care a straw for them; that he was
King, Emperor and Pope all in one so far as his own country was
concerned. But there were uneasy rumours that Charles was preparing for war in defence of his aunt. Hostilities involved money
for arms as well as the loss of England's best customer, and Parlia-

ment showed no enthusiasm for either consequence. The House fairly buzzed with accord when one Member rose to move that their sovereign should take back the Queen to wife and thus solve both problems.

The last deputation sent to attend on Katherine before the separation was large and imposing, but neither its numbers nor the importance of its personages could persuade her to withdraw her suit from Rome. To her the Pope was the mirror image of eternal Truth, and he alone could judge. She would not consider the case being placed before four English prelates and four English nobles, even when reminded once again of the King's troubled conscience crying out for settlement. "God grant my husband a quiet conscience," was her reply, "but I mean to abide by no decision excepting that of Rome."

A fortnight later Henry and Anne rode together from Windsor Castle as they had ridden often enough in the past, but this time they did not return. Katherine received no warning; man-like Henry could not bring himself to say good-bye. He sent instructions that she must move from Windsor to one of Wolsey's old houses, where she took up residence with a small household. "Go where I may," she said, "I am his wife, and for him will I pray." She blamed her former lady-in-waiting for edging him into heresy and disobedience to Rome. Anne and her father were described as more Lutheran than Luther; it was not, however, devotion to the Gospel which made them "true apostles of the new sect" but because the Pope had failed to produce the annulment.

Katherine never saw her husband again, nor her daughter who was parted from her about the same time. There is a pathetic item in the royal accounts, a payment by the King to Dr. Butts of a considerable sum for attending to his daughter Mary: the entry is dated the same month that he separated from her mother.

The parting of the daughter from the mother was Katherine's punishment for having a conscience of her own. That Mary was not allowed to visit her even on her death-bed was due to Anne Boleyn's vindictive temper. "The King himself is not ill-natured," the imperial ambassador was to write later, "it is this Anne who has put him in this perverse and wicked temper, and alienates him from his former humanity." Anne's jealousy of Mary was even stronger than her jealousy of Katherine, probably because she could not compete with Henry's affection for his daughter or his pride in her attainments.

Nothing is more characteristic of Katherine than the letters she wrote to Mary after they were parted. She prays God that the amendment in her daughter's health may continue, tries to reconcile her to the loss of the Latin lessons she used to give her by praising the superior qualifications of her tutor, and asks that sometimes she might be comforted by being sent some of her exercises to see. She signs this letter, breathing love through its self-control, "your loving mother, Katherine the Queen." She still signs herself thus two years later when Anne's marriage to the King had been proclaimed and she had been crowned as his queen.

In this letter she tells her daughter to obey the King her father in everything except in what she knows will offend God. "We never come to the kingdom of God but by troubles." The dictionary definition of religion is "the recognition of supernatural powers and of the duty lying upon man to yield obedience to these". Katherine's religion was the most important thing in her life, and this world was but a discipline to equip her for the next. There was nothing equivocal about her conscience: it was a sharp, shining sword separating right from wrong; there was no overlapping. Her daughter took after her in this respect, but Mary lacked her mother's sweetness and forbearance. Her rigidity was to earn for her a terrible opprobrium from the people and never the love and loyalty they bore her mother.

Henry spent that Christmas at Greenwich Palace, the family home where he had spent it since his childhood days, but now instead of his wife Katherine and his daughter he had Anne at his side. The festivity, glee and excitement of other years were banked against the walls, caught behind doors, the present making echoes of the past. Instead of mirth and merrymaking, there was lavish and sumptuous entertainment of the new French ambassador: Francis had to be courted. If dispute with Rome led to war with Charles, Henry must have as strong an ally as he could find.

In a house that had belonged to someone else, Katherine made Christmas as full of cheer as she could for her small train, and wept in the emptiness of the night to be bereft of Henry's overflowing presence; while their daughter, feeling like an orphan, wondered how anyone could call this Christmas, with no mother to turn to, no father to caress her or give her money to disport herself with and load her with gifts.

At Easter Henry was again at Greenwich, keeping the great services of the Church, always a solace to a man devout but fundamentally irreligious, creeping to the Cross on Good Friday, sitting among his courtiers on the Sunday listening to the sermon preached by a member of his favourite order, the Observant Friars.

In the chapel bright and glancing with jewel-like colours, rich with ceremonial, the preacher's words, after the divine Hallelujahs, Hosannas and *Te Deums* rising from choirs, suddenly sounded discordant as the knells of a bell. A stir passed over his congregation that did not subside as the stern voice continued to denounce the unlawfulness of the King's proposed new marriage. If he, like Ahab, did evil in the sight of the Lord, then, perhaps, history would record that the dogs licked up his blood as they had done Ahab's.

The following Sunday a royal chaplain was put into the pulpit to plead the King's cause, which he could do with good effect as his sovereign was present. He received short shrift from the warden of Greenwich convent who rose, fierce with anger, and routed him with a battery of blasting words.

The arrest of both malcontent priests did not silence the criticism which was cropping up all over the country, directed by the common people against Nan Bullen. Henry was affronted at such disapprobation: that his subjects should dare to disapprove of what he, their sovereign, approved. Nevertheless his annual hunting expedition into the counties north of the Thames was abandoned, lest it provoked popular demonstrations against the woman who would supplant her former mistress. But opposition always stiffened his determination to have his own way. He was going to marry Anne Boleyn and nothing or no one, Pope, preacher or subject, would stop him.

He raised her to the peerage, the first female peer ever to be thus created. So she was styled Marquis on the charter; he desired her to possess his family title of Pembroke in her own right. It was most unusual, this brief ceremony when the King in the presence of the assembled court slipped over her sloping shoulders the crimson velvet mantle and placed on her bird-like head the coronet. She received a pension of a thousand pounds a year for maintaining her new dignity, and her initials with Henry's, entwined with a true lover's knot, appeared on royal architecture, notably on Wolsey's

Cardinal College at Oxford, now known as King's. Katherine was bidden to surrender her jewels for her rival to wear, and Henry left no stone unturned to have her invited to France on his visit that autumn to Francis. Official French recognition would ensure the new Marchioness a cachet in the eyes of the world that Henry was quite unable to bestow.

Francis saw no necessity for a meeting with his fellow king, but Henry, determined to have French acceptance of Anne, was insistent, and good-humouredly Francis gave in, stipulating that everything was to be on the simplest scale and nothing ruinous like the Field of Cloth of Gold twelve years ago.

The problem now facing the French authorities was: which of their ladies was to receive the King of England's travelling companion? Francis's second wife, Queen Eleanor, was obviously out of the question as she was Katherine's niece. Even had she been willing, Henry made it clear he would as soon see the devil as a woman in Spanish dress. He foresaw no difficulty: there was always better cheer without women, and he would be quite content if Francis entertained Madame Anne by himself with great respect; but the French King's good humour did not stretch so far. His sister Marguerite's refusal to play hostess for him left only the Duchess of Vendome available, but because of the scandals associated with her Henry considered her totally unsuitable to welcome his Anne. He was forced to agree that at his meeting with his French counterpart he would be unaccompanied by the newly created Marchioness of Pembroke.

Anne nevertheless travelled with him to France. Henry had not given in yet. The two kings met at Boulogne to conclude an alliance against Charles, and Francis promised to intercede again in Rome on Henry's behalf. The French were realists, and if furthering the King of England's divorce was the price to be paid for winning Henry as an ally against Charles, with his monstrous encircling empire, it was a small one indeed to pay. Henry for his part could not do without Francis in case Charles made war on England. The friendship therefore between the two kings was genuine, as it had not been at the empty charade of the Field of Cloth of Gold.

Francis accompanied Henry back to Calais, where the English King broke the gentlemen's agreement on simplicity with a banqueting hall worthy for him to play host to his royal guest. It was hung with silver and gold tissue and decorated with golden wreaths encrusted with stones and jewels. He was attired in russet velvet covered with gold, pearls and precious stones, but the French King beat him at his own game. His doublet was so thickly embedded with diamonds and jewels it had no background to have a colour. Appraising eyes valued it at a hundred thousand crowns (£800,000 in the present day).

After supper eight masked ladies glided into the room to dance with the principal guests. Later Henry himself removed the visors to reveal the beauty they covered, and lo, the King of France found his fair partner was none other than Anne Boleyn whom he remembered as maid of honour to his first queen. Another of the dancers was her sister Mary. Francis rallied successfully, talking to the unmasked Anne for a little time apart, and next morning sent her the present of a costly jewel.

Altogether the visit to France could be counted a success, although Anne had not received the recognition Henry had worked for. But, inveterate gamester that he was, he had other cards up his capacious sleeve that would take more than one trick, and the Joker Fate had slipped him a trump shortly before he left for France. The aged Archbishop of Canterbury, the highest church dignitary in England, died.

Nervous and noisy with bulls ever since the Legates' court, the Pope had inhibited the King of England, under pain of excommunication, from making a second marriage, forbidden the Archbishop of Canterbury to judge the suit, warned the King of England not to cohabit with any woman other than Queen Katherine and, for good measure, prohibited all women to contract marriage with him. Little wonder that Henry found himself with Anne and her faction in the opposite camp, versus the old régime and the *status quo* symbolized by the Pope.

Henry had riposted with act after act passed through an anticlerical Parliament only too willing to legislate against the clergy, so craven and abject they did not make even the show of a stand. No longer was there a Wolsey to hold the door. The Church in England was stripped of its sanction to make laws except with the King's consent, and was thus stripped of its birthright. The Pope's authority for electing English bishops was abolished; henceforth they were to be licensed by the crown. Rome was no longer to be paid the fees known as Peter-pence when English bishops were consecrated, or like payments: Henry had not yet confirmed this particular act, as it was one of the tricks he kept up his sleeve to be played at a later date. The legislature was tempered by the sanctifying declaration that neither King nor realm meant to deviate from the articles of the Catholic Faith of Christendom. Neither King nor realm had any quarrel with Christendom's Catholic Faith; their quarrel was with the foreigner Pope meddling in their affairs and refusing an annulment. Henry was and remained stoutly orthodox; he was not attracted by Protestant doctrine with its rejection of mass.

The old Archbishop of Canterbury had not been a courageous man, but he had been unwilling to judge the King's suit, which was tantamount to declaring the King's marriage to Queen Katherine invalid, when the Pope had forbidden him to do so. Now his office was empty and could be filled by the King's nominee. Henry's choice fell on "a wonderful and grave wise man", who had written a book, founded on Leviticus (the Pope favoured Deuteronomy), proving that the King's marriage was against God's law, and so no Pope could make it lawful by dispensation.

Thomas Cranmer was recalled from abroad where he had been sent to win men over to the King's divorce and when he was taking his first tentative steps towards the new Lutheran teaching. A forty-three-year-old doctor of divinity, he had one of these malleable minds that are coloured and influenced by others, so that, chameleon-like, it changed with his company.

He left England believing what his master believed, that his union to Queen Katherine was against the word of God, and expediently closed his priest's eyes to the knowledge that his patroness, Anne Boleyn, was living in sin with their sovereign. Abroad he came in contact with men who did not view the King of England as the King of England viewed himself. They saw him as a man trying to be rid of a faithful wife that he could marry his concubine. These scholars did not believe in gleaning the Bible for convenient texts to prop up a dubious point of view but searching it for the truth by which the Church could be purged of erroneous doctrine. Under their influence, Cranmer began to blame what his master was doing against Queen Katherine and Princess Mary.

When the summons came from King Henry to return, his ambassador lost no time in starting, but once on the road he delayed his journey. Did he really want to become Archbishop of Canterbury? What about his grave doubts on the propriety of the King's conduct? Did he wish to be associated with another's actions, even if he were king, which he as a priest knew to be wrong? On the other hand, surely it was the duty of a subject to obey and serve his prince. He could not turn now, he had gone too far on the road back. Never would he desert his prince in the middle of a foreign mission. After all, his king was appointing him to the highest position in Church and State. If he held it, he could advance the new Lutheran teaching in England.

"Never man came more unwilling to a bishopric than I did," Cranmer could say. But he came. He was chosen by the King because he and the Boleyn faction felt he would be reliable, i.e. amenable, and they were right. The impress of Henry's forcible mind was to be stamped upon Cranmer's pliant one. If scruples, hesitations or doubts ever troubled the new Archbishop of Canterbury, they did not rise to the surface but wavered and floated in these wan regions of the mind, like fronds of seaweed so pulled and distorted with unseen tides they appear to be what they are not, rootless.

It was vital for Henry that the consecration of his new Archbishop should be recognized by the Pope, essential that the highest Church dignitary in England should have papal authority for his position. For Henry had a great deal for Cranmer to do. Anne was pregnant, and everything must be expedited that the prince to be born was legitimate.

He married Anne so secretly that to this day it is not known where the ceremony took place and who officiated; even Cranmer did not hear of it until a fortnight later. It was towards the end of January, 1533, about St. Paul's Day, probably at Greenwich Palace, by an Augustinian friar well known for his support of the King's cause, that Henry Tudor married Anne Boleyn.

Not a hint of the marriage must get abroad while the Pope was asked for the necessary bulls recognizing Thomas Cranmer as Archbishop of Canterbury. It was conveyed to his Holiness that if they were not forthcoming Henry would confirm the act forbidding the customary large revenues to be paid to Rome. No longer were English ambassadors allowed to chivvy and harry the Vicar of Christ, they were instructed to "use all gentleness towards him".

Two French cardinals made a timely appearance in Rome, asking Clement on behalf of their sovereign to acquiesce over the matter of Henry's bulls. London saw their sovereign arrive in state at the opening of Parliament, and who should have the honour to accompany him on his right hand but the papal nuncio.

Basking in this English sunlight, the Pope was heard to say the King of England was wiser and had a better nature than the King of France. In vain Chapuys, the imperial ambassador in London, who knew everything, sent warning dispatches not to believe the story that the King had given the Lady Anne the marquisate to compensate her for not having received the throne. The coronet had been conferred on her as an earnest of the crown, not by way of compensation. Urgently he wrote that the Pope must be persuaded not on any account to issue bulls unless he made it a condition that Cranmer swore not to interfere in the divorce case. Bitterly he remarked that his Holiness would not be so eager to admit Cranmer as Archbishop if he believed he was a Lutheran.

It all seemed harmless to Clement. He had refused the King of England so much and now this welcome opportunity had arisen when he could do something to please him. With astonishing and uncharacteristic alacrity he issued eleven bulls authorizing Cranmer's consecration, and sent the pall to England.

Henry was saved. Cranmer as papal legate could give judgement that his marriage to Katherine was against the law of God and invalid. He could pronounce that Henry's marriage to Anne was lawful. Never mind if criticism chattered up and down the country about their king marrying another wife before his marriage to his first was invalidated: his rude, ignorant and common people could or would not comprehend that since his marriage to his first was unlawful, he had never been married at all and so was free as any other single man to take a bride.

A bride who was bearing him a son. He was forty-two, in the prime of life, riding the tide when it was full. This was his midsummer, high noontide. His sun was at its zenith, and fulfilment was ripening before his very gaze.

It was Chapuys, the imperial ambassador, who said it. Did the King's Grace really think he would be able to produce more progeny? The Spaniard's voice, soft and sibilant, did not sound as though it were loaded and Henry was off his guard. But his reaction was instantaneous, rebounding before he knew he was struck. Three times he demanded as he blazed with anger, "Am I not a man like other men? Am I not a man like other men? Am I not a man like other men?" The blood that had rushed to his face took long to pale.

CHAPTER THIRTEEN

A KING BEWITCHED

"False luve, and hae ye played me this,
In the summer, mid the flowers?
I shall repay ye back again,
In the winter, mid the showers."

HE WAS to remember her when he was old as he had seen her that day, passing in her litter on her way to her coronation, her black hair so long and plentiful she appeared to him to be sitting in it. And when he had anointed and crowned her in Westminster Abbey, he remembered her joyful smiling face when she said "Amen". It was a day neither could ever forget, the petty squire's son who was Archbishop of Canterbury and the merchant's granddaughter who was now crowned Queen of England.

The citizens of London had lived in their streets these past few days, crowding to the wharves to watch the Mayor and aldermen in their scarlet robes bringing *her* from Greenwich Palace to the Tower, "the King's dearest wife Queen Anne", with all honour and might, their barges fluttering with streamers and banners and bristling with artillery. Music she had all the way, trumpets blowing and musicians following her in another float and every flag making gay the boats hung with little bells. Everything had been done to amuse and divert the citizens, with a furious dragon on the Lord Mayor's barge twirling its tail, capering for all it was worth and spitting wildfire into the Thames every few minutes.

That was *her* symbol, the white falcon—crowned it was and holding in one claw a sceptre, and that was her motto written large as life, "Me and Mine". You do see what it means, rising out of a tree with a golden stem bearing red and white roses? It means that the red rose of Lancaster and the white rose of York will continue through *her* and her line. "Me and Mine"—the pride of it, and

everyone knowing what she is, no better than she ought, no better
than any of us. The real Queen would never have chosen such a
motto—"Thee and Thine" it would have been with her.

Did you hear what the Bishop of London said?—pity there were
not more like him in high places. "The King's Grace, ye say, shall
have another wife and she shall bear him a prince. Who hath
promised him a prince?" Who has, unless the King himself? If
God did not grant a good woman like Queen Katherine one for
him, do you suppose He will stoop Himself to her?

The real Queen—it makes a difference, you know, when you're
the King of Spain's daughter and not just a Mayor's brat. Did you
hear what the real Queen did when they told her she was Prince
Arthur's widow and no longer King Henry's wife? She took her
pen and drew it through the words Princess-dowager wherever they
appeared on the citation. Ay, and she said her name of Queen she
would vindicate, challenge, and so call herself until death. "I stick
not so for vain glory," said she—true enough, not like some we
could name sitting there queening it in her golden dress. "But because I know myself to be the King's true wife"—what we all know,
every man-John of us.

King Hal should be ashamed of himself—mebbe, but kings even
more than ordinary folk are seldom what they should be. He's no
by her, you notice. She's sitting there by her lone self with only her
maidens around her. No, he's waiting for her at the Tower. He will
no be by her either when they crown her in a day or two. Yon will
be *her* day, you see, no his, just like today. No like when he married
the real Queen, and they were crowned thegither. Husband and
wife *they* were, no King and his —

So much to see, so much to hear, something happening every
minute the day before they crowned her, the city's fountains flowing
red and white wine for the refreshment of the citizens. She'll pass
by this way, her canopy of cloth of gold held over her by four knights.
By Fenchurch Street in her golden litter, pausing at the corner of
Gracechurch Street, hung with crimson and scarlet, to listen to the
speeches of Apollo and his attendants from Mount Parnassus, most
cunningly contrived. At Cheapside Cross, all cloth of gold and
velvet, wait the aldermen, where the city recorder hands her a
thousand marks of gold in a purse which she most thankfully receives. Most gracious she is with her bowings—well, she had the

mistress she served all these years to pattern herself on. Mebbe the Mayor and his men are trying to take the bad taste out of the King's mouth when folk at the Easter sermon walked out of a city church before the prayers for *her* could be read.

They have removed the real Queen into the country, to silence and hide her away. They say she stopped one of her gentlewomen from cursing *her*. "Rather pray for her," said she, "for even now is the time fast coming when you shall have reason to pity her, and lament her case." How could that ever be, when they are crowning her the morrow, and every bell in the city is ringing in her honour today?

Here *she* comes by Ludgate, stopping to listen to the choirs singing her praises—her ears will never weary of that. All the scutcheons and angels in Fleet Street have been new painted and, sudden with brightness, appear as though for the occasion. To Westminster Hall, hung with gold arras and newly glazed all because of her, where the King is awaiting her. Such glory and grandeur and triumph will last a lifetime. King Hal can do what he likes but I bare my head to my real Queen and not to her serving-maid, and no cheer will I give as she passes.

The morrow was her coronation day, and Henry watched through a hole in the wall the banquet given in her honour on her return. Earls were her carver, officer and chief butler and her cup-bearer, lords of the realm her lesser servants. That was Wyatt, the poet, who was pouring scented water over her hands. So she sat at table with her ladies—of all the dignitaries only Thomas Cranmer shared her board. Charles Brandon and Will Howard rode into the hall on horseback, escorting the officer and the Knights of the Bath when they entered bearing the first course for the Queen's table, twenty-seven dishes in all. Charles always managed to outshine everyone except Henry, and as Henry was not there his doublet and jacket sewn with orient pearl surpassed everyone else's. How heavy he was growing, his shoulders and back broad as he sat on his courser trapped to the ground with crimson velvet. Mary was not present. Mary was tethered to her manor house in the country. Would she have been there even if she were not ill? Her brother brushed the thought aside; it was of no consequence. The Earl of Sussex, Anne's officer, was kneeling before her with a spice plate so magnificent it took both his hands to hold—what a sweet tooth she had, his little love. Always munching comfets, nibbling at sweet-meats, making a feast of sugar plums.

There were lovers' tiffs even before the crown was secure on her head. Within six months of supplanting her mistress as his wife, Anne, angry with jealousy, was taking him to task for allowing his fancy to rove from her. But the days were past when she had him eating out of her small hand. Roughly he silenced her by saying she must put up with it as her betters had done before her, boasting he could degrade her as easily as he had raised her to the throne.

Her betters? She was his wife and queen, bearing his son. There was no one in the whole wide realm better than she. The law required the presence of the heir presumptive at the birth of the heir apparent. The Princess Mary was sent for, to be in attendance at the birth. Her father was too shrewd to disinherit her yet, lest he lose both Anne and his son in the hazards of childbirth, but when his wife was mother of his heir, then Mary would be degraded from royal rank—Anne would see to that.

The circular to be sent to the nobility announcing the birth of a prince was in readiness. He was to be christened Henry after his father or Edward after his kingly great-grandfather, and Francis had consented to become his sponsor. To think she, Anne Boleyn, was married to one king, had a second as sponsor, and was big with a child who would become a third.

She lay in the old palace at Greenwich waiting her happy hour, in a room where the tapestry on the wall illustrated the parable of the ten wise and the ten foolish virgins. Her long neck looked longer without its collar-band of jewels, and her dark skin was glossed with sweat as she entered travail. The child was not born until between three and four in the afternoon of that Sunday. It was a daughter, not a son.

Henry's disappointment was so great his eyes were sharp with tears, and Anne needed all her ingenuity to try to soften the blow for him. The circular dispatched to the nobility had an s added to the prince to indicate it was female. The child was christened Elizabeth after Henry's mother, and her birth was thought of so little consequence that Chapuys, the imperial ambassador, merely mentioned in his dispatches that the King's concubine had borne a bastard. No premonition warned him that the bastard was to become Queen Elizabeth who would break the power of Spain.

Henry's natural cheerfulness reasserted itself. His new daughter as a healthy child was but the herald of her brothers. He always put a good face on things to Chapuys and in a month or two was telling him he would have a son soon.

Never had he been merrier as he prepared to give such a buffet to the Pope as he never had before. No longer was there any necessity to deal gently with his Holiness, who was now known in England as the Bishop of Rome, all his papal powers having been transferred to the Archbishop of Canterbury. Henry had gone so far without being stopped; he was confident there were no limits to which he could not reach. When he was threatened with excommunication and imperial arms, he snapped his fingers. He would show the princes of the world how small was the real power of the Pope. As for the Spaniards, let them come—perhaps they would not return. He had successfully demonstrated to his subjects, to whom trade came first and foremost, that the Flemish could no more do without their merchandise than the English could do without their custom.

God and his conscience, he informed Chapuys, were on very good terms. He instructed him to tell his master, the Emperor, that the King of England took himself to be right not because so many said so but because he, being learned, knew it. A man, he announced bland with assurance, should rather endure all the censures of the Church than offend his conscience. His conscience was evidently bent on breach with Rome. And the loss of England to the close-knit Holy See was the beginning of the dissolution of the Roman Catholic Church. Impotence to bring its recalcitrant child back into the fold revealed the weaknesses of man-made canon and decree to its enemies, the Reformers, who came storming in with their thunderbolt from God—the Bible.

It has been said by his upholders that Henry VIII liberated the English Church, by his detractors that he enslaved it. In reality he did neither; what he did was substitute himself for the Pope. His subjects looked on in acquiescence, preferring the despotism of their native king to the despotism of a foreign prince of the Church. It must be remembered that their king's despotism did not affect the bulk of his people; it was a minority, chiefly the clergy, who felt its pressure and cutting edge.

The measures before Parliament and Church courts last year were reinforced by Parliament this year. Henry showed England and the world that what he threatened he was strong enough to perform. The English Church still paid the rich revenues they had paid to Rome in the past but now they jingled in their sovereign's pocket, for he was their Supreme Head, the Defender not of papal Faith but of his own. Parliament lopped the clergy's restraining clause "as far as the law of Christ allows", and passed the Act without it.

The Pope, forced to take notice of such defiance, solemnly pronounced sentence in Rome, seven years after the divorce case had first begun, that the marriage between Queen Katherine and the King of England was valid. He might as well not have spoken for all the difference his pronouncement made in England or to its monarch. "You never saw Prince nor man who made greater show of his horns or wore them more lightheartedly," an exasperated Chapuys exclaimed. He was forever appealing to his master, the Emperor Charles, to declare war on England, although Queen Katherine steadfastly refused to countenance hostilities against her husband or her adopted country.

In Rome bulls depriving Cranmer of his See and excommunicating Henry, Anne and Cranmer were drawn up but not published—yet. With the terrible sentence of greater excommunication dangling over the heads of their sovereign lord and lady, the English court sported, gamed and danced: ". . . Cut off from the Church as long as he lived, removed from the pale of Christian society and deprived of the solace of the rites of religion. When dead to lie without burial, and in hell suffer torment for ever."

That year Pope Clement died, and the Roman citizens forced their way into the room where he lay to stab his dead body again and yet again; they would have dragged his corpse through the streets had they not been prevented. Such savagery was the primitive impulse to destroy what was no longer sacred, to hack to pieces the sacred that had profaned itself.

The King of England's attitude towards the Supreme Head of the Church on earth had undergone cynical metamorphosis since the days he had enlisted himself with boyish ardour as the Pope's knight errant. Since then he had witnessed the Vicar of Christ grant absolution to those guilty of the sack of Rome for the return of his earthly territories. He had seen the men who held the keys of heaven prepared to barter them for unholy gain, to peddle their divine office like so many wares.

Henry VIII, King of England, was a better man than any Pope. Those who wanted proof had only to see how Henry's affairs always prospered because God knew his righteous heart. Let Clement or whoever took his place do what he liked in Rome, he could do what he liked in his own realm. If Paul III declared his predecessor's verdict void then Henry might be prepared to come and go on certain minor details, but he made reconciliation with Rome impossible by announcing his new style to the world, Supreme Head of the English Church, and sending to the block any who denied him the title.

An Act was brought in vesting the succession to the crown on the heirs of the King by Anne Boleyn. None quarrelled with that. Lawyers and clergy alike agreed it was within the rights of Parliament to fix the succession, but it was no longer enough for Henry to know he was in the right to marry again, not enough for the many to say so. Everyone must swear it.

So with the Act went an oath that prominent subjects and all clerics were required to take, swearing first that the King's former marriage was invalid and against the teachings of the Bible. Then, "Ye shall swear to bear faith, troth and obedience only to the King's Grace, and to the heirs of his body by his most dear and entirely beloved lawful wife, Queen Anne."

Now the bulk of Henry's subjects, clerics and laity alike, prominent and humble, were willing to allow, however shocking they considered their sovereign's second marriage, that since he had married again, Anne was Queen and the King's sons by her should succeed to the throne. It was one of these situations that was accepted as a *fait accompli*, no matter how strong the sympathy for the old rejected Queen and her only child. But Henry's nailing Act of Supremacy did not allow the saving grace of acceptance with mental reservations. It left no loophole for individual conscience; the word *only* securely dammed any exit. The King's conscience was to be sufficient for each and every one in his realm. Any who claimed to think for himself was guilty of treason, and worthy of death. Gone were the days when a man could hold high office although Henry knew he did not approve of his divorce, when he could tell his Lord Chancellor to serve God first and after God his king. For the King no longer thought of God and Henry as two separate Beings.

Parliament woke up to the fact, as he began to use them, that they had granted their monarch unlimited powers. He was to be not only king, not only pope, but God to them. Men he had walked with as friends and talked to about the New Learning made the short journey from Tower to block for denying the King's titles.

Sir Thomas More's legal mind could not accept the compromise with his conscience that Cranmer suggested to him, and died saying he was the King's good servant but God's first. The world shuddered at the brutal dispatch of so enlightened and famous a scholar.

John Fisher, with the visionary's far-sighted gaze, he who had spoken out loud and clear for Queen Katherine at the Legates' court, said the King could not possibly take the place of St. Peter's descendant the Pope, their only link with Christ. During his imprisonment Pope Paul, to anger the English sovereign, created him a cardinal; Henry's retort was he would send the new cardinal's head to Rome for the hat. The old man, upright as youth, walked to the block reading the New Testament; his last words were, "This is life eternal to know Thee, the only true God".

And a foreigner wrote home, "In England, death has snatched everyone of worth away, or fear has shrank them up."

Katherine's confessors were burnt alive; they, as members of Henry's favourite order, the Observant Friars, had solemnized and witnessed his first marriage. One, Father John Forrest, wrote from Newgate prison to comfort his queen whom he knew in the gentleness of her heart considered herself the cause of all his miseries: "Would it become, lady mine, an old man to be appalled with childish fear who had seen sixty-four years of life, and forty of these had worn the habit of glorious St. Francis? Weaned from terrestrial things, what is there for me if I have not strength to aspire to those of God?" Priors and vicars who refused to take the corporate oath for their religious houses were hanged, drawn and quartered. Many friars, monks and priests remained "unmoved, unshaken, unseduced, unterrified" after hideous torture for refusing to deny the authority of "the Bishop of Rome" in England.

Their deaths were Henry's defiance flung in the face of the Pope, of Spain and even of France, who had done all she could to effect reconciliation between Rome and England. Christendom trembled at such wickedness and held its breath, waiting for heaven to rain down judgement on its perpetrator. None came. But the constancy of men who refused to deny their conscience was not obliterated by the sickening thud of axe on block, the crackle of flames, or the deaths of prisoners chained to walls: on such sure foundations was the Protestant faith established.

Henry's evil genius was Thomas Cromwell, Wolsey's one-time secretary. It was he who enforced the carrying out of the Act of Supremacy. A man of no scruples, religious or otherwise, he had promised Henry to make him the richest king in Christendom and instilled in him the theory that to be very king his will and pleasure should be regarded as law. Henry preferred to make the laws his will, and had the strength and efficiency to carry his policy out.

Cromwell was now the power at court: the one-time money-lender had become Chancellor of the Exchequer, the merchant made Secretary of State, the soldier promoted to Vicar-General who could recommend bishops and clergy. It was to him one referred if one desired access to the King, he in whose ruthless hands the reins of government resided—for the King. It was to him Queen Katherine had to write, begging him to tell the King that what she desired above all else was to see her daughter who was ill: "A little comfort and mirth she would take with me, would be a half health to her. For my love let this be done."

Small wonder that Mary was ill; her fate was as unhappy as the stepdaughter in the fairy tale. Present at her half-sister's birth, nothing would induce her to call Lady Pembroke's daughter princess. "Sister," she said, setting her mouth straight, "I will call her, but nothing more." Threats made not the slightest difference to her, and when instructions reached her from her father to change her residence she wrote him trusting that he had not seen the order requiring the lady Mary, the King's daughter, to remove to the place aforesaid, as it left out the name of Princess.

"If I have a son, as I hope shortly, I know what will become of her," said Anne Boleyn. In the meantime Mary's considerable household was broken up and transferred to her half-sister Elizabeth, an establishment which had the magnificence of the rank of which Mary had been deprived. Anne allocated her aunt to be Mary's governess, and told her to box her charge's ears; Mary had to join baby Elizabeth's household where it was Anne's pleasure to make her serve as her half-sister's maid. The only comfort she had was her books, and it was probably the self-control of the girl whose father used to boast never cried that made Anne so vindictive against her. We are jealous of those to whom we feel inferior, and jealousy corrodes the subject, not the object. It says much for Mary's nature that she did not hate the baby who supplanted her but played with her and was amused by the bright little thing's antics.

Henry dare not let mother and daughter come together. He had two fears: one, that there would be a rising on their behalf among his subjects—together that danger was doubled, separate it was halved; the other, that Charles might yet declare war to redress his aunt's wrongs. He knew that Katherine had the power to wage as fierce a war against him as ever her mother Isabella had waged in Spain, but Katherine had no hatred in her except that of being the cause of bloodshed and suffering.

Everyone had to convince him of their loyalty by taking the Oath of Supremacy, and everyone included his first wife and elder daughter. Both refused. Katherine would never swear that Anne Boleyn was queen and Henry's lawful wife. To Catholics she was the King's mistress and her daughter Elizabeth illegitimate.

Suffolk was sent to break up her diminished household, he whom Katherine had shielded from Henry's wrath when he married his sister without permission. Mary, the youngest of them all, was dead now.

And here was Charles Brandon raging in upon her, trying to force her and her servants to take the new oath. Her old Spanish bishop implored her to yield to expediency, but expediency was not in Katherine's vocabulary, either Spanish or English. "We find here the most obstinate woman that may be," Suffolk wrote in his dispatch. Never had woman so faithful servants as she. They stiffly stood in their conscience that she was the Queen and the King's lawful wife. She told them to swear in Spanish the opposite of what the oath said. As she would not go of her own free will, she was forcibly removed in the dead of winter to an inhospitable stronghold with a handful of servants, and the old bishop who was allowed to go as her confessor. He was so timid her enemies considered him harmless, and a confessor she could not be denied.

Mary refused to take an oath dishonouring her mother and declaring herself a bastard. The degree of Henry's megalomania can be gauged when we read that he considered his daughter's refusal the height of ingratitude, just as in the past his feelings had been deeply wounded when her mother refused to temper her principles to the tenderness of his newly awakened conscience.

This inability to countenance anyone's point of view but his own where he personally was concerned can be explained by his upbringing and kingship. He had no sense of proportion, for he had not been schooled as his father had by hardship, deprivation and effort before he climbed the steps to the throne. He did not go softly all the days of his life, remembering the grace of God and a hawthorn tree on a battlefield from which the crown that now rested on his head had been plucked.

His days had been golden all his life with the grace of God which he accepted as his natural climate. The divinity that invested an anointed king clung to reigning monarchs long after Henry VIII's time, and he was robed in it. Not only in his realm but in other lands men praised and asked forgiveness from the crowned head who had sent them to the scaffold. Henry was accustomed to everyone, archbishop and bishop included, prostrating themselves at his feet. He, Sovereign Lord the King, never entered Parliament but he listened to it trusting to his most excellent wisdom, princely goodness, and fervent zeal for the promotions of God, honour and Christian religion, and also in his learning, far exceeding in his Parliament's judgement the learning of all other kings and princes it had read of. It was now second nature for him to believe not only that he could do no wrong but that everything he did was right. He never received a letter from his dearest, from his closest, relative, that did not humbly draw his attention to the unbridgeable difference stretching between him and the writer. But not from Katherine.

He held in his hands the last letter she was ever to send him, for she was on her death-bed.

Between the "My Lord and dear Husband" with which it began and the signature "Katherine, Queen of England", the writer forgave him for the way he had cast her into many calamities and himself into many troubles, and prayed God that He also would pardon him. She commended their daughter Mary to him, beseeching him to be a good father to her. "Lastly, do I vow, that my eyes desire you above all things."

Henry is said to have shed tears when he read her letter; he could overlook the signature now he knew this was the last time she would sign herself thus. He sent the Spaniard Chapuys to her, telling him to hasten and to greet her kindly from him. The ambassador reached her in time, although it was the end of December and the snow had begun to drive in air that clanged with cold.

Anne was pregnant, and all her vitality went into prayers that the child she was bearing be a son. She had not been married for three years yet and had less security with Henry as her husband than ever she had had with him as her lover. The court buzzed with gossip, for there was no privacy, about tiffs and quarrels, coldnesses and umbrage. No longer was Anne the one to hold the cheek, Henry the one to kiss, or rather no longer was Anne the love Henry chose to kiss. It was happening all over again down to the smallest detail: the King's roving fancy alighting on one of the Queen's maids-of-honour, the maid-of-honour squeamish to accept his advances in the initial stages out of reluctance to injure her mistress. But what added to the repetition's nightmare quality was that Anne was no longer the maid-of-honour, she was the mistress.

Henry made so little secret of his preference for the pale insipid Jane Seymour that it was palace common talk. A saying was being bandied amongst midwives, "It is never merry in England when there are three queens in it." To which one cackling crone rejoined, "There will be fewer soon."

Of course she meant Mary's mother who was ill and must die some day, put away with all her wits about her in a strong castle in the most inaccessible place that could be found. Anne was the only Queen in England, her predecessor no longer the King's wife or consort. And whoever heard of a lady-in-waiting being called a queen? The child Anne felt leaping in her womb was a son, she was convinced of that; the birth of England's hope would pull the world to rights once more for her and set her where none could assail. That ignorant old crone had probably said "There will be one fewer soon" and the one had been dropped in the repetition.

While she waited for her son to be born, Anne went *devoté*, listening to sermons by a preacher of the new teaching, reading the Bible, distributing alms. She sat amongst her ladies-in-waiting sewing as she used to see her former mistress sit, embroidering a tester for Henry's bed, and helping them to make shirts and other garments for the poor.

The news of Katherine's death followed hard on her last letter to

Henry, and the relief at court could be felt. "God be praised," Henry shouted, "we are free from all suspicion of war." Charles had delayed too long to send a punitive army to England; what he had not done to aid his aunt when she was alive, he would not do now she was dead. "Now I am indeed Queen," exulted Anne. They were at Greenwich, and the last of the Christmastide festivities for which Anne up to then had had little heart suddenly bounced with good spirits and cheer.

On the day of Katherine's obsequies—the service to benefit the soul of the departed, often performed by mourners at a distance—the King, his servants and the court attended dressed in mourning as he had commanded. He could wear yellow, the colour of gladness, when he heard of her death, but he had a strong sense of occasion and would not have dreamed of attending the obsequies of his one-time wife unsuitably garbed. Anne, however, dressed not only herself but her ladies-in-waiting in yellow; it was a gesture that cost her dear where her husband was concerned. All her giddy spirits had returned, but she was as jealous of Katherine dead as ever she had been of her living.

Great store was set in these days on how one met one's end. A lifetime could be redeemed by the resigning and repentance of dying, by the shedding of one's baser nature in preparation to meet one's Maker, sorrowing for the wrong one had done and throwing oneself on the mercy of God who alone could deliver, when the naked soul stood on the brink of eternity. And the talk up and down the country was of the good end Queen Katherine had made, of the serenity of a passing that fittingly crowned such a life. In death as in life Anne felt outrivalled by an old demeaned plain woman whose place she could only pretend to fill until she did what her predecessor could not do, present Henry with the gift of a son.

She was brought to bed before her time in the month Katherine died. The premature birth has been attributed by some to the fright Anne received when her husband fell so heavily in the lists he lay unconscious for two hours, by others to her shock when she surprised the mouse-like Jane Seymour sitting on the King's knee. The child she nearly lost her life to deliver was a stillborn son.

Henry upbraided her furiously for the loss of his boy, to which Anne replied with spirit he had only himself to blame, for it had been caused by her distress over his wench.

"Who hath promised the King a prince?" That was what Henry had promised his people when he put aside his first queen to marry his second, and look what had happened. If Katherine of Aragon had not borne him a son who had lived, Anne Boleyn was certainly never going to do so. The signs were unmistakable, God could not have made Himself clearer. He had denied Henry heirs with Katherine because she had first been married to his brother. He was denying Henry heirs with Anne Boleyn because of his former relations with her sister. No good was coming of their union. Henry did not know how he had ever come to marry her in the first place; the only solution to that riddle must be that she had bewitched him. But she could not bewitch God and God had opened his eyes that He refused to bless his second marriage. It would have to be dissolved as his first one had been, the speedier the better.

As always, God and Henry thought the same.

CHAPTER FOURTEEN

"COMMEND ME TO HIS MAJESTY"

"Oh, Death! rock me asleep,
Bring on my quiet rest,
Let pass my very guiltless ghost
Out of my careful breast.
Ring out the doleful knell,
Let its sound my death tell—
For I must die,
There is no remedy,
For now I die."
—written by Anne Boleyn
after her death sentence

NEVER again did the King share bed and board with her. No longer was he Henry to her Anne, no longer were they man and woman together, even husband and wife, but sovereign and his consort who had failed to bear his son alive. When she saw him at all it was in the open gaze of court life. Convention still kept up its play, and when she was strong enough to sit down to dinner, the King's waiter carried to her his Majesty's customary compliment of "Much good may it do you", but never again did he come himself or send for her to share his meal with him.

She who had loved delectable dishes of linnets and rare dotterels had lost her appetite; and even when she regained her health, her spirits flagged. Jane Seymour's absence was now more telling than her presence, and Anne took no part in court life. She spent her time sitting by herself in Greenwich Palace or in the quadrangle withdrawn into her thoughts which, from the expression on her face, were grey. Sometimes she would make a conscious effort to stir herself to play with her collection of little dogs, setting them to fight each other, but these sudden spurts of activity were short-lived, and she would revert into inertness once again.

The King had paid in October last year a visit to Wolf Hall, the family home of the Seymours, before Anne had been brought to bed at the end of January and before Katherine had died. It was after that his attentions to the eldest daughter of the house had become marked. Anne knew everything there was to know about Jane Seymour, a characterless creature with nothing to know except that she was the eldest of Sir John Seymour's eight children, so fair she paled into the background, considered the soul of discretion because she, who had no opinion to give, was never heard to voice one.

As Elizabeth had her own establishment at Hatfield, Anne had not her two-year-old infant to divert her, but she never seems to have yearned for her child. The fact that she was a girl when she should have been a boy coloured any maternal feelings she might have, and the only satisfaction she derived from her daughter was the overweening one of placing her above the King's Mary. In all the well-documented accounts of Anne's last days, only once does she refer to Elizabeth and that without tenderness.

Isolated by herself in Greenwich Palace, with her servants and ladies-in-waiting about her, she was cut off from that other world where wheels were set in motion; from the murmur of voices behind closed doors where a hint became an assumption and eye held eye under lifted brow; from the shuffling between question and answer when they were sorted out, from the little silence after the peroration.

Arrogance did not make for popularity, and Anne had never been popular. Her vituperative tongue had driven her uncle, the Duke of Norfolk, from court when, nerves taut after Elizabeth's birth, she accused him of changing sides and intriguing against her. The accusation was all the more hateful to the Duke because it happened to be true. Others looked upon her as an upstart: but for her usurpation of Katherine of Aragon's place, England would be bound in a profitable alliance to the Emperor Charles instead of to an unpopular one with Francis. And her unwise tongue, the levity of her manners, her familiarity with those who had been her equals before she was queen, and the coquetry of one well armed for the parry and thrust of the duel between male and female, all added grist to her enemies' mill.

"Why are you so sad?" she demanded of Mark Smeaton one

spring day when she saw him standing at the round window of her presence chamber. He was of humble origin but so skilful a musician she had elevated him to the office of groom of the chamber.

The reason of Smeaton's loitering at the window was probably to await the opportunity to warn her of what everyone at court but she knew: that William Brereton, friend of both her and the King, had been committed to the Tower after being subjected to examination by a secret committee formed of the Queen's enemies.

Taken off his guard by her question, he replied flurriedly, "It is no matter."

Anne, provocative with boredom and under the impression his pensive demeanour indicated love for her, smartly put him in his place with the rejoinder, "You may not look to have me speak to you as if you were a nobleman, because you are an inferior person."

"No, no, madam," he replied hurriedly, "a look suffices me."

That was on Saturday. On Sunday he was removed to the Tower where he was clamped into irons because, unlike Brereton, he was not of noble birth.

Monday was the first of May, a day celebrated that spring at Greenwich with a more than usual splendid tournament. The King and Queen shared the royal balcony with his close friends. Since his accident earlier that year when his life was miraculously spared, Henry had not jousted, nor was he ever to be able to do so again although he continued to ride and hunt. A spectator now where once he had been the leading exponent, he sat watching the flower of the nobility meet each other in the lists.

Anne's brother, Viscount Rochford, hung up his shield as principal challenger. The Boleyns were a small but close-knit family; they had lost their beautiful and noble mother early, and their father married again, beneath him this time, but their stepmother was always on affectionate terms with her husband's children.

Sir Henry Norris took up the challenge by touching George Boleyn's shield. He was friend of the Queen and so favoured by the King that he was the only person Henry ever permitted to follow him into his bedchamber, and one of the three witnesses of his master's secret wedding to Anne.

The story goes that the Queen, either by accident or design—and knowing Anne it is safe to say it was not by accident—dropped her handkerchief at the feet of Norris who, as any courtier would have done, kissed it when he picked it up.

Instantly Henry rose, his face blackening, and ostentatiously left the balcony, followed by six of his closest friends. He did not speak as he left, and Anne was never to see him again. Uncertainly the joust continued, but the Queen's perturbation was obvious to all, and when shortly she retired, the sports fell apart and broke up.

Versions vary as to when and where the arrests were made but all agree it was within the next couple of days. One report says that as George Boleyn and Henry Norris were leaving the tiltyard they were charged with high treason. At the same time on the same charge Sir Francis Weston was apprehended. Handsome, wealthy and young, he had played cards and dice with Henry and Anne in the past; the King, who unlike Anne was unlucky at games of chance, often lost to him.

Henry rode back to London that day, attended only by six men. One of them was said to be his prisoner, Henry Norris, with whom he rode apart, strenuously recommending him to secure mercy by acknowledging his guilt. Norris repudiated the suggestion that there had been illicit love between him and the Queen, and stoutly maintained his and her innocence. When Westminster was reached, he was sent to the Tower where the Queen's musician, Mark Smeaton, already lay, and whose confession was said to have provided evidence for the several arrests.

In an atmosphere where the very familiar bulked portentous, Anne went through the movements she would have made had everything been normal. As she seated herself at table the following day for the midday meal of dinner, she became aware that something was missing—the King had not sent his waiter to her as always with his compliments. The alarm she felt at this omission was mirrored in the averted faces of her ladies, and she saw some of her servants were crying, tears spurting from their eyes in the manner of their kind. Anne's own foreboding increased until the very air seemed to palpitate with it.

The meal passed in unbroken silence, course following course as though nothing were amiss, beef and mutton taking the place of salad, then fowl and fish, and when they were removed, game. The banquet or dessert was reached at last, all the dishes cleared from the table with the smaller cloth which had kept the larger one clean for the feast of pastries and sweetmeats.

Before they could be served men entered the room, led by her uncle, the Duke of Norfolk. She recognized them all—Cromwell was one, who always seemed to be holding papers in both his short-fingered strong hands—members of the King's council, every one of them, when she came to think of it. As she realized that, she thought, They have come from the King to comfort me for my brother's arrest—he has sent them to reassure me. Then she caught sight of Sir William Kingston. She had seen him only yesterday— only yesterday, a lifetime had dragged itself out since she had noticed Sir William Kingston at the tournament before Henry had left in dudgeon. Everyone had been there and there had been nothing out of the ordinary in his presence yesterday. But what about today? He was not on the council. What was he doing here, entering her presence with these others; what had he come to tell her, the Lieutenant of the Tower?

In terror she rose from her stool and demanded of them all, that she might lose the individual in the crowd, "Why have you come?"

Tersely came the reply, "We have come by the King's command to conduct you to the Tower, there to abide during his Majesty's pleasure."

"If it be his Majesty's pleasure," she replied quietly, "I am ready to obey."

She was put through a gruelling examination by the council before taken to her barge as she had sat at table, without change of habit. Her paramours, her uncle told her, had confessed their guilt. Anne's reaction was instant and passionate, protesting her innocence and imploring to see the King. The contempt in the Duke's replies had the cut of taunts.

She made the same journey from Greenwich Palace that she had made before she was crowned, when she was the King's dearest wife, Queen Anne. People came to the water's edge to wonder as she passed, sitting there by her lone self with men instead of her ladies around her. *He* had been waiting for her at his royal residence then, Henry the husband who used to write her love letters signing himself her servant. What was awaiting her now?

For five centuries the Tower of London had served its kings as citadel, stronghold and castle. Impregnable, it had never been captured, its turrets set with eyes of windows so small they gave it a blind look. From its stout bastions sovereigns had left for their coronation at Westminster Abbey, worshipped in St. John's Chapel embedded in a tower strong enough to last for ever, entrusted the Crown Jewels, kept lions and leopards, and incarcerated their prisoners.

The water slapped against the stone steps as she disembarked at Traitors' Gate and the Tower clock struck five. She could go no further. Slipping to her knees, she cried, "Oh Lord! help me, as I am guiltless of that whereof I am accused." Catching sight of the Lieutenant, who, now she had reached her destination, was prominent, she asked, "Mr. Kingston, do I go into a dungeon?"

"No, madam," he replied, "to your own lodging, where you lay at your coronation."

At that she burst into a paroxysm of weeping which gave way to wild laughter. When she had quietened, she looked about her in a bemused way and said, "Wherefore am I here, Mr. Kingston?"

She asked him to move the King's Highness to allow her to have the sacrament in her closet that she might pray for mercy: what she was asking for was not to communicate, but to have the Host in her oratory for the purposes of adoration. Although described by Roman Catholics as a spleeny Lutheran, she was never Protestant, and clung to the day of her death to the usages and solace of the old religion. She only found herself in the camp of the new reforming sect because Roman Catholics rejected her as the wife of a man who had married her when his first spouse was living, and who looked upon her daughter as a bastard.

"I am the King's true wedded wife," she repeated, denying with vehemence that she had wronged him. To her inquiries about where her "sweet brother" was, the Lieutenant made evasive replies. "I hear say," she said, "that I shall be accused with three men, and I can say no more than—nay. Oh, Norris! you have accused me? You are in the Tower and you and I shall die together. And Mark, you are here too!" She told the Lieutenant that her stepmother would die for sorrow when she heard of her arrest. Her mind flew from thought to thought, never quite alighting until she demanded, "Mr. Kingston, shall I die without justice?"

"The poorest subject of the King has that," the official responded, a reply that drew from Anne a laugh bitter with incredulity.

She asked to be attended by her favourite ladies-in-waiting, but found closeted with her Mrs. Cosyns whom she had never liked and whose position now made her insolent. Worse still, Mrs. Cosyns was accompanied by one of Anne's sworn enemies, her aunt Lady Boleyn. These two women never left her, sleeping at the foot of her bed and greedily reporting statements they said the Queen had made to them in a deposition which was accepted by the council as true. According to it Anne incriminated herself to women she knew to be set over her as spies. "The King knew what he did," she said, "when he put such women about me."

A. F. Pollard, the historian, sums up the case against Anne in his masterly *Henry VIII* thus: "On the other hand, her conduct must have made the charges plausible. Even in these days, when justice to individuals was regarded as dust if weighed in the balance against the real or supposed interests of the State, it is not credible that the juries should have found her accomplices guilty, that twenty-six peers, including her uncle, should have condemned Anne herself, without some colourable justification. If the charges were merely invented to ruin the Queen, one culprit besides herself would have been enough. To assume that Henry sent four needless victims to the block is to accuse him of a lust for superfluous butchery, of which he, in his most bloodthirsty moments, was not capable."

But one culprit besides Anne would never have satisfied Henry; that would have proved nothing to the world and been an insult to him both as man and king. He had to repudiate her as wife and woman, so she could not be made wicked enough, which was why to the accusations against her with three prepossessing accomplices and one low born, incest with her brother was added for good measure. The best that can be said for Henry is he believed what he wanted to believe.

Confession of the Queen's adultery could be wrung from none of the prisoners except from the musician Mark Smeaton and that only after he had been grievously tortured and told if he signed his life would be spared, which promise was not kept. Because he was of low birth, he was hanged, not executed. By his last words at the gallows foot, "Masters, I pray you all to pray for me, for I have deserved the death," he either meant the Queen had committed adultery with him or that he was receiving his desserts for having borne false witness against his mistress. Obviously she expected him to confess her innocence at his end, for when she heard of his death she exclaimed, "Has he not, then, cleared me from the public shame he has done me? Alas, I fear his soul will suffer from his false witness he has borne." The Day of Judgement was not a metaphor in those days but a dread reality; the *e* was still in aweful and it spelt eternity.

When the knightly Norris was offered mercy as the price of confession, he replied he would rather die a thousand deaths than accuse the Queen of what he believed her to be innocent. The four men were tried by a royal commission, and no records of their trials, or of Anne's or her brother's, have been preserved. "If the crown were prosecutor and asserted it," Wolsey once remarked, "juries would be found to bring in a verdict that Abel was the murderer of Cain."

George Boleyn was tried by twenty-six peers chosen by the council from a maximum of fifty-three. He defended himself with such force and point that at first he divided his twenty-six judges. They heard his wife, Lady Rochford, witness against her husband, and listened to the evidence put forward: that one day, when making some request to his sister the Queen, he leant over her bed and kissed her. Yet these men were living in a century when it was the custom for women to hold audiences from their beds, and when kissing was so prevalent in England that foreigners said it was the same as shaking hands among other nationalities.

Kinship would not have stopped the Duke of Norfolk from condemning the niece with whom he had quarrelled; rather the reverse, to prove to the King on whose side he stood. Wherever that massive figure shifted his weight, there would be found Thomas Howard taking up his stance.

There were political as well as marital reasons for the removal of Anne. The death of Katherine dislodged an insurmountable obstacle between Henry and improved relations with Charles and his Empire. Already Cromwell had been told by the Spanish ambassador that though the world—and by the world he meant his master the Emperor—would never recognize Anne as Henry's wife, it might be ready to recognize a new wife.

In the days that followed, as she moved about the rooms she had used when life was at its fullest, Anne's mood alternated between utter despair and hopes dizzy with height. One hour, the Lieutenant noted, she was determined to die, the next the very opposite. She was anxious about her father, and forever asking for her fellow prisoners. Sometimes she could not believe the King intended to harm her. This cruel handling was done to prove her, and at that thought her spirits rose as though she was already saved. "Ballads will be made about me," she said once, adding as an afterthought, "None could do better than Wyatt." He was preserved from sharing the fate of Anne's fellow prisoners, but in a sonnet he was to write later he refers to the danger which once threatened him in the month of May. His sister Mary was Anne's favourite lady-in-waiting who was amongst those brought to the Tower to attend her but, barring Lady Boleyn and Mrs. Cosyns, none was allowed to enter her rooms except in the presence of the Lieutenant and his wife. The notes in the high-pitched score of Anne's imprisonment are flattened occasionally by the comments, bald with common sense, of Lady Kingston, who slept outside the Queen's bedroom. Once Anne predicted there would be no rain in England until she was released, which brought from the Lieutenant the rejoinder, "I pray, then, it will be shortly because of the dry weather."

He was not an unkind man and Anne could have had a harsher warder. Cromwell, the powerful Vicar-General, acted as liaison officer between the King and the Constable of the Tower, and a letter from Anne reached Henry through Cromwell for, four years later, amongst his papers was found a copy marked "To the King, from the lady in the Tower." It was written four days after her arrest, and every aimed sentence reaches its mark as unswervingly as a barbed dart:

Sir,
    Your grace's displeasure, and my imprisonment, are things so strange unto me, as what to write, or what to excuse, I am altogether ignorant. Whereas you send unto me (willing me to confess a truth, and so obtain your favour) by such an one whom you know to be mine ancient professed enemy; I no sooner received this message by him, than I rightly conceived your meaning; and if, as you say, Confessing a truth indeed may procure my safety, I shall with all willingness and duty perform your command.
    But let not your grace ever imagine that your poor wife will ever be brought to acknowledge a fault, where not so much as a thought thereof preceded. And to speak a truth, never prince had wife more loyal in all

duty, and in all true affection, than you have ever found in Anne Boleyn, with which name and place I could willingly have contented myself, if God and your grace's pleasure had been so pleased. Neither did I at any time so far forget myself in my exaltation, or received queenship, but that I always looked for such an alteration as now I find; for the ground of my preferment being on no surer foundation than your grace's fancy, the least alteration, I knew, was fit and sufficient to draw that fancy to some other subject. You have chosen me from a low estate to be your queen and companion far beyond my desert or desire. If then, you found me worthy of such honour, good your grace let not any light fancy, or bad counsel of mine enemies, withdraw your princely favour from me; neither let that stain, that unworthy stain of a disloyal heart, towards your good grace, ever cast so foul a blot on your most dutiful wife, and the infant princess, your daughter; try me, good king, but let me have a lawful trial, and let not my sworn enemies sit as my accusers and judges; yea, let me receive an open trial, for my truth shall fear no open shame; then shall you see, either mine innocency cleared, your suspicion and conscience satisfied, the ignominy and slander of the world stopped, or my guilt openly declared. So that, whatsoever God or you may determine of me, your grace may be freed from an open censure; and mine offence being so lawfully proved, your grace is at liberty, both before God and man, not only to execute worthy punishment on me as an unlawful wife, but to follow your affection already settled on that party, for whose sake I am now as I am, whose name I could some good while since have pointed unto; your grace being not ignorant of my suspicion therein.

But, if you have already determined of me, and that only my death, but an infamous slander must bring you the enjoying of your desired happiness; then I desire of God, that He will pardon your great sin therein, and like-wise mine enemies, the instruments thereof; and that He will not call you to a strict account for your unprincely and cruel usage of me, at His general judgment-seat, where both you and myself must shortly appear, and in whose judgment, I doubt not (whatsoever the world may think of me), mine innocence shall be openly known, and sufficiently cleared.

My last and only request shall be, that myself may only bear the burthen of your grace's displeasure, and that it may not touch the innocent souls of those poor gentlemen, who, as I understand, are like-wise in strait imprisonment for my sake. If ever I have found favour in your sight; if ever the name of Anne Boleyn hath been pleasing in your ears, then let me obtain this request, and I will so leave to trouble your grace any further, with mine earnest prayers to the Trinity to have

your grace in His good keeping, and to direct you in all your actions. From my doleful prison in the Tower, this sixth of May,
    Your most loyal and ever faithful wife,

                                        Anne Boleyn

There would be Seymours at court instead of Boleyns. Jane Seymour's face was expressionless as the shell of a crescent moon. Two luminaries could not share Henry's firmament; as Anne waned she would wax, reflecting the golden light of his love.

Ten days after writing her letter, Anne walked into the great hall in the Tower for her trial. An eye-witness records that she presented herself at the bar with the true dignity of a queen. There was not a trace of hysteria in her demeanour as she curtsied to her judges, looking round about them without any sign of fear. The same twenty-six men had sat in judgement on her brother earlier, but he had been removed, condemned, before she was brought in. Standing, she heard the indictment read, after which she held up her hand and stated clearly, "Not guilty", when a chair was provided for her.

She saw the narrow beardless face with its hooked nose and peaked chin of her uncle as he sat in the president's chair; the Lord High Steward of England, he would pronounce sentence. She noticed his son, her cousin, sitting under him as deputy earl marshal, giddy with youth and life and a poet's fancy, all sail had he been a ship, known as the most foolish proud boy in England. And Charles Brandon, Duke of Suffolk—she would receive no mercy from that quarter. The King's illegitimate son, the seventeen-year-old Duke of Richmond, was also one of her jury. He was married to her cousin Mary, daughter of the Duke of Norfolk: strange to think she had brought that marriage about. She had been friendly with her uncle in those days and had so arranged things that he did not need to pay a dowry for his daughter. There was an empty seat where the Earl of Northumberland had sat earlier that morning, but he had been taken ill and had to leave the court. The man who had been Henry Percy in those love-lit days when she had come from France and they had plighted their troth, did not return.

It was reported outside the court that, with her ready wit and eloquence, she, without counsel or adviser, had cleared herself with a most wise and noble speech. Bishop Godwin stated that had the peers given their verdict according to the expectation of the assembly she would have been acquitted, but through the Duke of Suffolk, "one wholly given to the King's humour", they did pronounce her guilty. The Lord Mayor said *he* could not observe anything in the proceedings against her, but they were resolved to make an occasion to get rid of her. As far as can be gathered when all records of the trial have been destroyed, she was condemned on the ground of Smeaton's confession alone, but she was not confronted with him. When she protested that one witness was not enough to convict a person of high treason she was told that in her case it was sufficient.

She heard her doom, to be burnt or beheaded at the King's pleasure, without losing colour, and when she addressed her judges, her words did not falter.

". . . I have ever been a faithful wife to the King, though I do not say I have always shown him that humility which his goodness to me and the honour to which he raised me merited. I confess I have had jealous fancies and suspicions of him, which I had not discretion or wisdom enough to conceal at all times. But God knows, and is my witness, that I never sinned against him in any other way. Think not I say this in the hope to prolong my life. God has taught me how to die, and He will strengthen my faith. . . . As for my brother, and these others who are unjustly condemned, I would willingly suffer many deaths to deliver them; but, since I see it so pleases the King, I shall willingly accompany them in death, with this assurance, that I shall lead an endless life with them in peace."

Four days lapsed between her trial and hurried execution. The day before, she took the lieutenant's wife into her presence chamber, locked the door and before six of her ladies-in-waiting told her to sit down in the chair of state. Lady Kingston demurred; it was her duty to stand, not to sit, in her presence, far less upon her, the Queen's, seat of state. But Anne insisted, telling her that title was gone. "Well," said Lady Kingston, "I have often played the fool in my youth, and, to fulfil your command, I will do it once more in my age." No sooner had she seated herself under the cloth of state than Anne fell on her knees before her, imploring her, as she would answer at the Day of Judgement, to kneel thus before her step-daughter and ask for forgiveness for the wrongs Anne had done her.

The last toll had been exacted, the ultimate clearance imposed. Yesterday she had been taken to the Archbishop of Canterbury,

Thomas Cranmer, who had crowned her, sliding down the river to Lambeth Palace in the early morning light, and in a low crypt there heard the primate of England pronounce her three-year-old marriage to the King invalid, thus bastardizing their daughter. Now there was nothing left, and tomorrow could not come swiftly enough for the relief of death.

The King had granted the less cruel death, beheadal, and an executioner was sent for from France, there being none practised enough in England. The hour was not fixed, for the authorities did not want any crowds to witness their victim making a good death, and all strangers were expelled from the Tower.

"Mr. Kingston," she said to the Lieutenant, "I hear I shall not die before noon, and I am very sorry therefor, for I thought to be dead by this time, and past my pain."

"I told her," Kingston wrote to Cromwell, "that the pain should be little, it is so subtle."

At that she put her hands round her throat and said, laughing merrily, "I have heard the executioner is very good, and I have a little neck."

"I have seen men, and women also, executed," the official wrote soberly to Cromwell, "and they have been in great sorrow, but, to my knowledge, this lady has much joy and pleasure in death."

He led her to the block that day, inside the Tower precincts, on the green before the little chapel of St. Peter-in-Chains where the garrison worshipped. She was dressed in a robe of black damask and was said never to have looked more beautiful. One of her attendants was Mary Wyatt, to whom she was seen to whisper something as she knelt. A message she sent to Henry earlier on her execution day no one dared to deliver to him. It was: "Commend me to his Majesty, and tell him he has ever been constant in his career of advancing me. From a private gentlewoman, he made me a marchioness, from a marchioness a queen. And now he has left no higher degree of honour, he gives my innocency the crown of martyrdom."

Legend says she refused to have her eyes covered and that the French executioner, unarmed by the brightness of her eyes, could not do his work with his two-handed sword until, motioning to one of his assistants to attract her attention, he took off his shoes and stole swiftly up to her on the other side.

Anne of Cleves, Henry's fourth wife

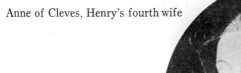

Katherine Howard, Henry's
fifth and youngest wife, said to
be the loveliest of all his brides

Katherine Parr, Henry's sixth
and last wife

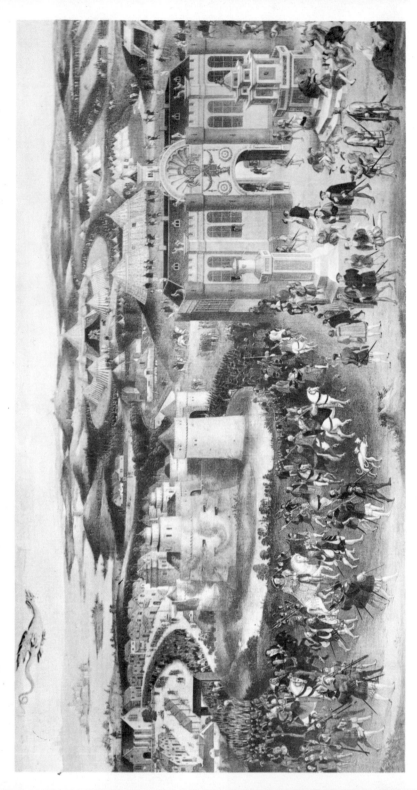

A contemporary picture of Henry VIII arriving at the Field of the Cloth of Gold

She had had to remove her coif herself because her ladies-in-waiting were too overcome to help her, but they reverently placed her body in the old elm chest waiting for it that had been used for keeping arrows, and it was hastily thrust away beside her brother in the soldiers' church.

The day before Anne Boleyn was beheaded, it was noticed at matins that the unlit tapers round Queen Katherine's sepulchre kindled with their own light and after *Deo Gratias* quenched themselves. The King, on being advised of this extraordinary occurrence, sent thirty men to witness it. Even from Katherine's tomb, he was receiving confirmation of the righteousness of his acts.

CHAPTER FIFTEEN

TRUMPETS FOR A PRINCE

"My little sweete darling, my comfort and joy,
Singe lully by, lully,
In beauty excelling the princes of Troye,
Singe lully by, lully."

As a dead moth disintegrates at a touch, like the garment it has eaten, so Henry's memory of Anne Boleyn and all she had once meant to him was effaced. He wore white on the day she was beheaded and, when the gun which was to give the signal she was dead sounded, rode at once to Wolf Hall. These two facts gave rise to the persistent legend that he married his third wife either on the day of his second one's death or the day after. In reality the wedding took place privately ten days later in London, and was solemnized by the Archbishop of Canterbury, the pliant Thomas Cranmer, in the Queen's closet at York Place.

A discerning nobleman noted that the richer Queen Jane was apparelled the fairer she appeared, whereas the better Anne Boleyn was dressed the worse she appeared; in short, Anne's looks did not depend on what she wore and Jane's did. Jane reaches us in her portraits with the impersonality of a queen on a playing card, for it is the beauty of the clothes she wears that makes the picture, not the wearer.

Anne had chosen as her motto "Me and Mine", Jane's was "Bound to Obey and Serve". It was her passivity and submissiveness that contented Henry after the demanding Anne and lofty-minded Katherine. He was beginning to tire now, and confided to Chapuys that he was growing old, the first time he had made such an admission.

Her docility made her the happiest of his six wives, and would have ensured her remaining so had fate decreed to extend her brief marriage. No party fermented round her in which she was active as yeast, like Anne; neither did her circumstances or personality ever warrant the devoted partisanship that Katherine could claim; but tall handsome brothers received important posts and while she was Queen it was very advantageous to bear the name of Seymour.

She had shown kindness to Henry's daughter Mary before her marriage, and after it did everything she could to reconcile father with daughter. Even taking into consideration that Jane would naturally prefer Katherine's offspring to Anne's, she was drawn to Mary and had understanding how she felt about religion. Henry's wives alternated between following the traditional faith and the new: Katherine had been an unwavering Roman Catholic, Anne favoured the Reformers. Now it was the turn of his third wife to be true to the established. Also, the treatment the girl had received from Jane's predecessor automatically justified the King's marriage with Anne's successor. Jane would have no difficulty in believing the charges brought against her former mistress; she had lived at court until after the Queen's miscarriage, which meant she knew all the scandal, intrigue and titillating gossip of that enclosed inbred world, which would serve to fill in, confirm and heighten the King's picture of his second wife.

The obstacle preventing Henry ever receiving his elder daughter into his presence was the Oath of Supremacy which she steadfastly refused to take. Mary's conscience was very much her own, high principled like her mother's and infallible like her father's. But at the same time as Jane was doing everything in her power to have Mary reinstated at court, pressures were being brought to bear on the girl herself to induce her to conform.

Chapuys visited her some five months after her mother's death in the month of June at the household she shared with her half-sister Elizabeth. The Spaniard believed if anything happened to the King, England would accept Mary as Queen, but if she continued in her obstinacy what had happened to Anne might well happen to her. After all, her lack of submission was dangerous to her father, for she could well supply even inadvertently a rallying point for his potential enemies. So the statesman advised her to obey the King unconditionally; some believe that, present when her mother was dying, he may even have carried a message from Queen Katherine telling her to submit. Advice from such a quarter as the Spanish

ambassador, her mother's countryman and confidant, could not fail
to carry weight: Mary thanked him for his good counsel and told
him she had already written to her father.

Chapuys was Mary's good friend at court. When he returned to
London he conveyed to the powers that be his surprise at the heavi-
ness of the Lary Mary's mourning. Hard on his visit came one from
the brother of the new Queen, bringing Mary the welcome present
of a riding-horse and telling her to send in a list of the clothing she
required to the King.

But still no attention was paid to the letters she was sending to
her father in the humblest fashion possible, venturing to congratulate him on the comfortable news of his marriage and telling him she
prayed God daily to send him a prince, signing herself Your Majesty's
most humble and obedient servant, daughter and handmaid.

Cromwell, who had obtained leave for her to write to her father
in the first place, sternly exhorted her to do better in her next by
telling her the kind of letter she should write.

Poor Mary could not think how to make herself more abject than
she had. She suffered all her life from headaches and indigestion,
caused by strain acting on a delicate constitution and highly strung,
reserved temperament. Now when she forced herself to do what
went against the grain, she was nagged with toothache, had a head-
ache that would not lift, and could not sleep. But she wrote out
Cromwell's pattern letter word for word—she could not endure
to make a copy—and sent it to the Vicar-General to convey to
the King.

A deputation from the privy council waited upon her to hear her
take the Oath, when Mary promised unconditional submission to
all the King required consistent with what she considered the laws
of God. But that was not the Oath at all: the Oath was the acknow-
ledgement that her mother's marriage was incestuous and illegal,
her own birth illegitimate and the King's supremacy over the
Church absolute. The deputation retired circumvented.

Mary received a stinging letter from Cromwell, telling her that
her folly would undo her and all who had wished her good. He took
God as his witness that she was the most obstinate and obdurate
woman that ever was. Unless she signed a book of articles he was
enclosing and wrote a letter declaring that she thought in her heart
what she signed with her hand, he would make no more effort with

the King to effect reconciliation. "If you will not with speed leave off all your sinister counsels, which have brought you to the point of utter undoing without remedy, I take my leave of you for ever . . . for I shall never think otherwise of you than as the most ungrateful person to your dear and benign father."

Mary signed, but that was not enough for Henry. He was taking no chances. She had to repeat her submission in the presence of his council. The only article that was excepted was that which stigmatized her own birth as incestuous.

Her household was re-established, every consideration given to her comfort and she was told she need no longer call Elizabeth princess but sister. As Parliament had made Elizabeth a bastard without declaring Mary legitimate this was not so generous as it sounded, but Mary showed becoming gratitude for permission to address her sister as she had done all along.

That she bore no grudge against the three-year-old Elizabeth is clear in her first letter to her father after her submission. Following its prefatory grovelling paragraph in which she describes herself as his bounden slave, Mary breaks free from Cromwell's tutorage to put in a good word for her demeaned half-sister: "My sister Elizabeth is in good health (thanks to our Lord), and such a child toward, as I doubt not but your Highness shall have cause to rejoice in time coming (as knoweth Almighty God)." And always when the child's name appears in Mary's accounts which she kept herself she is written in as "my Lady Elizabeth's grace".

So Mary's star rose in the ascendant until, through the good offices of Queen Jane, she found herself at court joining in the Christmas festivities at Greenwich Palace. It was nearly seven years since she had lived in the same household with her father but he had always been fond of her, although the impression is received that his pride in his child prodigy was slightly nonplussed when she as a mature woman joined his close circle. In the gay whirl of court life, one quality her contemporaries all ascribe to her and that was virtue.

She was twenty years old now, not unpleasing in appearance, with her father's penetrating small eyes, but tiny and without the attraction that so many small women do possess to captivate and charm. She was an accomplished musician with a swift deft touch and a fine singer, but her speaking voice was discordant and surprisingly strong coming from so little a person. A negotiable asset to her father, she must have been the most betrothed princess in history, but even if she had married, the seal of the spinster was already upon her. It was as an aunt rather than a mother she took charge of her sister Elizabeth at ceremonies, and visited the little brother she was so shortly to have, watching over him with care.

Life was pleasant for Henry in these summer months, showing off his new Queen to the Londoners, gliding down the river with her or joining in the prolonged and elaborate festivities of court life. He was being wooed by both Spain and France who were again at each other's throats. Even the Pope was making friendly advances to facilitate his return to the fold of the Roman Catholic Church, now Anne Boleyn, the bone of contention, was as dead as her predecessor Katherine. But the English King was not thinking of changing his religious policy. He talked with pride of "our Church of England"; the Roman had gone for good.

Monasteries were naturally the most influential centres of papacy in the country, and the lesser religious houses throughout the land were being systematically suppressed and their lands confiscated because of the corruption, slackness and manifest sin Cromwell was claiming to have uncovered in them. The Act was drawn up before his commissioners, called Visitors, returned from their investigations. Cromwell's boast that he would make his sovereign the richest king in Christendom was beginning to come true, for the wealth from the suppressed monasteries found its way by natural course into the coffers of the Supreme Head of the Church of England. Not that these lesser houses were particularly rich; it was the great cathedrals, abbeys and churches that had the wealth—Canterbury for instance with its jewelled shrine of St. Thomas à Becket. But it was comforting to know that the treasury, empty for so long, was beginning to fill.

Superstition too was to be plucked out of the land by its roots and of course everyone knew religious houses were the strongholds of superstition. Pilgrimages were to be suppressed, relics destroyed, saints' days celebrated as holidays abolished (holiday sprang from holy day), and wonder-working images pulled down. In the market-place at Maidstone it was exhibited to the people how the famous Rood of Boxley opened and shut its mouth by an ingenious mechanism and not through a miracle as they had always thought.

How these monks had imposed on their fathers who knew no better. . . .

Parliament had brought in these measures, summoned to repeal the Act which vested the succession to the crown on the King's offspring by Anne Boleyn. Members compared their sovereign to Samson for strength and fortitude, Solomon for justice and prudence, and to Absalom for beauty and comeliness. The House was asked to remember the perils and dangers he had suffered and sustained when he contracted his second marriage, and that the Lady Anne and her accomplices had met their due reward. What man of middle life, they were asked, would not after this be deterred from marrying a third time? Yet their most excellent Prince had condescended to contract matrimony again and had, on the humble petition of the nobility, taken to himself a wife whose age and fine form gave promise of issue. Parliament, like God and Henry, thought the same.

The new Act entailed the crown on any sons Henry and Jane might have, on any sons Henry might have by a future wife, and on Jane's daughters or any other legitimate daughters Henry might have. The Lords and Commons heartily desired their King's reign to last for ever, but they had to make suitable provision if, when their sovereign went the way of all flesh, he died without heirs. Henry saw to it there was to be no ruinous scramble for his crown after his death. Parliament gave him full authority to give, dispose, appoint, assign, declare and limit the imperial Crown of the realm "to such person or persons as shall please your Highness". It was a unique Act granting unique powers to a unique king. Even from the dead he would pronounce what was to be done by his servant Parliament.

If he had no heir—even his illegitimate son was not spared to him. The boy died of consumption, that scourge that stalked the Tudor race but which by the grace of God had never trailed him, England's sovereign Lord and King. In the meridian of summer at the age of seventeen, Henry Fitzroy, Duke of Richmond, died, whose charm and grace and love of letters reminded everyone of his father. The comely shoot of such a parent tree had been under sentence of death from his physicians for a year. To think that Norfolk's boy, Henry Howard, Earl of Surrey, whom Henry had allowed to be brought up with him, was still alive while he. . . .

Only a month or two ago, he had been the first because he was the youngest to pluck his hand from his sleeve and say "Guilty" at Anne Boleyn's trial. A few days later he had watched a queen die on the church green, and shortly before his death had appeared disguised as a Turk at a gay court revel.

Perhaps God never meant to grant Henry a son, but he must not countenance such a thought, only be prepared in case that should happen. He was forty-five, in his middle years but stronger, more active, resolute with health, than a man half his age, than his own son in the flower of his youth. And his third marriage was uncomplicated by these barriers to which God had taken such strong exception in the past.

It came from the north, the rattle of revolt, in autumn, an inconvenient season for warfare. That was where it would come if it came from anywhere. Populous London where he was known was the centre of his popularity; the further he travelled from his capital the less familiar he was to his thinning subjects, and he had never made progress far north. It was unenlightened, clinging to the old faith and a left-off way of living; it had not marched with the times like the south, in step with Henry. He considered his northern subjects rude and ignorant, the most "brute and beastly" of his whole realm.

Not that this rising was against him but against the low-born men in high offices: shear-man Cromwell and tavern-keeper Cranmer, for two. The northerners were demanding their dismissal, the burning of heretical bishops who favoured the Reformation, reconciliation with the Pope, the restoration of the monasteries and the remission of land taxes. It was known as the Pilgrimage of Grace. Thirty thousand men gathered as the army of the Church under a banner displaying the five wounds of Christ. They did not call themselves rebels but pilgrims, and asked to meet their sovereign lord that they could submit their grievances to him personally.

Henry had never heard anything like their presumption, taking upon themselves to amend his laws, as if, after being their king for twenty-eight years, he did not know how to govern his own realm. To pardon or parley with rebels he considered would disdain his honour, but he had no standing army and to treaty was necessary while one was mustered. So Norfolk was dispatched to play for time.

Norfolk was an astute choice. The most unpopular and difficult undertakings usually fell to him to atone for forebears who had fought on the Yorkist side and prove by success his allegiance to the Tudor line. But this commission had a kind of rough justice about it, for Norfolk was of exactly the same opinion as the rebels about the mean men who were his fellow councillors. Henry himself had heard him mutter against the thieves and murderers in high positions. He had snapped back if anyone would not serve as readily under the humblest person he had put in authority as under the greatest duke in the realm; his king would neither consider him a good subject nor allow him to go unpunished. As Norfolk was one of the two dukes in the King's realm, he was suitably crushed into silence.

With skill and vague promises he managed to soothe the leaders, dealing chiefly with one Robert Aske, a lawyer. Their king was a benignant prince and would grant a free pardon to all who had taken up arms if they would disperse. Their demands would be conveyed to and considered by the King himself. Aske must prepare a full statement of them. The King would visit the northern counties, and Parliament would be asked to reconsider the liberties of the Church. On such assurances Aske dispersed his well-disciplined troops while Norfolk in York gathered an army round him.

The lawyer was summoned to London in December to place before the sovereign his statement of the northerners' grievances. Henry, affable with good will, lent him the favour of his ear. Their complaints about the Faith were so general they were hard to be answered; the King intended always to live and die in the Faith of Christ. When the Queen was crowned, Henry would like nothing better than for her coronation to take place in York—in spring or summer next year when the roads were passable. Aske returned to Yorkshire secure with promises. All would be well, he told his fellow leaders, if only their monarch's just conditions were obeyed.

But all those who bore the Badge of the Five Wounds were not single-minded pilgrims; many were men with political and economic scores to settle. When these extremists saw no signs of the government fulfilling their promises, they broke the truce. This was the chance and now was the hour to recall the free pardon.

Henry examined the evidence sent to him against the plotters like a "detective policeman". Norfolk was instructed to cause dreadful execution upon every town, village and hamlet that had offended in this rebellion; all the leaders, including the innocent Aske, were executed. Instead of a Queen's coronation in the white city of York, courts were set up that spring and summer throughout the northern counties. Even those who had laid down their arms and fulfilled the royal obligations were not spared, and Norfolk was told to show no pity to abbots and monks who had joined in the Pilgrimage. Once and for all Henry would stamp out revolt in his realm and make rebels a terrible example to the rest of his subjects.

That January was so severe the Thames froze. It was remembered because the King and Queen, attended by their entire court, crossed it on horseback to Greenwich Palace. London learnt the Queen was with child when a service of thanksgiving was held.

Henry did not move about much that spring because his leg was troubling him again. This was a varicose ulcer in his thigh, called in contemporary accounts "the King's sore leg". It was described that year as somewhat sore, which was an understatement for the condition was now chronic, the patient never giving it a chance to heal, and this spring both legs were affected.

No longer did he hunt as in the old days, pursuing the chase with his hounds, but shot from a stand or butt. Riding must have been acutely painful because of his leg, but his subjects were unaware of that as they watched him pass on long progresses, visiting his ports and harbours, inspecting defences—more peremptory in his look perhaps but still benignant towards them, a little bigger each time he passed their way. For he was fast putting on weight. Unable to take the excessive exercise of earlier years, to join in the athletic pursuits in which he had no rival, he continued to eat enormously.

He remained near his consort while she was carrying his child, lest she should hear any sudden or unpleasant rumours blown about if he were absent from her. After all she was but a woman, and women were prone to idle fancies. He was remembering Anne's miscarriage which some believed was caused by the shock she sustained being told of his accident when he was thought to be dead, but which Anne herself attributed to her distress over his penchant for Jane Seymour.

His additions to Wolsey's rose-red Hampton Court were finished now, the splendid banqueting hall completed, a tiltyard added, butts for archery, bowling alleys and, for his favourite game, a tennis court—a prince of the Church's palace made into a country residence for an athletic king. The Queen's lodgings begun for Anne, whom he had brought here after her coronation at Westminster Abbey, were completed and, because London was sick with a visitation of the plague, were used for Jane's lying in. Her initials took the place of Anne's twined with his; in some of the true lovers' knots the J for Jane does not quite cover the superseded A. Henry's arms on the right of the chapel entrance faced Jane's on the left: the unicorn, with a collar of roses round its neck, was adopted for her as the emblem of chastity.

Her labour was a martyrdom of suffering; she endured thirty hours of travail. The story of the King's reply, "The child by all means, for other wives can easily be found," when asked whether his wife or child was to be spared can be discounted. No medical man or attendant would have dreamed of putting such a question; it went without saying that the child at all costs must be saved, to which the mother would have been the first to accede.

Jane gave to her husband the crown of his life, a son and heir. There were no doubts about whether he should be called Henry or Edward: arriving on the vigil of St. Edward, 12th October, 1537, the child decided for himself it was to be Edward.

The noise of that age was deafening and it was like an accompaniment to the King himself. Even when he went to a masque he was attended by sixteen torchbearers and the rat-tat of drums, and guns shot off at his landing for an evening's entertainment would rumble in the air like thunder.

Exaltation at the Prince's birth exploded into bell-ringing, gun-firing, singing, cheering, feasting, and music noisy with triumph and joy. Hampton Court rang, and the goodly sound of the trumpets at his christening was remarked upon for its loudness.

It took place three days after his birth and at night. The mother, wrapped in crimson velvet furred with ermine, was moved for the occasion from her bed to a pallet sewn in gold thread with the crown and arms of England. From this she handed her baby over to be baptized. At her side sat the King, and he remained there throughout the hours-long christening, and was not present as custom guided at the ceremony itself in the chapel.

It was midnight when they heard the trumpet flourishes at the entrance of the silver-stick gallery announcing the return of the procession. The Prince had been baptized by the Archbishop of Canterbury and proclaimed by Garter King-of-Arms: "God in His Almighty and Infinite Grace, grant good life and long to the most high, right excellent, and noble Prince Edward, Duke of Cornwall and Earl of Chester, most dear and entirely beloved son of our most dread and gracious lord Henry VIII."

They brought him in, their christened son, with trumpet notes, under a canopy of state, to hand him to his mother that she might be the first to call him by his Christian name. Nothing could ever take that moment from Jane Seymour. For all time she was rooted in the family tree of England's history.

Nothing would ever take that moment from Henry as he saw his own likeness in the face of his son, bone of his bone, flesh of his flesh, lying big-browed amongst the cushions with his little starfish hands.

CHAPTER SIXTEEN

ROSE WITHOUT A THORN

" 'Ten thousand times I'll kiss your face,
And sport, and make you merry.' "

THE Queen took so ill the day after the christening that all the rites
of the Roman Catholic Church were administered to her, but rallied
sufficiently to raise hopes of her recovery. The betterment, however,
proved to be the delusive pause that so often precedes death and she
died between sunset and sunrise twelve days after the birth of her
child.

Henry sent an exulting letter to Francis on the birth of his son:
now his rival had no advantage over him. Even the death of the
mother could not diminish the exaltation for a prince of the Tudor
line, although he felt the loss of his wife keenly. "Divine Providence," he wrote to Francis, "has mingled my joy with the bitter-
ness of the death of her who brought me this happiness."

He took his bereavement heavily. He did not want to be spoken
to and left Hampton Court as soon as he could, withdrawing into
himself. His council saw to the funeral arrangements, and his
daughter Mary as chief mourner kept nightly watch with the dead
Queen's ladies around the embalmed body. The obsequies lasted
for three weeks on the orders of the King: daily services, nightly
vigils, tapers burning on the altar night and day; the chapel close
round the treasure of its dead, the air heavy with incense; the
stumble of the unuttered prayers of the mourners, over-hung with
a suspension that grew unbearable until some movement, such as
the black-robed figures replaced by others, shifted the momentum
which began to mount imperceptibly again.

Jane was Henry's only wife for whom he wore mourning. He
hated black or anything that reminded him of death, and there was
a scene should someone inadvertently come into his presence in the

sable clothes that betokened loss. But for Jane his wife, the mother of his son, he wore mourning throughout Christmastide like his court, and did not change till Candlemas.

His genuine sorrow for his wife's death did not stop him taking preliminary political steps for providing himself with a new queen. He could make a French alliance which would annoy Charles and strengthen his friendship with Francis, or he could choose an Empire bride which would annoy Francis and strengthen his friendship with Charles. The surprising thing was neither Charles nor Francis appeared to set much store on gaining England's king as a marriage asset. Indeed the two rival kings were showing regrettable but unmistakable signs of wishing to terminate their mutual warfare which was draining their resources and benefiting only England. For, locked in hostilities with each other, neither could take advantage of Henry's vulnerability when his northern subjects rose in revolt.

Henry began hopefully enough by suggesting to Francis's ambassador that Frenchwomen suitable by birth and their good looks for his bride should be sent to Calais where he could inspect them in person, and get to know them some time before deciding. "I trust no one but myself," he told Marillac; "the thing touches me too near." The sardonic Marillac's reply in his native tongue about testing the ladies' charms sent the Englishman's colour flaming to his face.

He asked for the hand of the very tall young widow who had been born Marie of Guise, although she was already engaged to his nephew, the young King of Scots. But Henry had not the slightest doubt that when he appeared on the scene the promise to James would be broken and at the same time the traditional "auld alliance" between Scotland and France. Jovially he said he was big and needed a big wife. James, however, sitting so conveniently on his uncle's doorstep, was far too important an ally for Francis to offend. Henry was offered instead the plain, sickly princess his nephew had already rejected, which he could not be expected to take in good part.

The well-known story of the royal duchess who said that if she had two heads, one of them would be at King Henry's disposal, has been attributed to both Marie of Guise and Christina of Denmark. Christina came under her uncle, the Emperor's sphere of influence; she also was very tall and a widow although only sixteen. The

English King commissioned his court artist to paint the portraits of potential brides and Holbein executed Christina's in a three hours' sitting at Brussels. Henry's courtship of her went on for the best part of two years, blowing hot and cold as the political scene dictated, although he accused Charles of "knitting one delay to the tail of another", and instructed his envoys to assure Christina how earnestly "we have been minded to honour her with our marriage".

Cromwell was now ready to bring the greater monasteries into line with the lesser by suppressing them. They had escaped earlier because although his Visitors had revealed the smaller ones as dens of iniquity it was considered religion in the large solemn ones was right well kept and observed—for the time being. The hour was now ripe for them to receive visitation.

That there was slackness in religious houses is undeniable, and grave abuses in many. An Order does tend to grow laxer, never stricter, as time intervenes between it and its founder's pristine simple Rule. Throughout Henry's reign isolated bishops drew attention to monastic reclaim; they had discovered disorder in one, enormities in another. It was Wolsey's glorious opportunity to effect reformation but his hands were too occupied with statecraft, his eye too trained on the papal throne and its next occupant, to do more than write out detailed instructions for the improvement of monastic devotions.

Indeed he had been the first to suppress some twenty-three monasteries and three nunneries, putting the proceeds towards educational endowments dear to his heart, and many considered his fall was God's punishment for such robbery. True, each community he suppressed had dwindled to fewer than twelve surviving inmates but they had grown into their neighbourhood and their ejection was fiercely resented. The citizens were not appeased when told it was better to have forty of their children educated and afterwards sent to Oxford than to have six or seven canons living amongst them. Indeed at one place they turned out the agents Wolsey employed to enforce his instructions, reinstated the canons and told them if they were again molested, to ring their big bell, when they would have immediate assistance.

The Cardinal's two agents had been hated as they rode about the countryside from one religious house to another carrying out their master's orders and accepting large bribes to exempt certain communities. One rode accompanied by a train of hangers-on, as though he were making a royal progress. The other was Thomas Cromwell.

His programme for the dissolution of the large monasteries worked out ahead of schedule. The measures against these religious houses that had joined in the Pilgrimage of Grace had taken all the heart out of brother- and sisterhoods throughout the country; only a dozen out of hundreds had to be threatened into submission. Better to accept the pensions they were offered than lose them in an unavailing fight. The world had turned upside down, and there was no place in it for them now the splendour, wealth, authority and power of the old faith was being gripped by the crown. The ecclesiastical splendour, authority and power had themselves superseded the ancient Rule of poverty, chastity, obedience, which gave the founders that grandeur of the spirit that asked only for the essentials.

But it was not only nuns, monks and friars who were turned out of nunnery, convent and monastery. Every foundation had its own household, a community in itself, its servants and tradesmen not in holy orders, who found themselves without livelihood and home when the parent house was destroyed. And there were the skilled craftsmen, the makers of vestments, robes and copes, of altar cloths and wax tapers, crosses and crucifixes, beads, reliquaries and images, whose markets disappeared when shrines were rifled and altars plundered.

It took twenty carts to carry away the treasure of St. Thomas's shrine in Canterbury, England's mother church. The finest jewel in Europe, a French King's offering to St. Thomas four centuries ago, was made into a ring for Henry's big thumb. "A cloister without books," wrote St. Benedict, "is a fort without an armoury." Centuries of library-arsenals were destroyed at the dissolution of the monasteries, priceless illuminated manuscripts thrown out as though they were rubbish after being torn from their jewelled covers. And no one cared, not Henry, the patron of the arts, the enlightened lover of learning, in their greedy haste to get their hands on the Church's buildings, lands, wealth and possessions.

It was the monasteries who provided hospitals for the sick poor. London was full of them: St. Bartholomew's, St. Thomas's, St. Mary Spital, Elsing Spital for the blind, St. Mary of Bethlehem (Bethlem, Bedlam) for the insane, the House of St. Augustine Papey

Henry with his three children, Edward, Mary and Elizabeth, all of whom reigned

Edward, Henry's beloved son, known as England's Treasure

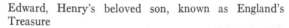

Charles Brandon, Henry's closest lifelong friend, who married Princess Mary

Thomas Wolsey, Cardinal of York, with the college he founded at Oxford in the background

for old priests. All disappeared. The city authorities wrote to the King about the great infection and other inconveniences this had caused, but Henry paid no notice until he needed money and credit from the city. Then he refounded St. Bartholomew's, only to take it back when he received what he wanted. His physicians, a band of wise and upright men, said the only way of getting the King to listen to reason was to have him fall ill.

The citizens of London went about their business as though unaware that no longer cowled monks in black, white or brown habits with rope girdles were to be seen. Only their own numbers were swollen disproportionately with an influx of vagabonds, rascals, masterless men and the wretched poor who were always with them, while their city fell suddenly and strangely silent without the chiming, ringing and pealing of cascades of bells.

No more processions to watch as abbot or friar went by in a forest of crosses and sconces and standards, or pause as the relics of the saint were borne past. There were no relics now: the Blood had been found not to be blood at all; the splinters of wood not from the Cross; the saint's shoe replaced when it wore out. It was still the people's duty to go to church on Sunday morning, to attend the services at Easter, Christmas, Trinity and Whit. Holidays might be abolished, but not fast days.

The King had commanded out of the goodness of his heart that a copy of the Bible should be placed in every church and that the priest should read from it to the people in their own tongue, that they might learn the Word of God. He was to recite the Lord's Prayer, the Creed and the Ten Commandments in English that his flock could learn them by degrees, and before anyone could receive the sacrament at the altar he must satisfy his shepherd he knew the rudiments of the faith.

The Lutherans saw in the dissolution of the monasteries the dawn of the Reformation breaking over England, but Henry's principal Protestant leaning was that towards the Bible which was to him "that most precious jewel, the Word of God". He hated Lutheranism, and upheld the doctrine of transubstantiation, celibacy of the clergy and the traditional liturgy of the Church.

The Reformers did not think of their, the Protestant, faith as new. It was called thus only to distinguish it from that of the Roman Catholic, for they did not abolish an old church to establish a new one in its stead. To them reform meant re-form, to make better by removing, or become better by abandoning, imperfections, innovations and faults. They claimed to re-form the Church of Christ in terms of the age of His first apostles. Gospel truth led them not to Rome but to where One sat with His disciples in a bare upper room. They replaced the infallibility of a Church with the infallibility of the Bible, and they freed the Lord's Supper from the elaboration, symbolism and ritual of the Mass.

Like most of his subjects Henry was orthodox to the core, and why he carried them with him in what he chose to do was because of this identification between them. He had that inestimable gift as a leader: he knew when to stop. Not only the Pilgrimage of Grace warned him not to go too far or he would alienate his subjects but his inclination.

Their giant of a King hung with jewels, in his ruby collar and his coat of cloth of gold buttoned with diamonds and rubies and sapphires, this great father figure more than life size like the embodiment of England, a transcendent prototype of the common man, personified both the best and the worst of his people.

If Henry's actions against the old faith heartened the Reformers, they shocked and horrified Rome, and dismayed his one-time allies Charles and Francis. Pope, King and Emperor all met at Nice where Paul negotiated a ten years' truce between the two rulers. In this atmosphere of fervent friendship, the long-cherished project of a joint attack on the outsider England was considered. The Pope as his contribution took upon himself to encourage Scotland to invade her neighbour at the appropriate time. Henry was isolated, without an ally.

Cromwell was more apprehensive of the situation than his sovereign. Henry at once set about seeing that the defences along the coasts and on the Scottish border were repaired and strengthened. The ulcer on his leg suddenly clogged that spring so that for ten to twelve days he was dangerously ill, black in the face, unable to speak, his breath stifled. But that did not deter him travelling a month or two later to inspect in person the fortifications he for years had been erecting at Dover at great cost. Everywhere his subjects surged forward to help, lining their shores with palisades, repairing beacons, digging dykes and throwing up ramparts. Even women and children worked with shovels at trenches and bulwarks. Let them come, Scot, Spaniard, Frenchie—England was ready for them, England and her King, her King who was England.

Cromwell was not a religious man but his politics inclined him towards the radical Reformers and away from the reactionary old faith. For some time he had advocated an alliance between England and the strong Protestant princes in Germany who were as much a thorn in Charles's side as his neighbour Scots were to Henry. Such a bloc of united interests would seriously threaten the Emperor's hold on his Dutch dominions, so vital to English trade. But Henry had been lukewarm because of his distaste for the uncompromising Lutheranism of his proposed allies. Only when Charles began to accumulate guns and ammunition in the Antwerp area, preparatory to invasion of England, was he prevailed upon to form a precautionary alliance with them and Denmark.

To make his plan doubly secure Cromwell was pushing for all he was worth the marriage nostrum which, despite the lessons of the past, was still believed to act as cement binding nation to nation in indissoluble union. Who more suitable for a bride for the King of England than a member of the House of Cleves? With his family claims to the Duchy of Guelders, the Duke of Cleves was the very barb of the thorn in Charles's side, his lands most favourably placed for invasion of Charles's dominions should the need arise. And he had sisters for the picking.

Holbein was dispatched to paint the portraits of the two sisters Anne and Amelie; Anne was chosen. Henry, and posterity, considered his court artist excellent at making likenesses but he has been accused on this occasion of flattering his subject. So delectable did he portray her that the legend arose he fell in love with his sitter, a fellow German, as he was painting her. Even a plain woman has her moments, and Anne's moment may well have chimed with Holbein's hour.

Her very age might have given Henry's advisers pause: she was thirty-four, old in those days for a woman. And the pen of Henry's ambassador did not run away with him, whatever happened to Holbein's brush. His description is a decided monotint. "The said lady" occupied her time with her needle; her virtues of gentleness, sobriety and gravity which he mentions are all estimable but unsprightly. She could read and write her own language. There her attainments began and ended for she knew no other, nor could she sing or play any instrument. The ambassador took some pains to point out the Germans considered it unseemly for their great ladies to be learned, and music a frivolous pastime. He was of the opinion she would soon learn English once she put her mind to it, but he obviously could not picture the said lady disporting herself at Henry's sophisticated court. He inferred her brother, the Duke of Cleves, was serious enough but lively compared to his sister Anne.

It was Cromwell who assured his King that everyone praised the beauty of Anne of Cleves, both of face and body, and that she excelled the lovely Christina as the golden sun did the silver moon.

The marriage treaty was concluded and Henry had the satisfaction of the man who discovers on doing his duty he is pleasing no one so much as himself. He agreed to forego a dowry since his brother-in-law was in financial straits. For two years he had been wifeless and was agog to meet his bride.

She travelled towards the end of the year and was stormbound at Calais for well over a fortnight, which meant she had to spend Christmas on her journey instead of with her bridegroom. But she was received with all pomp in the port town, and admired the King's ships *Lyon* and *Sweepstakes* until they let off a hundred and fifty rounds in her honour which caused so much smoke none of her lengthy train could see any of the others. The time waiting for a prosperous wind was spent pleasantly enough with the English lord admiral trying to teach her cards, a very necessary accomplishment for the bride of the gamester King of England.

Henry, on the other side of the Channel, could hardly restrain his impatience. When he heard she had disembarked at Deal, he determined he had waited long enough. It would be days before her train reached London on winter roads for her state entry. He told Cromwell that he sore desired to see her grace and intended to visit her secretly next day, "to nourish love".

Accompanied by eight lords-in-waiting, all dressed the same as he was, travelling incognito, he posted to Rochester where his bride-to-be was resting to present her with his New Year's gifts in person. Boyish with eagerness, he entered her presence.

The interview is said to have lasted only a few minutes, and scarcely twenty words were exchanged. Anne's German was guttural high Dutch, and German was not one of Henry's five languages. Henry withdrew almost at once. An eye-witness testified that he had never seen his Highness so marvellously astonished and abashed. It is the one occasion on record that Henry was at a loss for words.

He found his voice when he sent for his lord admiral and demanded, "How like you this woman? Do you think her so personable, fair and beautiful as she has been reported to me?" Cleverly the sailor evaded a direct reply by remarking he would call her complexion brown, not fair; and he would have none of it when Cromwell tried to shift the responsibility on to his shoulders. So he should have detained her at Calais, should he, and told his sovereign she was not as handsome as she had been reported? But he had been invested with no such authority; his commission was to bring her to England, which he had done.

"If it were not that she is come so far into my realm," Henry declared, "and the great preparations that my states and people have made for her, and for fear of making a ruffle in the world, and of driving her brother into the hands of the Emperor and the French King, I would not now marry her."

There was no remedy. He had to put his neck into the yoke and wed what he called a Flanders mare.

Someone would have to pay for this. His head was not too much to ask for placing his sovereign before the whole world in so humiliating a position, making him a laughing-stock. Cromwell had no friends: he was too successful, too rich, too ruthless to have accumulated goodwill as he battled to power. Now his enemies gathered round the cockpit to glory in watching the conqueror, all spurs and crop, conquered at last.

They had to wait a month or two. When it was rumoured abroad he was tottering, Henry raised him to Earl of Essex. The King's small mouth pinched itself even smaller as his face stoutened round it, his watchful small eyes withdrew even further, like a mole's that are buried in its fur to protect it from the dust and grit it throws up.

The wedding took place almost at once. Both the French and Empire ambassadors had been invited to witness a ceremony that was to have been a diplomatic and personal spectacle of triumph. No expense had been spared, with the coffers bursting with monastery gold. Marillac noted that five thousand horsemen rode in the procession.

Henry put on as gallant a face as he could, lovingly embracing and kissing his bride in public. He was dressed magnificently in a crimson satin coat slashed and embroidered, his cloth of gold doublet raised with large silver flowers and richly furred. His Queen's costume was every bit as costly, thickly embroidered with pearls, but it was made in the unbecoming Dutch fashion without a train. Her jewelled crown sat on a wig of long luxuriant yellow hair. Marillac described her as "tall of stature, pitted with the smallpox, and has little beauty. Her countenance is firm and determined."

Henry had the endearing habit of calling all his wives Sweetheart, and he addressed Anne thus when they were together. In public he treated her with the courtesy due to his Queen. But he averred from the first he would never have a child by her, and his distaste of the whole situation grew more and more pronounced until he had not the palate to continue it. He was accustomed to the society of cultured women: Katherine had been his intellectual equal, Mary and Anne Boleyn had both been educated in France, and Anne's vitality made her like an arrow that was always travelling. This woman's phlegm was not Jane's docility: she was not submissive, she was stubborn, and the clatter of her ugly tongue was an affliction to his musical ears. They had no common ground on which to meet.

That she found sharing the King of England's bed as unpleasant an experience as he found it with her can be judged from her reply when some English court ladies tried to inveigle her into saying that the King had neglected her. She denied he had done any such thing, affirming she had received quite as much of his Majesty's attention as she wished.

Perhaps the best testament of Anne of Cleves is contained in the few words of the English historian who wrote, "Well, it pleased his Highness to mislike her grace, but to me she always appeared a brave lady."

Marillac ran his practised eye over her German ladies-in-waiting and pronounced them even inferior in looks to their mistress, their dress so tasteless that a beauty would have looked a fright. Anne had hoped to keep them beside her as companions in a foreign country, but it was made clear her household must be English.

There had been a scramble for the coveted appointments of lady-in-waiting amongst young Englishwomen before her arrival, strings pulled, influence brought to bear, presents of Gascon wine and barrels of herring placed in the right quarter. The maids of honour to Queen Jane had an advantage over newcomers. Having access to the King, they could make offerings of quince marmalade and damson cheese, writing to their mothers in high glee to send more as soon as could be, so acceptable were they proving.

Young Katherine Howard had not been one of Queen Jane's attendants and she had no mother to press her suit for her. Nevertheless she won her heart's desire, an appointment at court, because she was niece of the great Duke of Norfolk.

She had red hair and was always laughing, her dimples snug in her pretty cheeks, a young girl but so diminutive she could have been taken for a child. No one would have guessed looking at her that she was so experienced a child. Her aunt had warned her she would spoil her beauty if she were not careful, but her beauty was not spoiled. She knew how to look after herself.

All these days were behind her now, she was as maidenly as any of her court companions. Life was quite different from what it had been when she had been sent to her step-grandmother, the redoubtable Dowager Duchess Agnes, to learn all housewifely arts, sharing the long dormitory with her grandmother's highly-born attendants and their servants. But learning how to govern and direct house and kitchen, embroider and play the virginals, did not occupy all Katherine's time in the Norfolk country mansion at Lambeth, embowered in orchards and gardens that ran to the very edge of the Thames. Not when her music master was Henry Manox. They used to meet in the little room the Duchess used behind the chapel. How fond he had been of her, how very fond, suing her to give him a token of her love. She had soon put him right there—as though a low-born music teacher could expect a token from her with Plantagenet blood in her veins.

But blue blood did not mean wealth. Her soldier father, whose valour and military skill had been largely responsible for the Flodden victory, had never been rewarded and was penurious. Katherine had ached for silks, satins and velvets.

Dereham, her young kinsman, used to give her things: sarcenet to make a little quilted cap, a fine Holland shirt embroidered with point and needlework to make into articles for her wardrobe, a silk pansy and another artificial flower called a French fennel they said all the ladies at court were wearing—before she dare wear that, she had to prevail on indulgent Lady Brereton to say she had given it to her.

Dereham belonged to what her uncle called his household troop, all gentlemen and most kin to him, whom he kept handy to be ready in times of strife or neighbourly quarrels. Dereham and other young gallants used to steal up to the long dormitory for midnight feasts, bearing with them delicacies left over from the banqueting table in the great hall below—wine, strawberries, apples and other rare things to make good cheer. There was a convenient little gallery where the young men could hide should a suspicious Duchess Agnes happen to pay a reconnoitring visit.

They had exchanged love tokens, she and Dereham, and he had called her wife. How they had kissed, clinging to each other with their lips like two sparrows. Her grandmother had surprised them once and had boxed Katherine's ears, asking them if they took her home for the King's court.

When it was discovered there had been more than kissing, Katherine was beaten and her lover fled. Their stolen farewell had been tempestuous with grief, and Katherine had employed one Jane Acworth, a readier writer than herself, to carry on a secret correspondence with him for a time.

She did not know where he had gone; some said it was out of the country, and now she did not care. She was well quit of him with his possessiveness. Manox, Dereham and the ready writer, the nurse Mary Lassells who had slept in the dormitory—every single one of them had been swept clean out of her mind. The present was sufficient for her, the scintillating irresistible present—maid-of-honour to the Queen, at the King's court full of gentlemen-in-waiting, gentlemen of the privy chamber, gentlemen this and gentlemen that, and the handsomest of them all, her cousin Thomas Culpeper. The very mention of his name had made Dereham blacken with jealousy.

She was in the brush and stir of court life, heard all the gossip going its rounds. Do you know what his Majesty said when he heard the Princess Elizabeth ardently desired to see the new Queen? "Tell her," he said, "that she had a mother so different from this woman, that she ought not to wish to see her." That was the first time he had ever been heard to mention Anne Boleyn since . . . She of course was Katherine's cousin, which made little Elizabeth her niece.

Her uncle the Duke had newly returned from France where he had been taking soundings. He told his sovereign the French King was not likely to join in any alliance against England. It was Cromwell and his ecclesiastical policy of which Francis disapproved, not Norfolk's king.

Everyone had known, when the Emperor dispersed his fleet last year, that England had no longer anything to fear from that quarter. They had known that even before the Cleves marriage treaty had been signed. Why then had it been signed? The only answer was Cromwell—it was his doing from first to last, no one else's. Already the need for the Cleves alliance had passed (Norfolk was of the opinion it had never existed) and was proving nothing but a blunder and an embarrassment.

And what about the King and his marriage, saddled to a wife he could not love, with whom he had known the first time he had slept with her he could not have a child? A sad day for England that their sovereign could never have any more children because his minister Cromwell was plotting to bring in Luther's heresies. His Highness himself had not only said how detestable and abominable they were but had written a book against them.

Cromwell, so arrogant in council, so ambitious of others' blood. Only yesterday he had threatened Norfolk and the Bishops of Winchester, Durham and Bath and Wells, all because he knew they, like their king, hated the new teaching. Norfolk was stout to defend the old faith now their king, whose learning knew no end, had been wise enough to make the Pope the Bishop of Rome. Cromwell and Cranmer would have the whole country Lutheran if they could.

But Norfolk had not only the well-worn string of Cromwell to harp upon. His *bonne bouche*, the feather in his cap, the trick up his sleeve, was his pretty little niece with her red hair, hazel eyes and uptilted nose.

Marillac kept his sovereign posted stage by stage about the English King's affection for another lady, reported to be a great beauty. The Queen was sent to Richmond, and the King promised to follow in two days, but the caustic Marillac predicted his steps would take him in the Lambeth direction instead. They were saying at court that Queen Anne had gone to Richmond of her own accord to remove herself from the plague. Marillac did not believe a word of that tale. If there had been any suspicion of plague in London, the King would have been the first to flee: everyone knew it was the one thing of which he was timid. It was even said that the marriage between him and the young lady of extraordinary beauty had already taken place and was being kept secret. Marillac could not tell how far that report was true.

A deputation instead of her husband waited upon the Queen some three weeks after her arrival at Richmond. Now, Anne knew it was openly said in European courts Henry's first wife had been poisoned; she knew he had beheaded his second and that his third had received an early grave. Before the commissioners could tell her a word of their mission, she, believing they had come to carry her to the Tower, fell to the floor in a dead faint.

Her relief was unspeakable when, soothed and comforted, she was brought round to hear the King's most tender conscience was troubling him again. He did not believe he and she were married. There was that pre-contract of marriage with the Duke of Lorraine that had been made for her when both were minors—the King and his advisers, spiritual and temporal, did not consider it had ever been legally terminated. It was his Majesty's gracious intention to adopt her as a sister; all she would require to do to win that outstanding privilege was to resign the title of Queen. The King would see she would have precedence over every lady at court except his daughters —and of course his future consort. A handsome pension was to be hers, with manors and estates. These were forfeited by Cromwell, now in the Tower on the charge of treason, arrested by Norfolk in the name of the King. And freedom to live abroad or in England, exactly as she chose, although of course if she chose abroad she could neither take her handsome pension nor estates. As for her marriage with the King, it had already been annulled. The nation had to be considered: it had a great interest in their king's having more issue, and the King had never given inward consent to his marriage with her grace, or completed it.

Anne of Cleves had not one objection to raise. She signed the necessary deeds and documents with alacrity and returned Henry's wedding ring in the most affable fashion possible. Never since her arrival in England six months ago had she been happier, holding her own little court. This was her honeymoon without the drawback of a husband swelling visibly with portent and disfavour. Every day she put on a rich new dress of extraordinary fashion from her trousseau.

She took everything in good part, which Marillac said was marvellous prudent of her although some considered it stupidity. Even her recent husband's new bride—she greeted her with acclaim, so glad was she to see another by his side. And when Henry visited her, their meeting was amiable enough to encourage him to stay to sup, when they were merry together as they had never been as husband and wife.

The wedding of the King of England to Katherine Howard took place seven months after his marriage to Anne of Cleves, on the day Cromwell was executed. It was an unproclaimed affair: she was introduced as his wife when she took her seat at chapel beside him. That Sunday she was prayed for in churches throughout the realm as Queen of England.

Never, reported the French ambassador, had he seen the King in such good spirits or in so good a humour. The effect of marriage to his young bride was instantaneous, and love acted on him like elixir. All the buoyancy and vigour of youth returned to him, sending the blood singing in his veins. He was up in the morning at five and hunting until ten, declaring how much better he felt in the country than London. He could not keep his hands from fondling and caressing her, his pretty little nosegay of a bride. Never, he declared, had he been so happily wedded. He chose the rose as her symbol, and called her his rose without a thorn.

CHAPTER SEVENTEEN

BACKSTAIRS SCANDAL

"And, oft before tempestuous winds arise,
The teeming stars fall headlong from the skies,
And shooting through the darkness gild the night,
With sweeping glories, and long trains of light."

THEY came out of the past like beetles from under a stone, sensitive to change of light; and she was the light. She heard from the ready writer even before the Anne of Cleves marriage was annulled, loading her with all the good wishes of the sender and asking her, once she was in the Queen's place, to find room for her, "the nearer I were to you the gladder I would be of it," a letter which ended that she knew the recipient would not forget her secretary.

Katherine made her one of her bedchamber women, and also took into service Katherine Tylney, her cousin, who had slept with her in the Lambeth dormitory and shared in the midnight feasts, and Margaret Morton, another former room-mate. Her one-time music-master, Manox, is said to have been appointed a royal musician, and there is no doubt that she employed Dereham as her usher and secretary for a short time, an act of such folly that it must have been exacted from her to buy his silence.

Dereham had returned to England before her name had been linked with the King's. A young couple were considered married in the eyes of God and the law without engagement or religious ceremony, if they agreed to it between themselves and agreement was accompanied by carnal knowledge. Dereham therefore considered himself and Katherine Howard man and wife, and sought her out to tax her with the court gossip that Thomas Culpeper was to be her husband. Katherine's reply was that he must not trouble her about that "for you know I will not have you". Dereham was not the type to take such a disclaimer lying down, but when the King fell in love with her he did not press his prior claim, although he confided to a friend that if the King were dead he would step into his shoes. As for Thomas Culpeper, he lost no time consoling himself elsewhere and Katherine saw him ingloriously worsted at the jousting celebrations to mark her wedding.

The besotted King lavished gifts, jewels, furs and an elaborate household upon his young bride. Never had Katherine dreamed when she yearned for rich stuffs that there were such fabrics in the world and that she should ever be clothed in them. Greedy as a child for the pleasures and sensations of the moment, she was as emotionally unreliable as a demi-mondaine. With all the petting from her royal lover, she grew plump and merry, wearing her clothes, fashioned like a Frenchwoman's, tight about the bodice to reveal her new curves. Marillac voted her face very delightful, and said the King was so enamoured of her he was at a loss to demonstrate his affection. Her motto was "No other than his".

Henry was forty-nine when he took his fifth wife, a panorama of a man, the landscape of his face unfurrowed, the bluff of his brow unlined, the promontory of his nose only beginning to coarsen. And for these idyllic months of early marriage he was able to hold his winter at bay. This was his Indian summer. Something of the old agility returned to that gargantuan frame. In Katherine he recovered his lost youth, when he and life and the world had been at high noontide, and she who brought him this miracle was like a goddess.

He took her to Windsor, dispensing as much as possible with the pomp and restriction of court life while he enjoyed her tirelessness for the round of feasting and dancing, her bubbling naïve pleasure finding herself in his arms, her full red lips to kiss. They made a little progress together, through country towns and landscape yellowing with autumn. The report that a certain Windsor priest, with members of his community, had spoken disrespectfully of the Queen's grace cast no shadow, for the King knew there was no substance behind it. The man was told to confine himself to his own diocese and to be more temperate in the use of his tongue in the future.

Christmas was spent at Hampton Court without the presence of any members of his council to disturb with business a festival elate with present happiness and past childhood memories. Amongst the gifts he bestowed on his bride were a diamond and ruby brooch edged with pearls and a muffler of black velvet furred with sables and gemmed with rubies and hundreds of pearls. Rubies were fitting to give one whose price was far above them, and whose husband praised her. He went up to London to see to business in the New Year but returned in three days after he had transacted it.

It was during Lent that the first ruffle appeared on the placid waters of the eight-month marriage. The King had an attack of fever which left him irascible and melancholy. The ulcer on his leg flared again, distorting his face with pain, and when he could manage to walk he had to hobble miserably on a stick.

Physical disability cracked the delusion that he could put the clock back. His Golden Age had not returned. News of a small rising in the north raised his choler and deepened his depression although this time it was abortive, stamped out almost before it had begun. He said he had an evil people to rule. The very youth of his inconsequential wife irked him, and for over a week he refused to see her. Instead of a royal bridegroom, Katherine came face to face with a frightening, obese, quarrelsome man, sagging into gloom or shouting with rage.

She beguiled the tedium of these days while the King lay sick amusing herself with Thomas Culpeper who, as gentleman of the privy chamber, was about the court. When she gave him a velvet cap garnished with a jewelled brooch, she told him to put it under his cloak that nobody would see it. And she wrote him the only letter of hers in existence, a love letter: she was not literate like Katherine of Aragon or Anne Boleyn, but wrote and expressed herself like a child.

As soon as Henry could resume his normal activities he did, flouting his doctors. The belief that Katherine was with child cheered him and he determined, if it proved true, to have her crowned at Whitsuntide. Unfortunately it was a false surmise, so his little Queen forfeited her coronation for the present. But the rising in the north had reminded him of his promise five years ago during the Pilgrimage of Grace negotiations that he would make a progress to that unvisited quarter of his realm.

Arrangements were at once put in hand, for the planning and provisioning of such an undertaking was prodigious. This was to be no ordinary progress: Henry was not only going to show himself to his seditious subjects as their king but what manner of king he was.

His whole court accompanied him, and it took two hundred tents to house them alone, also nearly all his council. The barbaric north was to be dazzled by the choicest royal tapestries, the finest plate and the King's richest wardrobe, and impressed by the size of the army marching alongside. The enormous cavalcade included five thousand horses to carry men and supplies. Eighty archers with drawn bows preceded them when they entered a city.

It was a life that suited Henry, constant movement to absorb his tremendous energies, the strong northern air, the stimulus of new scenes and sights. This was his realm although he had never set foot on it before, these forests of oak, wastes of scrub, brushwood and thickets, moorland and mossland where grey sheep cropped, their tangled wool parted by the wind; each town fringed with fields and run-rigs of land wrested from the wilderness surrounding it. Standing on its rocky height, his keep or castle awaited him, their grey walls tough to withstand the assault and battering-ram of storm and man.

And these were his subjects. His keen huntsman's eye glinted over them whose fathers and fathers' fathers had fought for the white rose of York against the red. They were bigger than the men in the south, their features craggy and projecting from their faces, which made them look like the corbel heads in his father's chapel. Yes, these were his subjects, whether he or they liked it or not.

He sent proclamation before him that if any found themselves grieved for lack of justice, they were to have full access to declare their complaints to him, that they could have right dealt them at the hand of his Majesty. Hard on the proclamation followed his Majesty in person, formidable with bulk, not like a man as they were men, but powerful as the State, iron-bound as the Law, sacrosanct as the Church, their anointed king.

It was triumph all the way for Henry, extending his royal pardon, accepting humble submission from kneeling civic authorities, receiving expiatory gifts and propitiating bags of gold at every halt.

He reached the walled city of York in the middle of September, his health recovered, jocund and active, supervising the construction of a vast lodging outside the city. At first it was thought he intended to have his Queen crowned in York Minster, whose pale stone glowed with the gold of past summers. But soon it was discovered this was to be the scene of another Field of Cloth of Gold, not so spectacular of course, although Henry marshalled all the resources at hand to make a fine display, but a rendezvous that would, he felt, bear more lasting fruit.

Instead of Francis I of France, his counterpart this time was to be James V of Scotland, who had promised to ride across the border and hold tryst with his uncle and neighbour King. Their meeting would be a worthy climax to a progress that had been a paean of satisfaction. Henry had no doubts that he had but to meet his nephew to prove to him that his uncle's friendship was more valuable than the French King's.

Greenwich, Hatfield, Lincoln, Pontefract, York—the summer months swung by for Katherine, dressing herself in different dresses of crimson velvet except when she entered a city, when her gowns were of silver. She was Queen of the England she was passing through, second to none but her lord and sovereign, receiving homage, adulation and honour every mile of the way, and it was not enough. Satiated with plenty, she hungered for forbidden fruit.

Her principal lady-in-waiting was Lady Rochford, who had kept her position at court throughout the reigns of Anne Boleyn, Jane Seymour and Anne of Cleves. She had been the wife of George Boleyn, against whom she had borne witness, a woman with an obsession for playing with fire and edge tools. She now acted as intermediary between the young Queen and presentable young Thomas Culpeper, carrying messages, arranging assignations late at night, the only one to be present with the Queen when he came lurking up the backstairs.

"Jesus! is not the Queen abed yet?" Katherine Tylney asked Margaret Morton one hot night at Lincoln when their mistress was still in Lady Rochford's room at two o'clock. The doors were barred from the inside at Pontefract once the King came to spend the night with his wife, and there was some delay before he was admitted. None of the Queen's attendants ever saw or heard who was supposed to be closeted with her and Lady Rochford, but she betrayed her infatuation for Culpeper to her servants simply by the way she looked and spoke to him in daily intercourse.

His royal uncle waited twelve days at York for James who did not come; the French party were in ascendancy in Scotland and his nephew begged to be excused. Henry was very angry indeed. Instead of blandishing the Tudor charm, he had to prepare for his return journey. The great pavilion was taken down which was to have staged history in the making, the tapestries rolled up, the plate carried away whose richness was guaranteed to make any Scot blink. Throughout the journey back Henry was vocal on the subject of his nephew, rumbling with threats of vengeance.

But this disappointment was the one discordant note in the whole progress. When he arrived home at Hampton Court towards the end of October he, touched and gratified by the humility and devotion of his northern subjects, was at peace with himself and all the world. Those members of his council, including Cranmer, who had been in charge of the government in his absence, were there to welcome him.

On All Hallows Day a mass of thanksgiving took place for the safe return of the King's Grace. He expressed his gratitude to his Maker for the good life he was leading and trusted to lead with his present Queen after the troubles he had suffered through his earlier marriages. He was a ship that across tempestuous seas at last reaches haven, and he instructed his confessor to make like prayer publicly and give like thanks with him.

Twenty-four hours later as he left his private chapel, Cranmer handed him a letter, thrusting it at him in his importunity to be rid of it, requesting him in a low voice to read it in private.

The Archbishop told through his pen what he could not say to his King by word of mouth. The Queen upon whom his affection was so marvellously set had lived most corruptly and sensually.

Sometimes an avalanche can be caused by the dislodgement of a pebble. One John Lassels said to his sister Mary, a servant of Duchess Agnes who had shared the dormitory with her granddaughters, why did she not ask for a place in the Queen's household as the others had done? Mary replied she had no wish to enter the Queen's service, but she pitied her. "Why so?" inquired her brother. "Marry!" came the reply, "because she is light both in conditions and living."

John Lassels was a fervid Protestant, and religious zeal would not permit him to sleep on such disclosures. He asked for an interview with the Archbishop of Canterbury, well known for his Protestant leanings. Immediately aware of the weight and importance of what he had heard, Cranmer relayed it at once to his two fellow council members who had not gone, like Norfolk, on the northern progress.

The conclusion arrived at was inevitable: the King must be told. The scandal was not unwelcome for it offered an opportunity of undermining the Howard predominance at court, but no one wanted the painful duty of being the one to tell him. They knew his anger. It could rend and tear apart anyone who dared reveal what the love of his heart and the light of his eye really was. It was Cranmer who undertook to write and deliver the letter. He was probably motivated by his duty to his royal master more than the others, who seized the chance to bring about the downfall of the Duke of Norfolk and the Roman Catholic party.

The King's reaction was totally different from what anyone had expected. He did not tower with rage. He was not disturbed, except that the calumny against Katherine should be investigated and the perpetrators punished. Not a word of it did he believe. He had only to look at his bride of little more than a year with the bloom of youth and the dew of freshness upon her to be assured. He had lived long enough in the world to know all about the malice on idle and lying tongues. Quietly he ordered that no stone should be left unturned to discover the falsity of the rumours, and continued in high spirits for the rest of the week.

On the Sunday morning, 6th November, 1541, Henry attended in person at Hampton Court a full meeting of his council, an unusual proceeding; but the circumstances were unusual and he had to learn the siftings of the scandals against his Queen that appropriate punishments might be dispensed.

Instead he heard proof after proof of her looseness before her marriage. Mary Lassels said Manox, the music-teacher, knew a private mark on Katherine's body. Manox admitted guilty familiarity with her but said Dereham had supplanted him in her affections. Dereham confessed he and Katherine had had intercourse but there was no guilt in it as their precontract made her his wife.

They saw the King age as they looked at him when disbelief at last gave up the struggle. For a moment he was a giant again, shouting for a sword with which to slay the girl who had betrayed him and swearing that she would never have such delight in her incontinency as she would have torture in her death. As suddenly he collapsed, like a tower whose foundations have shifted, and they turned their faces away not to see their king weeping, a strange sight in one of his courage.

The man who left the council chamber was not the same as the man who had entered it. He was never to be the same again. Time at last made up on him, vanquishing all the magniloquence of youth, and the greyness of age took root. He rode to London that afternoon, taking a few musicians with him and without saying where he was going.

Cranmer, with four members of the council, visited Katherine's apartments and accused her of failing to disclose her immorality before she married the King. Throughout all the lengthy inquisitions and interrogations that were to follow she acted true to her type, extenuations depriving too full confessions of their context, her defence weakened by deception, crawling remorse overridden by the anxiety to remove the blame to her partners. Unable to extricate herself from the ever-developing situation, she unconsciously took refuge in hysteria. That Sunday night it was thought she would lose her reason.

A gallery at Hampton Court is still called the haunted gallery because it is said her ghost frequents it. That Sunday, knowing the King would be at mass in his chapel, she tried to reach him but was caught and forced back to her apartments. Her shrieks tearing up and down the gallery are said to echo there today.

Cranmer was instructed on the Monday to bring home to the Queen how grievously she had offended, to make much of the punishment she deserved, and then to inform her the King was graciously pleased to pardon her and remit these dread punishments. Instead she was to be degraded from the rank of Queen and confined in custody.

Seeing the condition Katherine was in, Cranmer wisely told her about the pardon first, which steadied her to a certain extent. Taken off her guard the day before, she had instinctively denied everything with all the strength she could summon. Now she admitted that she had allowed him, through flattery and fair persuasions on the part of Manox, to take liberties with her, and confessed that Dereham by many persuasions procured her for his vicious purposes. But she would not agree there was anything like a precontract between them, as that would have made it even more heinous for her to have gone through a form of marriage with the King of England when she knew she was already married to Francis Dereham. Also she had for long wanted not to be tied to but finished with him.

Questioned whether she had ever called him husband and he her wife, she had to agree that happened many times. She supposed it was true that at one time he kissed her very often, and that once when some spectators remarked on it, he answered, "Who should hinder me from kissing my own wife?" But she slipped through the questioners' net each time by saying she had not appreciated such behaviour constituted marriage.

When she thought of what she had lost and for what, Katherine could not contain her grief and remorse. Even through her statement of guilt addressed to the King, sufficient in itself to warrant the death penalty, there emerges a picture of the man to whom she is writing as she remembers him, his unfailing goodness, always so gracious and loving a prince to her.

The news that a second niece of his had proved herself an unworthy escort for the King struck the Duke of Norfolk like a thunderbolt. He wrote at once to Henry beseeching him to forgive him the sins of his seditious family and to continue his good and gracious Lord. Katherine's unchastity before her marriage may have been and probably was hidden from her uncle, but to prove his shock and horror he had to draw attention to them. He disowned all his relations sent to the Tower who had known of Katherine's past, uncovered incriminating evidence against his stepmother, Duchess Agnes, who had commended her granddaughter to the King as worthy of the honour to be his wife; accompanied Cranmer on several occasions to interrogate the degraded Queen; and as he sat with the rest of the council at the male prisoners' trial, laughed loudly when the prosecution scored a point. He was all for having his "ungrateful niece" burned alive for her sins.

It was the King who showed patience and some compassion. Katherine Howard's treatment was gentle compared to that meted out to Anne Boleyn. It was carefully stipulated that her keys were not to be taken from her, which meant that she could move about her rooms with some freedom, and she was to choose four gentlewomen and two chamberers as her attendants. But her jewels were taken from her, all cloth of state removed and her most sumptuous dresses.

Cranmer broke up the Queen's household at Hampton Court, and she was sent under guard to the suppressed monastery of Syon. Believing the worst was over, the enormity of her faults and sins diminished to more conventional size, and she became cheerful again. She dressed herself from her restricted wardrobe as carefully as she had done when she was Queen and was said to be plump and pretty as ever. But it was noticed she was more imperious and difficult to please than she had been when she was the King's wife.

The Council determined to suppress, quite illegally, the pre-contract evidence because it would assist the defence. Their difficulty was Dereham could not be found guilty of having lain with his wife either before or after her marriage to the King, and Dereham must be inculpated. Accused of having renewed their former intercourse during the short space he was the Queen's secretary, he, to prove himself innocent, protested that Culpeper had succeeded him in the Queen's affections.

Thomas Culpeper, gentleman-in-waiting, favourite at court! They were after the new scent in full cry. The unsuspecting gallant was apprehended while he was hawking, and Katherine was questioned about her relationship with him.

She admitted the backstairs assignations as did Culpeper, who added the detail that the Queen, not unnaturally, was in great fear lest somebody should come in. Katherine even confessed to calling him her little sweet fool and giving him a cap and a ring, but both he and she denied adultery. Her explanation of the midnight meetings was Culpeper wanted them and they had been engineered by Lady Rochford for some dark reasons of her own.

Lady Rochford's evidence was verbose but contradictory. She had never wanted to act as go-between, but the Queen and Culpeper forced her to it. She had never heard what the Queen and Culpeper said to each other, but thought Culpeper must have known the Queen carnally, considering all the things she had heard and seen between them.

Both Culpeper and Dereham were tortured although torture was illegal in England. There was no one to question the persecution (Katherine had no trial); if so, their answer would have been that in a case that involved the royal person of the King all means were lawful. Both men refused to confess, even on the rack, they had committed misconduct with the Queen after her marriage. But Katherine's doom was sealed as well as his own when Culpeper admitted he intended and meant to do ill with her and that in like wise she so minded to do with him.

This woman had been Queen of England, this woman might, but for the grace of God, have borne a son during the short time she shared the King's bed. She and her lovers had committed the worst crime that could be committed; they had confounded the succession.

Not bigamy but adultery! His young wife had made a cuckold of him. He might be King of England but to her he was an old man. He who had believed Henry Tudor was not like the common run, that his place could never be filled as long as he drew breath, saw himself displanted by nincompoops who could only boast their youth.

Both Culpeper and Dereham asked to be beheaded instead of the traitor's death of hanged, drawn and quartered. The King granted the boon to Culpeper but not to Dereham.

Lady Rochford was executed on the same day as her young mistress. Her mind gave under the ceaseless questioning; she had probably been streaked with insanity all along, and a bill was brought in that the State could proceed against those who had lost their reason. However, she made the conventional "good death" of exhortation, edification and repentance, although one observer did feel she took too long cataloguing her offences. One of these was that she had brought this shameful death upon herself because of having contributed to her husband's fate by her false accusation of Queen Anne Boleyn.

Parliament saved the King the pain of signing the Queen's death warrant. It also brought in an Act which declared it treason for any woman to marry the King if her previous life had been unchaste. "Few, if any, ladies now at court would henceforth aspire to that honour," was Chapuys's comment to that.

Katherine was taken from Syon to the Tower. She knew what lay before her, but as she was being escorted to the barge and saw the galleys that were to escort it, she would have turned. Struggling, she was put on board.

The night before she was to die she asked that the block be brought into her cell so that she might learn how to place her head on it. On the day of her execution her brother and cousin paraded themselves, making merry and ostentatiously dressed in festival finery, in the streets of London. "It is the custom," the laconic Marillac noted, "and must be done to show they did not share the crimes of their relatives."

No man chose death rather than say Katherine Howard was not guilty as four did for the sake of Anne Boleyn. No stories reach us of the love her ladies-in-waiting bore her as they bore her elder cousin. No token of hers was handed down from generation to generation like the one Anne Boleyn gave on her execution morning to the officer on guard because of his unfailing respectful conduct towards her. Katherine Howard stands almost alone in that she has no mourners, unless she was remembered in the heart of an ageing king.

Henry had to carry the knowledge that what was said against Anne Boleyn, except the incest, was true of Katherine Howard. What he would have given to have heard a Dereham or a Culpeper proclaim he would rather die a thousand deaths than accuse the Queen of what he knew her to be innocent. Instead, to save themselves, they had placed the blame at her door as she had at theirs.

The King seemed very old and grey to Marillac when he next saw him; he reported he took such grief that of late it was thought he had gone mad, and Chapuys wrote that he had been low-spirited ever since he heard of the late Queen's misconduct.

CHAPTER EIGHTEEN

THE LAST BARGAIN

"This ae nighte, this ae nighte,
Everie nighte and alle,
Fire and sleet and candle-light,
And Christe receive thy saule."

WHILE Henry was on his northern progress, his son Edward fell
ill with a quartan fever. He was four years old and his portraits
confirm the reports that he was a handsome boy, blond and broad-
browed like his father. There is a cameo which represents them
both; Henry's arm is round his shoulder, clamping him to him like
a lion its cub. But although the boy recovered from the ague, it left
him delicate, and his doctors realized that after all he had not inherited his parent's constitution, while his pictures begin to portray
him still good-looking but fragile and thin. Highly intelligent, like
all Henry's children, from the beginning he took the liveliest interest
in all that was going on around him. He was a scholarly boy who
played the lute, was thrilled by the stars, and learnt Latin, Greek,
French and Italian. Beloved by his father's people, they called him
England's Treasure.

News that his sister Margaret had died in Scotland reached
Henry when he was restlessly moving from place to place as his
councillors inquired into the abominable demeanour of his Queen.
Margaret, older than he, had never meant to him what his younger
sister Mary had, but her death coming at such a time depressed
him. Now he alone was left. He sent to learn whether his sister
was really dead and if she had left a will.

The clouds that had threatened so long at last broke into open
warfare between England and Scotland. The northern country was
an irritant to Henry who became more and more impatient as he
grew older. He could not induce James to break with Rome (his

uncle's suggestion that he should imburse himself by despoiling the monasteries struck the Scots King as blasphemous, although like most men, and all kings, he liked well to be rich), and Scotland's ancient alliance with France made her a source of potential danger to her English neighbour.

The first round went to James, whose success over his uncle greatly elated him. Henry ordered Norfolk to avenge the defeat, issued a plausible manifesto regretting he was compelled to use arms against his nephew, and sent a warning to James that he still had the same rod in his keeping which had chastised his father.

Norfolk entered Scotland on his punitive expedition with twenty thousand men. The Scots side of the border was a much richer country than the English side, which meant the English could wreak immeasurably more harm quicker when they crossed into Scotland than the Scots could when they crossed into the barren bog and harsh moorland that edged England. Another Scottish disadvantage was their capital of Edinburgh was within easy striking distance of the border, whereas London was buried deep in England.

It was October and the harvest garnered in what was the granary of Scotland. Norfolk reduced it to ashes, and sacked and fired farms, villages, towns and abbeys along the Tweed. He had no intention of making organized war; it was far too late in the year for that, and after inflicting as much damage as he could, as a lesson to the Scots for not complying with his master, he wheeled his army and made to fall back on his home country.

The cry from the borders reached the Scots King who, hot to invade England, pursued the enemy with thirty thousand men; but when the tide of battle could have turned in his favour, his nobles, whose disaffection was chronic, withdrew their support. They allowed the English to cross safely over the Tweed, and dispersed to their homes.

James had been King of Scotland for the twenty-nine of his thirty years, having inherited the crown when his father was killed at Flodden. He had the Stewart red hair, oval face, heavy lids, and above all the Stewart blood, with its mixture of charm and passion, its wayward weakness allied to great nobility, and its undiluted personal courage. He made a good ruler to his people, but his nobles were too strong, too lawless, too factious, to be subdued: the only counter he had to keep them in check was the Church. For four years he had been married to French Marie of Guise, whom his uncle had wanted and whom he had won, and she had borne him two sons, both of whom had died within a few days of each other. James began to show signs of his grandfather's melancholy and could not sleep. Now his Queen wife was in Linlithgow Palace for her third lying-in.

It was the Church which provided him with another army after his nobles' defection, and the King marched west with it where he fell ill. It was now November, too late for warfare, but James may well have reasoned that it was better to use an army when he had one to use. Too sick to lead the men himself, he made the disastrous decision of sending them forward into enemy country. The Scottish force crossed the Esk during the night. The men believed the King was with them and only discovered he was not when dawn broke over the flats of the treacherous Solway Moss. Dissension broke out as to who was to lead and into the confusion rode an English force a quarter their number.

This had none of the heart-breaking heroism of Flodden. This was panic, rout, abject defeat. Hundreds of high-ranking prisoners were taken by the English. News of the disaster was carried to the sick Scots King. He had one more blow to sustain before he succumbed, when he heard on his death-bed before the end of the year that his queen was safely delivered—of a daughter. Crying out, "The deil take it! The deil take it!" he turned his face to the wall. The child he never saw was Mary, Queen of Scots before she was a week old.

Henry saw in the birth of his great-niece at her father's death providence working for him, and he seized the opportunity in his strenuous hands. There was another process now than costly warfare by which the Scots crown could be seized—marriage. It had been tried before; each king, except his father, who had sat on the English throne had attempted to subject Scotland through either conquest or marriage, but never had such an opportunity as this presented itself, with so many influential prisoners to play their part in Henry's game. And throughout this game played without rules, he never lost sight of the ball, the small Scots Queen.

Union of marriage must be effected between the newborn Queen and Prince Edward—on Henry's terms. He sold their freedom to the Solway prisoners on condition they agreed, on their return, to have the child straightway delivered to his guardianship. But it was one thing to promise the King of England everything he demanded on English soil, another to fulfil their promises on their return when the mother of the proposed bride was a Frenchwoman and their fellow Scots had no intention of selling either their country or their Queen to their hereditary enemies.

The best the Solway lords could achieve for the English monarch was that Mary should be espoused to Edward and sent to England in her tenth year. Henry had to modify his terms which he did with a poor grace, for the Scots saw to it that the marriage treaty left no loophole for annexation. One Scots nobleman voiced what all his countrymen were thinking when he said, "I dislike not so much the marriage as the manner of the wooing."

If Henry had been content, as he would have been content earlier, with the marriage of the Scots Queen to his son, all the patient and skilled negotiations of his former years might well have borne fruit. His deteriorating health contributed something to his diminishing statesmanship where Scotland was concerned, but he had grown into a despot and despotism and conciliation do not go hand in hand. He had completed the union of Wales with England and was now King of Ireland. Scotland alone prevented his title to Emperor of Great Britain, and the possibility of a British Empire was ruled out so long as his weaker but stubborn neighbour had the aid of rich and powerful France.

Francis at present had his hands full as he had declared war on Charles when their ten-year-old friendship had still six years to run. When it suited Henry he concluded an alliance with Charles and declared war on Francis, ostensibly to recover his ancient rights in France and because Francis had committed the unpardonable sin against Christendom by giving entry into Europe to the hordes of infidel Turk, but in reality to destroy the support which enabled Scotland to resist union with England.

The wheel had turned full circle, the three powers were back where they had been at the start of their reigns: Spain and England versus France.

Francis could not believe it. When Henry's ambassador presented him with his letters of recall, the French King spoke of the English sovereign as his good brother, his best brother, his best beloved brother who assuredly could not be his enemy. He offered liberal terms if Henry would make a separate peace with him, but Henry kept his pledge to Charles. Francis, who was gaining ally after ally with every victory against the morose Emperor, was his rival as Charles could never be.

Seventeen months after the execution of his fifth wife, Henry married his sixth, Katherine Parr. She was aged thirty-one and had been twice widowed. Their wedding was no hole-and-corner affair like those of the Howard cousins but took place at Hampton Court with all due observances, in the presence of his two daughters, although without the pageantry that marked that to Anne of Cleves. But this was no political union to impress the world; it was the marriage of a sick king in need of a helpmeet.

On the 12th July, 1543, in the Queen's closet, the bride, in love with another man who was to be her fourth husband, promised, "I Katherine, take thee, Henry, to my wedded husband, to have and to hold from this day forward, for better for worse, for richer for poorer, in sickness and in health, to be bonair and buxom in bed and at board, till death us do part."

The woman who stood beside her sovereign and husband that day was small in stature, with a serene brow and hazel eyes, her features delicately clear cut as those on a miniature. A contemporary Spanish chronicler tells us she was quieter than any of the young wives the King had had, and as she knew more of the world got on well with him, and had no caprices. But, he adds, she kept her ladies very strictly, perhaps no bad thing when the histories of recent ladies-in-waiting are considered.

The man who stood beside her was fifty-two years old, unwieldy with corpulence, his small eyes needling in his stoutening face. His sands of time were running out; he had not four years to live, but magnificence still clung to him: it was his person—not the monstrous body one saw on his wedding-day—amiable and benign on so pleasant an occasion.

The only tart comment on the marriage came from Henry's fourth wife in her contented if retired little court. Anne of Cleves was a prudent housewife, generous to her servants, who remained throughout on affectionate terms with Mary and Elizabeth, Henry's daughters. When she heard of her former husband's sixth essay at wedlock she remarked, "A fine burthen Madam Katherine has taken on herself."

The fine burden never shut the door against Katherine Parr as he had against some of his former wives. Her soothing presence was always welcome to him. She was not afraid of him when, goaded with pain, he raged and blamed. Something of the tenor of life with Katherine of Aragon returned with Katherine Parr, although circumstances were as different as age from youth, but both women were tender, tactful, humane, and in their devotion put him first not so much because he was their sovereign but because he was their husband.

Another characteristic his new English wife shared with her Spanish counterpart was both were learned. His marriage to Katherine Howard had swung the religious balance towards the Catholic side, his last marriage swayed it towards the Reformers. Katherine Parr liked to discuss theological subjects, and was earnest for reform. Once her tongue ran away with her to such an extent that Henry considered she was poaching on his preserves. He was heard to mutter what were things coming to when women turned priests and he in his old days was taught by his wife. It never happened again. At once Katherine said it would be unbecoming in her to assert opinions contrary to those of her lord; her remarks were only intended to minister talk. "Is it so, Sweetheart?" he replied, "then we are perfect friends."

At first Henry directed the course of hostilities with France from his court. He dispatched a general with the resounding name of Wallop at the head of six thousand troops to reinforce Charles's army in the Netherlands, while he tried to raise money to pay for a war that had scarcely begun and whose cost was already reaching astronomical sums. As his father's fortune had long ago disappeared, so had the one accumulated for him by Cromwell. A hard-pressed King levied forced loans, debased the coinage, sold crown lands and raised loans in the Netherlands at ruinous rates of interest, while his people asked in their grumbling way what were they gaining fighting France except exposure to war on two fronts.

The ink was hardly dry on the marriage and peace treaties with Scotland than the bridegroom's father seized Scots merchant ships in his high-handed way. Edinburgh rose. The English envoy escaped only in the nick of time when the house where he lodged was burnt down by the populace. He wrote to Henry complaining of the beastly liberties the Scots enjoyed, concluding with the remark that he would rather be among Turks. Hastily the Scots arranged the coronation of their Queen. The ceremony, performed with crown, sceptre, sword and baby, exacerbated Henry. The Scots declared the English treaties null and void, and renewed their alliance with France.

It was more than Henry would tolerate. Determined to be Mary's father-in-law, he sent an army into Scotland to take her by force. His instructions, which were carried out to the letter, were to inflict all the misery it could, lay waste the country, and put to fire and sword man, woman and child. The royal child was hurried from one stronghold to another before the destructive arm of the English King, who with every blow strengthened the French party in Scotland. The army returned to England, leaving desolation in its wake, but without the bride or beating Scotland to its knees.

Henry was very ill that year, suffering severe pain and fever caused by his sore leg. The ulceration was not syphillitic in origin but varicose, the veins on his leg becoming plugged or thrombosed. He would sit with it on his wife's lap, or lie in bed disputing with his doctors.

Nothing would stop him crossing the Channel to lead his army in person against the French King. His physicians said it was madness, his Council was horrified and even Charles sent a special envoy to dissuade him. The envoy arrived and was given audience by the King, whom he found so determined upon the voyage he did not dare attempt to dissuade him. Henry boasted his strong and robust constitution enabled him to stand illness, but the ambassador noted his face clearly showed he was much worse than he was making out.

Henry arranged with Charles, who was to invade France from the north-west, to effect a junction with their armies and together march on Paris. In July he sailed from Dover to Calais in a ship with sails of cloth of gold. With him went his new armour, as he had outgrown his old, and a heavy charger specially selected and trained to carry his increased bulk.

Sometimes he had to be borne on a litter and to leave his troops to Suffolk, old now but his ablest general, and Norfolk, older still and not so successful on foreign soil as he was on home ground. But Henry was an old campaigner, and amongst men, horses and arms he felt strong and more than able for the stir, clatter and challenge of battle. He camped in torrents of rain and thunder and spent all day in the fields.

The English sat down to besiege Boulogne, which upset Charles, who wanted them to meet him as soon as possible striking west. But Boulogne was a prize Henry had been done out of twenty-one years ago, when Wolsey and his imperial allies had prevailed on him to forego it, and twenty-one years was a long time to wait for Henry to get something on which he had set his heart.

He and Charles might be on enemy soil as allies but neither was in the least interested in the other's objects for going to war, only in his own. While Henry besieged Boulogne and Charles St. Dizier, Francis's envoys were working overtime trying to drive a wedge between them by plying each with separate olive branches and tempting concessions. Henry informed Charles most sedulously of all French peace-feelers, which he loftily spurned, but the reticent Charles was not so forthcoming.

In the agreeable letters Henry wrote home we catch echoes of those he wrote thirty-one years ago to Katherine of Aragon in the same circumstances. He told his wife how busy he had been, seeing and caring for everything. In September he broke the good news that the outworks of the castle had been taken under his command, and the French were unlikely to recover them again (after this sentiment he appended "so we trust" in brackets). Progress was delayed because provision of powder had not come out of Flanders as expected, but he had no doubt that, with God's grace, castle and town would follow the same trade. "No more to you at this time, Sweetheart, but for lack of time and great occupation of business, saving, we pray you, to give in our name our hearty blessings to all our children. . . . Written with the hand of your loving husband, Henry R."

It might have been Katherine of Aragon holding the pen when Katherine Parr wrote of the capture of a Scots ship at Rye, with many Frenchmen as well as Scots on board, bearing letters to the French King which she had examined and was sending the most important to him; also any further information which could be extracted from the prisoners. Although it was not many days since he departed, yet already it seemed a long time to her who felt the want of his presence. She told him my lord Prince and the rest of his children were all, thanks to God, in very good health, concluding "Your Grace's most humble loving wife and servant".

Katherine was a tender stepmother to the three children and while

Henry was abroad the family lived together, for the most part at Hampton Court. All three loved, looked up to and patterned themselves on their gifted stepmother. Edward copied her beautiful handwriting, and the way she expressed herself made him think how poor were his own compositions. She encouraged Mary and Elizabeth to translate passages from the Scriptures, and each compiled a little manual of devotions in Latin, French and English and dedicated it to her.

There were only a few years between Mary, aged twenty-eight, and Katherine Parr. Not even their different religious emphasis separated them; indeed at her stepmother's instigation Mary undertook the translation of a Reformer's Latin paraphrase of St. John.

The last few years of Henry's life, while he was married to his sixth wife, mark a pleasant interlude on Mary's calendar. Her father, even had he so desired, could not will away the crown from his legitimate son, but he could pronounce who was to inherit it in the event of Edward's death. Failing Edward, it was to fall to Mary; failing Mary and her heirs, to Elizabeth. Neither sister wished their adored little brother to die, but the fact that they were accepted in the direct line of succession made a difference to their prestige and circumstances.

Mary's love of flowers did not begin and end there. She made a study of them, and delighted in rare seeds and roots brought from abroad—to watch a Spanish plant establish itself in English soil. It was Spain, her mother's country, that she loved. She had her collection of clocks and dogs (Italian greyhounds were her favourites), and a pet white lark.

At twenty-eight she was still unmarried. Two years ago, when relations between Francis and Henry were more cordial, there was talk and even negotiations about marrying her to the Duke of Orleans, Francis's second son, but the fathers could not agree on the dowry. Francis demanded a million crowns, Henry coolly offered 200,000, saying that was fair enough because the Duke was but a second son. The French ambassador heaved twenty sighs, cast his eyes up to heaven as many times and crossed himself. Henry was told the French would rather take the lady Mary in her kirtle than a mean 200,000 crowns, and the alliance fell through like all the others. Mary was like one of her own seeds kept too long which never flourished as it should.

Her half-sister Elizabeth was eleven. She had not the fair skin of Henry's other children but was sallow like her mother, and her eyes had some of Anne Boleyn's beauty. Already she knew she had pretty hands and took care that others noticed them. She was going to be tall, and whereas Mary was always ailing she was spirited and strong. She was as well educated as her elder sister, without the same need for application and study, so that later she was to carry her learning with panache. In temperament she was far more like her father than was Mary; so like, indeed, that sometimes their contact had the action of metal against metal. He had been so angry with Elizabeth shortly after his last marriage that he had refused to see her or permit her to write to him for a whole year, and had passed over to France without a sign that he knew of her existence. But Katherine was waging her pen adroitly on her young stepdaughter's behalf, and her father's message to *all* his children showed Elizabeth she was forgiven. She was eloquent with gratitude to her stepmother for having brought about the reconciliation.

Boulogne surrendered in September, and Henry had the glory of entering the city at the head of his troops. Now he was ready to join up with Charles for their march on Paris. But Charles, in a tight corner with his army endangered, was convinced Boulogne was all that Henry wanted and that the English would never advance to support him. So, five days after it fell, he made a separate peace with Francis.

It had happened all over again, what had happened more than once in the past. England's Spanish ally had left her in the lurch. As the campaigning season was now far advanced and sickness had broken out among his troops, there was nothing for Henry to do but return home, leaving his prize of Boulogne strongly fortified.

The winter passed uneasy with portent. Henry told Chapuys he was ten times better at Boulogne than he had been since, and the ambassador described him as much broken since his return. Even Henry could not get away with the enormous demands he made on his physical strength. In February the Scots with a small force defeated an English army, and Francis, liberated from war with Charles, prepared to launch an armada on England.

The hour his enemies had promised themselves had at last struck for Henry VIII. He stood alone, without an ally in the world, the Scots victorious in the north, the French about to descend on him from the south. Now his people would rise up against their excommunicate King who had brought them to this pass, their prosecutor, a blood-thirsty tyrant, the enemy of the Church. Seventy-two thousand persons were said to have been put to death during his reign; if that were so it was nearly two and a half per cent of the total population of England. Their blood cried out for vengeance on their slayer.

But his people did not rise against him. Their King was coining his plate and mortgaging his estates for their defence; surely they could pay loans, subsidies and benevolences to help him. He had always seen to the defences of the country from the beginning, inspecting them himself to see they were kept in repair. They must say that for him. He had built castles of granite on the coast especially to accommodate artillery. There was really no one like him, their King. Look at the fleet he had built; as long as any of them could remember he had been adding ships to it. No, there wasn't a king in the whole world equal to him. Only he could go over to France and take a city like Boulogne from under the Frenchies' noses. They say his Council wanted him to strike a bargain with the French King, sell Boulogne back to him for a fortune, and save us trying to victual and garrison it on enemy soil. But he wouldn't hear of that, not their good King Hal. He wouldn't let a prize like that out of his hands. Neither would we. After all, we've the ships to provision it, haven't we? We're like our King, we'd rather spend all we had and risk everything to keep a trophy like Boulogne.

Spring brought the invading ships from France, two hundred of them. Henry's much vaunted fleet of half their number seemed very small in comparison. Some foreign soldiers landed but when the English destroyed a bridge so that they could not cross, they appeared undecided what to do. Enemy ships tried to force their way into Portsmouth harbour but French navigators knew nothing about the swirl of English contending tides or native hidden sandbanks, and the attempt failed. God was most certainly on the side of the English, for a westerly breeze sprang up from nowhere and the French had to drop down before it along the Sussex coast.

Henry's *Mary Rose* sank with all hands on board, but that was the one disaster. English ships followed the French and the two fleets anchored for the night almost within gunshot. There was no engagement the following day for there was no enemy to engage.

When the light of dawn pierced the sky, it revealed the horizon swallowing the last French ship as their fleet lurched back to home waters. Disease had broken out on board and taken such toll there was hardly a soldier fit to bear arms. Yes, God was on Henry's side. He always had been and always would to the end of the chapter.

Henry saw Katherine wore as many wonderful jewels as her slight form could carry when plenipotentiaries arrived from France to discuss peace. It was the New Year and the entertainment of the foreign dignitaries made resplendent the grey chill of January. But for all their splendour, there was something of afterglow about the festivities, for they were the last ever to gild Henry's court.

The treaty was favourable to him in every respect. England was to hold Boulogne and district for eight years, when France was to redeem it for two million crowns. France was to resume paying Henry his pension (the clause to have it back-dated was the only one Henry waived), and help him to force the Scots to renew the marriage and peace pacts they had declared null and void.

He, the King of half an island, was recognized as an equal in Europe by Francis and Charles. But the world scene was changing; characters who had dominated the stage for so long had played out their parts. There were others ready to take over their roles waiting in the wings, that limbo draughty with the past, shuffling with the present, empty of the future.

Henry VIII, Francis I and Charles V—Henry had only a year to live, Francis little more. The solitary Charles was not like the two rivals, competing for the centre of the stage, cutting in on the other's lines. He did not wait for his cue from death to force him, still talking, to make his exit, but resigned one crown after another before retiring to a monastery.

All that year Henry was ill on and off: when his leg broke out he had to rest; restored, he rose from bed to resume the day's activities until it flared again. That he lasted so long must be attributed to a spirit that refused to accept defeat, and to his doctors' skills. He set off for his customary progress in September, only this time he spared himself the fatigue of receiving many addresses and deputations, and stayed at manor houses and country seats far removed from towns.

He went first to the only palace he ever built, for he was not a builder in the sense that Wolsey was. This was a favourite resort of his which he called None-Such, and he was right. No such edifice has ever been erected like it, for it sprang from his fertile brain, larger and more colourful than any other, too long for its height until a commandingly tall tower was added at either end, all turrets, cupolas and domes. The ground floor alone was built of stone; the lofty storeys above were constructed of timber and plaster. The plaster was painted with pictures that told a story, the timber covered with lead and gilded. When the sun shone on this fantastic building, it was a sight worthy of its royal builder's eye.

On his return he moved from castle to palace and back to castle. He suffered from winter colds but still gave audiences to foreign ambassadors, his ministers and Chancellor, still hunted from a butt and persisted each day in taking outdoor exercise. He had to be assisted to mount his horse, and indoors was carried from room to room up and down stairs in a chair. Sometimes he would dress to go to mass or into the palace gardens, and instead sat brooding where he was. The ulcers on his legs had spread and had to be cauterized, an extreme and painful treatment, yet he transacted state business up to the day before he died.

The scales between the two factions in his Council which he kept balanced as he thought fit weighed towards the Reformers: this indicated the regency council he would nominate in his will to act for his son. It was his strength that he kept them fairly equal; preponderance one way or another was dangerous and he was far too astute to commit himself to either party. That autumn he discussed with Cranmer ways and means of turning the mass into a communion service.

Suddenly the balance was destroyed. Norfolk and his mountebank son Surrey were both sent to the Tower, the father made to suffer for the son, who had quartered his coat-of-arms with the royal arms and asked who had more right to be Protector when the King died than his father.

The royal prerogative was challenged. The Norfolks with their blue blood could well cause trouble during Edward's minority when his father was no longer there to keep them in their place. Henry had shown in the past his unanswerable method of dealing with possible pretenders, and he was taking no chances where his son was concerned.

Silent crowds watched the poet Surrey go to his death, he who had threatened the inheritance of their rightful little Prince whose reign was to inaugurate a golden world. His father's execution was stayed only because the King who ordered it died before it could be carried out.

What was he thinking as he lay in Wolsey's palace of Whitehall? He had so much to remember, yet it is not the large scenes that crowd the mind as the self withdraws, but little things, fugitive as the few notes of a full score.

Did he remember the pounding of his horse's hoofs as he chased the French in the Battle of the Spurs? These were the days he had breath to blow the captain's whistle on one of his new ships until it sounded like a trumpet. Did bugle notes reach him from a little hill when his sun was high in the heavens? It was winter now, January 1547, when there was no meridian, and he was old, in the fifty-fifth year of his age and the thirty-eighth of his reign.

He had always hated to hear of death, and his doctors dare not tell him because his own Act of Parliament made it treason to prophesy the King's demise. It was his chief gentleman of the chamber who boldly told him what case he was in that he might prepare himself for the end. His King demanded what judge had sent him to cast this sentence upon him, to which Sir Anthony Denny replied, "Your Grace's physicians."

He was asked if he would like to speak to any of his bishops but he said, "I will see no one but Cranmer, but not him as yet. Let me repose a little, and as I find myself, so shall I determine."

When he woke he felt the feebleness of death upon him and told Denny to send for Cranmer. The Archbishop arrived after midnight to find the King unable to speak. He saw he was recognized, for his master stretched out his hand to him and would not let his go. Cranmer spoke comfortably to him, urging him to give some sign by eye or hand that he put his trust in God through Jesus Christ. With his last strength, Henry wrung his Archbishop's hand hard.

A Chronology of Henry VIII

hi story

1485   Accession of Henry VII.
       Birth of Katherine of Aragon.
1491   Birth of Henry.
1501   Marriage of Katherine of Aragon and Arthur, Prince of Wales, Henry's brother.
1502   Death of Arthur.
1503   Marriage of Margaret, Henry's sister, to James IV of Scotland.
1509   Death of Henry VII.
       Marriage of Henry to Katherine of Aragon.
       Coronation of Henry.
1513   Battle of the Spurs.
       Battle of Flodden.
1514   Marriage of Mary, Henry's sister, to Louis XII.
1515   Marriage of Mary, Henry's sister, to Charles Brandon, Duke of Suffolk.
1516   Birth of Mary, daughter of Henry and Katherine of Aragon.
1519   Birth of Henry Fitzroy, illegitimate son of Henry and Elizabeth Blount.
1520   Field of Cloth of Gold.
1530   Death of Wolsey.
1533   Marriage of Henry to Anne Boleyn.
       Death of Mary, Henry's sister.
       Birth of Elizabeth, daughter of Henry and Anne Boleyn.
1536   Death of Katherine of Aragon.
       Execution of Anne Boleyn.
       Marriage of Henry to Jane Seymour.
1537   Birth of Edward (later Edward VI), son of Henry and Jane Seymour.
       Death of Jane Seymour.
1540   Marriage of Henry to Anne of Cleves.

1540   Marriage of Henry to Katherine Howard.
1541   Death of Margaret, Henry's sister.
1542   Battle of Solway Moss.
       Execution of Katherine Howard.
1543   Marriage of Henry to Katherine Parr.
1547   Death of Henry.

Index

A

Adrian VI, Pope, 67, 92
Alençon, Duchess of, 83
Angus, Earl of, 52, 53
Anne (Boleyn), Queen, *see* Boleyn
Aragon, Katherine of, Henry VIII's first wife: engaged to Prince Arthur, 14; arrives in England, 17–20; sent to Ludlow Castle with bridegroom, 22; death of Arthur, 23–4; engaged to Prince Henry, 25; marries Henry VIII, 30–31; happiness in her marriage, 32; first child stillborn, 33; birth and death of son; 33–4; 35, 39, 41, 42, 44–5, 46; her baby son dies, 47; her daughter Mary born; 51; 52, 54, 56; last pregnancy a stillbirth, 57, 58; accompanies Henry to Field of Cloth of Gold, 61, 62; 63, 68, 73; steps taken to annul her marriage, 79–83; with Campeggio, 90–91; faces Henry at Legates' Court, 94–6; 104, 108; abandoned by Henry, 109, 110; loved by the Londoners, 84, 92, 96, 119–20; refuses to take Oath of Supremacy, 127; writes Henry on her death-bed, 128; dies, 129
Ardes, 61
Arthur, Prince of Wales, Henry VIII's elder brother: 11, 13; engaged to Katherine of Aragon, 14, 15; meets his bride, 18; their wedding, 19; sent to Ludlow Castle with bride, 22; his death, 23; mentioned, 96
Aske, Robert, 153, 154

B

Baynard's Castle, 55
Blount, Elizabeth, 57, 75, 79
Boleyn, Anne, Henry VIII's second wife: description of, 67, 78–9, 104; Wolsey dissolves her engagement to Henry Percy, 78; Henry VIII in love with her, 79, 83–6; her unpopularity, 85, 88, 118–20; 136; waspish with frustration, 103–104, 108; Henry's mistress, 109; Lutheran leanings, 109, 129; jealous of Princess Mary, 109–10, 126–7; created Marquis of Pembroke, 111; accompanies Henry to France, 112–13; Henry marries her, 115; her coronation, 118–20; gives birth to Elizabeth, 121; pregnant, 129; triumph at Katherine's death, 130; has stillborn son, 130; Henry withdraws from her, 132; at May Day tournament, 134–5; taken prisoner, 136; in the Tower, 137–45; her letter to Henry, 140–42; her trial, 142–3; execution, 144–5; mentioned, 168
    George, Viscount Rochford (Anne's brother), 134, 135, 139
    Lady (Anne's aunt), 138, 140, 176, 181, 182
    Mary (Anne's sister), 45, 67, 68, 79, 113
    Sir Thomas (Anne's father), 67, 83
Bosworth Moor, Battle of, 12, 16, 39
Boulogne, 112, 191, 193, 195
Brandon, Charles, later Duke of Suffolk, 14, 40, 44; in love with Mary Tudor, 46; joins ambassade to look after Mary when widowed, 48; marries Mary Tudor, 49; 53, 87; takes part in Anne Boleyn's coronation, 120; 127; one of Anne Boleyn's judges, 142, 143; 190
Brereton, William, 134, 138
Butts, Dr. William, Henry VIII's favourite physician, 109

C

Calais, 32, 38, 72, 112, 164
Campeggio, Cardinal Lorenzo, 86; comes to England to try King's case, 88, 89–91; presides at Legates' Court, 94–7
Canterbury, 60, 150, 160
    Archbishop of, *see* Cranmer, Thomas
    Archbishop of, *see* Warham, William
Chapuys, Eustace (Imperial ambassador), 116, 121, 122, 129, 147, 148, 182, 183, 193

Charles, later Charles V, Emperor of the ✓ Holy Roman Empire, 21; engaged to Henry's sister Mary, 26; the engagement renewed, 42; jilts Mary, 44; 48; succeeds Ferdinand as King of Spain, 51; 57; description of, 60; 63, 65-6; second visit to England, 69; signs treaty to marry Henry's daughter Mary, 70; 72; his restraint in victory, 73; does not fulfil his obligation to marry Princess Mary, 74-5; 133, 139, 158; makes non-aggression treaty with Francis, 162; prepares to invade England, 163; disperses his invasion fleet, 169; unites with Henry against Francis, 187, 189-91; betrays Henry by making separate peace with Francis, 193; 195

Christina of Denmark, 158-9, 164

Claude, Queen of France, 48, 62, 67, 75

Clement VII, Pope, 72, 77; taken prisoner, 82; approached about Henry's annulment, 85-6, 93-4; his secret instructions to Campeggio, 88, 97; 107; publishes bulls against Henry, 113; authorises Cranmer's consecration as Archbishop of Canterbury, 115-16; 122; dies, 123

✓ Cleves, Anne of, Henry VIII's fourth wife: description of, 163-4, 166; Henry sends her to Richmond, 169; happily agrees to be divorced, 170-71; 188

Duke of, 163, 164

Cosyns, Mrs., 138, 140

Cranmer, Thomas: created Archbishop of Canterbury, 114-15; crowns Anne Boleyn, 118; 120, 123, 144, 146, 152; deals with Katherine Howard's immorality, 177-80; at King Henry's death-bed, 197

Cromwell, Thomas, 103, 126, 136, 139, 140, 144, 148-9, 150, 152, 159-60, 164, 165, 169, 170, 171

Culpeper, Thomas, 168, 172-3, 174, 176, 181, 183

D

Denny, Sir Anthony, 197

Dereham, Francis, 167, 168, 172-3, 178, 180, 181, 183

Dover, 45, 60

Dover Castle, 45, 60

E

✓ Edward, Prince, Henry VIII's legitimate son: born, 155; description of, 184; 186, 192, 197

Eleanor, sister of Charles V, 21, 112

Elizabeth, Henry VIII's younger daughter: born, 121; 126-7, 133, 168, 192; description of at eleven, 193

Elizabeth of York, Henry VIII's mother: description of, 13; 19, 20; comforts husband on death of their son, 23; dies, 24

Esher Palace, 101, 102

F

Ferdinand, King of Aragon, 14, 17, 21, 24, 26, 31, 32; his treachery, 33, 37, 43, 44; jealous of Henry, 41; his death, 51; mentioned, 82

Field of Cloth of Gold, 61-3

Fisher, John, Bishop of Rochester, 96-7, 106, 125

Fitzroy, Henry, Henry VIII's illegitimate son, 57; created Duke of Richmond and Somerset, 75-6; 142; dies, 151-2

Flodden, 41

Forrest, John, 125

Francis I, King of France: rival of Henry VIII, 48; 49, 59; meets Henry, 61-2; 65, 66; Henry declares war on him, 70, 72; defeated by Charles at Pavia, 73; 75, 80, 112-13, 133, 157, 158; makes non-aggression pact with Charles, 162; breaks it, 187; tries to separate Henry and Charles, 191; 192; makes separate peace with Charles, 193; his forces invade England, 194; makes favourable treaty with Henry, 195

G

Goodwin, Bishop, 142

Gravelines, 63

Greenwich House or Palace, 13, 30, 104, 110, 111; Elizabeth born in, 121; 130, 132-3, 134, 136, 149, 154, 176

Guildford, "Mother", 45, 46, 47

Guisnes, 61

H

Hampton Court, 58, 100, 154; Edward born in, 155-6; 173, 177, 178, 179, 180, 192

Hatfield, 133, 176

Henry VII, King of England; founder of the House of Tudor, 11; description of, 12, 16; wins Battle of Bosworth Moor, 12; has Earl of Warwick executed. 16; insists on seeing Infanta, 17-18; 19, 20, 21, 22; learns of death of elder son, 23; death of his wife, 24; 25, 26; death and funeral, 27-8

Henry VIII, King of England: born, 11; appearance of, 11, 15, 27, 59, 62, 173, 175, 188; love of music, 11–12; honours heaped on him, 12; entertained by London when a child, 15–16; escort to the Infanta at her wedding to Arthur, 18–19; 20; heir to the throne, 23; engaged to Katherine of Aragon, 25; repudiates his engagement, 26; acclaimed King, 28; the new reign, 29–30; marries Katherine of Aragon, 30–32; first child stillborn, 33; son born, 33; his popularity, 33–4, 59, 162–3, 194; baby son dies, 34; 35; joins Ferdinand against France, 36; anger at the return of his troops, 37; lands in France, 38, 40–41; returns from France, 42; 43; makes pact with France, 43–4; visits her father's treachery on Katherine, 45; builds ships, 45–6; celebrates Katherine's recovery, 47; jealous of Francis I, 48; receives Mary and her bridegroom favourably, 49; 50; delighted at birth of his daughter Mary, 51; reunion with his sister Margaret, 53; his anger at Evil May Day riots, 54; pardons apprentices, 54–5; fears sweating sickness, 55–6; relationship with Wolsey, 56, 58; his illegitimate son, 57; goes to France for Field of Cloth of Gold, 59–62; meets Charles, 60, 63; returns to England, 63; doubts his marriage, 63–4; champions Pope against Luther, 66; receives title of Defender of the Faith, 65; his disloyalty to Francis, 65–6, 70; handles state affairs himself, 66; his mistresses, 67; 69, 71–2; his delight at Francis's defeat, 73; 74, 76; in love with Anne Boleyn, 79, 83, 92–3; tells Katherine they are not married, 81; declares war against Charles, 86–7; with Campeggio, 89–90; expounds his great matter to London, 91–2; with Katherine before Legates' Court, 94–6; present to hear verdict, 97–8; his development, 99–100; use of Parliament his strength, 99, 101, 103, 122–3; hardens, 100, 106; assumes title of Supreme Head of the Church and Clergy of England, 106; warns Pope Clement, 107; leaves Katherine, 109; priests protest before him about divorce, 111; goes to France, 112–13; legislates against Clement, 113–14; marries Anne Boleyn, 115; disappointed, child is daughter (Elizabeth), 122; prepares to break with Rome, 122; he neither liberated nor enslaved the English Church, 122; his changed attitude towards the Vicar of Christ, 123–4; Acts of Succession, 124, 151; Oath of Supremacy, 124–5, 147–9; his megalomania, 127–8; weeps over Katherine's last letter, 128; his fancy roves, 129, 133; relief at Katherine's death, 130; blames Anne for loss of son, 130; leaves Anne at May Day tournament, 135; his responsibility for Anne's fate, 138; no compunction over Anne, 146; marries Jane Seymour, 146; contented with new marriage, 150, 152; deals with Pilgrimage of Grace, 152–3; his "sore leg", 154, 174, 190, 196; his son born, 155–6; sorrow at Jane's death, 157; enters marriage market, 158; orders Bible to be placed in every church, 161; his religion, 162; isolated when Charles and Francis make non-aggression pact, 162; prevailed on to marry Anne of Cleves, 163–4; disappointed in her, 165; marries her, 166; falls in love with Katherine Howard, 169; on good terms with Anne of Cleves after their divorce, 171; marries Katherine Howard, 171; his Indian summer, 173; his northern progress, 174–7; returns at peace with himself and all the world, 177; hears of Katherine Howard's looseness, 177; does not believe it, 178; truth forced on him, 178–9; her guilt a nemesis for Henry, 183; at war with Scotland, 185–7, 189–90, 193; unites with Charles against Francis, 187, 189; marries Katherine Parr, 168; insists on invading France in person, 190; writes home, 191; betrayed by Charles, stands alone, 193; his people's loyalty, 194; France invades, 194; France makes peace, 195; recognized as an equal power by Charles and Francis, 195; his last year, 195–7; death, 197

Holbein, Hans, the Younger, 163

Howard, Katherine, Henry VIII's fifth wife: description of, 167, 169, 173; early love affairs, 167–8; Henry falls in love with, 169; Henry marries her, 171; prior contracted marriage with Dereham, 172–3; her dangerous dalliance with Culpeper, 174, 176; accused of immorality before her marriage, 179–80; her treatment gentle compared to Anne Boleyn's, 180; her assignations with Culpeper uncovered, 181; Culpeper's admission seals her doom, 181; executed, 182–3

Howard, continued
    Thomas: *see* Norfolk, 2nd and 3rd
    Dukes of

I

Isabella, Queen of Castile, 14, 17, 21, 25;
    mentioned, 90, 127
Isabella of Portugal, 74, 75

J

James IV, King of Scotland, 21; engaged
    to Margaret Tudor, 22; 25; makes war
    on England, 39; death at Flodden, 41;
    mentioned, 185
James V, King of Scotland, 43, 52, 158,
    176-7, 185-6
Jane Seymour, *see* Seymour, Jane
Julius II, Pope, 64

K

Katherine (of Aragon), Queen, *see* Aragon,
    Katherine
Katherine (Howard), Queen, *see* Howard,
    Katherine
Katherine (Parr), Queen, *see* Parr,
    Katherine
Kingston, Lady, 140, 143
Kingston, Sir William, 136-7, 140, 144

L

Lassels, John, 177
    Mary, 168, 177, 178
Leicester Abbey, 106
Leo X, Pope, 64, 65, 66
Lincoln, 176
Linlithgow Palace, 186
London, 13, 15, 17-19, 22, 24, 27, 54-5,
    73, 118-20, 135; full of hospitals,
    160-61; 182
Londoners, 16; take Katherine of Aragon
    to their hearts, 18; 53, 81; back Kath-
    erine, 84-5; 92, 96, 100, 118-20, 196
Louis XII, King of France, 33, 36, 40,
    43-5, 46, 47
Ludlow Castle, 22, 75, 80
Luke, Anne, 12

M

Maidstone, 150
Manox, Henry, 167, 172, 178, 179
Margaret of Savoy, 40
Margaret Tudor, elder sister of Henry
    VIII: description of, 14, 18, 20, 21;
engaged to James IV of Scotland, 22;
    goes to Scotland as Queen, 25; 39, 43,
    45; marries again, 52; returns to Eng-
    land, 52-5; contemplates divorce, 57;
    achieves divorce, 76-7; death, 184
Marguerite de Valois, sister of Francis I,
    112
Marie of Guise, 158, 186
Marillac, Charles de (French ambassador),
    158, 165, 166, 169, 170, 171, 173, 182,
    183
Marseilles, 72
Mary, Queen of Scots, 186, 187, 190
Mary Tudor, younger sister of Henry
    VIII, 14; descriptions of, 15, 42, 47;
    18, 20; engaged to Charles, 26; her
    engagement renewed, 42; jilted by
    Charles, 44; engaged to Louis XII, 44;
    goes to France to marry Louis, 45-6;
    Louis dies, 47; prevails on Charles
    Brandon to marry her, 48-9; returns to
    England, 49; 51, 53, 54; meets Charles,
    now Emperor, who jilted her, 60; 62;
    loses her only son, 87; ill, 120; death
    mentioned, 127
Mary Tudor, elder daughter of Henry
    VIII: born, 51; 56, 57, 63; betrothed
    to Charles, 69-70; her engagement
    broken, 74-6; ill when parents separate,
    109; 110-11; at Elizabeth's birth, 121;
    refuses to call Elizabeth Princess, 126;
    not vindictive, 127, 149; refuses to
    take Oath of Supremacy, 127, 147-9,
    143; signs Oath of Supremacy, 149;
    description of, 149-50, 192; 157
Maximilian I, Emperor, 26, 40, 42, 43, 44,
    57
Monasteries, suppression of, 150-51,
    159-61
More, Sir Thomas, 125
Morton, Margaret, 172, 176

N

Nonesuch, Palace of, 195-6
Norfolk, Agnes, Dowager Duchess of,
    167-8, 177, 180
    Thomas Howard, 2nd Duke of:
    description of, 39-40; created Duke of
    Norfolk, 41; 45, 46
    Thomas Howard, 3rd Duke of, 76;
    hatred of Wolsey, 83; 96; demands the
    Great Seal from Wolsey, 100; 108, 133,
    136, 139; presides at Anne Boleyn's
    trial, 142; 152-4, 168-9, 178; learns of
    Katherine Howard's immorality, 180;
    185; sent to Tower, 196-7
Norris, Sir Henry, 134, 135, 137, 139

Northumberland, Earl of, *see* Percy, Henry

P

Paris, 40, 72
Parr, Katherine, Henry VIII's sixth wife: her wedding to Henry, 188; description of, 188-9; writes to Henry in France, 191; a tender stepmother, 191-2
Patch, Henry VIII's fool, 65
Paul III, Pope, 124, 162
Pavia, 73
Percy, Henry, later Earl of Northumberland, 67, 78, 105-106, 142
Pilgrimage of Grace, 152-4
Plantagenet, Edward, Earl of Warwick, 16-17, 82
Pollard, A. F., 138
Pontefract, 176

R

Richmond Palace, 13, 22; Henry VII dies at, 27; 83, 169, 170
Rochester, 164
Rochford, Lady Jane, 139, 176, 181, 182
Rome: sacked, 82, 85
Rye, 191

S

St. Benedict, 160
St. Paul's, 27, 55, 73
St. Thomas à Becket, shrine of, 150, 160
Seymour, Jane, Henry VIII's third wife, 129, 130, 133, 142; Henry marries her, 146; description of, 146-7; kind to Princess Mary, 147; pregnant, 154; has a son, 155-6; death, 157
Shrewsbury, Earl of, 96
Skelton, John, 13
Smeaton, Mark, 133-4, 135, 138-9
Spurs, Battle of the, 40
Suffolk, Duke of, *see* Brandon, Charles
Surrey, Henry Howard, Earl of, 142, 196-7

Syon, 257, 260

T

Therouanne, 39, 40
Tourney, 40
Tower of London, 16, 136-7, 182
Tylney, Katherine, 172, 176

W

Wallop, Sir John, 189
Warham, William, Archbishop of Canterbury, 25, 80, 106, 113
Westminster Abbey, 27, 31, 137, 155
Weston, Sir Francis, 135, 138
Windsor Castle, 13, 109
Wolsey, Thomas: description of, 35-6; his unpopularity, 37, 56, 71, 73-4, 78, 87; lands in France with King, 38; subtle, 43; ambitious, 43-4; 46, 49-50, 51, 53; pleads for apprentices, 54; nearly dies of the sweating sickness, 56; arrogance, 56, 57; relationship with Henry, 58; 60; at Field of Cloth of Gold, 62-3; 64, 65; his reasons for aligning England with Empire, 66; his bids to be chosen Pope, 66, 72; tries to raise money for war, 70-71, 73; 72, 80; goes to and returns from France, 83; his relationship with Henry never the same, 84; 86; with Campeggio, 89-90; officiates at Legates' Court with Campeggio, 94-8; his downfall, 100-103; takes up pastoral duties at York, 105; arrested for high treason, 105-106; dies on way to London, 106; mentioned, 139, 159
Wyatt, Mary, 140, 144
Thomas, 67, 120, 140

Y

York, 105, 153, 175, 176
York Palace, 100